DATE DUE

~~AP 2'99~~ RENEW		
~~AP 27 98~~		
~~NO+1 ON~~		
~~DE 3'03~~		

DEMCO 38-296

'THE AMUSEMENTS OF THE PEOPLE'
AND OTHER PAPERS
Reports, Essays and Reviews

1834–51

THE DENT UNIFORM EDITION OF DICKENS' JOURNALISM, Vol. I
Sketches by Boz and Other Early Papers 1833–39 (1994)

THE DENT UNIFORM EDITION OF

DICKENS'
JOURNALISM
Volume 2

THE AMUSEMENTS
OF THE PEOPLE
AND OTHER PAPERS:
REPORTS, ESSAYS AND REVIEWS

1834–51

EDITED BY MICHAEL SLATER

Ohio State University Press

COLUMBUS

R

Copyright © 1996 by the Ohio State University Press

Introduction, preliminary material, headnotes and index
© J. M. Dent 1996

Published in the United States by the Ohio State University Press
Published simultaneously in Great Britain by J. M. Dent

Library of Congress Cataloging-in-Publication Data
Dickens, Charles, 1812–1870.
  The amusements of the people and other papers: reports, essays,
and reviews, 1834–51/edited by Michael Slater.
      p.   cm.—(The Dent uniform edition of Dickens' journalism; v. 2)
  Includes bibliographical references and index.
  ISBN 0–8142–0724–3 (alk. paper)
    1. England—Social life and customs—19th century.   2. Popular
culture—England.   I. Slater, Michael.   II. Title.   III. Series:
Dickens, Charles, 1812–1870.   Journalism: v. 2.
  PR4572.A83S58   1996
  824'.8—dc20   96–24142
                                                                              CIP

The Amusements of the People and Other Papers: Reports, Essays and Reviews 1834–51
first published by J. M. Dent in 1996

Chronology from *The Dickens Index* by Nicolas Bentley, Michael Slater and Nina Burgis
(1988); reprinted by kind permission of Oxford University Press.

Filmset in Baskerville by Selwood Systems, Midsomer Norton
Printed in Great Britain by Butler & Tanner Ltd, Frome and London

The paper used in this publication meets the minimum
requirements of American National Standards for Information
Sciences – Permanence of Paper for Printed Library Materials.
ANSI Z39.48–1992.

9 8 7 6 5 4 3 2 1

CONTENTS

'THE AMUSEMENTS OF THE PEOPLE' AND OTHER PAPERS

PREFACE

The Dent Uniform Edition of Dickens' Journalism presents, for the first time in annotated form, all the journalism that Dickens published in collected form during his lifetime, *Sketches by Boz, Reprinted Pieces* and *The Uncommercial Traveller*. It also includes an early pamphlet, *Sunday Under Three Heads*, and a substantial selection of the many essays and reviews that were never collected by Dickens himself yet contain much material of outstanding interest. The earliest of these papers, those contributed to *Bentley's Miscellany*, were first collected as *The Mudfog Papers* by G. Bentley in 1880 (reprinted 1984). The later essays and reviews were first gathered together by B.W. Matz, the first editor of *The Dickensian*, in 1908, as part of the National Edition of Dickens's works. The *Miscellaneous Papers*, as they were called, were reprinted with additions and retitled *Collected Papers* by Matz's successor, Walter Dexter, in the luxurious limited Nonesuch Edition (1937). Since then there has been one reprint of *Miscellaneous Papers* (1983) but the great mass of all this vintage Dickens writing has remained largely unobtainable outside libraries.

In order to fully understand and appreciate Dickens's journalistic achievement the modern reader inevitably needs a certain amount of background information and explanatory annotation. This Uniform Edition supplies such help in the form of headnotes preceding each piece, supplemented at the end of the volume by an index that is also a glossary and a dictionary of proper names. It is hoped that this combination will, while avoiding a proliferation of footnotes, provide readers with all necessary information.

M.S.

INTRODUCTION

In the summer of 1834 a long-established but now faltering London paper, the *Morning Chronicle,* was bought by a trio of bankers and stockbrokers led by a self-made man called John Easthope. The object was to make the *Chronicle* a more effective supporter of the Whig Government in all the post-Reform Bill measures it was carrying out against virulent Tory opposition, opposition most trenchantly and influentially expressed in *The Times.* In particular, Easthope wanted the *Chronicle* to be a strong champion of the New Poor Law, the centrepiece of the Whigs' legislative programme. He retained the colourful old Scots bibliophile John Black as editor (Black had held the post since 1817), but set out to recruit some good new reporting staff. One of the new appointments was young Thomas Beard from the *Morning Herald* and he successfully recommended a friend of his, the twenty-two-year-old Charles Dickens.

Beard had worked alongside the freelance Dickens in the gallery of the old House of Commons (burned down in 1834), and as they strove accurately to record what Dickens later scornfully referred to as 'the drone of the Parliamentary bagpipes' he had developed the highest admiration for him. 'There never *was* such a reporter,' Beard was later quoted as saying; 'In the dazzling swiftness of his zigzag notes, no less than in his rapid transcript from them afterwards, he distanced the fleetest of his companions.' Dickens, having mastered the 'savage stenographic mystery' of Gurney's system of shorthand, was working for his barrister-uncle John Barrow's publication *The Mirror of Parliament,* launched as a rival to Hansard in 1828, and from the spring of 1832 he was also working for a new ultra-Whig, or even Radical, evening paper, the *True Sun.* Although he would have been earning good money while Parliament was sitting, the appointment to the regular staff of the *Chronicle* at five guineas a week must have been very welcome to him, a good reason for celebrating with the purchase of that new hat and 'very handsome blue coat with black velvet facings, the corner of which he threw over his shoulder *à l'espagnole*.'[1]

Black was a 'keen politician' and 'an ardent disciple of Jeremy Bentham', but he had also, according to his sub-editor Charles Mackay, 'a heart overflowing with kindness and a warm sympathy with all literary talent'. Dickens had already published, for no pay, several comic stories (later collected in *Sketches by Boz*) in the *Monthly Magazine* and now found, as he recalled later, that his 'faculty for descriptive writing' was 'seized upon' as soon as he joined the *Chronicle*.[2] 'Omnibuses', the first of his 'Street Sketches', appeared in the paper on 26 September, a week or so after he and Beard had covered their first big assignment, the Edinburgh 'Grey Festival' (see pp. 3–8), and four more sketches followed before the end of the year.[3] He always remembered 'dear old Black' with affection, calling him 'my first hearty out-and-out appreciator'.[4] According to Mackay, Black wanted Dickens treated with special distinction:

> It was of my duty ... to confer with ... Mr Black on the employment of the Parliamentary reporters during the recess ... and to utilize their services in the general work of the paper, – such as attendance at public meetings, reviews of books, or notices of new plays at the theatres. Mr Black desired to spare Mr Dickens as much as possible from all work of this kind, having the highest opinion of his original genius, and a consequent dislike to employ him on what he considered the very inferior work of criticism. 'Any fool,' he said, in his usual broad Scotch, 'can pass judgment, more or less just or unjust, on a book or a play – but "Boz" can do better things; he can create works for other people to criticize. Besides, he has never been a great reader of books or plays, and knows but little of them, but has spent his time in studying life. Keep "Boz" in reserve for great occasions. He will *aye* be ready for them.'[5]

Although this reminiscence of Mackay's tends to crop up in every Dickens biography, it is hard to reconcile it with the evidence. The Grey Festival apart (and maybe we could also include the Hatfield fire – see pp. 22–5), few events occurred during Dickens's time on the *Chronicle* that could be called 'great occasions' and, as may be seen from the listing of Dickens's known or probable contributions to the paper between 1834 and 1836 in Appendix B (see pp. 373–5), he certainly did a great deal of routine reporting work. One 'great occasion' he definitely was used for, however, was the sensational Norton *v.* Melbourne trial (22 June 1836), when the Prime Minister, Lord Melbourne, was prosecuted for 'crim. con.' (i.e., adultery) with the society beauty Mrs Caroline Norton by her estranged husband. These farcical proceedings later provided rich copy for Ch. 34 of *The Pickwick Papers*, but the *Chronicle*'s report is devoid of any comic glossing. There is, however, a complaint at the beginning of it which does strike a note of prickly assertion of personal or professional dignity tinged with class resentment that is very characteristic of Dickens. It was apparently difficult to get in and out of the crowded courtroom and this was, says the report,

... wholly occasioned by the very indecent behaviour of a large concourse of barristers of small standing, young 'gentlemen' who being never called into Court by any higher motive than curiosity, would appear to have acquired but a very imperfect understanding of the behaviour of gentlemen when they get there. From professional gentlemen of long standing ... the Reporters received every accommodation ...; but from these youths, from the very first moment of their preventing the progress of business, by their self-important cries of 'Room for the bar,' down to the last moment of the trial, they experienced nothing but a series of gratuitous annoyances and ungentlemanly interruptions....[6]

As regards regular political reporting, it seems clear enough that Black regarded Dickens as one of his star performers. He sent him to Exeter in May 1835, for example, to cover the Home Secretary, Lord John Russell's offering himself for re-election, and Dickens and his *Chronicle* colleague had a glorious race back against the *Times* reporters ('... the Times and I changed horses together; they had the start two or three minutes: I bribed the post boys tremendously & we came in literally neck and neck – the most beautiful sight I ever saw ...'). Dickens clearly delighted in this work, the challenge and excitement of it as well as the sense of excelling in a fiercely competitive trade. Thirty years later, addressing a dinner of the Newspaper Press Fund, he vividly recalled his *Chronicle* days, before the railway and the electric telegraph had utterly transformed the reporter's profession:

I have pursued the calling of a reporter under circumstances of which ... many of my modern successors, can form no adequate conception. I have often transcribed for the printer from my shorthand notes, important public speeches in which the strictest accuracy was required, and a mistake in which would have been to a young man severely compromising, writing on the palm of my hand, by the light of a dark lantern, in a post chaise and four, galloping through a wild country, all through the dead of night, at the then surprising rate of fifteen miles an hour. The very last time I was at Exeter, I strolled into the Castle Yard there to identify, for the amusement of a friend, the spot on which I once 'took', as we used to call it, an election speech of my noble friend Lord Russell, in the midst of a lively fight maintained by all the vagabonds in that division of the county, and under such a pelting rain, that I remember two good-natured colleagues, who chanced to be at leisure, held a pocket handkerchief over my notebook after the manner of a state canopy in an ecclesiastical procession. [*Laughter.*] I have worn my knees by writing on them on the old back row of the old gallery of the old House of Commons; and I have worn my feet by standing to write in a preposterous pen in the old House of Lords, where we used to be huddled together like so many sheep [*laughter*], kept in waiting, say, until the woolsack might want re-stuffing. [*A laugh.*] I have been, in my time, belated on miry by-roads, towards the small hours, in a wheelless carriage, with exhausted horses and drunken postboys, and have got back in time for publication, to be received with never-forgotten compliments by the late Mr Black, coming in the broadest of Scotch from the broadest of hearts I ever knew. [*Hear, hear.*][8]

Dickens knew how much his exceptional abilities were valued by his editor. Relations with Easthope (nicknamed 'Blasthope' by his employees) were less easy and when the success of *Sketches by Boz* and the 'rocket-like' ascent of *Pickwick* in popular favour enabled Dickens to resign from the *Chronicle* staff, he parted somewhat bitterly from his Scrooge-like employer: 'with the satisfaction', he wrote, 'of knowing that there is not another Newspaper Office in London where [my] services [to the *Chronicle*] have not been watched and appreciated ... I can afford to part with the thanks of the Proprietors....'[9]

Dickens emerged from his *Chronicle* engagement as 'the best reporter in London',[10] but with no signs of developing into a political journalist. He clearly participated with zest in the Tory-bashing that characterised the *Chronicle*,[11] and could throw off a clever satirical squib like 'The Story without a Beginning' (pp. 10–13), but his attention rested on the frequently farcical or grotesque surface of political life, the blatant electoral mal-practices in the constituencies or the many absurdities of Parliamentary procedures and of the behaviour of individual MPs. He published two comic sketches of Parliamentary life in the *Evening Chronicle* in the spring of 1835, but never tried his hand at any analytical or reflective political piece, maintaining always a cool ironic distance from the actual business of politics. This was tempered only by admiration for a few politicians, notably Lord John Russell, whom he had watched steering the Reform Bill legislation through the House of Commons. 'I am sufficiently behind the scenes to know the worth of political life', he was to make David Copperfield write; 'I am quite an Infidel about it, and will never be converted.'[12]

What his reporting experiences had given him, besides this 'infidelity', was wonderful material for his early fiction – for creating the Eatanswill election in *Pickwick*, or for portraying the ineffable Mr Gregsbury MP in *Nicholas Nickleby*, for example. The one political measure that we know he did feel very strongly about, and often debated with Black, the New Poor Law, also became material for fiction, the superbly powerful propagandist fiction of *Oliver Twist*, rather than for journalistic articles. As Dickens realised a few years later, when he abandoned his promise to write an article for the *Edinburgh Review* on the appalling findings of the Children's Employment Commission and wrote *A Christmas Carol* instead, it was through the creations of his mythopœic imagination rather than through straight journalism that he could most powerfully influence contemporary social and political attitudes.

Oliver Twist was published in a new monthly magazine, *Bentley's Miscellany*, of which Dickens was the first editor (January 1837), his second journalistic engagement. Unable to tolerate his proprietor Richard Bentley's persistent interference in matters of editorial concern and irritated too by a squabble over the extent of his own contributions, Dickens resigned after two disputatious years.[13] He remained haunted, however, by the desire to edit his own journal, one modelled on those eighteenth-century periodicals, the *Tatler, Spectator* and Goldsmith's *Bee*, which had so entranced him as a child.[14] But the journal he envisaged was to be 'far more popular both in the subjects of which it treats and its mode of treating them'. It was to contain 'pleasant fictions', 'amusing essays' and so on, but also an occasional series of 'satirical papers' focusing particularly on the administration of justice ('to keep a special look-out upon the magistrates in town and country, and never to leave those worthies alone').[15] An illustrated weekly miscellany called *Master Humphrey's Clock* (1840–1), written entirely by himself (though this was not the original intention), was the outcome of Dickens's negotiations with his publishers about this matter. The Humphrey formula (which did not, in the event, include any 'satirical papers') proved unpopular and Dickens rapidly transformed his weekly into merely a vehicle for the hugely popular *Old Curiosity Shop*. As soon as this ended, *Barnaby Rudge* began its run and after that had finished the *Clock* stopped for ever.

Meanwhile Dickens had become associated with another journal as a result of his growing friendship with John Forster. Forster was a Newcastle grammar-school boy who had come to London as a law student in 1828, but who by the late 1830s was well launched on a career in literary journalism. He had worked on the *True Sun* at the same time as Dickens, but the two young men did not become acquainted until afterwards.[16] In 1833 Forster joined the staff of the distinguished political/literary weekly *The Examiner*. This paper, founded by Leigh Hunt and his brother in 1808, had started life as a Radical journal, exposing both the Tory Government and the Prince Regent's Court to constant witty attack. Leigh Hunt's imprisonment (1812) for libelling the Prince had made the journal something of an icon of the Radicals, but it languished during the 1820s. Its fortunes revived after it was bought by Albany Fonblanque in 1830. Fonblanque, reputed as 'the wittiest journalist of his day', was 'outstanding in his ability to expose the fallacies in an opposing argument, either through the ingenious corollary or through the use of the *reductio ad absurdum*'.[17] He was an admirer of Melbourne and moved *The Examiner* closer to the Whigs, but without its becoming a sort of unofficial government organ like the *Chronicle*. The front pages of each sixteen-page issue were devoted to politics and social issues, after which there followed review sections ('The Literary Examiner' and 'The Theatrical Examiner'), foreign, commercial and miscellaneous news (including police reports), and advertisements.[18] Ample space was given to the review sections and in 1833 Forster was put in charge of them. Francis Espinasse, looking back to the 1830s from the end of the century, recalled that *The Examiner*

> partly through [Forster], but still more through the pungent political articles of . . . Fonblanque, had, after a period of decadence, regained the old position won for it by Leigh Hunt and his coadjutors. In his own department Forster had brought things so far that praise of a new book or a new play in the *Examiner* was a feather in the cap of an ordinary author or dramatist.[19]

It was as one of Forster's reviewers that Dickens first began to write for *The Examiner*; later he was to contribute topical articles also. All contributions to the journal were anonymous, but over forty have been positively identified as by Dickens, several more have been plausibly attributed to him, and it is very likely that there may be still more waiting to be identified.[20] As can be seen from the listing in Appendix B, his work for *The Examiner* fell into two periods, 1837–43 and 1848–9. In the first period Dickens contributed mainly theatre and book reviews, a notable item here being his eager plunge into the controversy over the ruin of Sir Walter Scott (see pp. 32–8). The political crisis of 1841, which resulted in August in the securing in power of the Tories under Sir Robert Peel, inspired Dickens to contribute to *The Examiner* in another way. He wrote a series of scathing anti-Tory verse squibs signed 'W': 'The Fine Old English Gentleman. New Version (*to be said or sung at all Conservative Dinners*)', 7 August; 'The Quack Doctor's Proclamation', 14 August; and 'Subjects for Painters', 21 August. The last verse of 'The Fine Old English Gentleman' gives the flavour:

> The bright old day now dawns again; the cry runs through the land,
> In England there shall be dear bread – in Ireland, sword and brand;
> And poverty, and ignorance, shall swell the rich and grand,
> So, rally round the rulers with the gentle iron hand,
>> Of the fine old English Tory days;
>> Hail to the coming time!

Forster comments about these verses when reprinting them in his *Life of Dickens*: 'I doubt if he ever enjoyed anything more than the power of thus taking part occasionally, unknown to outsiders, in the sharp conflict the press was waging at the time.'[21]

After a six-month 'sabbatical' in America (1842), Dickens contributed further occasional reviews to *The Examiner* and at least two more satirical pieces, both prose, one on the State and one on the Church (see pp. 51–5 and 59–63), before the end of 1843. His urgent social concerns about the poor and the desperate need to provide them with better living conditions, more equitable treatment before the law and, above all, some decent education, found expression through his public speeches and through his fiction, especially the first two Christmas Books, rather than through his journalism, and it was not until after his return from a year's residence in Italy in the summer of 1845 that he began again to hanker after involvement with the press. He revived the idea of a journal of his own, a weekly to be called *The Cricket* ('A cheerful creature that chirrups on the hearth'):

> ... partly original, partly select; notices of books, notices of theatres, notices of all good things, notices of all bad ones; *Carol* philosophy, cheerful views, sharp anatomisation of humbug, jolly good temper, papers always in season pat to the time of year, and a vein of glowing, hearty, generous, mirthful, beaming reference in everything to Home and Fireside.[22]

In the event, this quintessentially Dickensian conception dwindled down into a little Christmas volume, the weekly-journal project having been, as Forster puts it, 'swept away by a larger scheme', nothing less than the founding of a new national daily newspaper to be called the *Daily News*, with Dickens as its first editor.

The *Daily News* was founded by a group of capitalists, including Joseph Paxton, the future architect of the Crystal Palace, to champion Liberal, Free-Trade principles (editorial after editorial would denounce the Corn Laws as the greatest evil of the day) and to give a voice particularly to the Railway interest; as the *Pilgrim* editors note, 'railway money supplied most of the capital ... and railway advertising part of its revenue'.[23] It was obviously a good publicity stroke to appoint the most popular novelist in England as editor, but Dickens soon found the position untenable. He resigned after only seventeen issues and Forster took his place for a few months. After he too had extricated himself from the editorship Dickens wrote to congratulate him (26–29 October 1846): 'we'll have ... the old life again, as it used to be before those daily nooses caught us by the legs and sometimes tripped us up'.[24] Dickens began his brief editorship with high hopes and great confidence, however, as reflected in his first editorial which set out the paper's creed:

> The Principles advocated by THE DAILY NEWS will be Principles of Progress and Improvement: of Education, Civil and Religious Liberty, and Equal Legislation; Principles such as its conductors believe the advancing spirit of the time requires: the condition of the country demands: and Justice,

Reason and Experience legitimately sanction. Very much is to be done, and must be done towards the bodily comfort, mental elevation, and general contentment of the English People. But, their social improvement is so inseparable from the well-doing of Arts and Commerce, the growth of public works, the free investment of capital in all those numerous helps to civilisation and improvement to which the ingenuity of the age gives birth, that we hold it to be impossible rationally to consider the true interests of the people as a class question, or to separate them from the interests of the merchant and manufacturer.

Dickens also touched on another objective, which, after his bruising experience of the American press, would have been close to his heart:

> We seek, so far as in us lies, to elevate the character of the Public Press in England. We believe it would attain a much higher position, and that those who wield its powers would be infinitely more respected as a class, and an important one, if it were purged of a disposition to sordid attacks *upon itself*, which only prevails in England and America.... The stamp on newspapers is not like the stamp on Universal Medicine-Bottles, which licenses anything, however false and monstrous....[25]

Apart from this editorial, Dickens's other contributions to the *News* during his brief editorship consisted of the beginning of a series of 'Travelling Letters' describing his year in Italy (published later in the year as *Pictures from Italy*); another verse squib, 'The British Lion' (24 January); and a letter on Ragged Schools (4 February). He also contributed, under Forster's editorship, a remarkable series of five letters on capital punishment, advocating its total abolition 'for the advantage of society, for the prevention of crime, and without the least reference to, or tenderness for, any individual malefactor whatever'. Discussing them in his *Dickens and Crime* (1962), Philip Collins comments:

> He presents his case against capital punishment lucidly, marshalling very ably the several kinds of objection to hanging. He uses psychological insight, emotional appeal, statistics, and pertinent references to the literature on the subject. He argues at unusual length, too (some twelve thousand words); I cannot, indeed, recall his *arguing* at such length about any other social question.[26]

After the last of these letters, Dickens wrote no more in the *Daily News* and, indeed, wrote no journalism for nearly two years.[27] During this time, he was again resident abroad for a period ('The Retreat to Switzerland', Forster rather grandly calls it), and busy with writing *Dombey and Son*, as well as with his work for Miss Burdett-Coutts's 'Home for Homeless Women' and performances by his 'Strolling Players' to raise money for the projected Guild of Literature and Art. Meanwhile, Forster had succeeded Fonblanque as editor of *The Examiner* and Dickens became once more a contributor in February 1848, with a substantial review (see p. 80) of a new book about ghosts, a subject always of the deepest interest to him.

Over the next twenty-one months, Dickens wrote regularly for *The Examiner*, often perhaps responding to a specific invitation from Forster to review a book or a dramatic performance.[28] It would be most interesting to know whether it was at Forster's suggestion, or on his own initiative, that he undertook the review of Hunt's *Poetry of Science* (see p. 129), which reveals a greater familiarity on his part with pre-Darwinian evolutionary theories than he is usually credited with. Above all, he found *The Examiner*, with its enlightened middle-class readership,[29] an ideal medium for the expression of his urgent social concerns. Sometimes he would use a book review as the vehicle for setting out his views, as in the case of his notice of Cruikshank's *The Drunkard's Children* (see p. 102), but mostly he would be inspired to write by some news item, such as a court case, some government statistics, or a royal burial. Among the most powerful of such contributions are his scorching denunciation, in a whole series of articles, of the scandalous Tooting baby farm and the official negligence and incompetence that allowed it to continue (see pp. 147–56), and his withering attack on fanatical temperance reformers in 'Demoralisation and Total Abstinence' (see pp. 159–69). These articles are unlike anything he had written before, though they echo much in his speeches of the previous few years, and they look forward to the superlative social journalism that he was soon to be regularly publishing in *Household Words*. As K.J. Fielding and A.W. Brice comment, 'In contributing to the *Examiner*, he learned to be a journalist rather than a reporter. The connection fostered and helped form his interest in society, and it may even be said to have helped shape his style as well as his thought.'[30]

His work for *The Examiner* during 1848–9 was indeed preparing him for the 'conducting' of his own journal, *Household Words*, which began publication at the end of March 1850.[31] It sometimes also suggested material for his fiction, e.g., the Borioboola-Gha enterprise and the character of Guster in *Bleak House* (see p. 109).

Dickens's writings for *Household Words*, and the nature of the journal itself, will be more fully discussed in the Introduction to Vol. 3 of this edition, which will consist entirely of articles from it. The present volume only includes what would now be called Dickens's 'mission statement' for his enterprise (see pp. 177–9) and a generous sampling of the articles he published in it through June 1851. Among these are two of his richest pieces of investigative journalism in the field of popular entertainment –

'The Amusements of the People' and 'Some Account of an Extraordinary Traveller'. A comparison of the latter with his earlier report for *The Examiner* on Banvard's Panorama will show how dramatically (here very much the adverb *juste*) he has moved from the mode of lively reportage to that of brilliantly inventive and entertaining journalism. Learning, perhaps, from his admired friend Carlyle, he begins to invent nonce-characters like Joe Whelks of the New Cut, Lambeth, or the Pickwickian Mr Booley, life and soul of the Social Oysters club.[32] These become the reader's enthusiastic companions in the exploration of such delights as a performance of *Eva the Betrayed* at the Old Vic (as the Royal Victoria Theatre came later to be known) or Mr Brees's 'Colonial Panorama' of New Zealand in Leicester Square.

In a number of his satirical social-comment pieces Dickens makes exuberant use of the dramatic monologue form, or communication from an imaginary correspondent, a device he had first used in his 1844 'Threatening Letter to Thomas Hood from an Ancient Gentleman'. Whether it is the aggrieved Raven in 'Perfect Felicity', the disturbed young art-lover in 'The Ghost of Art', the steady-going narrator of 'A Poor Man's Tale of a Patent', the meanly complacent Mr Snoady in 'Lively Turtle', the hapless Mr Meek, or the King of the Bill-stickers, Dickens makes us hear and relish the sound of a highly individual voice, a device by means of which, in the best examples (Mr Meek is perhaps rather too conventional a joke), we are given a strange but illuminating perspective on some aspect or aspects of the contemporary scene. These monologues also look forward to the great triumphs in this genre that Dickens was later to achieve in his *Christmas Stories* – Mrs Lirriper and Christopher the waiter in 'Somebody's Luggage'. And in the virtuoso writing of such a piece as 'On Duty with Inspector Field' we can see Dickens mastering the technique of free indirect speech ready for the spectacular use he will make of it in *Bleak House*.

'Keep *Household Words* imaginative!' was Dickens's constant 'conductorial' injunction to his sub-editor W. H. Wills and to his 'young men', staff writers like G. A. Sala and Henry Morley. No one, having read the articles from the journal reprinted in this volume, can doubt that he himself set a dazzling standard in this respect. As journalist no less than as novelist he showed himself fully worthy of his self-conferred title, 'The Sparkler of Albion'.

MICHAEL SLATER
Birkbeck College, University of London, 1996

NOTES

1. The phrases 'drone of the Parliamentary bagpipes' and 'savage stenographic mystery' come from *David Copperfield*, Chs 47 and 43 respectively. Quotations from Beard come from Charles Kent, 'Dickens as a Journalist', *Time*, Vol. 5, July 1881, pp. 363 and 365. On Dickens and shorthand, see W.J. Carlton, *Charles Dickens Shorthand Writer* (1926). The description of Dickens's new clothes comes from J. P. Collier, *An Old Man's Diary, Forty Years Ago* (see John Forster, *The Life of Charles Dickens*, ed. J. W. T. Ley [1928], p. 67).

2. *Pilgrim*, Vol. VIII, p. 131.

3. For the detailed publication history of Dickens's Sketches, see Vol. 1 of this edition, pp. xxiii–xxvi.

4. Forster, *op. cit.*, Book 1, Ch. 4. When in 1843 Easthope dismissed Black from the editorship of the *Chronicle*, Dickens wrote that he was 'deeply grieved. . . . Sorry from my heart's core' and organised a dinner in Black's honour to console him (Forster, *op. cit.*, p. 295).

5. 'Mr Charles Mackay's Recollections' in F. G. Kitton, *Charles Dickens: By Pen and Pencil* (1890), pp. 133–5.

6. *Morning Chronicle*, 23 June 1836, p. 2, col. 1. Dickens's concern about 'ungentlemanly' treatment in this passage is very understandable in the light of the following comments in an article on 'Newspaper Reporting' in *The Metropolitan Magazine* (1832), p. 284: 'the greatest and most extraordinary anomaly in society is the condition of reporters . . . they must be men of integrity and of gentlemanly feeling, for their responsibility is great, and their functions often require a delicate discernment, and a nice sense of propriety. Notwithstanding this, no class of men is so little regarded – none so completely out of the pale of respectable society – none so impoverished, or so subject to mortifications, insult, and gross impositions.' (Quoted by G. Mott in his ' "I Wallow in Words", Dickens, Journalism and Public Affairs 1831–38', unpublished Ph.D. thesis, University of Leicester, 1984, p. 154.)

7. *Pilgrim*, Vol. 1, p. 58.

8. K. J. Fielding (ed.), *The Speeches of Charles Dickens* (1960), p. 347.

9. *Pilgrim*, Vol. 1, p. 197.

10. The great journalist William Howard Russell, who reported the Crimean War for *The Times*, said of Dickens, 'he was the best reporter in London, and as a journalist he was nothing more' (J. B. Atkins, *The Life of Sir William Howard Russell* [1911], Vol. 1, p. 58).

11. Mott (*op. cit.*, p. 112) quotes a choice specimen of the *Chronicle*'s rhetoric applied to the Tory press: 'The poor old *Times* in its *imbecile ravings*, resembles those unfortunate wretches whose *degraded prostitution* is fast producing neglect and *disgust*' (15 June 1835).

12. *David Copperfield*, Ch. 43.

13. For Dickens's work on *Bentley's*, see Vol. 1 of this edition.

14. For an excellent recent account of Dickens's response to these journals, see G. Smith, *Charles Dickens: A Literary Life* (1996), pp. 60–5.
15. Forster, *op. cit.*, Book 2, Ch. 6.
16. Forster first met Dickens during the winter of 1836–7 (*Pilgrim*, Vol. I, p. 240).
17. Mott, *op. cit.*, p. 174.
18. Writing in the *Times Literary Supplement*, 23 November 1967, Robert Gittings described *The Examiner* for a modern audience as 'like a mixture of the *New Statesman*, *The Times* (new style) and (in good measure) *The News of the World*'. He was writing about Hunt's *Examiner*, but the mixture had not greatly changed under Fonblanque's editorship.
19. F. Espinasse, *Literary Recollections*, (1895), p. 114.
20. See Appendix B, pp. 372–8.
21. Forster, *op. cit.*, Book 2, Ch. 12. Forster continues: ' "By Jove, how radical I am getting!" he [Dickens] wrote to me (13th August). "I wax stronger and stronger in the true principles every day." '
22. *Ibid.*, Book 5, Ch. 1.
23. *Pilgrim*, Vol. VI, p. xiii. For an excellent, illuminating discussion of Dickens's work with the *Daily News*, see David Roberts, 'Charles Dickens and the *Daily News*: Editorials and Editorial Writers', *Victorian Periodicals Review*, Vol. 22 (1989), pp. 51–63. Roberts notes that 'A deep, pervasive, and intense hostility towards the landed classes and their privileges, not economic reality, underlay the *Daily News*' denunciation of the Corn Laws.' How sympathetic this attitude would have been to Dickens can be seen from his 1844 assault on 'the Agricultural Interest' in the *Morning Chronicle* (see p. 64). For a critical contemporary view of Dickens as editor of the *News*, see K. J. Fielding, 'Dickens as J. T. Danson Knew Him', *The Dickensian*, Vol. 68 (1972), pp. 151–61.
24. *Pilgrim*, Vol. IV, p. 649.
25. *Daily News*, 21 January 1846, p. 4, col. 1.
26. *Dickens and Crime*, p. 227. At the time that Collins wrote only four of the letters were known. The first in the series, bringing the total up to five, was discovered by Kathleen Tillotson and published by her in the *Times Literary Supplement*, 12 August 1965 (p. 704). These letters, together with the earlier one on Ragged Schools, were considered as articles rather than letters by the *Pilgrim* editors and so not included in Vol. IV of their edition, where one might have expected to find them. All are included by David Paroissien, however, in his *Selected Letters of Charles Dickens* (1985). These letters took the place of the article 'on the Punishment of Death, and sympathy with Great Criminals' that Dickens had in July 1845 promised to write for the *Edinburgh Review*; like previous such promises it remained unfulfilled (see *Pilgrim*, Vol. IV, p. 340).
27. Dickens made one further verse-contribution to the *Daily News*, the entirely serious anti-Corn Law 'Hymn of the Wiltshire Labourers' (14 February).

28. Occasionally Forster seems to have persuaded Dickens to shape an article out of a private letter sent to him by Dickens – see pp. 99 and 104.

29. James A. Davies notes in his *John Forster: A Literary Life* (1983), p. 223, that *The Examiner*'s appeal 'was to a comfortable, affluent, intelligent middle class, as was evident from its advertisements for books, cutlery, life assurance, patent medicines and opera subscriptions at 200 guineas a year'. Davies quotes (p. 224) a eulogy of the middle classes from the issue for 15 April 1848: 'To the virtue of our institutions we owe the existence of the most numerous and best-conditioned middle class in the world. . . .'

30. Alec W. Brice and K. J. Fielding, 'A New Article by Dickens: "Demoralisation and Total Abstinence" ', *Dickens Studies Annual*, Vol. 9 (1981), p. 1.

31. Dickens took the editorial title of 'Conductor' for *Household Words*. All contributions, including his own, were published anonymously.

32. The MP for Whitened Sepulchres in 'The Sunday Screw' (pp. 253–6) is another good example.

ACKNOWLEDGEMENTS

My deepest debt is to those two great Dickens scholars, Professor
Philip Collins and Professor K.J. Fielding, whose friendship, practical
guidance and unfailingly generous encouragement I have had the
privilege of enjoying in all my work on Dickens ever since my
graduate-school days. In the case of the present volume I am especially
in their debt for it is they above all who, together with Professor
Harry Stone, have done most, over the past thirty years or so, to
deepen and extend our knowledge of the range and significance of
Dickens's journalistic writings. Without Professor Fielding's many
notable articles on *The Examiner*, including those published jointly with
Dr Alec W. Brice, this edition would have been infinitely harder to
undertake, as it would have been also without the benefit of Professor
Collins's classic study *Dickens and Crime* and many other writings as a
rich resource for the compilation of so many of the headnotes in this
volume.

Professors Fielding and Collins have added to all their past kindnesses
to me by reading drafts of *The Examiner* and *Household Words* sections
respectively and making numerous valuable comments. I am also grateful
to Dr John Drew and my friend Mr John Grigg for reading through all
of the headnotes, spotting several errors, and making a number of most
helpful suggestions; to Dr Klaus Stierstorfer for much help with textual
collating; to Dr Jean Elliott and Mr Julian Sheather for research assistance; and to Mr Michael Rogers for meticulous help with proof-
reading.

Dr David Atkinson with his computer expertise has been not a tower
but a whole Castle of strength in helping me compile the Index and
Glossary as well as the Appendix listing all Dickens's known journalism
from 1833 to the end of June 1851.

For help and information on particular points I am indebted to the
following friends and colleagues: Professor Richard D. Altick, Professor
Jon Arms, Ms Gillian Avery, Dr Michael Baron, Mr Christopher Date,
Dr Robin Howells, Dr Tom Keymer, Mr George Newlyn, Dr David
Parker, Professor Robert L. Patten, Dr Adam Roberts and Mr Anthony
Williams.

Finally I would like to thank my editor, Linda Osband, for all her quite invaluable help; and to acknowledge with gratitude the financial support for this edition received from the Research Priority Fund of the Centre for Language and Literature at Birkbeck College.

M.S.

NOTE ON THE
PROVENANCE,
Selection and Treatment of the Texts

Dickens's writings for the *Morning Chronicle* have never been collected but
have been reprinted individually in *The Dickensian* from time to time as
they have been identified by scholars, notably the late W. J. Carlton. The
work of the *Pilgrim* editors in their first volume (1965) enabled the
identification of still more examples. The selection presented includes
good examples of the different kinds of work done for the paper by
Dickens – reports, reviews, a satirical squib – apart from his 'Boz'
sketches, which appear in Vol. 1 of this edition.

Twenty of Dickens's anonymous contributions to *The Examiner* were
first identified (one erroneously) by B. W. Matz from MSS. in the Forster
Collection at the Victoria and Albert Museum and were reprinted by
him in *Miscellaneous Papers* (1908). Over twenty more have since been
identified and reprinted in *The Dickensian* and elsewhere by Professor K. J.
Fielding, Dr Alec W. Brice and other scholars. The twenty-four *Examiner*
pieces presented in this volume have been selected on the basis of their
intrinsic interest and as particularly effective examples of Dickens's work
in this genre (and, as with the *Chronicle* pieces, I have tried to strike a
balance between reviews of various kinds and topical comment, also of
various kinds). Where an article was succeeded by others on the same
topic, these have been summarised in an end-note.

Matz also included in *Miscellaneous Papers* Dickens's two stray pieces
written to help his friends Thomas Hood and Douglas Jerrold, printing
the latter ('The Spirit of Chivalry in Westminster Hall') from the MS. in
the Forster Collection rather than from Jerrold's *Shilling Magazine*. Both
these articles find a place in this volume and I have followed Matz in
the text chosen for the Jerrold piece.

Dickens collected only twenty-six of his host of articles written for
Household Words, reprinting them, together with five of his Christmas
Stories from the same journal, under the title *Reprinted Pieces* to fill out
the second volume of *The Old Curiosity Shop* in the Library Edition of his
works (1858). The rest of his contributions were first identified by Matz,
using the journal's Contributors' Book, and included in *Miscellaneous
Papers*. I present in this volume twenty-four of the thirty-three full-length

articles solely written by Dickens during the first fifteen months of *Household Words*'s existence. My selection is based on the same criteria as for the *Examiner* pieces. One of his 'Raven' pieces may stand for the whole series and the 'Three "Detective" Anecdotes', included in *Reprinted Pieces*, has also been omitted as being 'more of the same'.

With the one exception of 'The Spirit of Chivalry', the text of each report, essay or review in this volume is the text as first published in the relevant newspaper or magazine, with any obvious misprints silently corrected and the original spelling and punctuation, italicisations, etc., preserved with three exceptions: in accordance with standard modern usage, single quotation marks are used before double ones, the full stop has been omitted after Mr, Mrs, Dr, etc., and words like 'today', 'downstairs', 'anybody', 'juxtaposition', that were printed as two words in the nineteenth century, or else hyphenated, are here printed as single words. The location of any manuscript and/or corrected proof version is recorded in the relevant headnote and any interesting variants noted. Substantial alterations made when Dickens republished one of the *Household Words* essays in *Reprinted Pieces* are also recorded.

M.S.

ABBREVIATIONS

ATYR	*All the Year Round*
Forster	John Forster, *The Life of Charles Dickens*, ed. J. W. T. Ley (1928)
HW	*Household Words*
MP	*Miscellaneous Papers*, ed. B. W. Matz, 2 vols (1908)
Nonesuch	*The Letters of Charles Dickens* (The Nonesuch Edition), ed. Walter Dexter, 3 vols (1938)
Pilgrim	*The Letters of Charles Dickens* (The Pilgrim Edition), eds Madeline House, Graham Storey, et al. (1965–in progress)
RP	*Reprinted Pieces* (1858)
Stone	*The Uncollected Writings of Charles Dickens: Household Words 1850–1859*, ed. Harry Stone, 2 vols (1969)

SELECT BIBLIOGRAPHY

Note: Not included here are books or articles primarily relevant to only one particular item. These will be found cited in the appropriate headnote.

ACKROYD, Peter, *Dickens*, Sinclair-Stevenson, 1990. The best modern biography (though difficult to use for reference purposes) – an astonishing combination of exhaustive research and insight into the workings of Dickens's imagination.

ALTICK, R. D., *The Shows of London*, Harvard University Press, 1978. A magisterial and magnificent account, very fully illustrated, of London public entertainments, which provides detailed background for many of the pieces in this volume.

BRICE, Alec W., 'Dickens and *The Examiner*: Some Newly Identified Essays', unpublished M.Litt. thesis, University of Edinburgh, 1968. Provides much valuable context for Dickens's writings in *The Examiner*, several of which are here identified for the first time.

CARLTON, W. J., 'Charles Dickens, Dramatic Critic', *The Dickensian*, Vol. 56 (1960), pp. 11–27. Identifies and reprints with commentary many reviews written by Dickens for the *Morning Chronicle* 1834–6.

COLLINS, Philip, *Dickens and Crime*, Macmillan, 1962 (reprinted in paperback, 1995). Comprehensive and authoritative survey of the subject, which pays great attention to its central place in Dickens's social journalism.

FIELDING, K. J., *The Speeches of Charles Dickens*, Oxford: Clarendon Press, 1960; new edn, 1988. Essential companion volume to any collection of Dickens's writings on public affairs.

FORSTER, John, *The Life of Charles Dickens*, ed. J. W. T. Ley, 1928. Useful modern edition of the classic Dickens biography by his lifelong friend (first published 1872–4).

HOBSBAUM, Philip, *A Reader's Guide to Charles Dickens*, Thames and Hudson, 1972. Brief but trenchant discussions of Dickens's journalism in Chs 10 and 13.

HOUSE, Humphry, *The Dickens World*, Oxford University Press, 1942 (Oxford Paperback, 1960). The first study of Dickens to pay detailed attention to his social journalism and the connections between it and his fiction. Still very important.

House, M., Storey, G., et al. (eds), *The Letters of Charles Dickens* (The Pilgrim Edition), Vols 1–6 (1820–52); Oxford University Press, 1965–88.

Lohrli, Anne (ed.), *Household Words. A Weekly Journal Conducted by Charles Dickens. Table of Contents. List of Contributors and their Contributions based on the Household Words Office Book in the Morris L. Parish Collection of Victorian Novelists Princeton University Library*, University of Toronto Press, 1973. Superbly informative volume with a substantial and illuminating introduction.

Mott, Graham, ' "I Wallow in Words": Dickens' Journalism and Public Affairs 1831–38', unpublished Ph.D. thesis, University of Leicester, 1984. Valuable detailed discussion and contexting of Dickens's journalistic writings in the *Morning Chronicle* and elsewhere.

Philip, Neil, and Neuburg, Victor, *A December Vision: Dickens' Social Journalism*, Collins, 1986. Reprints, with commentary and parallel passages from the novels, eleven examples of Dickens's social journalism including 'Pet Prisoners', 'A December Vision', 'A Walk in a Workhouse' and 'On Duty with Inspector Field'.

Schlicke, Paul, *Dickens and Popular Entertainment*, George Allen and Unwin, 1985. Excellent comprehensive study of the topic highly relevant for 'The Amusements of the People' and several other pieces in this volume.

Scott, P. J. M., 'Introduction to the Present Reprint Edition. *Dickens's Journalism*', Dickens: *Miscellaneous Papers* (2 vols), Kraus Reprint, 1983.

Smith, Grahame, *Charles Dickens: A Literary Life*, Macmillan, 1996. Contains an important chapter on 'Periodicals, Journalism and the Literary Essay'.

Stone, Harry, *The Uncollected Writings of Charles Dickens: Household Words 1850–1859* (2 vols), Allen Lane: the Penguin Press, 1969. Meticulously edited and lavishly illustrated presentation of Dickens's so-called 'composite' articles, i.e., those written in collaboration with others, with a substantial and important introductory essay on Dickens as journalist and as editor.

DICKENS'S
LIFE AND TIMES 1834–51

<table>
<tr><td>CD's Personal Life</td><td>Writing Career</td><td>Historical and Literary Background</td></tr>
<tr>
<td>1834 Becomes reporter on the Morning Chronicle and meets Catherine Hogarth (Aug.). Takes chambers at 13 Furnival's Inn, Holborn (Dec.).</td>
<td>Six more stories published in the Monthly Magazine, also one in Bell's Weekly Magazine; five 'Street Sketches' published in the Morning Chronicle.</td>
<td>Poor Law Amendment Act (the New Poor Law). Transportation of 'Tolpuddle Martyrs'. Destruction by fire of old Houses of Parliament. Ainsworth's Rookwood, Balzac's Père Goriot, Lady Blessington's Conversations with Lord Byron, Bulwer Lytton's Last Days of Pompeii and Marryat's Peter Simple published. Deaths of Coleridge and Lamb.</td>
</tr>
<tr>
<td>1835 Becomes engaged to Catherine Hogarth (?May).</td>
<td>Two more stories in the Monthly Magazine, twenty 'Sketches of London' in the Evening Chronicle, ten 'Scenes and Characters' in Bell's Life in London.</td>
<td>Municipal Reform Act. Browning's Paracelsus, Clare's The Rural Muse, and Wordsworth's Yarrow Revisited, and Other Poems published.</td>
</tr>
<tr>
<td>1836 Moves into larger chambers at 15 Furnival's Inn (Feb.). Marries Catherine Hogarth at St Luke's, Chelsea (2 Apr.). Honeymoon at Chalk (Kent). Leaves staff of the Morning</td>
<td>Two more 'Scenes and Characters' in Bell's Life, two contributions to The Library of Fiction and one to Carlton Chronicle, four 'Sketches by Boz, New Series' in the Morning Chronicle. Sketches by</td>
<td>Chartist Movement begins. Forster's Lives of the Statesmen of the Commonwealth, and Lockhart's Life of Scott begin publication; Marryat's Mr Midshipman Easy published.</td>
</tr>
</table>

Chronicle (Nov.). First meeting with John Forster (?Dec.).

Boz: First Series published (8 Feb.). *Pickwick Papers* begins serialisation in 20 monthly numbers (31 Mar.), *Sunday Under Three Heads* (June). *The Strange Gentleman* produced at the St James's Theatre (29 Sept.) followed by *The Village Coquettes* (22 Dec.). *Sketches by Boz: Second Series* published (17 Dec.).

1837   First child (Charles) born (6 Jan.). Moves to 48 Doughty Street (Apr.). Death of Mary Hogarth, CD's sister-in-law (7 May). First visit to Europe (France and Belgium – July) and first family holiday at Broadstairs (Sept.).

First number of *Bentley's Miscellany* (ed. by CD) appears (1 Jan.). First of the 'Mudfog Papers' appears in it. *Oliver Twist* serialised in *Bentley's* in 24 monthly instalments from the 2nd number. *Is She His Wife?* produced at the St James's (3 Mar.). *Pickwick Papers* published in one volume (17 Nov.).

Death of William IV, accession of Victoria. Carlyle's *French Revolution* published. Death of Grimaldi, the clown.

1838   Expedition to Yorkshire schools with H. K. Browne (Jan./Feb.). Second child (Mary) born.

Sketches of Young Gentlemen (10 Feb.) and *Memoirs of Joseph Grimaldi* (26 Feb.). *Nicholas Nickleby* begins serialisation in 20 monthly numbers (31 Mar.). *Oliver Twist* published (9 Nov.).

Anti-Corn Law League founded in Manchester. First Afghan war breaks out. Daguerre–Niepce method of photography presented to the Académies des Sciences et des Beaux Arts, Paris.

1839   Resigns editorship of *Bentley's Miscellany* (31 Jan.). Third child (Kate) born. Moves to 1 Devonshire Place, Regent's Park.

The Loving Ballad of Lord Bateman published (June). *Nicholas Nickleby* published in volume form (23 Oct.).

First Opium War between Britain and China. Turner paints *The Fighting Téméraire*. Ainsworth's *Jack Sheppard* published.

1840

Sketches of Young Couples published (10 Feb.). First number of *Master Humphrey's Clock* issued (4 Apr.). *The Old Curiosity Shop* published in 40 weekly numbers in *Master Humphrey's Clock* from 25 Apr. *Master Humphrey's Clock*, Vol. 1 published (Oct.).

Victoria marries Albert. Introduction of the Penny Post. Sir Charles Barry begins building new Houses of Parliament. Nelson's column erected in Trafalgar Square. Ainsworth's *Tower of London,* Browning's *Sordello,* Poe's *Tales of the Grotesque and Arabesque,* and Thackeray's 'A Shabby Genteel Story' (*Fraser's Magazine*) published.

1841　Fourth child (Walter) born. CD declines invitation to be Liberal Parliamentary candidate for Reading. Granted the Freedom of the City of Edinburgh (29 June).

Barnaby Rudge published in 42 weekly numbers in *Master Humphrey's Clock* from 13 Feb. *Master Humphrey's Clock*, Vols 2 and 3 published (Apr. and Dec.). Publication of *The Old Curiosity Shop* and *Barnaby Rudge*, each in one volume (15 Dec.).

Peel succeeds Melbourne as Prime Minister. John Tyler becomes tenth President of the USA. *Punch* founded. Carlyle's *On Heroes and Hero-Worship*, J. F. Cooper's *The Deerslayer,* and Poe's 'The Murders in the Rue Morgue' (*Graham's Magazine*) published.

1842　Visits America with Catherine (Jan.–June). Visits Cornwall with Forster and other friends (Oct.–Nov.).

American Notes published (19 Oct.). *Martin Chuzzlewit* begins serialisation in 20 monthly numbers (31 Dec.).

Weber–Ashburton Treaty between Britain and America defines Canadian frontier. Tennyson's *Poems*, Macaulay's *Lays of Ancient Rome*, and Gogol's *Dead Souls* published.

1843　Presides at opening of the Manchester Athenaeum (5 Oct.).

A Christmas Carol published (19 Dec.).

Launching of SS *Great Britain*, and building of Thames Tunnel between Rotherhithe and Wapping. Carlyle's *Past and Present*, Hood's 'Song

1844 Fifth child (Francis) born. CD breaks with Chapman and Hall; Bradbury and Evans become his publishers. Resides in Genoa from 16 July. Visits London to read *The Chimes* to his friends (30 Nov.–8 Dec.).

Martin Chuzzlewit published in volume form (July). *The Chimes* published (16 Dec.).

of the Shirt' (*Punch*), and Vol. 1 of Ruskin's *Modern Painters* published. Marx meets Engels in Paris. Turner paints *Rain, Steam, and Speed*. Disraeli's *Coningsby*, Kinglake's *Eothen*, and Thackeray's *Barry Lyndon* published.

1845 Visits Rome and Naples with Catherine, returns to London from Genoa. Directs and acts in Jonson's *Every Man in His Humour* for the Amateur Players (Sept.). Sixth child (Alfred) born.

The Cricket on the Hearth published (20 Dec.).

Layard begins excavations at Nineveh. Wagner's *Tannhäuser* produced in Dresden. Browning's *Dramatic Romances and Lyrics*, Disraeli's *Sybil*, and Poe's *The Raven and Other Poems* published.

1846 Editor of the *Daily News* (21 Jan.–9 Feb.). Resides in Lausanne (11 June–16 Nov.), and then in Paris.

Pictures from Italy published (18 May). *Dombey and Son* begins serialisation in 20 monthly numbers (30 Sept.). *The Battle of Life* published (19 Dec.).

Famine in Ireland. Repeal of Corn Laws. First Christmas card designed. Browning marries Elizabeth Barrett. Balzac's *Cousine Bette*, Lear's *Book of Nonsense*, and Thackeray's 'Snobs of England' (in *Punch*) published.

1847 Returns from Paris (28 Feb.). Seventh child (Sydney) born. Arranges lease of house for Miss Burdett-Coutts's 'Home for Homeless Women' (Urania Cottage). Performs with The Amateur Players in Manchester

First Californian gold rush. First British Factory Act (restricting hours worked by women and children). Charlotte Brontë's *Jane Eyre*, Emily Brontë's *Wuthering Heights* and Prescott's *The Conquest of Peru* published.

and Liverpool.

Thackeray's *Vanity Fair* begins serialisation in monthly numbers (Jan.).

1848 Directs and acts in London and provincial performances by the Amateur Players (May/July). Death of CD's beloved sister Fanny.

Dombey and Son published in volume form (Apr.). *The Haunted Man* published (19 Dec.).

'The Year of Revolutions' (in Paris, Berlin, Vienna, Rome, Prague, and other cities). Outbreak of cholera in London. End of the Chartist Movement. Pre-Raphaelite Brotherhood founded. Mrs Gaskell's *Mary Barton* and first two volumes of *Macaulay's History of England* published. Thackeray's *Pendennis* begins serialisation in monthly numbers (Nov.).

1849 Eighth child (Henry) born.

David Copperfield begins serialisation in 20 monthly numbers (30 Apr.).

Death of Poe. Dostoevsky sentenced to penal servitude in Siberia. Matthew Arnold's *The Strayed Reveller and Other Poems*, Charlotte Brontë's *Shirley*, and Ruskin's *Seven Lamps of Architecture* published.

1850 Ninth child (Dora) born. CD founds the Guild of Literature and Art with Bulwer Lytton to help needy writers and artists.

Household Words, a weekly journal edited by CD, begins publication (30 Mar.). *David Copperfield* appears in volume form (Nov.).

Restoration of Catholic hierarchy in England. Wordsworth dies, Tennyson succeeds him as Poet Laureate. Millais's *Christ in the House of His Parents* exhibited (attacked by CD in *HW*). Hawthorne's *The Scarlet Letter*, Kingsley's *Alton Locke*,

		Tennyson's *In Memoriam*, Turgenev's *A Month in the Country*, and Wordsworth's *The Prelude* published.
1851	Amateur theatricals at Rockingham Castle. Illness of Catherine Dickens, treatment at Malvern where CD visits her. Deaths of John Dickens (31 Mar.) and baby Dora (14 Apr.). CD directs and acts in Bulwer Lytton's *Not So Bad As We Seem* at Devonshire House (in aid of Guild of Literature and Art).	*Child's History of England* begins serialisation in *Household Words* (Jan.).	Death of Turner. Verdi's *Rigoletto* performed. The Great Exhibition in London. Melville's *Moby Dick*, Harriet Beecher Stowe's *Uncle Tom's Cabin*, and first part of Ruskin's *Stones of Venice* published.

ILLUSTRATIONS

'THE AMUSEMENTS OF THE PEOPLE' AND OTHER PAPERS

I

Report from Edinburgh on Preparations for the Grey Festival

Morning Chronicle, 17 September 1834

Dickens's first major assignment after joining the staff of the *Morning Chronicle* in the summer of 1834 was to go to Edinburgh with his friend and colleague Thomas Beard to cover the so-called 'Grey Festival', at which Scotland honoured the man chiefly responsible for the passage of the Reform Bill of 1832. The great Whig statesman Earl Grey had become Prime Minister in 1830, but by July 1834 he was not in good health and was eager to leave office. He found an opportunity to do so after Cabinet disagreements over the Irish Coercion Bill and Lord Melbourne took over the Premiership. 'Few Prime Ministers', comments E.A. Smith in his *Lord Grey* (1990), 'have retired to such a chorus of tributes' (p. 307). Scotland had benefited even more than England from the Reform bill, its electorate being increased from a mere 4,500 to 65,000 and eight new Parliamentary seats being created; hence the decision there to honour Grey with a grand public banquet.

Dickens and Beard had an exhilarating journey by sea to Leith, vividly described by Charles Kent, drawing on Beard's memories, in his 'Charles Dickens as a Journalist', *Time*, Vol. 5 (1881), pp. 361–74. Beard identified the following report as having been written entirely by Dickens.

EDINBURGH – SEPT. 13
(From Our Own Correspondent)

The city is extremely full of visitors, but the persons of note who have yet arrived are not numerous. The Earl of Durham is here, and the Lord Chancellor arrived about three o'clock this afternoon: his Lordship immediately proceeded to the scientific meeting; and it is understood that he will reside until after the dinner, on Monday, at the house of a private friend in the immediate vicinity of Edinburgh. I obtained a view of the temporary banqueting hall (the Grey Pavilion, as it is called) this morning. It is erecting in the High-School grounds on Calton Hill and, according to the estimate of the Committee, is capable of dining fifteen hundred individuals, and of affording accommodation, after removal of the cloth, to an indefinite number of persons. I confess I do not entertain very sanguine anticipations as to the accuracy of either of these calculations. The room is a square one with seven entrances, and, as far as I can judge from the unfinished state in which I saw it this morning, is very elegantly fitted up. It is, however, very ill adapted for hearing, and as to ventilation, it seems to have been forgotten that the two thousand persons who will meet together on this great occasion will require an occasional breath of fresh air. I hope I am mistaken, but I fear some confusion and much disappointment will arise from a large number of persons having purchased tickets, and the accommodation being such as necessarily to prevent a considerable portion of the company from witnessing, at all events, the preliminary part of the festival.

'A promenade' took place this morning in St Andrew's-square for the benefit of the Blind Asylum, the Deaf and Dumb Institution, and the House of Refuge. It was most respectably attended, but a lamentably dull affair. A marquee was erected in the centre of a parched bit of ground, without a tree or shrub to intercept the rays of a burning sun. Under it was a military band, and around it were the company. The band played, and the company walked about; and when the band were tired, a piper played by way of variation, and then the company walked about again; and when the piper was tired, such of the visitors as could find seats sat down, and those who could not looked as if they wished they had not come; and the poor blind-school pupils, who occupied the warmest seats in the inclosure were very hot and uncomfortable, and appeared very glad to be filed off from a scene in which they could take little interest, and with which their pensive careworn faces painfully contrasted.

To describe the bustle and animation and beauty of the city would be impossible. The advantages of its situation, the magnificence of the public buildings and the picturesque appearance of the old town, with which so many historical associations and local legends are connected, would form materials for a volume at any time; but thronged as the streets are now by a continued crowd of well-dressed strangers and bustling visitants, they present an exciting and exhilarating appearance which can hardly be imagined by those who have not been fortunate enough to witness it.

I have only time to express my hope, that the arrangements in progress for the long-expected dinner may meet with that success to which the spirit in which they are dictated fully entitles them.

2

Report of the Edinburgh Dinner to Lord Grey, 15 September 1834

Morning Chronicle, 18 September 1834

The full report of Grey's triumphal progress on Monday, 15 September, from Oxenfoord Castle via Dalkeith to Edinburgh, the presentation to him of the Freedom of the City and the proceedings at the dinner occupies eleven columns of the *Chronicle*. The detailed reports of the many lengthy speeches bear impressive witness to the skill and stamina of Dickens and Beard. The *Chronicle* proudly notes in a leader that it provides its readers with a report of all the proceedings 'down to one o'clock on Tuesday morning when our Express left Edinburgh, as the company were on the point of breaking up'. The *Times* express left one hour earlier, however, and enabled that paper to print its report of the day's events and most of the speeches at the dinner on 17 September (seven columns); the rest of the speeches were reported the following day.

For the introductory paragraphs of the *Chronicle*'s report, identified as Dickens's by Beard and describing Grey's progress to Edinburgh, see *The Dickensian*, Vol. 31 (1935), pp. 5–10. The description of the dinner itself, given here, is unmistakably Dickensian, and in his tale 'The Steam Excursion', published in the October *Monthly Magazine*, Dickens referred back to his account of the man who could not wait to begin eating. After the words 'blood to the head' in the paragraph about Mr Hardy towards the end of 'The Steam Excursion' (Vol. 1 of this edition, p. 387), the *Monthly* text continues:

> Having been for some months past subject to indigestion, he was recently persuaded to try a keener air and a more northern climate for the removal of the one, and the improvement of the other. We are credibly informed that he was present at the Edinburgh dinner, and, moreover, that he is the individual to whose eager appetite on that occasion we find allusion made in the *Morning Chronicle* of a few days since.

The *Times* reporter also commented on the 'rather indecent proceeding' of 'a general demolition of the eatables' before the chairman had appeared ('there arose an almost universal clatter of knives and forks'), but his account has none of Dickens's humorous observation.

Beard told Kent that it was at this dinner, as they worked furiously to get the speeches down, that Dickens 'began first to be affected by that intense dislike for Lord Grey's style of speaking, for his fishy coldness, his uncongenial and unsympathetic politeness, and for his insufferable though most gentlemanly artificiality, against all of which peculiarities Dickens years afterwards inveighed ... exclaiming in allusion to [Grey], with a serio-comic shudder, "The shape of his head (I see it now) was misery to me and weighed down my youth" ' ('Charles Dickens as a Journalist', *Time*, Vol. 5 [1881], p. 369).

THE DINNER

The greatest exertions having been made to secure the completion of the temporary building erected for the occasion in the High School Yard on Calton Hill, the whole of the arrangements were finished and the pavilion ready for the reception of the fortunate holders of tickets at an early hour of the afternoon. To prevent confusion notices had been extensively circulated, informing the visitors that they would be admitted into the area in which the building was situated at four o'clock; that they would then be required to form themselves into 60 sections containing 30 persons in each, and that the acting stewards (60 in number) each heading a section, would proceed with them into the dining room, the order of priority being determined in the presence of the company by ballot. The number of white tickets originally issued was 1,500, it having been estimated that the room was capable of dining that number of persons; but as the applications for an increased number of tickets were very numerous, some four hundred buff tickets were issued, on the understanding that the holders of those admissions should dine as best they might, in the rooms belonging to the school, and be admitted into the pavilion immediately after the removal of the cloth. As we were admitted into the building at three o'clock, we had an opportunity of observing the result of these arrangements, and certainly nothing could be better: for by half past five o'clock every table (with the exception of those allotted to the chairman and croupier) was completely filled, without the slightest confusion having occurred.

On the principal side of the spacious apartment was the chairman's table, on a raised platform reserved for the strangers and distinguished visitors. Immediately opposite, on the other side of the pavilion, was the croupier's table; and behind it, extending the whole width of the building, was the ladies' gallery, a small portion of which was assigned to the musicians. Long tables, extending across the room, from the chairman's table to that of the croupier, were prepared for the ordinary guests. A handsome chandelier, borrowed for the occasion from the Theatre Royal, was suspended from the ventilation in the centre of the ceiling. There were also four smaller chandeliers – one at each corner of the room. The walls were ornamented with the armorial bearings of the Duke of Hamilton and the Earl of Rosebery, and the arms of the cities of Edinburgh and Glasgow, which were extremely well executed. The ceiling was tastefully painted in compartments and supported by crimson pillars, ornamented with a circular foliage of gilt laurel leaves. The remainder of the apartment was painted a faint stone-colour, and the effect of the whole was extremely light and elegant.

It had been announced that the dinner would take place at five o'clock precisely; but Earl Grey, and the other principal visitors, as might have been expected, did not arrive until shortly after six. Previous to their arrival, some slight confusion, and much merriment, was excited by the following circumstance: A gentleman who, we presume, had entered with one of the first sections, having sat with exemplary patience for some time in the immediate vicinity of cold fowls, roast beef, lobsters, and other tempting delicacies (for the dinner was a cold one), appeared to think that the best thing he could possibly do, would be to eat his dinner, while there was anything to eat. He accordingly laid about him with right good-will; the example was contagious, and the clatter of knives and forks became general. Hereupon, several gentlemen, who were not hungry, cried out 'Shame!' and looked very indignant; and several gentlemen who were hungry cried 'Shame!' too, eating nevertheless, all the while, as fast as they possibly could. In this dilemma, one of the stewards mounted a bench and feelingly represented to the delinquents the enormity of their conduct, imploring them for decency's sake, to defer the process of mastication until the arrival of Earl Grey. This address was loudly cheered, but totally unheeded; and this is, perhaps, one of the few instances on record of a dinner having been virtually concluded before it began.

On the arrival of the distinguished guests, Earl Rosebery took the chair, in consequence of the absence of the Duke of Hamilton (who was to have presided) through illness. This circumstance involved the necessity of appointing a new croupier, and the Lord Advocate was selected to fill the office.

[Here follows a para. listing the guests at the principal tables.]

The Chairman intreated the assembly to postpone the commencement of the dinner for a few moments. The Reverend Mr Henry Grey was in attendance for the purpose of saying grace; but he was outside the room, and the crowd was so great that he could not get in. Under these circumstances he intreated them to pause for a few minutes.

As the major part of the company had already dined, they acceded to the request with the utmost good humour. The Rev. Gentleman arrived; grace was said; and the same ceremony was repeated at the conclusion of the dinner, which soon arrived. *Non Nobis Domine* having been sung, another trifling delay was occasioned by the entrance of the gentlemen who had dined in the school-room with the Buff tickets, for whose accommodation seats were hastily placed in the spaces which had been previously occupied by the waiters.

The Chairman inquired of the stewards whether all the company were yet seated? Several of the stewards replied in the negative; and various gentlemen corroborated the assertion, by exclaiming that it was entirely impossible they could sit down anywhere.

A glee having been directed in the meantime, 'The King of Merry England,' by Robert Gilfillan, was sung.

The room being now quite full, and no more complaints being heard –

The Chairman rose (proposed toast of The King).
[Here follow reports of the various speeches, toasts and glees and the report as a whole then ends as follows:]

Lord Grey, and the noblemen and gentlemen who accompanied him, were most enthusiastically cheered on their retiring from the pavilion, and during their progress to the city.

The company then departed, apparently much gratified with an entertainment of a most memorable nature, both with reference to the occasion itself, and the splendid and novel scale on which it was celebrated.

We cannot conclude this report without expressing our admiration of the excellent arrangements made by John Gracie, Esq., to whom the arduous task of supervising the extensive preparations had been confided. We are under great obligations to that gentleman for his unremitting attentions, and are most happy to have this opportunity of acknowledging them.

3

Theatre Review: *The Christening* by J.B. Buckstone

Morning Chronicle, 14 October 1834

J.B. Buckstone was a highly popular comic actor (his 'voice offstage would set the audience roaring, and his face was irresistibly funny', Michael Booth, *Theatre in the Victorian Age* [1991], p. 128) and a prolific provider of melodramas, farces and interludes for the stage. By 1834 he had written over forty pieces, many of them having been produced at the thriving Adelphi Theatre in the Strand, described in 1835 as 'by far the most fashionably attended theatre in London' (quoted by R. Mander and J. Mitchenson, *The Theatres of London* [1963], p. 17). J.P. Wilkinson and Mary Anne Keeley were also celebrated comedians, so it is not surprising that the piece enjoyed a long run.

Buckstone's farce seems, as Dickens humorously points out here, to have been inspired by his own comic story about another old curmudgeon forced into becoming a godfather, 'The Bloomsbury Christening', published in the *Monthly Magazine* (April 1834) and subsequently included in *Sketches by Boz* (see Vol. 1 of this edition, p. 448). Buckstone has, as Dickens admits, introduced much extra comic business (two babies instead of one, etc.), but the lack of any acknowledgement to his story moved Dickens to publish a humorous letter in the November *Monthly Magazine* protesting against Buckstone's 'kidnapping' of his 'offspring' (see *Pilgrim*, Vol. 1, p. 42).

When *The Christening* was revived at the Adelphi nearly a year later, Dickens renewed his complaint of plagiarism in his review (29 September 1835; quoted by W.J. Carlton in his 'Charles Dickens, Dramatic Critic', *The Dickensian*, Vol. 56 [1960] p. 14):

> Who is the author of this piece? We read a tale in the *Monthly Magazine*, a couple of years ago, we believed, of which *The Christening*, as represented, seems to be little more than a transcript, with a change in the names of the characters.

ADELPHI

A new trifle, in one act, by MR BUCKSTONE, was produced here last night, and met with complete success. It would be hardly fair to detail the plot of an amusing interlude, which is principally made up of unlooked-for situation, and humorous *équivoques*. We will, therefore, only say that the principal features of the peace [*sic*] are the distresses of *Grum* (MR WILKINSON), a surly misanthrope, who is entrapped into becoming sponsor for the first child of *Mr Hopkins Twiddie* (MR BUCKSTONE), and the confusion arising from certain mistakes occasioned by a changing of children, and confounding of people, which frequently take place on the stage, and never occur elsewhere. The acting of MRS KEELEY in the part of a busy, meddling godmother, who entices the unfortunate godfather to make presents he never meant, and concessions he never intended, was extremely good. WILKINSON himself was excellent in *Grum*; we had no idea he could act so well, or so differently from his usual style. BUCKSTONE's portraiture of the happy, bustling father, and subsequently of the angry, jealous husband, was admirable; and the remainder of the *dramatis personae* acquitted themselves with great spirit. We hailed one or two of the characters with great satisfaction – they are old and very particular friends of ours. We met with them, and several of the jokes we heard last night, at a certain 'Bloomsbury Christening' described in 'The Monthly Magazine' some little time since. We make this remark in no spirit of ill-nature to MR BUCKSTONE, who has added excellent materials of his own, and produced a very sprightly and amusing interlude, which we hope and believe will have a long run. He obtained permission to attempt the christening of his bantling every evening until further notice, without a dissentient voice, and amidst great applause. He is an old, and a very successful caterer for the amusement of the public and deserves their approbations as much as any author who has appealed to their favour for years past.

4

'The Story without a Beginning'
(Translated from the German by Boz)

Morning Chronicle, 18 December 1834

Dickens's first essay in political satire, this piece was published under his 'Boz' pseudonym and relates to William IV's abrupt dismissal of Melbourne and the Whigs on 15 November. Apprehensive generally about the pace of political reform, the King had become alarmed above all by the Government's attitude towards Irish Church reform and so 'for the last time in British history a monarch ... dismissed his political servants' (Norman Gash, *Sir Robert Peel* [1972], p. 79) and sent for the Duke of Wellington to form a Tory administration, which Wellington did with Peel as Prime Minister. Liberal and Radical opinion was outraged by the King's action and Dickens's piece is expressive of this. As he was later to use his beloved *Arabian Nights* for the purpose of political satire during the Crimean War (see Vol. 3 of this edition), so here he uses a German *märchen*, *Das Märchen Ohne Ende*, written by the religious philosopher F.W. Carové and translated into English as 'The Story without an End' by Sarah Austin in 1834. A sugary little moral-allegorical tale about growing up, Carové's story describes a child discovering, with the aid of a friendly dragonfly, the wonder and

beauty and joy of Nature (he has 'a little flower-garden behind his cottage
... where he knew that all the flowers would nod kindly to him'). It was
enormously popular in England and Dickens drew on it again, for a very
different effect, many years later when he wanted 'something tender for an
early number of *HW* (see p. 186). He did not read German, so knew the
story only in Austin's translation, the style of which he perfectly captures.

The child clearly represents William IV, the flowers his people (the green
flowers being, of course, the Irish), the 'insects and reptiles' the Tories, and
the industrious gardener-bees the Whigs. The 'burrows' that had 'become
close and rotten' are the so-called 'rotten boroughs' that sometimes returned
not one but two members ('carcasses') to the Commons and were intended
to be swept away by the Reform Bill.

And the child was happy, and he trod on soft carpets, and feasted on
rich delicacies, and listened to the sound of music, and his mind was
easy, and the child was quite at home, for it was not his first childhood,
but his second childhood. And people gaily clad, wearing fine glittering
stars upon their breasts, like the beautiful diamond drops that twinkle in
the blue sky on a frosty night, flattered the child, and praised his wisdom;
and the unsuspecting child – for he knew no guile – believed them. Now
the child had beds of flowers that loved him; and when he walked among
them, they clustered around him so fondly in the bright noon-day, that
they fanned him with their pure breath, and protected him from the
sun's glare. And the insects and reptiles that bask in sunshine, and retreat
to small dark corners when the air is cold, hated the flowers and stung
them, and tried to spoil their growth. But the flowers grew and flourished;
and as they reared their noble heads, and gradually developed their
bright colours more and more, the insects grew frightened, and shrunk
back to their holes. But when the flowers were lulled to sleep by the
calm air of a peaceful summer's night, the insects crawled to the child,
and crept into his ear, and left their poison there; and the child, confused
by the constant buzzing of the insects, forgot his old dear friends the
flowers, and left them. There was one bed of flowers which had been
beautiful; they blossomed still, a bright, bright green, but they hung their
heads, and were fast fading away. They had been forced in their youth,
and cut down, and grafted on an old stem; their natural juices were
dried up, and they withered fast. But when they drooped and asked the
child to prop them up, and keep such blossoms as they had, from falling
to the ground, he only forced them the more. Their opening buds were
rudely torn off, and the insects devoured them, and drew the very life
and sap from the flowers; and the child looked playfully on, for he forgot
the days when the old green flowers were the bravest part of the triple

chaplet that adorned his brow. The other flowers, conscious of their own neglect, and smarting under the stings of the insects, saw all this, sullenly enough; and as they beheld their neighbours bending to the very earth, and withering for want of nourishment and culture, they felt angry that the child should ever have gathered their blossoms, and sorry that he should have shared them with the greedy insects.

Now, the child had gardeners who ministered to the flowers. They were bees – active, hard-working bees; they found the roots choked up by weeds; and their growth impeded by the remains of some burrows that had become close and rotten. They were very small, but they harboured rats in myriads, and some of them had the magical property, when one body was dissolved, of disgorging two carcasses on the neighbouring commons; and at last the corruption became quite insupportable. So the bees went actively to work, and let streams of running water into the burrows, and pulled up the weeds by the roots; but the insects had always lived in the weeds and burrows; and as they were now turned out of their retreats, and had no means of getting to the commons, they crawled to the child, and cried bitterly. The child was tender-hearted, and cried too; then the insects cried the more, and then the grand persons with the bright stars began to cry, and then they all cried, like slimy crocodiles. The bees, who were still engaged in grubbing up old weeds, thought this crying was a hum; but they were mistaken, for the child got bewildered, and, with the assistance of a small quantity of brimstone, turned the bees out of their hive, and put the insects in their places. The care of the flowers was consigned to their new masters; and the insects, who had lain torpid for some time before, expanded their wings, and fluttered into a butterfly existence.

But the insects were disappointed, and the child was deceived. He looked on – lightly at first, then attentively, and then sadly. He saw the gay flowers, whose gently waving heads used to greet him fondly, turn coldly from him; the sun seemed no longer to smile on them, and the cold shade was on him. He saw the other bed fast dwindling away; its beauty melting like the thin ice that vanishes before the morning sun and its flowers dying before his eyes; and as the mildew and the rot blighted them in groups, he thought, in his agony, that he had better even have adopted the advice which one of the insects had given him long before, and put the whole bed under the still water for a day and a night. He saw the once cheerful flowers closing their beautiful petals, and refusing to yield one drop of moisture to the humbled insects who begged it in vain for their and his support. He looked in vain for the glad welcome they once gave him; and oh! how painfully he thought of the time when they freely scattered their rich blossoms in his path. He cast himself on the ground, and cursed the insects, now fast perishing around him. At length he appealed to his former friends the flowers, and conjured them by the recollection of their old attachment and companionship to take pity on his helpless loneliness. But the flowers, who had been obliged to support one another when their natural protectors deserted them, turned a deaf ear to his earnest prayers; and the child found, to his grief and sorrow, that the appeal had been made too late.

5

Report on the Tory Victory at Colchester

Morning Chronicle, 10 January 1835

The Government formed by Wellington and Peel at William IV's request in November 1834 sought a mandate from the electorate at a general election held in January. Dickens was sent to cover the elections in Essex and Suffolk and filed the following report from Colchester, followed by others from Braintree (12 January), Chelmsford (13 January), Sudbury (14 January) and Bury St Edmunds (17 January) – see *Pilgrim*, Vol. I, pp. 52–4.

COLCHESTER
(From Our Own Correspondent)

Friday – The ceremony of chairing the successful candidates for the representation of this town, took place this morning at twelve o'clock. Long before that hour the streets presented an unusually lively and bustling appearance. Numerous groups of the neighbouring yeomanry and gentry, well mounted and bearing the Tory colours – blue and white – galloped through them at intervals, and the streets [*sic*] fronting the Three Cups Inn, which was the place of rendezvous, was thronged ·with spectators. The windows of the opposite houses were strongly barricaded or closely shut up, and the balconies and roofs were filled with people.

Notwithstanding the strong party feeling which had prevailed through-out the election, and the disappointment experienced by the Liberal party in the defeat of the Whig candidate, perfect order was preserved, and no strong manifestation of feeling exhibited. A few boys who were stationed in the principal street, attempted to hiss Sir Henry Smyth, but the formidable disturbance was gallantly quelled by several gentlemen on horseback, who forthwith rode up to the spot, and put as many of the unfortunate offenders into the cage as they happened to catch.

Shortly after twelve o'clock the procession started. It was preceded by a numerous body of gentlemen on horseback; then followed a band of music; then several banners, with such inscriptions as, 'We live to uphold, and will defend our King and Constitution'; – then there were the Union Jack and the Royal Standard, and then a Crown elevated on a long pole, the general appearance of which forcibly reminded one of May-day. The successful candidates followed, in an open carriage drawn by four grey horses, and a barouch [*sic*]. These were followed by a stage coach, and the stage coach was followed by the mob, and the procession went round the town and came back again. It will be recollected that Sir Henry Smyth quitted the House of Commons in disgust on the passing of the Catholic Relief Bill. Time, however, has, happily for the Legislature of the country, softened down his recollection of that dreadful measure, and he has fortunately been induced again to solicit a return to Parliament, even after the additional enormity of the Reform Bill.

A public dinner took place at the Three Cups, at four o'clock, at which the attendance of the friends of the candidates, and the supporters of the Conservative cause was earnestly requested.

6

Grand Colosseum Fête

Morning Chronicle, 10 July 1835

The Colosseum, designed by the young Decimus Burton, was built 1824–9 on the east side of Regent's Park to house, in its great Rotunda, a vast panorama of London as seen from the top of St Paul's Cathedral. The drawings for this had been made on site by the Colosseum's projector, Thomas Hornor, and were translated into a huge continuous painting by a young artist, Edmund Parris. The Colosseum was also designed to be a luxurious pleasure-palace with a 'Saloon of Arts' and other elegant attractions. Before the building was completed, Hornor's chief financial backer absconded to the United States and Hornor followed him a few months later, leaving his creditors to try to recoup their losses as best they could (hence Dickens's reference to 'Mr Horner [*sic*] ... of Colosseum notoriety' in his *Evening Chronicle* sketch, 'Greenwich Fair', 16 April 1835 – see Vol. 1 of this edition, p. 115). By 1835 the wealthy tenor John Braham and the popular actor and theatre-manager Frederick Yates had become owners of the Colosseum and on 8 July Dickens reported on a private view of 'the extensive improvements' they had made to it, including a 'glittering "Hall of Mirrors" ... a superb apartment, literally lined with looking-glass, and supported by chrystal columns' and 'the Colossus of Rhodes, with a revolving light in his hand'. He described Yates as 'that Colossus of stage management and theatrical contrivance ... quite as much at home, and even more energetic, bustling, and vehement, than he used to appear in his old sphere of action – the Adelphi Theatre'. Edward Stirling later in the century recalled Yates as a man who 'loved extremes. ... Anything to attract, from a tame elephant to a gnome fly, nothing came amiss, to draw the public, with Yates' (*Old Drury Lane* [1881], Vol. 1, p. 97). For the full text of Dickens's report and the first reprinting of the report on the fête, see Patrick J. McCarthy, 'Dickens at the Regent's Park Colosseum: Two Uncollected Pieces', *The Dickensian*, Vol. 79 (1983), pp. 154–61. McCarthy was the first to identify the 8 and 10 July reports on the Colosseum as having been written by Dickens. For a detailed account of the Colosseum itself and its history, see Ch. 11 of R.D. Altick's *The Shows of London* (1978). A ticket for the grand fête described in the following passage cost 25 shillings; evidently, it was aimed at attracting a very exclusive clientèle.

The grand opening *fête* of this delightful place of public amusement took place last night; the proceeds to be devoted to the benefit of the London, Westminster, and Charing Cross Hospitals. We are happy to say that the attendance was as numerous and fashionable as the best wishes either of those meritorious institutions or of the enterprising proprietors of the Colosseum could possibly desire. We had prepared a list of the principal nobles and fashionables we noticed in the different rooms, but it swelled so rapidly, and we entertained so little hope of arriving at the conclusion of our task within any reasonable period, that we gave up the attempt in despair, and must content ourselves by saying – everybody was there. It was originally intended, we believe, that the company should be admitted at the great entrance in the park, and from thence, after traversing the cave of Flora and being duly initiated into the Eleusinean mysteries, conducted into the ball-room. The project, however, was abandoned from a feeling of consideration, we believe, for the peace and quiet of the inhabitants of the park, and a temporary entrance (leading directly to the principal apartments) was formed in Albany-street. The extensive nature of the preparations, and the long lines of carriages, created no small degree of excitement in the immediate neighbourhood of the building. The balconies of the opposite houses were crowded with spectators; and a numerous concourse of people were assembled in the road, who beguiled the time and enlivened the occasion, as the different carriages set down, by urgently entreating the visitors to 'flare-up'; imploring smartly-dressed gentlemen 'not to cut it too fat, but just to throw in a bit of lean to make weight', and similar *facetiae*. The dancing commenced at ten o'clock, and in another hour the rooms, passages, staircases, conservatories, glens and caverns, were crowded by a dense mass of people. The great majority of the company were in their customary full-dress costume; but there was a plentiful sprinkling of fancy dresses in the manufacture of which, however, we should be disposed to say but little fancy or money had been expended. Their awkward and melancholy-looking wearers contrasted very disadvantageously with the rational portion of the company. The band was stationed in the Egyptian tent; the Hall of Mirrors, superbly ornamented and illuminated, served for the principal promenade; and the supper was served at one o'clock in the Saloon. When we add to this, that the ball, as far as the company were concerned, was like all other public balls – that there were match-making mammas in abundance – sleepy papas in proportion – unmarried daughters in scores – marriageable men in rather smaller numbers – greedy dowagers in the refreshment-room – flirting daughters in the corners – and envious old maids everywhere – we have said all we need.

Of the Colosseum itself – of the scale on which the whole fête was conducted, the liberality which was displayed, or the attention and civility which were everywhere experienced, it is impossible to speak too highly. The best taste, an utter disregard of expense, and a scrupulous attention to the comforts of the visitors, are the characteristics of the place, and were the prominent features of the entertainment last night. Refreshments of every description were provided during the whole of the evening, and the supper was the best we ever saw, even from Gunter. Every one appeared to be disposed to be pleased, and on all sides we heard nothing but expressions of delight and approbation. The different attractions combined to form a perfect scene of enchantment, and cannot fail we think to prove most attractive.

We have only to add our earnest hope that the benevolent object of the fête has been attained, and that the institutions to which we have already adverted will derive substantial assistance from it. The proceeds of last night could not be devoted to a better or a nobler purpose; for of all the charitable institutions with which London abounds, none diffuse their charity and benevolence over a wider sphere than its public hospitals, affording as they do, relief, ease, and comfort, at a time when of all others the poor, the aged, and diseased, stand most in need of consolation and support. The donation of the fête reflects the highest credit on the proprietors of the Colosseum – we hope its result will reflect credit on the public.

7

The Reopening of the Colosseum

Morning Chronicle, 13 October 1835

Following the grand fête described in the previous article, the Colosseum continued to attract what the *Court Journal* (quoted by McCarthy, in the article cited on p. 15) described as 'crowds of rank, beauty, and fashion' for some time, but attendance declined in the late summer and early autumn. After closing for a short while, Braham and Yates sought to rekindle public interest with the gala reopening described here. Proof of their determination to make a splash was the guest appearance of the hugely popular equestrian performer Andrew Ducrow, manager of Astley's Amphitheatre, which Dickens had lovingly sketched for the *Evening Chronicle* five months earlier (see Vol. 1 of this edition, pp. 106–11). Ducrow had first devised the show that he put on at the Colosseum in 1830. Called *Raphael's Dream*, it consisted of his striking a succession of classic poses ('Brutus condemning his Son to Death', etc.) while an actor playing Raphael moralised upon them at some length. For a full description of the show, see A.H. Saxon, *The Life and Art of Andrew Ducrow* (1978), pp. 226–32.

Dickens's lack of enthusiasm for the attractions on offer seems to have been shared by others. McCarthy quotes a *Sunday Times* report of 18 October: 'The Colosseum, during Ducrow's performances, has been a miserable affair, and this attempt has been abruptly terminated. The average receipts of each night, it is said, have not exceeded 10£....'

On two former occasions we have availed ourselves of an opportunity of expressing our satisfaction in the different arrangements made for the amusement of the visitors to this pleasant place of public resort. It re-opened last night for the winter season, and we regret that the entertainments were not of a character to justify a similar degree of praise. The principal novelties of the evening – we quote the bills – were 'The courses of the Enchanted Chariot, and round flights of the Mechanical Peacock,' described as an elegant 'diversion arranged for the lady-visitors to display their skill with the Silver Arrow, and Jeu de la Bague, and their fortune with the White Dove and Rosebud.' Now the Enchanted Chariot was a pantomimic car, and the Mechanical Peacock was harnessed to the said car, and the Mechanical Peacock and Enchanted Car performed the round flights together, by travelling in a groove, which went completely round the Rotunda, and along which it was propelled by men and machinery. The car held two ladies at a time, and the fortunate fair who knocked off the greatest number of wreaths, or rosebuds, or something of that kind, was entitled to a free admission for herself and friend for the current week. The car was a complete failure: first of all the ladies wouldn't go, and when the ladies did the car wouldn't; and when at last both parties consented to go together, the company unanimously pronounced it to be 'no go' at all. The ladies having thus delighted themselves and everybody else, an opportunity was afforded to the gentlemen to display their skill on the 'War Hobby' – a mimic horse of large dimensions, accoutred, like John Reeve in *Quadrupeds*, with petticoats in lieu of legs, which half concealed the men who forced it along. This was also childish to absurdity – the only amusement derivable from it being that consequent upon an experimental trip made by Yates himself with some fun and considerable good-humour. Ducrow's performances, in the *Dream of Raphael*, displayed all that wonderful skill and taste for which he is eminently remarkable in a department of his art peculiarly his own; but it was too long: *Raphael* is decidedly the most prosy individual that ever presented himself on any stage, and his introductory descriptions were melancholy in the extreme. The remainder of the entertainments were familiar to the frequenters of Astley's, and presented nothing new. The Rotunda has been improved and beautified, and the suite of apartments is well supplied with warm air, except the upper room, which is intolerably cold. We wish we could say anything more in praise of the present attractions of the establishment, but we really cannot: and we regret it the more, when we consider the trouble and expense which have been again incurred by the enterprising proprietors. When the difficulties and imperfections of a first night have been removed, they may possibly tell better; if so, we shall be happy to report to that effect. For the present we have made a true deliverance according to our consciences; and can do no more.

8

Theatre Review: *The Dream at Sea* by J.B. Buckstone

Morning Chronicle, 24 November 1835

The beautiful and talented comedienne Louisa Nisbett leased the Adelphi Theatre from the actor-managers Charles Mathews, Junior, and Frederick Yates for five months from November 1835, securing the services of most of the theatre's regular stars. Dickens hailed her venture in a notice in the *Chronicle* on 17 November, which concentrated on her and her company rather than on the pieces performed, 'on each and every one of which', he wrote, 'we have pronounced our opinion at the time of its appearance'. Mrs Nisbett was following Madame Vestris, who became manager of the Olympic Theatre in 1830 and had made a dazzling success of the venture. In his 17 November notice Dickens comments that the Adelphi's stage appointments 'bore all that character of taste and propriety which Lady-Managers seem to have a peculiar talent of imparting to such things. Admirable managers they are, and the influence they possess is really extraordinary.... There must be a Salique law in theatricals, or there is really no telling where all this will end.'

Buckstone's *Dream at Sea* was the first 'novelty' produced by the Nisbett management. In his review, as in his later one of *Pierre Bertrand* (see article 11), we see Dickens beginning to develop that humorous skill in recounting the preposterous plots characteristic of contemporary melodramas that he was later to use so brilliantly in the Crummles scenes in *Nicholas Nickleby*. The allusion to 'an Ecclesiastical Court' at the end of the third paragraph concerns the fact that for most people at this date divorces could only be obtained through the Court of Arches, the consistory court of the Arch-bishop of Canterbury, which was held at Doctors' Commons (see Vol. 1 of this edition, p. 89). Mr Laing (p. 22) was Allan Stewart Laing, magistrate since 1820 at the police court in Hatton Garden and notorious for his harshness and bad temper. The *Chronicle* for 20 November had carried an amusing report of his having a little boy taken up for ringing a muffin-bell in Hatton Garden during the sitting of Laing's court. Dickens lampooned him as 'Mr Fang' a year and a half later in the July 1837 instalment of *Oliver Twist* (Ch. 11). He also later ridiculed the clog dancers Brown, King and Gibson in his March 1837 paper for *Bentley's Miscellany* (see vol. 1 of this edition, p. 503) as the Adelphi's 'three unchangeables who have been dancing the same dance under different imposing titles, and doing the same thing under various high-sounding names for some five or six years last past'.

Literary allusions (p. 21) 'dying on the Parisian principle': i.e., like the County Paris in Shakespeare's *Romeo and Juliet*, Act 5, Sc. 3.

ADELPHI THEATRE

A new drama, by MR BUCKSTONE, called *The Dream at Sea* was produced at this theatre last night. It is stated in the bills, to be 'founded on fact.' Truth is decidedly stranger than fiction, if it be. As nearly as we can undertake to recapitulate the 'facts' upon which the piece is founded, they are to the following purport: – At the opening of the drama *Richard Penderell* (HEMMING) is shipwrecked on the coast of Cornwall, to which place he has voyaged for the purpose of marrying his cousin, *Ann Trevanion* (MISS DALY), who, like a true dramatic heroine, has previously formed another attachment for *Launce Lynwood* (VINING). The Land's End, Cornwall, is infested by wreckers, one of the chief of whom is *Black Ralph* (O. SMITH); and *Black Ralph* and his companions are on the point of pillaging and murdering the unhappy *Richard*, who exhausted with fatigue can offer but a faint resistance, when he is saved by the timely interposition of his rival, who, having previously rescued him from a watery grave, preserves a valuable casket of jewels and gold belonging to him, from the clutches of the wreckers, and sends him unscathed to the residence of his destined bride. The treasure, however, has not escaped the eager glance of *Black Ralph*. Impelled by misery, and urged to desperation by the hungry cries of his starving children, he sits in his wretched hut vainly endeavouring to devise some mode of obtaining possession of the glittering casket, when *Launce Lynwood* enters, announces his intention of quitting for ever a place which only reminds him of his blighted hopes and lost happiness, and his own wardrobe being scanty, and ill adapted for sea-voyaging, begs to exchange his own cloak and hat for those of *Black Ralph*, which happen to be in better condition. *Ralph* consents with singular Christian charity and kindness – for *Launce* had stabbed him in the arm some half hour before – and subsequently disguised in *Launce*'s attire, secretes himself in a closet during the ceremony of the wedding, and, having heard from his place of concealment where the casket is deposited, rushes into the bride's bed-room to secure it, just as she has retired. *Ann Trevanion* utters the name of her old lover: shrieks are heard, and the mansion is alarmed. Rendered desperate by his situation, *Ralph* strikes her to the ground, secures the valuables, and escapes by the window. A scene of confusion and an excellent tableau conclude the act. At the opening of the second act, we learn that *Ann* has died of the wound inflicted by *Ralph*, and that the guilt of her murder is unanimously attributed to *Launce*. *Launce*, however, unexpectedly presents himself to

Ralph, and informs him that his sudden reappearance is occasioned by a frightful dream which has haunted him thrice, and visited his pillow on land and sea. It was, that *Ann Trevanion* had died, and some mysterious agency urged him, with an impulse he could not resist, to return to the place he had so lately quitted. *Ralph* acquaints him with the realization of his vision; and *Launce,* still under the influence of the same agency we suppose – a most mysterious one certainly – tears the inanimate object of his love from the family vault to a lone hovel, where he shuts himself up with the body, and after carefully examining the chinks in the apartment, lights a charcoal fire, and lies down to die on the Parisian principle. Now comes the principal 'fact' in the piece. The lady is not dead, but to the very natural surprise of *Launce* suddenly awakens and imitates *Juliet* to the life. *Launce* has been recognized and pursued; he has just time to secrete his beloved in a dark recess, when his pursuers burst in upon him; he is at once charged with the murder of *Ann* and very wisely thinking that the shortest way of refuting the charge satisfactorily will be to produce the lady herself – he desires the recess to be searched. The recess is searched, and *Ann* is not found there: she having been, by a little theatrical hide and seek, removed by *Ralph,* by whom she is carried – we did not exactly understand how – to the *Pendeen Vau,* or Haunted Cave, where the faithful *Launce,* who has again escaped from his pursuers, finds her, and where his pursuers find him soon afterwards. *Ralph,* who has fallen off a rock, and damaged himself irreparably, then confesses his share in the affair, and dies melo-dramatically. *Mr Trevanion* (GALCOT) learning that *Miss Trevanion* has been brought to life by means of *Launce,* suggests to his nephew, *Mr Trevanion* the younger, the propriety of giving up his wife to her preserver. To this little family arrangement, *Mr Trevanion, junior,* at once accedes in the most handsome and gentlemanly manner, and they are made happy without the intervention of an Ecclesiastical Court, or any such tedious common-place proceeding. There is an under-plot arising out of the humours of Alley Croaker, an overseer and tax-collector (WILKINSON), who is constantly calling upon the *dramatis personae* for 'two quarters' poors-rates', and incessantly deploring the badness of the times, and the cries of *Tom Tinkle,* the village muffin-man (BUCKSTONE) and his sweetheart *Biddy Nutts* (MRS NISBETT). In this underplot there is little novelty. The *Overseer* gets knocked down the usual number of times: *Mr Tinkle* has a cow-skin waistcoat bequeathed him by his grandfather, much to his disappointment at first, but greatly to his joy afterwards: for the cow-skin waistcoat is discovered to be lined with bank notes, and the property thus acquired enables him to marry *Biddy Nutts.*

Such are the incidents of the piece. If we were to say that they were probable, our good humour would exceed our common sense; if we were to report that they were unskilfully managed by the Dramatist, we should not deal justly by him; but if we were to add that his last production is in any respect equal to *The Wreck Ashore, Victorine*, or any of the numerous dramas which have rendered his name so popular, we should do him a far greater injustice. At the conclusion of the piece MR BUCKSTONE was loudly called for, and announced it for repetition every evening till further notice, amidst great applause.

Having said that the scenery was beautiful, and the whole 'getting up' of the piece admirable, it only remains to speak of the acting. VINING had the most to do, and did it well; many of his scenes exhibited great feeling and power, and would have done infinite credit to many actors of far greater pretensions – he played excellently throughout. O. SMITH was admirably dressed, and acted in his best manner – no slight praise at any time. BUCKSTONE, as the Muffin Boy, was as quaint and humorous as ever, and tinkled his bell as merrily as if there were no such wiseacres as Mr Laing in existence, and no Hatton-garden law on record. Mrs Nisbett had a lively part, to which she did full justice, and the remainder of the *dramatis personae* did their best. There was a Cornish clog dance by Messrs BROWN, KING and GIBSON, which the gallery encored – rather unnecessarily, for they see the same thing in every new piece produced here, and have seen the same thing for seasons past.

MR BUCKSTONE's dramas have attracted full audiences to this house, and afforded general delight to the play-going public. We are happy to see such a return to the old system as the production of any piece by him; but we should be more happy to see one in his old pleasant domestic style, where the situations are not wholly improbable, nor the incidents palpably absurd.

9

Report on the Fire at Hatfield House

Morning Chronicle, 2 December 1835

During the night of 27 November a fire broke out in the west wing of Hatfield, the Hertfordshire seat of the Marquess of Salisbury, and, the flames fanned by the high wind that was blowing, all that part of the great mansion was destroyed. It was only a change in the wind, towards dawn, that enabled the firemen to get the blaze under control and save the rest of the building. The Dowager Marchioness of Salisbury, aged eighty-five, perished in the fire. Nicknamed 'Old Sarum' and 'Old Sal', she was a very colourful character, of Anglo-Irish stock, much addicted to hunting, gambling, rich dresses and a general parade of wealth, all of which passions she carried vigorously into old age.

It was thought that she had been writing and that the feathers in her high-piled hair – she still wore it in the fashion of her youth – had caught in the candle and so started the fire. Besides her bones a few scraps of metal were discovered, thought to be what was left of the family jewels that she should long since have handed on to her daughter-in-law. Further investigation, however, suggests that most of these had been already sold to pay gambling debts. [David Cecil, *The Cecils of Hatfield House* (1975), p. 196]

Dickens was sent to report on the fire on 1 December, 'receiving', he wrote aggrievedly to his fiancée, Catherine Hogarth, 'only three hour's [*sic*] notice, and being previously out of bed until three o'Clock' (*Pilgrim*, Vol. 1, p. 100). He had to linger on the scene awaiting the recovery of the Marchioness's remains and filed two further reports, on 3 and 4 December. In the second of these he expresses the view that since 'it is evident ... that the walls must be pulled down eventually before any preparation can be made for re-building the western wing ... I cannot help thinking that the shortest mode of proceeding would have been to have thrown them down at once, in which case the search for the remains of the Marchioness might have been almost immediately recommenced'. As a different course had been taken, 'there is little doubt that many days will elapse before the search is attended with any successful result', which indeed proved to be the case. The inquest was eventually held on 16 December, by which time Dickens was in Kettering (see next article).

THE LATE CALAMITOUS EVENT AT HATFIELD HOUSE
(From Our Own Reporter)

Hatfield, Tuesday evening – The body of the unfortunate lady who fell a sacrifice to the fire which has so recently destroyed a considerable portion of this magnificent residence, has not yet been found. Workmen have been employed during the whole day in digging among the ruins, and conveying away large masses of rubbish; but as a considerable quantity still remains to be cleared, it is not probable that they will arrive at the conclusion of their labours before tomorrow morning at the earliest.

I had an opportunity of visiting the ruins this morning. They are still smoking, and the whole of the west wing of the mansion (to which the ravages of the fire were fortunately confined) presents a melancholy picture of ruin and desolation. The fire extended to no less than forty-five apartments, many of which were lofty and noble rooms, splendidly furnished, adorned with rich oak carvings of considerable antiquity, marble chimney-pieces, and magnificent decorations of every kind. When the fire was at its height, the different doors communicating with the beautiful old chapel and south front of the building were hastily bricked up to a considerable thickness; and to this precaution, combined with the judicious direction of the different engines, and the indefatigable exertions of the firemen and others on the spot, the preservation of the remainder of the habitation can alone be attributed. Its escape, even with these precautions, appears most miraculous. Huge oaken beams lie strewed upon the ground in all directions, scorched and charred by the action of the flames till reduced to a mere shadow of their former size. Heaps of brickwork and stone, mingled with bars of iron and masses of molten lead, render the approach to the ruins difficult and toilsome; and the lofty walls, tottering above the head of the spectator, appear as if a breath of wind would level them to the ground, and involve the workmen in the destruction by which they are surrounded. One or two portions of the ruin present a frightful appearance; strong iron girders have been ingeniously bound to the most dangerous parts, but a considerable space is necessarily, from the very construction of the building and the difficulty of employing the workmen with effect in its present state, wholly undefended.

There appears every reason to suppose that the ill-fated lady suffered little from burning, and that she was most probably suffocated by the dense smoke at a very early period of the fire. She made no reply when the door was opened and her name pronounced, at which time the smoke would have rendered any attempt to enter the room certain destruction; and it is worthy of notice that a favourite dog, which was in her dressing-room at the time, did not avail himself of that opportunity to escape. The inference is, that the strong smoke with which both the dressing-room and bedroom were filled before the draught of air from the suddenly opened doors made the flames burst forth, caused suffocation almost instantaneously, and that the aged lady thus escaped the dreadful torment of being burnt to death. The grief and horror of the Marquess of Salisbury on ascertaining the danger of his mother's situation were extreme. He rushed up the staircase calling frantically on her name, burst open the door of her chamber, and would have infallibly perished in the act of exploring it, had he not been forcibly seized by two members of the household, both strong men, who removed him from the door by main force, and stood with their backs against it until the increasing heat of the flame compelled them to retire. But, however regardless of his own personal safety, the presence of mind and energy of the Noble Marquess were of material assistance in checking the progress of devastation. He was on the spot for many hours superintending the operations of the firemen, and in one instance even directing the engine with his own hand.

Some idea of the fury and rapid progress of the flames may be derived from the construction of the edifice, and the means taken to prevent a fire diffusing itself throughout the building, in the event of its extending to a portion of it. The flooring in the attics and servants' apartments was covered with a layer of composition three inches thick, the surface of which was paved with thick tiles, which, together with other rubbish, were lying about in heaps so hot, that the hand could hardly bear to touch them. The ruins were still smoking when I visited them, and buckets of water were thrown over the loads deposited on the lawn, to prevent the possibility of their being reignited by the action of the air. The chapel roof has fallen in, and the interior is consequently considerably damaged; so much so, that it is feared its repair will be nearly as expensive as the erection of a new building. The flames did not penetrate to the library, although they slightly cracked a part of the wall which divided it from the apartments entirely consumed. The valuable books and MSS were, we are happy to say, preserved, although in the hurry and confusion inseparable from such an occasion, the doors of the different presses were wrenched from their hinges and strewed about the room.

The house is, perhaps, the finest remnant of the Elizabethan age extant. The south front, in particular, is the most beautiful specimen of the picturesque architecture of the period that can be imagined. The principal suites of rooms are princely, and worthy of the residence of a monarch. The cloister, long gallery, banquetting-room, and hall, are magnificent apartments, and though they present at this moment an appearance very different from that which they usually bear, and have worn for many years past, they are not the less interesting on that account. The confusion and disorder which pervade them – the hurried jumbling together of the costly furniture in the anxiety to preserve it from destruction – rich couches and sofas, handsome mirrors, high-backed damask-covered old chairs, and fantastic cabinets of ancient date, with Turkey carpets, chrystal ornaments, pictures, and suits of armour, and a thousand other heterogeneous articles – contrast singularly enough with the old heavy chimney-pieces, and oaken pannels which have worn the same appearance for centuries, and seem to defy the ravages of time as proudly as that of the edifice which is now a mass of ruins did but a few days since.

IO

Report on the Northamptonshire Election

Morning Chronicle, 16 and 19 December 1835

At the 1835 general election North Northamptonshire returned one Tory and one Whig MP. The premature death of the latter, Viscount Milton, caused a by-election at which the Whig candidate, William Hanbury, was opposed by the Tory Thomas Maunsell.

Party feeling ran very high. Dickens wrote to his fiancée from Kettering on 16 December (*Pilgrim* Vol. I, p. 106f.), and, referring to his report of the tumult at the hustings below, he commented:

> As the Tories are the principal party here, *I* am in no very good odour in the town, but I shall not spare them the more on that account in the descriptions of their behaviour I may forward to head quarters. Such a ruthless set of bloody-minded villains, I never set eyes on, in my life. In their convivial moments yesterday, after the business of the day was over, they were perfect savages.

As is evident from the following report, he did indeed not pull any punches in describing the incident. The *Times* reporter also commented disapprovingly on the behaviour of the Tory horsemen and on the Rev. John George's pistol-flourishing, but in far more restrained terms.

NORTHAMPTONSHIRE ELECTION
(By Express)
(From Our Own Reporter)

Kettering, Tuesday, Dec. 15 – This being the day appointed for the nominations, the town presented an unusual scene of life and bustle at a very early hour. Bands of music paraded the streets, a variety of banners with appropriate inscriptions were displayed, and the friends of both candidates thronged into the town in one continued stream.

The hustings had been erected on the Market-hall, and in the front of them is a tolerably large piece of open ground, on which the crowd began to collect so early as nine o'clock. Ten was the time appointed, and long before that hour a vast concourse of spectators had assembled before the booth. These people were principally the friends and supporters of Mr Hanbury, and were all on foot. Perfect order and good humour existed among them, and would no doubt have continued to prevail, but for an outrage of the most disgraceful nature I ever witnessed. Before the arrival of the sheriff, and when the friends of the two candidates had taken their places on the hustings, a large body of horsemen in Mr Maunsell's interest arrived, with bludgeons and leaded riding or hunting whips, galloped up to the spot, and actually charged the mob, making their way to the hustings amidst every opposition, and bearing down all before them with a degree of ruffianly barbarity, and brutal violence, of which no description could convey an adequate idea. The whole of this cowardly and unmanly proceeding was preconcerted. I heard last night that it was in contemplation, but could not believe it was really intended.

This body was headed by a parson of the name of John George, of Bythorn, who dashed his horse among the defenceless people, with a reckless disregard of lives and limbs, and laid about him in all directions with a thick ash stick. The confusion and disorder thus occasioned were excessive; and when it was at its height, and before a single missile had been thrown by the Buff party, this man George produced from his coat pocket a pistol, and levelled it at a person in the crowd. His hand was arrested by some member of his own party, and a cry of 'Seize him!' 'Carry him off!' 'Constables do your duty!' was immediately raised. The horsemen, however, crowded about him, and screened him from the just indignation of the crowd. A large party of constables and banner-bearers of Mr Hanbury's rushed forward to seize his horse's bridle, and some person threw, I think, a piece of stick, which struck him on the nose, and fetched a little blood. The man, foaming with passion, again produced the pistol, levelled it, cocked it, and in another instant would, in all probability, have committed murder had not his arm been forcibly seized and held down by two of his horsemen, who kept him pinioned, and struggling all the while, until the arrival of the sheriff, and the indignation of the crowd and gentlemen on the hustings induced him to desist. It is worthy of remark that no one speaker on the Conservative side made the slightest allusion to, or expressed any regret for, this disgraceful proceeding. We heard Mr Maunsell himself appealed to on the hustings. His reply was that the other (the Buff) party had taken the ground first, with the addition of some other words which we were unable to hear.

Dickens's account, which occupies two-and-a-half columns, continues with
reports of the speeches by the Sheriff vainly urging the horsemen to move
to the back of the crowd, the nomination speeches for Maunsell, his own
acceptance speech (he looked forward to the time when 'England might
again be governed by honest and upright Englishmen, and not by a set of
factious demagogues'), and, after renewed confusion, the nomination speeches for Hanbury and his acceptance, defending himself against the charge
of being an 'O'Connellite'. Hanbury's proposer refused to proceed until
the Rev. George had been forced to surrender his firearm and Dickens
comments: 'It will hardly be credited that the pistol was a double-barreled
one, and was *loaded*.' The Sheriff called for a show of hands and, 'as the
numbers appeared to be nearly equal, ... refused a second show, and
declared it to be in favour of Mr Hanbury' (according to the *Times* reporter,
however, the show of hands 'was very decidedly in favour of Mr Maunsell').
The Tories demanded a poll and this was fixed for the following Friday.
The conclusion of Dickens's report makes special mention of how

> a very eccentric person, of the name of Lucas, who had been addressing
> the crowd from the hustings before the proceedings commenced, singing
> 'The Death of Nelson', and complaining that some gentleman present
> had stolen his wife, also ineffectually attempted to address the electors.
> After performing an inaudible duet with Mr Tryon [Maunsell's seconder],
> which lasted about ten minutes, they both gave up the attempt.

The *Chronicle* for 17 December carried a further report from Kettering,
presumably by Dickens, with transcripts of speeches by the Tory Sir George
Robinson and the Whig MP for Northampton Vernon Smith (Sydney
Smith's nephew). On the first of the two polling days he sent the following
report, which appeared in the *Chronicle* on 19 December:

(By Express)

Kettering, Friday night, seven o'clock – The Liberal interest has, I regret
to say, suffered a defeat today, which no efforts that can be made
tomorrow will be able to repair. No artifice has been left untried, no
influence has been withheld, no chicanery neglected by the Tory party;
and the glorious result is, that Mr Maunsell is placed at the head of the
poll, by the most ignorant, drunken, and brutal electors in these kingdoms,
who have been treated and fed, and driven up to the polls the whole
day, like herds of swine.

The rest of the report consists of a transcript of Maunsell's victory speech, characterised as 'a few desultory observations' which 'were nearly drowned by the vociferous howlings of his own party, and the hooting of the other', and a somewhat wistful comment that the next day's polling might possibly reduce the size of the Tory majority (in fact, it increased it).

II

Theatre Review: *Pierre Bertrand* by Frederic Lawrence

The Examiner, 17 December 1837

The Haymarket Theatre (rebuilt by Nash in 1821) was the only London theatre, apart from Covent Garden and Drury Lane, legally permitted to present straight plays, though only for limited periods during the year. The popular comic actor Benjamin Webster became manager in 1837 and under him it became, over the next twelve years, the home of 'legitimate' comedy. Both Julia Glover and Harriet Waylett were celebrated comic actresses and this perhaps encouraged the audience in their hilarious reception of Lawrence's unhappy essay in domestic drama. The *Times* reviewer, like Dickens, ridiculed the play (15 December 1837) while praising Ranger's acting ('clever to a wonder'):

> a gentleman in the boxes had burst into a hearty laugh at one of the pathetic scenes, and on hearing a suggestion from several parts of the house that he should be 'turned out', excused himself by vociferating 'It is so funny!' The audience, struck by the critical acumen displayed in this remark, adopted the sentiment, and from that moment every pathetic situation was acknowledged by the heartiest roars of merriment.

The play was taken off after two performances.

HAYMARKET

On Thursday night an original domestic drama (advertised in the bills as the work of one Mr Frederic Lawrance [*sic*]) was produced at this house, and was received in play-bill phraseology with 'roars of laughter' – meeting, in short, with a reception which would have been most delightful to the author's feelings if the piece had been intended to be funny, but which (his intention apparently being that it should be very affecting) was calculated to awaken feelings of quite an opposite description in his mind – if he has such a thing about him, which we rather doubt.

The *dramatis personae* are *Pierre Bertrand* (MR RANGER), an amiable Frenchman, reduced to the small but honourable independence derivable from breaking stones for the parish; *Albert*, his friend (MR HUTCHINGS); *Colonel Lacy*, everybody's friend (MR STRICKLAND); *Hardheart*, nobody's friend and an overseer (MR RAY); *Richards*, a landlord (MR WORRELL); *Trusty*, a servant (MR T.F. MATHEWS); *Madame Clement*, a mourning bride of eight and twenty years' standing (MRS GLOVER); and *Agnes Lacy*, a ballad singer of private life (MRS WAYLETT).

The plot is by no means complicated. *Pierre* speaks broken English, walks about in muddy inexpressibles and no linen; and in the absence of a flannel waistcoat wears next his heart the picture of an unknown mother, who gave him up to a tutor who never told him who he was and becoming naughty left him to take care of himself. In this stage of his fortunes the pupil took to making love and gaming, and becoming poor forsook the young lady and took to sentimentalising and stone-breaking. Well; he gets very poor indeed, and then his landlord comes for his rent, and as he can't pay it wonders why he don't go out with his flageolet (for he has a flageolet which all parties had forgotten) and play under the windows of the nobility and gentry. Upon this *Pierre* goes into transports and out with the flageolet, and playing in the streets receives a shilling's worth of half-pence instantly to go away, and is going away, when a servant comes out and says he must come in and see his missis, for his missis is fond of vagrants, especially French vagrants, and requests the honor of his company. He goes in accordingly, and is introduced to an elderly lady of a stout figure, with a damp pocket-handkerchief, who first asks him to take a glass of wine and then to tell his history, which he does, and pending its relation the stout lady becomes agitated and asks what his name is, and he says what his name is, and the stout lady screams, and holding out a miniature says that's his father, and *he* screams, and holding out a miniature says that's his mother, and the stout lady says 'that's me,' and the son says 'oh!' and the mother says 'my son!' and the son says 'my mother!' and, they are just going to fall into each other's arms when a noise is heard in the street, upon which they each strike an attitude and look – as people always do upon the stage when unaccountable noises are heard – into the flies for an explanation. Now this noise is no other than a verse of a song, sung by a young lady whom the old lady is very fond of, because, being low-spirited, her sad songs console her, and who, having knocked a double knock, is just passing away the time by singing as loud as she can in the street until the door is opened; and the young lady comes in all pretty and unconscious, and screams out very loud, for the flageolet player is her long lost lover, and then the stout lady looks up at the place where the chandelier ought to be, and clasps *her* hands and joins *theirs*. And finally they sit down in chairs, and the stout lady says that she was unfortunately obliged to desert her son, because if she hadn't, her husband couldn't have got a situation at Court, which could only be held by a bachelor, to which the son replies that he is perfectly satisfied, and begs she won't mention it. A letter arrives in the very nick of time to say that the old gentleman who was supposed dead (why, the supposers best know) is alive, and, having made his fortune, is coming home by the next coach, whereupon another old gentleman, apparently insane, habited in a blue surtout, and agitated without cause, rushes in and going up to the stage lights without ever stopping, says that's the reward of honor and affection and runs back again with a bow as the curtain falls.

Of all the insults ever offered to the understanding of an audience this is the greatest.

The production of such wretched despicable trash is disgraceful to Mr Webster, and most unworthy treatment of the clever actors and actresses who are compelled to utter the mawkish absurdities set down for them. 'What's in a name?' observes Mr Frederic Lawrance, indignantly. 'Everything. Nothing is to be done without one.' We know one, at all events, by which nothing will ever be done, and that is the name of Mr Frederic Lawrance.

We had almost omitted to make mention of MR RANGER, whom we are most anxious to see in some better character. He is evidently possessed of great intelligence; is easy, and gentlemanly, and, to all appearance, well accustomed to the stage. He appears to possess every requisite for genteel comedy, and we trust may be found an able and efficient representative of many characters which at present have no representative at all.

12

Review: *Refutation of the Misstatements and Calumnies contained in Mr Lockhart's Life of Sir Walter Scott, Bart respecting the Messrs Ballantyne.* By the Trustees and Son of the late Mr James Ballantyne.

The Examiner, 2 September 1838

This was the first of three articles on the Scott/Lockhart/Ballantyne controversy that Dickens wrote in *The Examiner*. It was first identified and reprinted by K.J. Fielding in *The Dickensian*, Vol. 46 (1950), pp. 122–7. The two later articles had been included by Matz in *MP*.

John Gibson Lockhart married Scott's daughter in 1820 and published his seven-volume biography of his august father-in-law in 1838. The *Refutation* pamphlet attacks Lockhart for belittling and misrepresenting the role played by Scott's printer and business partner James Ballantyne and his publisher brother John in the collapse of Scott's finances in 1826. Dickens would have had private information about the matter from his father-in-law George Hogarth, whose sister had married James Ballantyne, and who had given Scott financial advice, but tells Forster when sending him the review ('very moderate in tone if not in length') that he has eschewed using this and 'taken all the facts from the refutation itself' (*Pilgrim*, Vol. 1, p. 428). His vehement championing of Lockhart stems partly from his admiration for Scott but surely also, as the *Pilgrim* editors note, 'from the way Scott *v.* the Ballantynes typified Author *v.* Publisher' (at this period Dickens was having his own troubles with a publisher, Richard Bentley, the 'Burlington Street Brigand' as he called him). The 'veracity' of Lockhart's narrative, defended so strongly by Dickens, has been a good deal 'impeached' by modern scholars, in particular the noble deathbed scene and dying words that Dickens quotes here – see the authorities cited by John Sutherland in his *The Life of Walter Scott* (1995), p. 355.

This pamphlet – most fortunately, as we cannot help thinking, for its authors – makes its appearance under circumstances calculated, if not to disarm criticism, at least to blunt its sharpness. The feeling which prompts it is one with which the public generally cannot fail to sympathise, inasmuch as it is the laudable and natural desire to vindicate the character of a deceased friend and relation.

There is an old proverb, however, about good intentions and the place they pave, not altogether inapplicable to this production. That its authors, losing sight of their intentions, and the most probable method of inducing right-minded persons to respect them, have conceived their 'Refutation' in a violent spirit, and clothed it in coarse and irritating terms, must be obvious to every reader. We hold that neither its manner nor its matter is at all likely to serve the object sought to be attained. We think indiscriminate and blustering abuse of Mr Lockhart, and the constant endeavour to fix upon that gentleman the guilt of wilful falsehood or concealment of the truth, as little calculated to impeach the veracity of his narrative as the production of a few unexplained and isolated items from the Trust accounts is calculated to throw any clear or satisfactory light upon the so much talked of and so very complicated partnership affairs of Ballantyne and Company.

Before proceeding to the matter of this pamphlet, let us illustrate our objection to the manner. In the very outset there is something excessively disgusting and offensive in the selection of a few most affecting words – among the last Scott spoke – for the motto: –

> ' "Lockhart," said Sir Walter Scott, when his son-in-law was called to his death-bed. "I may have but a minute to speak to you. My dear, be a good man – be virtuous – be religious – be a good man. Nothing else will give you any comfort when you come to lie here." '

This is a touching fragment of a most solemn scene. The dying words of Scott should be held more sacred, and not caught for the motto of a personal controversy, because a vulgar point may be made in the first page, and an empty boast held out how the refuters will show that Mr Lockhart is neither virtuous, religious, nor good. It is an unworthy and indecent proceeding, and the trustees and son of the late Mr James Ballantyne should, of all people living, have known better than to resort to it.

As further specimens of the style which pervades the pamphlet, we would cite the constant use of such terms as 'foul aspersions' – 'misstatements and calumnies' – 'libellous misrepresentations' – 'bitter personalities' – 'pandering to a depraved taste' – 'cruel and ridiculous distortions' – 'vulgar wit and ribald exaggeration' – 'scandalously abused' – 'gross and libellous caricature' – and many other expressions of similar scurrility, which will be found plentifully scattered over almost every page.

The matter, which from its want of arrangement it is no easy task to make an abstract of, appears to resolve itself into two heads. First, that Mr Lockhart designedly and with malice aforethought has, in his biography of Sir Walter Scott, sought every opportunity of blackening the character of Messrs Ballantyne, and of holding them up to vulgar ridicule and merriment; and, secondly, that he has, by a falsification of the accounts of the printing firm (intentional in part, and in part arising from his ignorance), attempted to practise upon the credulity of his readers, by leading them to believe that Scott's embarrassments were in some degree occasioned by his business connexion with the Messrs Ballantyne, and not wholly and solely by his love of improving Abbotsford, his passion for land, his fondness for old books and old armour, and the most signal and extraordinary improvidence.

With reference to the first charge – that of holding up the Messrs Ballantyne to ridicule – we must say, without the least intention of wounding the feelings of any surviving member of their family, that the Messrs Ballantyne seem all along greatly to have mistaken their own position. Mr James Ballantyne was a respectable small tradesman, doing business originally in the small town of Kelso, whence he gladly removed to Edinburgh, in compliance with the invitation of Sir Walter Scott. Mr John Ballantyne had succeeded his father in the business of 'a dealer in goods of all sorts,' or in one branch of the business – what branch it was we are not informed – and kept a shop in Kelso from 1795 to 1805, when he went to settle in Edinburgh, where his brother James was then established. The brothers had been well educated. Mr James Ballantyne corrected the proof-sheets of the Waverley Novels, and wrote criticisms thereupon to Scott as they passed through the press – not always, we think, with a precise recollection of their relative positions in the world of letters, or with the most delicate regard to Sir Walter's state of health or spirits at the moment. He was, however, a gentleman by manners and acquirements, and wrote theatrical critiques in the *Edinburgh Weekly Journal,* of which he was a proprietor.

Now it is perfectly clear to the most obtuse person in existence that the whole importance of Mr James Ballantyne, or his brother, or both, was solely and wholly derived from their connection with SCOTT; that but for SCOTT Mr James Ballantyne would have lived and died a printer in Kelso; that but for SCOTT Mr John Ballantyne would have lived and died in the one branch of the business of the dealer in goods of all sorts; that but for SCOTT nobody but the worthy burghers of Kelso, and perchance a few friends or relatives in Edinburgh, would have had the smallest curiosity or interest in the Messrs Ballantynes's affairs. Then what means the grandiloquent declaration of this pamphlet, that Mr Lockhart has pandered 'to that depraved taste which gloats over all sorts of revelations calculated to *lower to the level of the vulgar herd those who had before appeared to occupy elevated stations!*' – and why the soreness occasioned by Mr Lockhart's presuming to call the Messrs Ballantyne 'printers,' or 'the Ballantynes'; speaking and writing of them as other most respectable persons in the same way of business are spoken and written of every day? If SIR WALTER SCOTT, in the kindness of his nature and that comprehensive goodness of heart which extended itself to everything and everybody within the sphere of his influence, distinguished Mr James Ballantyne by his intimacy and honoured his board with his presence, his descendants should be only too proud to trace their deceased relative's notoriety to its true source. And they should entertain too much respect for the memory of the great man who thus distinguished him, and by pale reflection them, to presume to discuss his expenditure, and comment on the tastes he indulged, as if they were his equal, or as if his wishes and aspirations could be bounded by the measure of their own.

In fact, so far as Mr James Ballantyne is concerned, we take Mr Lockhart's real offence to have been simply this – that throughout his biography he has [properly] considered him as a man made by Scott, having no previous or other existence as a public man, and achieving his position in society solely through his means, and by the magic of his name. We confess that we think Mr Lockhart might have abstained from the frequent use of the nicknames applied to the Messrs Ballantyne, but it is no great stretch of imagination to assume that knowing them to have been bestowed by Scott in moments of thoughtlessness and good humour, he preserved them rather as little traits of his cheerfulness and hilarity to those by whom he was surrounded, than as throwing any slight or disparagement upon those gentlemen. The soreness upon this head again is only an additional proof to us that the trustees and son of the late Mr James Ballantyne always appear to consider *him* the great object of interest with Mr Lockhart's readers, and to forget that he is only interesting as a second- or third-rate actor in the sad drama of Scott's life and death.

With regard to the description of Mr James Ballantyne's dinners, his manner, or his speeches, we see nothing whatever in it, at which any sensible man would feel disposed to take umbrage. We rose from the perusal of those portions of Mr Lockhart's book, at the time they appeared, with anything but an unfavourable impression of Mr James Ballantyne, and certainly without the remotest idea that the lively sketches were conceived or executed in an ill-natured spirit.

In the early history of Mr John Ballantyne, Mr Lockhart appears to have been led into some errors – not very important, however, if we except the statement that his goods were once sold in Kelso for the benefit of his creditors. This is denied in the pamphlet before us, but the denial is so brief and so strictly confined to the terms of Mr Lockhart's assertion, that it leaves us in some doubt whether Mr John Ballantyne did not at that time *compound* with his creditors, which would reduce Mr Lockhart's mistake very considerably. From the evidence produced on both sides it would appear pretty clear that Scott was angry with him one day, and in good-humour another, as the vexations and exigencies of the business arose and vanished. There are very few persons placed in the same positions with reference to each other for any length of time, whose correspondence would not present similar contradictions.

Of this gentleman, then, we will only say that it is evident from all the circumstances in which he was an actor, as well as from Sir Walter Scott's own letter (quoted in this pamphlet with a complimentary passage in large capitals as a distinct proposition, and the preliminary '*if*' in the usual type) that he was not a man of business; that his want of knowledge of, or want of attention to business, seriously involved his partners on several occasions; and that both to him and his brother, Mr Lockhart bears honourable testimony in the following passage: –

> The early history of Scott's connexion with the Ballantynes has been already given in abundant detail; and I have felt it my duty not to shrink, at whatever pain to my own feelings or those of others, from setting down plainly and distinctly, my own impressions of the characters, manners and conduct of those two very dissimilar brothers. I find, without surprise, that my representations of them have not proved satisfactory to their surviving relations. That I cannot help – though I sincerely regret, having been compelled, in justice to Scott, to become the instrument for opening old wounds in kind bosoms, animated, I doubt not, like my own, by veneration for his memory, and respected by me for combining that feeling with a tender concern for names so intimately connected with his throughout long years of mutual confidence. But I have been entirely mistaken if those to whom I allude, or any others of my readers, have interpreted any expressions of mine as designed to cast the slightest imputation on the moral rectitude of the elder Ballantyne. No suspicion of that nature ever crossed my mind. I believe James to have been, from first to last, a perfectly upright man: that his principles were of a lofty stamp – his feelings pure even to simplicity. His brother John had many amiable as well as amusing qualities, and I am far from wishing to charge even him with any deep or deliberate malversation. Sir Walter's own epithet of 'my little picaroon' indicates all that I desired to imply on that score. But John was, from mere giddiness of head and temper, incapable of conducting any serious business advantageously, either for himself or for others; nor dare I hesitate to express my conviction that, from failings of a different sort, honest James was hardly a better manager than the picaroon.

Much is attempted to be made in the 'Refutation,' of Mr Lockhart's use of this word 'Picaroon,' and the meaning he intended it to bear, which, it is angrily contended, is an 'odious imputation.' These passages at least might have been spared, since Mr Lockhart here distinctly shows that he does not understand the term as implying any deep or deliberate malversation. A great deal is said, too, about Mr Lockhart's writing to Mr James Ballantyne on his death-bed, for his recollections of Scott, and calling them 'precious.' That he really considered them so is sufficiently proved by their insertion in the Biography. There is a note of admiration, too, because Mr Lockhart subscribes himself 'Truly and cordially yours,' and a dozen lines of great declamation, terminating with the remark that 'these letters require no commentary' – in which we quite concur.

With regard to the second charge, the falsification of accounts by Mr Lockhart, intentionally or in ignorance, to blacken and defame the Messrs Ballantyne, we shall offer but very few words. An article in the *Standard*, as ably-written as it was justly felt, called forth by a groundless charge in this same pamphlet, forcibly pointed out the very unsatisfactory nature of any more extracts from accounts of such magnitude extending over so many years, and further reminded the reader that this 'Refutation' assumed that when Sir Walter Scott first became connected with the Ballantynes, he had no private means or fortune whatever; which was notoriously untrue. In the confusion and entanglement of these affairs, Mr Lockhart may very possibly have fallen into some technical mistakes relative to bills; but that he has in the main, in any material degree, perverted the sum and substance of the matters of account between Scott and Messrs Ballantyne we do not believe. We have no satisfactory evidence to show us that he has; and we have the strong presumptive evidence of his position, his character, and the mode in which he has executed his task (never unduly exalting Scott, but, in his desire to be impartial, sometimes leaning more than we should have supposed necessary the other way), that he has not.

Besides which, and we would impress what we are about to say most strongly on the reader, let these considerations never be lost sight of – that the firm was to all intents and purposes, SCOTT, and SCOTT alone; that without his support it never could have crawled through one lingering year; that it existed in the full height and zenith of his fame, and had the incalculable advantage of producing before the world the most brilliant and successful of his creations; that if SIR WALTER SCOTT drew his means of subsistence from its funds, Mr James Ballantyne likewise drew his for many years, during which he lived in an elegant manner, and mingled with expensive society; and that if SIR WALTER SCOTT had 'an ambition to become a landed proprietor and endow a family,' as this pamphlet with some impertinence remarks, he had, of all men living, a right to entertain it. Foremost and unapproachable in the bright world of fiction, gifted with a vivacity and range of invention scarcely ever equalled and never (but in the case of Shakespeare) exceeded; endowed, as never fabled enchanter was, with spells to conjure up the past, and to give to days and men of old the spirit and freshness of yesterday; to strip Religion of her gloom, Virtue of her austerity, and present them both in such attractive forms that you could not choose but love them – combining with all these things a degree of worldly

success never before attained through the same path, and coining gold
with the rapidity of even *his* thought – who ever had a right, if SCOTT
had not, to look to the endowment of those who bore his great name,
and to encourage the ambition of raising an edifice whence he might
gaze with swelling heart on scenes he had painted in colours scarcely
less glowing than those in which they lay spread out before him; where
his children might be reared in that land of which every glen and rock
and blade of heather bore the impress of his genius; and through whose
halls his descendants of the third and fourth generation might one day
lead pilgrims from some of the many lands to which his works had
penetrated, and show them where HE lived and died?

Let us hear no more dissertations when Mr James Ballantyne knew,
and when he ceased to know, that Abbotsford stood between him and
ruin. The owner of Abbotsford had stood between him and ruin for
many long years, and that is enough.

Dickens reviewed Lockhart's response to the *Refutation, The Ballantyne Humbug
Handled*, on 31 March 1839 and was a good deal more vitriolic about the
Ballantynes than in his first piece, e.g., 'Of Mr John Ballantyne, the less
said the better. If he were an honest, upright, honourable man, it is a
comfort to know that there are a plentiful store of such characters living at
this moment in the rules of our Debtors' Prison.' Drawing on the details
set out by Lockhart, Dickens seeks to demonstrate (at great length) that

> the extravagance, thoughtlessness, recklessness, and wrong have been
> upon the part of these pigmies, and the truest magnanimity and for-
> bearance on the side of the giant who upheld them, and under the
> shadow of whose protection they gradually came to lose sight of their
> own stature, and to imagine themselves as great as he.

As to the authors of the *Refutation*, James Ballantyne's son and his Trustees,
'this attempt to blacken the memory of the dead benefactor of their house
would be an act of the basest and most despicable ingratitude, were it not
one of the most puling and drivelling folly'. He concludes that Scott's

> repeated forgiveness of his careless partners, and his constant association
> with persons so much beneath a man of his transcendent abilities and
> elevated station, lead us to fear that he turned a readier ear than became
> him to a little knot of toad-eaters and flatterers.

Ballantyne's son and his Trustees responded to Lockhart's pamphlet with
another of their own, which was briefly and contemptuously noticed by
Dickens in *The Examiner* on 29 September 1839; he was particularly outraged
by the appending to this pamphlet various private notes from Scott to

Ballantyne asking him to send money or settle bills, etc. For the full texts of these last two articles, see *MP.* The controversy continues. For a different view of the respective responsibilities of Scott and the Ballantynes for the financial crash, see Sutherland, *op. cit.*, Chs 14 and 15, and the authorities cited by him.

13

Review: *Hood's Comic Annual for 1839*

The Examiner, 3 February 1839

The career of the poet, humorist and engraver Thomas Hood was beset by money and health troubles. In 1829 he began editing his *Comic Annuals,* or 'Anniversaries of Literary Fun', as they were described on the wrappers, abundantly illustrating them with his own grotesque little woodcuts, frequently a visual rendering of a pun. They were a cheeky parody of the annuals so much in vogue during the 1830s. These superfine volumes were the 'coffee-table books' of their day. Generally edited by an aristocratic lady, who would solicit her literary and artistic acquaintances for contributions, they took the form of anthologies of verse and prose, profusely embellished with engravings and published under such titles as *Friendship's Offering* or *The Forget-me-Not.* The productions were much mocked for their elaborate decor and blatant snob-appeal as well as for the general feebleness of their literary contents. The ferocity of Dickens's 'A Word in Season', contributed to Lady Blessington's 1844 annual, *The Keepsake* (see p. 60), was exceptional.

Writing to his friend, John Forster, while at work on this review of the last of the Hood annuals, Dickens describes the book as 'rather poor', adding, 'but I have not said so, because Hood is too, and ill besides' (*Pilgrim,* Vol. 1, p. 505). Dickens's judgment is confirmed by a modern biographer of Hood: noticing that during the 1830s 'the greater part of his income depended upon the financial success of his yearly volume', John Clubbe comments, 'A survey of the ten *Comics* ... leads irresistibly to the conclusion that they show a decided fall-off in creativity within his comic vein' (*Victorian Forerunner: The Later Career of Thomas Hood* [1968], p. 20). Four years later Dickens went even further out of his way to assist Hood by writing something for his magazine (see p. 67).

Literary allusions (p. 40) 'land annuals and water annuals': echoes 'land rats and water rats', Shakespeare, *The Merchant of Venice*, Act 1, Sc. 3.

'The tenth *Comic Annual* is now in the field; and, luckily, it is a field of which no tithe can be demanded in kind or unkind.'

So says Mr Hood in his preface, and with truth and good reason, for of the originality of these ten little tomes, and of the pleasant and inoffensive nature of their sparkling humour, all men must be satisfied.

The very irregularity with which this eccentric dish is placed before us, adds to the piquancy of its flavour. Other annuals come as regularly as Lord Mayor's day, or that solemn holiday whereon geese are plucked and sheriffs plumed: there be land annuals and water annuals; and there be annuals wherein land and water are both so impartially depicted, that each has something of the properties of the other, and it is hard to tell the difference between them. But all these are true to certain times and seasons. 'About such and such period,' Francis Moore, or even Mr Murphy, might safely prophesy a good twelvemonths beforehand, 'about such and such period there will be a heavy fall of annuals – Literature at its lowest temperature' – and straightway the prediction would be fulfilled to the very letter. But Mr Hood defies all seers and conjurors, weatherwise or otherwise. He is a perfect marvel in this respect – always out of season and always in it. You give him up for lost; hold that he has made up his mind to return no more; and suddenly, like a late spring, he comes upon us one fine day, all smiles and sunshine, as we remember him of yore; and we give him house-room and a hearty welcome, as if he had made a special appointment with us for that very hour when we shook hands last year.

We love to look upon these rough woodcuts of square-headed, Dutch-built men and women, strained into all manner of extravagant attitudes as Mr Hood twists words and phrases for his purpose – and yet not half so extravagant or grotesque as the smooth-faced ladies and gentlemen who attitudinize in dearer books. We would gladly transfer one or two to our own columns, but as that is not to be done with a stroke of the pen, we will present our readers with a taste of Mr Hood's quality in prose and most undoubted verse.

There follow two columns of prose and verse extracts from the *Annual*.

14

'Theatrical Examiner'

The Examiner, 26 July 1840

When Dickens contributed this round-up of the London theatre scene to *The Examiner*, his own new weekly periodical *Master Humphrey's Clock* was five months old and in it Little Nell and her Grandfather were already launched upon their wanderings. Tyrone Power, the brilliant and highly popular Irish comedian, was making his last appearance on the London stage; the next year he went down in the ship on which he was returning to Britain from his American tour. Bulwer Lytton's *Lady of Lyons*, first produced in 1838, was one of the most popular high-class melodramas of the Victorian age, but Thomas Talfourd's ponderous *Glencoe; or, The Fate of the Macdonalds*, produced in May, had fallen flat and, despite Dickens's loyal promoting here of his beloved friend's work, was not to be revived.

The French composer and conductor Louis Antoine Jullien began his shilling Promenade Concerts at Drury Lane on 8 June 1840. These were a great success and he went on to conduct regular end-of-year concerts in one London theatre or another until 1859. Dickens's reference to 'a temple of obscenity' alludes to the notoriety of the Drury Lane Theatre as a haunt of prostitutes, who would promenade the grand saloon attached to the boxes (William Charles Macready put a stop to this practice when he became manager at the end of 1841). The 'hundred virgin warriors' appeared in J.T. Haines's drama *Jane of the Hatchet or, The Women of Beauvais* which opened at the Surrey Theatre on 20 July. Set in the France of Louis XI, this 'Gorgeous and Interesting Historical Spectacle' featured, according to the playbill (British Library), 'a Most Extraordinary Effect ... a mass of Disciplined and Variously Armed Females! Elate with their Victory, and determined on defending their homes, in Imposing Martial Array'. The second piece, *Mungo Park or, The Arab of the Night*, starred Isaac Van Amburgh ('The Last Nights of his Appearance in England') and his 'Matchless Collection of Lions, Leopards and Tigers'. Van Amburgh, the celebrated American lion-trainer, had made his debut at Astley's in 1838 and had drawn huge crowds, including the young Queen Victoria several times, to Drury Lane during 1838–9. For Ducrow and Astley's, see p. 17. Ducrow and Van Amburgh had fallen out, hence the former's production at Astley's of a rival American wild-beast trainer, a handsome six-footer named John Carter, who was English by birth. Billed as 'the Lion King', one of Carter's special effects was to drive a harnessed lion up a stage mountain. The mulatto Joseph Hillier had been with Ducrow for over ten years and had been trained by him in daring equestrian feats. 'The Courier of St Petersburg' was Ducrow's most famous and spectacular act, first performed by him at Astley's in 1827; it involved the management by a single rider of five or more galloping horses (see A.H. Saxon, *The Life and Art of Andrew Ducrow* [1978], pp. 142–4).

The Pavilion, Whitechapel, built in 1829, was one of the leading East End theatres. Samuel Butler made his reputation as a Shakespearian actor at the Surrey and other 'minor' theatres; he also developed a series of lectures on Shakespeare and this is perhaps what Dickens refers to here. 'The Wizard of the North' was the conjurer and illusionist known as Professor Anderson (J.H. Anderson), whose '*Soirées Mystérieuses*' were extremely popular.

Literary allusions (p. 43) 'a marvellous proper man': Shakespeare, *Richard III*, Act 1, Sc. 2.

There has been no novelty in theatrical politics at the Haymarket. The *Lady of Lyons* was repeated on Thursday to a house crowded to the ceiling, despite the counter attractions of the opera over the way; and Mr Phelps has thrice during the week played his character of *Macduff* in the tragedy *not* of that name, with great applause. Power, as rattling and vivacious as ever, has sent merry audiences laughing to their beds, and is now on the eve of another trip to America, whence let all lovers of rich humour pray for his speedy and safe return. The bills announce that the tragedy of *Glencoe* is shortly to be repeated. Its reception on the last night of its performance was a brilliant one, and more than justifies the announcement.

At Drury Lane the summer concerts have filled the house every night, and walls long unused to aught but empty benches have rung with the clapping of hands and tread of promenading feet. We are glad of this, for, besides that the nightly appropriation of the building to these purposes is a good practical illustration of the wisdom of the patent which gives it a monopoly in doing that which it never does, the concerts are exceedingly well conducted, well selected, and well performed. The entertainment is a very agreeable one, and the theatre is not a temple of obscenity – which (its old-established character in that respect being remembered) is worthy of remark.

The minor theatres placard the walls bravely, and give a new impulse to the art of wood-engraving on a large scale. One hundred virgin warriors, completely armed and accoutred in the costume of their time, whatever their time may be, make war-like demonstrations at the Surrey, and diffuse the love of Amazons over Lambeth and the Borough, turning the heads of steady 'prentices, and firing them with thoughts of Alexander the Great. Here, too, are Van Amburgh and his animals; but who can wonder at the docility of the latter? Time was when one virgin was more than a match for the boldest forest lion, who crouched at her tender feet, but one hundred virgins flocking round a captive lion, half blind and stupified already with sleeping behind dark scenes by day, and gaping and winking in the gas by night! Let Mr Van Amburgh no longer be prevailed upon to delay his journey to Saint Petersburg, but fly with his prostrate lion ere the virgins prove too many for him, and he dies.

Astley's, under the management of Ducrow, of course, exhibits another Van Amburgh in the person of 'Carter, the Lion King,' who drives wild beasts over bridges, and puts his legs and arms into their jaws, when he would go to sleep comfortably, with a coolness most remarkable. Those who admire such feats will perhaps prefer the Lion King to his rival, as he is a marvellous proper man, and displays a comical kind of *bonhommie* in compelling his beasts to their performances, which is foreign to his rival's nature. For the rest, there is a gorgeous drama about the Trojan war, in which the contending powers fight, sometimes on one side, and sometimes on the other, with romantic valour; and there are good scenes in the circle, in which Mr Hillier, the rider, in the *Courier of St Petersburg*, and a very humorous clown, whose un-theatrical name is Bullock, deserve especial mention.

The Pavilion has been furnishing the dwellers in the East with 'Rich Shaksperian Treats,' and 'Mr Butler, the great Tragedian' – but only for a few nights, for such things are too precious to be rendered common. Into the Strand Theatre, late the Mystic Temple of the Wizard of the North, a most impotent impostor, one 'Signior Frangopulos from Greece,' has intruded himself, and exhibits performances which would disgrace a race-course. *The* Wizard is, or has been, at home at the Saint James's Bazaar, and we hope with success – for he really deserves it.

The English Opera House, the Victoria, the Queen's Theatre, Sadler's Wells, and all other theatres within five miles of the Post office have been pursuing their beaten track; playing romantic dramas of intense interest and with terrific *dénouements*, where the mischief-working character is a being so terrible that he cannot be named, but is expressed in the playbills by a thick black dash and a corpulent note of admiration.

15

Review: *A Letter to Lord Ashley, MP, On the Mines and Collieries Bill* by C.W. Vane, Marquess of Londonderry, GCB

Morning Chronicle, 20 October 1842

Public opinion had been deeply shocked in May 1842 by the horrific facts revealed in the First Report of the Parliamentary Commission for Inquiring into the Employment of Children in Mines and Manufactories. The woodcut illustrations, based on sketches done on the spot, showing women and children labouring underground in brutal conditions had contributed greatly to the Report's impact. As a result, there was very widespread support for Lord Ashley's Bill, one of the main provisions of which was to outlaw the employment underground of children under thirteen and of women, and it passed the Commons on 5 July. It then went to the Lords, where it was strenuously opposed by colliery-owning peers, led by Charles Vane, 3rd Marquess of Londonderry, who, with his wife, owned extensive coalfields at Seaham in County Durham. On 25 July, when the Bill was due to be considered in Committee by the Lords, Dickens published an impassioned letter of support in his old paper the *Morning Chronicle*, which had consistently championed Ashley and his Bill. The letter was signed 'B', perhaps inviting connection with 'Boz'. For the full text, which pours withering scorn on the arguments against the Bill advanced by Londonderry, see *Pilgrim*, Vol. III, pp. 278–85. Towards the end of the letter Dickens writes:

> In these times, when so wide a gulf has opened between the rich and poor, which, instead of narrowing, as all good men would have it, grows broader daily; it is important that all ranks and degrees of people should understand whose hands are stretched out to separate these two great divisions of society.... Therefore it is that I implore your readers closely to watch the fate of this measure....

The Bill finally passed the Lords on 1 August, but with many watering-down amendments such as the one lowering the minimum age for employment of children underground to ten. The papers began to advertise the imminent publication of an open letter from Lord Londonderry to Lord Ashley, and the *Chronicle* editor accepted Dickens's offer to review it.

The allusion to Londonderry's 'book of travels' in the first paragraph refers to the Marquess's *A Steam Voyage to Constantinople ... in 1840/41, and to Portugal, Spain, etc. in 1839* (2 vols, 1842). The Earl of Shaftesbury mentioned on p. 47 was Lord Ashley's father; and the King of the Sandwich Islands

(Hawaii), who lodged at the Adelphi Hotel (p. 49), was King Kamehameha
II, who came to London in 1824 (both he and his Queen died of measles
before they could meet George IV).

The 'trapper boys' referred to on p. 49 were very young children who
were employed to open and shut the many 'traps', or doors, for the coal-
carts. They would sit alone in the dark by their doors for periods of twelve
hours or more a day.

Literary allusions (p. 46) 'Not even Lord Londonderry's self ... parallel':
adapts a line from Lewis Theobald's pseudo-Shakespearian tragedy *Double
Falsehood* (1728): 'None but Itself can be its Parallel' (Act 3, Sc. 1); (p. 46)
'Triton among the minnows': Shakespeare, *Coriolanus*, Act 3, Sc. 1; (p. 47)
'strangled by the Herods ... in their cradles': combines allusion to the
Biblical Herod's massacre of the innocents with the Classical legend of the
infant Hercules strangling serpents in his cradle; (p. 51) 'Don Quixote ...
little finger': Cervantes, *Don Quixote*, Part One, Ch. 32: it is, in fact, not
Don Quixote but a priest who mentions a knight 'of such great natural
strength that he could stop a millwheel, in its greatest rapidity, with a single
finger' (World's Classics edn, p. 306).

MS. The John Rylands Library, University of Manchester; published in
Moses Tyson (ed.), *A Review and Other Writings by Charles Dickens* (1934)
Tyson's edition includes the numerous manuscript alterations and can-
cellations which, Tyson observes, 'show the care with which Dickens
prepared his articles for the Press'. One major cancellation worth retrieving
is a continuation of paragraph 2, as follows:

> Nor can we too much exalt the grand simplicity, with which the noble
> Marquess, dating his letter 'to the Right Honorable Lord Ashley, MP,'
> from Wynyard Park, and beginning it 'My Lord,' and ending it 'My
> Lord, Your Lordship's most obedient servant,' in strict accordance with
> the forms presented in every genuine edition of the Polite Letter Writer,
> gradually slides, as he warms with the delivery of this printed speech,
> into the debating customs of the House of Peers, and does so in such
> passages as—'it is not necessary to say more to Your Lordships' and 'I
> have now to point out to Your Lordships' and 'it appears, My Lords,
> evident to me' and so forth. In like manner we have seen young
> gentlemen, newly summoned to the benches of the House of Commons,
> address the chairman of a Charity Dinner at Freemason's Hall as 'Mr
> Speaker,' and always with a strong effect upon their audience.

The Marquess of Londonderry has recently distinguished himself by the
production of a book of travels which for its exquisite good taste, its
surpassing modesty, its high gentlemanly feeling, its extensive information,

and its numerous beauties of style and composition has no companion in the Literature of any age or country. The Marquess of Londonderry has now still further distinguished himself by the production of a pamphlet, entitled as above, which in respect of all these points of excellence goes so far beyond the Book of Travels, that even that panting precedent toils after it in vain, and not even Lord Londonderry's self can be cited as Lord Londonderry's parallel.

As it is one of the most charming and graceful characteristics of this remarkable production that it has no one thought, or argument, or line of reasoning, in its whole compass, but is entirely devoted to the display of its noble author's exquisite taste and extreme felicity of expression (which might, by carping critics, be objected to as a blemish; the world being already possessed of ample information on these two points) we may be pardoned if we make them the principal topics of our brief and insufficient homage. But first it becomes our grateful duty to render our poor meed of praise to the noble and accomplished Marquess for expressing his sentiments in this form, and not upon the floor of the House of Lords. The delivery of speeches in pamphlets is a practice which cannot be too strongly commended. It is at once an economy of the public time; an encouragement to the printing, publishing, and paper trade; and an interesting exhibition of the orator in his own proper dress, undisguised by any of those shreds of style and grammar, with which Parliamentary reporters love to deck him out; to the great detriment and injury of such a nobleman of nature as the most noble the Marquess of Londonderry.

It is scarcely necessary to mention that, in reference to the Mines and Collieries Bill (as we learn from this letter) everybody was wrong except the Marquess of Londonderry; because whenever there is one intellect so vastly in advance of the rest of the world as the Marquess of Londonderry's is universally felt and admitted by all men to be, this result will inevitably follow. Forgetful for an instant, of this circumstance, we had expected to find that Lord Ashley was particularly, if not exclusively in the wrong, and were at first somewhat surprised to discover that he had for his colleagues in evil doing the Earl of Devon, Lord Hatherton, the whole House of Commons, every member of the present government from the Prime Minister downwards, and even the Duke of Hamilton; but a moment's reflection upon the stupendous character of Lord Londonderry's mind set us right, and shewed us, not only that this was quite intelligible, but that it must be, and is inseparable from the existence of such a Triton among the minnows of creation as this most noble marquess, 'whose humble services,' as he observes, 'are before the public and Europe,' and whose consolation, under all the Lillupitian [*sic*] arrows aimed at his mighty head by pigmies, is to be found 'in the recorded testimonials of great and enlightened warriors and statesmen' – which are neatly framed and glazed, at Wynyard Park, and may be seen on application to the housekeeper any Wednesday afternoon between the hours of two and four o'Clock.

We have said that our first head of remark should be, Lord Londonderry's exquisite good taste. There are so many instances of it in the short compass of the one hundred and forty-five pages to which this pamphlet extends, that we are rather puzzled which to adduce as a specimen; but perhaps the refined and witty attack on MR HORNER, a prominent member of the Children's Employment Commission, and a gentleman well known to the public for his valuable and zealous services in the cause of Humanity, and Human Improvement, is the best. The cutting humour, and bitter sarcasm, of printing in large capitals 'EXTRACTS FROM VARIOUS PUBLICATIONS, SHEWING MR HORNER'S VINDICTIVENESS, HIS QUARRELSOME DISPOSITION, HIS LACK OF MORAL COURAGE, ETC.,' is in the spirit of true manly nobility, and if Lord Londonderry were not already 'most noble' by courtesy, we should have ventured to suggest that he be called so, to distinguish him, in after ages, from less notable inheritors of his title; as society, conferring distinctions of its own on honors which descend from a great, great, grandfather to a small, small grandson, is wont to say, the Great Duke of Marlborough, or the famous Lord Nelson.

The mention of Doctor Southwood Smith, in a single line, as 'another commissioner *and an Unitarian*' is also full of generous point and purpose. So is the following passage, which, in its reference to some talk that may have been held among the footmen in the waiting-room of the House of Lords, touching the Earl of Shaftesbury or his plush-breeched representative in the Servants' parliament, is almost worthy of Mrs Honour.

'*It was said* that one noble Earl (and a very important person to your Lordship too) declared in an assembly, "That he knew better than to undertake the fathering of such a bill as yours, through the Lords." How well His Lordship knew the House of Lords!'

Doubtless very well indeed, and not the less intimately by reason of his long experience as chairman of its Committees. If the Earl of Shaftesbury, or the Earl of Shaftesbury's footman ever did say anything to this purpose, he spoke wisely. All measures which have for their object the improvement of the popular condition, or the elevation of the popular character, are very troublesome children to their fathers in the House of Lords. They cost a world of trouble in the bringing up; and are, for the most part, strangled by the Herods of the Peerage, in their cradles.

Lord Londonderry takes credit to himself in this letter for 'generously pointing out,' that there was no clause in the bill obliging the coal-owners to find the means of sending the Inspectors down into the pits; and that if an Inspector were sent down into a mine, he might, for any means the bill afforded him of coming up, be left there by the owner. On reference to the debate of the first of August, it will be found that the noble Marquess and elegant author expressed himself to this effect. 'For his part, if an Inspector came to *him*, and asked permission to inspect *his* works, he should say "get down how you can; but when you get down, you may get back how you can" ' – which speech, and which reference, are at once tasteful, generous, pleasant, and whimsical.

The 'disgusting pictorial woodcuts' which accompanied the report still haunt the nobleman of taste, who complains 'that they were seen in the *salons* of the Capital, and that the ladies were all enlisted in the cause of their own sex, thus represented in so brutal a manner.' And to be sure it was a sad depravity of taste to pity them, and in the very worst taste for any lady or gentleman to look into the rooms at Wynyard Park, and see those brutal forms reflected in the glittering plate, and polished furniture, and even bordering, in fantastic patterns, the pages of the bankers book of the most noble the Marquess of Londonderry, in account with Coutts and Co.

But our space is limited, and some few happy turns of expression and elegancies of composition should be extracted, as a sample of the rest. They may prove useful, too, as exercises for charity boys in their first quarter.

The following paragraph is hardly less admirable for beauty of construction and remarkable clearness and vigour of style, than for the profound philosophy of its sentiment:

'Before I conclude this letter, I shall develope my own views as contradistinguished from your Lordship's as to the impolicy of legislative interference with the management and labouring classes working the mines and collieries of England; and although I do not imagine I can alter the sentiments of those who, led astray by false reports, allow themselves to be guided by the representations of unqualified and ignorant authorities, nor of those who seek to build their fame on a new species of modern philosophy, by raising the standard of mistaken humanity, and advocating the theories of general education and overstrained morality, and still less by those who, in their excited and exalted enthusiasm, *forget that men are not all born to read and write, but that they must obtain by the sweat of their brow the food for the mouth as well as the mind*. From such as these, I look not for converts; but I flatter myself I shall be able to afford the public and the unprejudiced world such information upon the subject now at issue between us, as will remove many of the absurd and exaggerated statements your Lordship and the Commissioners' Reports have put forth.'

That all men are not born to read and write, is a very wise and profound remark. It is full of truth. There be Lords who are not born to write one correct sentence in the language of the country they have represented abroad; and who, if they be born to read at all, are born to be never the better for it.

Here are two sentences, which for their terseness, strength, and perspicuity, might have been written by SWIFT:

> 'Lord Devon, I understand, on perusing the Bill, as sent up from the Commons, contemplated and saw all its probable effect with dismay; but his Lordship was pleased with the field it afforded for his able and experienced pruning-knife, to undertake its management. And he then took those measures in private conference with your Lordship, to modify, change, and alter the clauses in such a manner as to render them innocuous, and no longer bearing the semblance of their first character: all this happened, as the preface to the noble Earl's moving the second reading of the Bill.'

Another:

> 'Here, then, is the end of your Lordship's bantling, dressed in your swaddling-clothes, it was stripped and despoiled before you took it back to your nursery, where you were doomed to accept it naked and deformed, not cognisable by its own parent, while its enemies had the satisfaction of contemplating its creation and its fall as perfectly harmless and inoperative.'

Another, unequalled, perhaps, save in the earliest English Exercises of the King of the Sandwich Islands, penned when he first took lodgings at the Adelphi Hotel, and began to study the language:

> 'As this Bill was brought in originally, it would have revolutionised the coal-trade, and vitally affect many of the working classes.'

Another, of singular beauty:

> 'Up to the age of *ten* allows sufficient time to acquire the rudiments of education on which to build in future, when occasion may require.'

The following is a passage from a letter received by the noble author, containing, as he says, 'many good observations'; and signed 'A Trapper Boy.' It is so obviously the writing of a trapper boy, and is so very interesting in that view for its simple artlessness, that it is worth attention. The allusion to the *piscina* is particularly natural, for it is well known that trapper boys are always thinking of piscinae, and from their earliest infancy constantly ruminate, at the bottoms of mines, in the Latin tongue:

> 'Without waiting to notice the Commissioners' exceedingly exaggerated Report, or to call in question the benevolent intentions of many of those

gentlemen to whom the Commissioner has had access, and from whom he has collected so many observations, I would beg leave to say, that the legislative enactment now under consideration will present something like the vicar's "*piscina*," completely choking up the conduit-pipes through which the stream of charity has flowed to many an indigent family for many years.'

Again:

'Is it possible then that your Lordships should place such implicit confidence in the Commissioners' report now on your Lordships' table, when you consider how and by whom it has been constructed, and be induced to legislate on and create these new authorities over private property, without *creditable* and proper evidence, and the examination of practical men?'

To this piece of writing, however, we cannot award the praise of originality. Both Winifred Jenkins and Mrs Malaprop use 'creditable' for 'credible.' So do hackney coachmen frequently, and costermongers always.

But in one of the noble author's concluding remarks, we thoroughly concur. It is, that the subject has been handled with great indecency, and is disfigured, by a vast amount of most reprehensible and disgraceful blunders. There is no doubt whatever of the fact; Lord Londonderry's own evidence in regard to it, being quite irresistible.

There are only fourteen original pages in the whole one hundred and forty-five of this letter; the remainder being devoted to a recapitulation of the discussions on the mines and collieries bill in the House of Lords, with an improved edition of the noble author's speeches in the front row. We have been in some pain lest from the excessive scantiness of its materials it may not be destined to answer the expectations, either of the noble Marquess, its author, or Mr Colburn, its publisher; but one mode of proceeding has after some reflection occurred to us, which we venture to suggest, as being full of promise and prospective advantage to both.

It is simply this: – that the one hundred and thirty-one pages of old matter should be summarily cancelled, and that the remaining fourteen should be distributed over a tolerably large number of very small sheets, and published at a cheap price under the name of The New Polite Letter Writer, or Noble Scholar's Companion.

Formerly there used to be displayed in certain shop-windows a Sixpenny Letter Writer with a highly colored frontispiece, representing a lady in a blue riding habit, holding above her head a red smear for a parasol, entering a bookseller's place of business, and saying:

A Letter Writer, if you please,
That I may learn to write with ease:

To which a grave and wealthy citizen behind the counter, clad in a light blue coat and yellow small-clothes, and politely holding forth a book as he spoke, replied:

> Globwog's Edition is the best;
> I sell more o' that, than all the rest.

Now, in the present case, with a new Globwog in the costume of the day offering this Polite Letter Writer of Lord Londonderry's to any noble Lord in search of the means of honorable distinction, an illustration in the same style, would tell exceedingly well. And he might be represented as saying – not even in verse, but in plain prose – 'The Vane Edition is the one, My Lord. There is no Letter Writer, but the Vane Letter Writer. The author is a person of quality, My Lord. He has had every possible advantage in the way of station and education; he entertains a high contempt for everything that is not polite and lofty: his bear never dances but to the genteelest of tunes; and here you behold his truly refined feeling, and his truly English Grammar, all condensed within the limits of one little book, price sixpence.' And if any additional recommendation were wanting, H.B. might furnish a vignette representing the most noble the Marquess of Londonderry; in the character of that stalwart knight, referred to by Don Quixote who stopped a windmill with his little finger; stemming the tide of public indignation and compassionate remembrance of the wronged and suffering many, with his gray goose-quill.

16

Snoring for the Million

The Examiner, 24 December 1842

First identified as Dickens's work by the *Pilgrim* editors on the basis of his letter to *The Examiner*'s editor, Albany Fonblanque, of 22 December (*Pilgrim*, Vol. III, p. 399: '... I haven't had time to do that "Snoring for the Million" yet ...'). 'Singing for the Million' was a catchphrase of the day, which originated in 1841 when the Privy Council's Committee on Education encouraged John Pyke Hullah, who had made his name by composing the music for Dickens's opera *The Village Coquettes* (1836), to set up singing classes for elementary schoolteachers at Exeter Hall following the system developed in Paris by Guillaume Wilhem. These classes proved hugely popular and were extended to the general public, who were no less enthusiastic. The Privy Council's Prefatory Minute to Hullah's *Wilhem's Method of Teaching Singing adapted to English Usage* (1841; rev. edn 1842) made the political agenda very explicit:

> Amusements which wean the people from vicious indulgences are in themselves a great advantage; they contribute indirectly to the increase of domestic comfort, and promote the contentment of the artisan.... The national legends, frequently embodied in songs, are the peasant's chief source of that national feeling which other ranks derive from ... history. The songs of any people may be regarded as an important means of forming an industrious, brave, loyal and religious working class.

J.E. Cox (*Musical Recollections of the Last Half-Century* [1872], Vol. 2, pp. 51–2) wrote: 'About this period the metropolis witnessed frantic efforts to make its inhabitants suddenly proficient in music ... by public lectures and class-teaching ... pompously placarded as being under the Committee of Council of Education.' Lord Wharncliffe was at this time Lord President of the Privy Council.

Exeter Hall (built in the Strand 1829–31 and demolished in 1907) was one of Dickens's *bêtes noires*. It was the venue for mass meetings of Evangelicals and what he would have regarded as the worst kind of patronising do-gooders, hence a fitting place for Hullah's classes for contented workers. The 'hypnologist' showman Gardner has not been identified. Lord Ellenborough was Governor-General of India (1841–4) and a controversial figure; 'After successful termination of the [Afghan] war [late 1842] he indulged in grandiose displays which have been universally ridiculed' (*Dictionary of National Biography*). The Home Secretary at this time was the highly unpopular Sir James Graham.

In the *Examiner* review of the Drury Lane pantomime *Harlequin and William Tell, or, The Ribstone Pippin* (31 December 1842, probably by Dickens; see *Pilgrim*, Vol. III, p. 401, n. 2) appears the comment: 'The cleverest hit is at the Singing for the Million, at the close of the burlesque of which, the stage is suddenly filled with innumerable kettles, singing lustily their earlier and happier English song.'

Literary allusions (p. 55) 'the ravelled sleeve of Care': Shakespeare, *Macbeth*, Act 2, Sc. 1.

Singing for the million is the great reform of the nineteenth century. All the human birds who have hitherto mistrusted their own vocal powers, and who couldn't sing and wouldn't sing, may now be made to sing, as tavern dinners are provided, on the shortest notice and the most reasonable terms. The popular superstition that a man may have 'a singing face' has become obsolete; it being clearly established that any man with any face at all can sing if he will. Nobody gets anything by teaching the million to sing. A new sect of philosophers has sprung up among us, akin in spirit to the wise men of the old time, who never bartered knowledge for gold and silver. The singing sages walk barefoot into Exeter Hall and other large assembly rooms, and call upon the million to come and mortify them, and steep them to the very eyebrows in poverty; while the good Lord Wharncliffe looks upon the sight in tearful wonder, and thanks his stars for having cast him on such pious times.

The Privy Council teaches the people to be vocal. The Government seeing the million with their mouths wide open, naturally thinks that they must want to sing; for it only recognizes two kinds of forks, the silver fork and the tuning fork, between which opposite extremes there is nothing. 'John,' said the frugal lady to her thirsty footman, 'when you go into the cellar to draw the beer, be good enough to whistle all the time.' 'John,' says the Government to its starving servant, 'when you ramble up and down the market-places, dying of hunger, be careful, above all things, to sing perpetually.'

The progress of this wise and happy institution, and its singular freedom from any tinge of humbug, has suggested to us the expediency of establishing another on similar principles, though with a different object. We desire to propound a system of Snoring for the Million.

It appears, by public advertisement in the newspapers, that one Doctor Gardner, sole keeper and warder of the leaden gate of that great science, hypnology, is lately dead; but that he has, happily for the world, left his key behind him. Now hypnology is (as we learn from the same source) the art of sending people to sleep without the use of opiates or animal magnetism; and as the great hypnological mystery is to be sold cheap by the Doctor's executors, we propose that it be instantly purchased by the Privy Council, and that a normal school on the purest hypnological principles be immediately founded.

That Exeter Hall is the natural place for such an establishment will be at once apparent, by reason of its never having yet been used but for purposes of unquestioned charity, utility, and benevolence, tending, beyond all doubt, to the enlightenment and happiness of the many. The normal foundation being instituted within the walls of a building endeared to the people by so many delightful associations, and having in due course attained perfection, and sent forth able teachers into every part of the country, we would suggest that Exeter Hall be henceforth made the central school of Snoring for the Million; and that classes be opened there every night in the week, Sunday excepted, four nights being allotted to artizans and labourers, one to the middle classes, and one (this would be a very select night) to persons of quality and members of the

Government. It is unnecessary to make any separate and distinct provision for the bishops, as they are pretty well known to be sound sleepers and very heavy snorers already; though whether they shall give to the clergy under their care periodical lessons in snoring, on the method of Gardner, instead of delivering them, as at present, on their own method of pastoral charges, may be matter for future consideration.

The mode of instruction will be extremely simple. The professor, reclining in an easy chair, or on a couch, placed in an elevated position in the centre of the hall, will impart to his pupils the great Gardnerian charm, or secret, which the pupils will repeat after him. At a certain point the whole company, including the professor, will fall asleep, and the snoring will immediately commence.

Should the classes conceive a great affection for the professor in their waking moments, and be desirous to present him publicly with some token of their affectionate regard, an embroidered pillow or a laced nightcap will readily suggest itself as an appropriate gift.

It only remains to consider some of the great advantages which cannot fail to result from carrying this system into practical operation; and, firstly, let us contemplate it with reference to the select class, composed of persons of quality and members of the Government.

The comfort which many persons of quality will certainly derive from having increased and frequent opportunities of self-forgetfulness, it would be difficult to exaggerate: and there are not few of this order who will not find it an unspeakable happiness to become oblivious of the Reform Bill, with its long train of ungenteel and revolutionary consequences, as exemplified in the increased and increasing audacity of the millions who demand to live. As to the members of the Government, a large proportion of them will draw their consolation from the same sources, while from their harmless repose the country can scarcely fail to derive inestimable benefit. To perceive the force of this remark, it is only necessary to consider how much more honourably for the credit and renown of Britain affairs in India would be managed, if Lord Ellenborough were comfortably tucked up in bed, in which case he would be worth at least double his present salary; or what a blessing it would be, if the Home Secretary, instead of occasionally bestirring himself in that somnambulistic state, in which people, with a muddled remembrance of their real duties, are apt to do things by halves and then to do them wrong, were but sound asleep and incapable of mischief.

To the middle classes, one night's unconsciousness of the Income Tax would be worth, at the lowest estimate, twenty times the cost of a whole course of snoring lessons; while it is impossible to set a price upon the luxury of forgetting the existence of a Minister who so handsomely cajoled and so worthily deceived them, as did the Right Hon. Baronet who is now at the head of her Majesty's Government.

But it is, in its effects upon the lower classes; upon the million; the labourers and artizans; the vulgar men of toil and sweat, and want and rags; that this system has peculiar claims upon the present Administration. No more complaints of hunger, when the starving poor may sleep and dream of loaves at will! No more pinching of the Landed Interest's corn in its good old gouty shoe! The ravelled sleeve of Care which flutters in the murky streets of our manufacturing towns, shadowing strange shapes in its dreary gambols, will be sewn up by the quickest process in the world. Oppressive and unequal laws will be no more remembered; the justice dealt out by Magistrates to Poverty, instead of being placarded on every little news-shop in bye-places, goading the irritated on to fury, and arming the wicked and designing with their sharpest weapons, will be forgotten save in dreams; the madness of that Church Establishment which, in its intolerant and bigoted insanity, loves, in its greatest danger, ever to exhibit itself with its hand at its own throat, will be evident to no man; there will be no fast-widening gulf between the two great divisions of society: all will be peace and comfort: there will be forgetfulness for those who have nothing, and undisturbed enjoyment for those who have everything.

How much better than Singing for the Million! How much easier than Legislating for the Million! How much quieter than the old system of Snoring for the Million, which had for its active agents cannon-balls and sabre-edges! But such is the difference between the Toryism of King George the Third's reign, and the Conservatism of Queen Victoria's! We undoubtingly confide our project to the present Ministry.

17

Theatre Review: Macready as Benedick

The Examiner, 4 March 1843

Since Christmas 1841 Dickens's admired friend William Charles Macready had been manager of Drury Lane and had struggled hard to restore its dignity as one of the two great homes of the national drama after the years of Alfred Bunn's management (Bunn 'was simply a showman and he made Drury Lane only a big booth', H. Barton Baker, *The London Stage* [1889], Vol. 1, p. 109). Appreciation of Macready's managerial efforts doubtless contributed to the immense enthusiasm with which he was received by a packed house on his benefit night (24 February). He recorded in his *Diaries*: 'Acted Benedict [*sic*] very well. The audience went with the play and with *Comus*. They called for me after both pieces'; he also noted on 26 February: 'Dickens called and sat for a short time.' They perhaps discussed the *Morning Post*'s unfavourable comments (25 February) on both Macready's performance ('especially and signally a character which lies beyond his range') and his choice of plays. The *Post*, which aimed at an aristocratic readership – hence Dickens's remarks about the 'nobility and gentry' – commented: 'the name of Shakespeare cannot prevent us from yawning over the vague tenuity of the earlier portion of *Much Ado about Nothing* ... profane brutes that we are', and 'candidly [owned] ... to nodding over the morality of Milton in the most pertinacious manner'.

Literary allusions (p. 57) 'primrose path': Shakespeare, *Macbeth*, Act 2, Sc. 3.

MS. Forster Collection, Victoria and Albert Museum. The printers garbled Dickens's text in three or four places, including the quotation from *Comus* where *The Examiner* text reads 'stabbed wolves' for 'stabled wolves'. These errors have been silently corrected.

Much Ado about Nothing and *Comus* were repeated on Tuesday to a crowded house. They were received with no less enthusiasm than on the night of Mr Macready's benefit, and are announced for repetition twice a week.

We are desirous to say a few words of Mr Macready's performance of *Benedick*; not because its striking merits require any commendation to those who witness it – as is sufficiently shown by its reception – but because justice is scarcely done to his impersonation of the character, as we think, by some of those who have reported upon it for that class of the Nobility and Gentry (not quite so limited a one as could be desired, perhaps), who seldom enter a theatre unless it be a foreign one; or who, when they do repair to an English temple of the drama, would seem to be attracted thither solely by an amiable desire to purify, by their presence, a scene of vice and indecorum; and who select their place of entertainment accordingly.

There are many reasons why a tragic actor incurs considerable risk of failing to enlist the sympathies of his audience when he appears in comedy. In the first place, some people are rather disposed to take it ill that he should make them laugh who has so often made them cry. In the second, he has not only to make the impression which he seeks to produce in that particular character, but has to render it, at once, so obvious and distinct, as to cast into oblivion for the time all the host of grave associations with which he is identified. Lastly, there is a very general feeling abroad in reference to all the arts, and every phase of public life, that the path which a man has trodden for many years – even though it should be the primrose path to the everlasting bonfire – must be of necessity his allotted one, and that it is, as a matter of course, the only one in which he is qualified to walk.

First impressions, too, even with persons of a cultivated understanding, have an immense effect in settling their notions of a character; and it is no heresy to say that many people unconsciously form their opinion of such a creation as *Benedick*, not so much from the exercise of their own judgment in reading the play, as from what they have seen bodily presented to them on the stage. Thus, when they call to mind that in such a place Mr A. or Mr B. used to stick his arms akimbo and shake his head knowingly; or that in such another place he gave the pit to understand, by certain confidential nods and winks, that in good time they should see what they should see; or in such another place, swaggered; or in such another place, with one hand clasping each of his sides, heaved his shoulders as with laughter; they recall his image, not as the Mr A. or B. aforesaid, but as Shakespeare's *Benedick* – the real *Benedick* of the book, not the conventional *Benedick* of the boards – and missing any familiar action, miss, as it were, something of right belonging to the part.

Against all these difficulties Mr Macready has had to contend, as any such man must, in his performance of *Benedick*, and yet before his very first scene was over on the first night of the revival, the whole house felt that there was before them a presentment of the character so fresh, distinct, vigorous, and enjoyable, as they could not choose but relish, and go along with, delightedly, to the fall of the curtain.

If it be beyond the province of what we call genteel comedy – a term which Shakespeare would have had some difficulty in understanding, perhaps – to make people laugh, then, assuredly, Mr Macready is far from being a genteelly comic *Benedick*. But as we find him – *Signior Benedick* of Padua, that is, not the *Benedick* of this or that theatrical company – the constant occasion of merriment among the persons represented in *Much Ado about Nothing*, 'all mirth,' as *Don Pedro* has it, 'from the crown of his head to the sole of his foot'; and as we find him, in particular, constantly moving to laughter both the *Prince* and *Claudio*, who may be reasonably supposed to possess their share of refined and courtier-like behaviour; we venture to think that those who sit below the salt, or t'other side the lamps, should laugh also. And that they did and do, both loud and long, let the ringing walls of Drury lane bear witness.

Judging of it by analogy; by comparison with anything we know in nature, literature, art; by any test we can apply to it, from within us or without, we can imagine no purer or higher piece of genuine comedy than Mr Macready's performance of the scene in the orchard after emerging from the arbour. As he sat, uneasily cross-legged, on the garden chair, with that face of grave bewilderment and puzzled contemplation, we seemed to be looking on a picture of Leslie. It was just such a figure as that excellent artist, in his fine appreciation of the finest humour, might have delighted to produce. Those who consider it broad, or farcical, or overstrained, cannot surely have considered all the train and course of circumstances leading up to that place. If they take them into reasonable account, and try to imagine for a moment how any master of fiction would have described *Benedick*'s behaviour at that crisis – supposing it had been impossible to contemplate the appearance of a living man in the part, and therefore necessary to describe it at all – can they arrive at any other conclusion than that such ideas as are here presented by Mr Macready would have been written down? Refer to any passage in any play of Shakespeare's, where it has been necessary to describe, as occurring beyond the scene, the behaviour of a man in a situation of ludicrous perplexity; and by that standard alone (to say nothing of any mistaken notion of natural behaviour that may have suggested itself at any time to Goldsmith, Swift, Fielding, Smollett, Sterne, Scott, or other such unenlightened journeymen) criticise, if you please, this portion of Mr Macready's admirable performance.

The nice distinction between such an aspect of the character as this, and the after love scenes with *Beatrice*, the challenging of *Claudio*, or the gay endurance and return of the *Prince*'s jests at last, was such as none but a master could have expressed, though the veriest tyro in the house might feel its truth when presented to him. It occurred to us that Mr Macready's avoidance of *Beatrice* in the second act was a little too earnest and real; but it is hard dealing to find so slight a blemish in such a finished and exquisite performance. For such, in calm reflection, and not in the excitement of having recently witnessed it, we unaffectedly and impartially believe it to be.

The other characters are, for the most part, exceedingly well played. *Claudio*, in the gay and gallant scenes, has an efficient representative in Mr Anderson; but his perfect indifference to *Hero*'s supposed death is an imputation on his good sense, and a disagreeable circumstance in the representation of the play, which we should be heartily glad to see removed. Mr Compton has glimpses of *Dogberry*, though iron was never harder than he. If he could but derive a little oil from his contact with Keeley (whose utter absorption in his learned neighbour is amazing), he would become an infinitely better leader of the *Prince*'s Watch. Mrs Nisbett is no less charming than at first, and Miss Fortescue is more so, from having a greater share of confidence in her bearing, and a somewhat smaller nosegay in her breast. Both Mr Phelps and Mr W. Bennett deserve especial notice, as acting at once with great spirit and great discretion.

Let those who still cling to the opinion that the Senate of ancient Rome represented by five-shillings' worth of supernumerary assistance huddled together at a rickety table, with togas above the cloth and corduroys below, is more gratifying and instructive to behold than the living Truth presented to them in *Coriolanus* during Mr Macready's management of Covent Garden, – let such admirers of the theatre track the mazes of the wild wood in *Comus*, as it is now produced; let them look upon the stage, what time

> 'He and his monstrous rout are heard to howl,
> Like stabled wolves, or tigers at their prey,
> Doing abhorred rights to Hecate
> In their obscured haunts of inmost bowers,'

– and reconcile their previous notions with any principle of human reason, if they can.

18

Report of the Commissioners Appointed to Inquire into the Condition of the Persons Variously Engaged in the University of Oxford

The Examiner, 3 June 1843

'I find I am getting horribly bitter about Puseyism,' Dickens wrote to Fonblanque on 13 March 1843. 'Good God to talk in these times of most untimely ignorance among the people, about what Priests shall wear, and whither they shall turn when they say their prayers ...' (*Pilgrim*, Vol. III, p. 462). 'Puseyism', or the Anglo-Catholicism identified with the Oxford Movement in the Church of England (often also called 'Ritualism'), had been much in the news since May, when Oxford University's Vice Chancellor and Heads of Houses had suspended Dr Pusey, Regius Professor of Hebrew and one of the leaders of the Movement, from preaching in the University for two years following a sermon on the Eucharist held by his opponents in the Church to be heretical; it was reported by the *Morning Chronicle* under the title 'Dr Pusey's Public Profession of Roman Catholic Doctrine'. All his life Dickens was impatient and intolerant of doctrinal disputes in the Church of England (particularly when any hint of 'Romanism' was involved – see article 55) when, he fervently believed, the Church should have been concentrating its energies on relieving social misery and combating ignorance and injustice. The close parodying of the format of the Report of the Children's Employment Commission (see p. 44) in the following piece gives a bitter edge to the satire. Shortly after writing it, Dickens expressed similar views in a poem entitled 'A Word in Season', written for Lady Blessington's annual *The Keepsake* (reprinted in Forster, Book 4, Ch. 1). In it he writes of a country where

> ... brutal ignorance, and toil, and dearth
> Were the hard portion of its sons and daughters:
> And yet, where they who should have oped the door
> Of charity and light for all men's finding
> Squabbled for words upon the altar-floor,
> And rent The Book, in struggles for the binding.

The 'Report' appeared as a leading article on the first page of *The Examiner*. On p. 341 of the same issue appeared an approving review of another anti-Pusey satire, referring to 'that cold hash of stale traditions of which the Pusey banquet is composed'.

MS. Forster Collection, Victoria and Albert Museum. Annotated at the top in another hand: 'A leader – Bourgeois [name of a certain type-face] Be very careful with the titles and the capital letters of this article.' Dickens would seem to have introduced two softening-down touches in proof: the phrase 'whereof almost every one shall contradict the others', which appears after 'nine-and-thirty articles at once' in the MS., is omitted in the printed version and in the last paragraph of the piece 'Clerical degrees' becomes 'Learned degrees'.

It can scarcely be necessary for us to remind our readers that a Commission under the Great Seal was appointed some months since, to inquire into the deplorable amount of ignorance and superstition alleged to prevail in the University of Oxford; concerning which, the representatives of that learned body in the Commons' House of Parliament, had then, and have since, at divers times, publicly volunteered the most alarming and astounding evidence. The Commission was addressed to those gentlemen who had investigated the moral condition of the Children and Young Persons employed in Mines and Manufactories; it being wisely considered that their opportunities of reporting on the darkness of Colleges as compared with Mines, and on the prejudicial atmosphere of Seats of Learning as compared with Seats of Labour, would be highly advantageous to the public interest, and might possibly open the public eyes.

The Commissioners have ever since been actively engaged in pursuing their inquiries into this subject, and deducing from the mass of evidence such conclusions as appeared to them to be warranted by the facts. Their Report is now before us, and though it has not yet been presented to Parliament, we venture to give it entire.

The Commissioners find:

First, with regard to EMPLOYMENT —

That the intellectual works in the University of Oxford are, in all essential particulars, precisely what they were when it was first established for the Manufacture of Clergymen. That they alone have stood still (or, in the very few instances in which they have moved at all, have moved backward), when all other works have advanced and improved. That the nature of the employment in which the young persons are engaged is, by reason of its excessive dust and rust, extremely pernicious and destructive. That they all become short-sighted in a most remarkable degree; that, for the most part, they lose the use of their reason at a very early age, and are seldom known to recover it. That the most hopeless and painful extremes of deafness and blindness are frequent among them. That they are reduced to such a melancholy state of apathy and indifference as to be willing to sign anything, without asking what it is, or knowing what it means; which is a common custom with these unhappy persons, even to the extent of nine-and-thirty articles at once. That, from the monotonous nature of their employment, and the dull routine of their unvarying drudgery (which requires no exercise of original intellectual power, but is a mere parrot-like performance), they become painfully uniform in character and perception, and are reduced to one dead level (a very dead one, as your Commissioners believe) of mental imbecility. That cramps and paralysis of all the higher faculties of the brain are the ordinary results of this system of labour. And your Commissioners can truly add, that they found nothing in the avocations of the miners of Scotland, the knife-grinders of Sheffield, or the workers in iron of Wolverhampton, one-half so prejudicial to the persons engaged therein, or one-half so injurious to society, as this fatal system of employment in the University of Oxford.

Secondly, with regard to the PREVAILING IGNORANCE —

That the condition of the University of Oxford, under this head, is of the most appalling kind; insomuch that your Commissioners are firmly of opinion that, taking all the attendant circumstances into consideration, the Young Persons employed in Mines and Manufactories are enlightened beings, radiant with intelligence, and overflowing with the best results of knowledge, when compared with the persons, young and old, employed in the Manufacture of Clergymen at Oxford. And your Commissioners have been led to this conclusion: not so much by the perusal of prize poems, and a due regard to the very small number of Young Persons accustomed to University Employment who distinguish themselves in after life, or become in any way healthy and wholesome; as by immediate reference to the evidence taken on the two Commissions, and an impartial consideration of the two classes of testimony, side by side.

That it is unquestionably true that a boy was examined under the Children's Employment Commission, at Brinsley, in Derbyshire, who had been three years at school, and could not spell 'Church'; whereas there is no doubt that the persons employed in the University of Oxford can all spell Church with great readiness, and, indeed, very seldom spell anything else. But, on the other hand, it must not be forgotten that, in the minds of the persons employed in the University of Oxford, such comprehensive words as justice, mercy, charity, kindness, brotherly love, forbearance, gentleness, and Good Works, awaken no ideas whatever; while the evidence shows that the most preposterous notions are attached to the mere terms Priest and Faith. One young person, employed in a Mine, had no other idea of a Supreme Being than 'that he had heard him constantly damned at'; but use the verb to damn, in this horrible connection, with the Fountain Head of Mercy, in the active sense, instead of in the passive one; and make the Deity the nominative case instead of the objective; and how many persons employed in the University of Oxford have their whole faith in, and whole knowledge of, the Maker of the World, presented in a worse and far more impious sentence!

That the answers of persons employed in the said University, to questions put to them by the Sub-Commissioners in the progress of this inquiry, bespoke a moral degradation infinitely lower than any brought to light in Mines and Factories, as may be gathered from the following examples. A vast number of witnesses being interrogated as to what they understood by the words Religion and Salvation, answered Lighted Candles. Some said water; some, bread; others, little boys; others mixed the water, lighted candles, bread, and little boys all up together, and called the compound, Faith. Others again, being asked if they deemed it to be matter of great interest in Heaven, and of high moment in the vast scale of creation, whether a poor human priest should put on, at a certain time, a white robe or a black one; or should turn his face to the East or to the West; or should bend his knees of clay; or stand, a worm on end upon the earth, said 'Yes, they did': and being further questioned, whether a man could hold such mummeries in his contempt, and pass to everlasting rest, said boldly, 'No.' (*See evidence of Pusey and others.*)

And one boy (quite an old boy, too, who might have known better) being interrogated in a public class, as to whether it was his opinion that a man who professed to go to church was of necessity a better man than one who went to chapel, also answered 'Yes'; which your Commissioners submit, is an example of ignorance, besotted dulness, and obstinacy, wholly without precedent in the inquiry limited to Mines and Factories; and is such as the system of labour adopted in the University of Oxford could alone produce. (*See evidence of Inglis.*) In the former Commission, one boy anticipated all examination by volunteering the remark, 'that he warn't no judge of nuffin'; but the persons employed in the University of Oxford, almost to a man, concur in saying 'that they ain't no judges of nuffin' (with the unimportant exception of other men's souls); and that, believing in the divine ordination of any minister to whom they may take a fancy, 'they ain't answerable for nuffin to nobody'; which your Commissioners again submit is an infinitely worse case, and is fraught with much greater mischief to the general welfare. (*See the evidence in general.*)

We humbly represent to your Majesty that the persons who give these answers, and hold these opinions, and are in this alarming state of ignorance and bigotry, have it in their power to do much more evil than the other ill qualified teachers of Young Persons employed in Mines and Factories, inasmuch as those were voluntary instructors of youth, who can be removed at will, and as the public improvement demands, whereas these are the appointed Sunday teachers of the empire, forced by law upon your Majesty's subjects, and not removable for incompetence or misconduct otherwise than by certain overseers called Bishops, who are, in general, more incompetent and worse conducted than themselves. Wherefore it is our loyal duty to recommend to your Majesty that the pecuniary, social, and political privileges now arising from the degradation and debasement of the minds and morals of your Majesty's subjects, be no longer granted to these persons; or at least that if they continue to exercise an exclusive power of conferring Learned degrees and distinctions, the titles of the same be so changed and altered, that they may in some degree express the tenets in right of which they are bestowed. And this, we suggest to your Majesty, may be done without any great violation of the true Conservative principle: inasmuch as the initial letters of the present degrees (not by any means the least important parts of them) may still be retained as Bachelor of Absurdity, Master of Arrogance, Doctor of Church Lunacy, and the like.

All which we humbly certify to your Majesty.

THOMAS TOOKE (L.S.)
T. SOUTHWOOD SMITH (L.S.)
LEONARD HORNER (L.S.)
ROBERT J. SAUNDERS (L.S.)

WESTMINSTER, *June* 1, 1843

19

The Agricultural Interest

Morning Chronicle, 9 March 1844

This appeared as second leader in the paper. Forster, commenting on Dickens's state of mind in early 1844, when he was completing *Martin Chuzzlewit*, says (Book 4, Ch. 3), 'the old radical leanings were again rather strong in him ... and he had found occasional vent for them by writing in the *Morning Chronicle*'. The following ironic assault on the entrenched opponents of the repeal of the Corn Laws is, however, the only article in the paper that can be attributed to Dickens (see *Pilgrim*, Vol. IV, p. 62).

The reference to Indictments for Conspiracy in paragraph 1 alludes to the trial of the Irish leader Daniel O'Connell in Dublin in February before a packed jury of Conservative Protestants. He was found guilty, but sentence was suspended until May and the whole trial was a 'mixture of inefficiency and absurdity' (Norman Gash, *Sir Robert Peel* [1972], p. 424). The Attorney-General for Ireland, Thomas Barry Smith, at one point challenged one of the defence lawyers to a duel, hence Dickens's allusion to his 'sword' (p. 65) and 'pistol' (p. 66). At another point, the Lord Chief Justice of Ireland, who presided, referred to the defence as 'the other side', hence Dickens's jibe at the end of paragraph 7. The Duke of Buckingham, acclaimed as 'the farmer's friend', was a 'fanatic agriculturist' (Gash, p. 313) and Richard Cobden was one of the foremost leaders of the Anti-Corn Law League, strongly supported by the manufacturing interest which wanted the cheaper bread that the end of Protectionism would bring. James Morison, the self-styled 'Hygeist', was a manufacturer of an immensely popular quack panacea called 'Morison's Vegetable Universal Pill' at his establishment in the New Road (now Euston Road), which he called the British College of Health (see R.D. Altick, *The Presence of the Present* [1991], p. 551).

Literary allusions (p. 65) 'sword into a ploughshare': Isaiah 2: 4; (p. 65) 'inscribed ... upon the walls': alludes to Belshazzar's Feast, Daniel 5; (p. 65) 'They who run ... may read': Keble's 'There is a book, who runs may read' (derived from Habakkuk 2: 2), *The Christian Year*, 'Septuagesima'; (p. 66) 'poorly furnish forth': Shakespeare, *Hamlet*, Act 1, Sc. 2; (p. 66) 'Do the professors ... fail in their truth': the anonymous popular song, 'Has she then failed in her truth?/The beautiful maid I adore', set to music by Bishop; (p. 66) 'The world is too much with us ...': Wordsworth, *Miscellaneous Sonnets*, Pt. 1, no. 33; (p. 67) Dante: this allusion is not quite accurate; the sinners Dickens means are those Dante finds just inside the Gates of Hell, before he enters the First Circle; these are they who had passed their lives 'in a state of apathy and indifference both to good and evil', who 'for themselves/Were only' (*Inferno*, trans. H.F. Cary [1805], Canto III, 'Argument' and ll. 37–8).

The present Government, having shown itself to be particularly clever in its management of Indictments for Conspiracy, cannot do better, we think (keeping in its administrative eye the pacification of some of its most influential and most unruly supporters), than indict the whole manufacturing interest of the country for a conspiracy against the agricultural interest. As the jury ought to be beyond impeachment, the panel might be chosen from among the Duke of BUCKINGHAM's tenants, with the Duke of BUCKINGHAM himself as foreman; and, to the end that the country might be quite satisfied with the judge, and have ample security beforehand for his moderation and impartiality, it would be desirable, perhaps, to make a slight change in the working of the law (a mere nothing to a Conservative Government, bent upon its end), as would enable the question to be tried before an Ecclesiastical Court, with the Bishop of EXETER presiding. The ATTORNEY-GENERAL for Ireland, turning his sword into a ploughshare, might conduct the prosecution; and Mr COBDEN and the other traversers might adopt any ground of defence they chose, or prove or disprove anything they pleased, without being embarrassed by the least anxiety or doubt in reference to the verdict.

That the country in general is in a conspiracy against this sacred but unhappy agricultural interest, there can be no doubt. It is not alone within the walls of Covent Garden Theatre, or the Free Trade Hall at Manchester, or the Town Hall at Birmingham, that the cry 'Repeal the Corn-laws!' is raised. It may be heard, moaning at night, through the straw-littered wards of Refuges for the Destitute; it may be read in the gaunt and famished faces which make our streets terrible; it is muttered in the thankful grace pronounced by haggard wretches over their felon fare in gaols; it is inscribed in dreadful characters upon the walls of Fever Hospitals; and may be plainly traced in every record of mortality. All of which proves, that there is a vast conspiracy afoot, against the unfortunate agricultural interest.

They who run, even upon railroads, may read of this conspiracy. The old stage-coachman was a farmer's friend. He wore top-boots, understood cattle, fed his horses upon corn, and had a lively personal interest in malt. The engine-driver's garb, and sympathies, and tastes belong to the factory. His fustian dress, besmeared with coal-dust and begrimed with soot; his oily hands, his dirty face, his knowledge of machinery; all point him out as one devoted to the manufacturing interest. Fire and smoke, and red-hot cinders follow in his wake. He has no attachment to the soil, but travels on a road of iron, furnace wrought. His warning is not conveyed in the fine old Saxon dialect of our glorious forefathers, but in a fiendish yell. He never cries 'ya-hip,' with agricultural lungs; but jerks forth a manufactured shriek from a brazen throat.

Where *is* the agricultural interest represented? From what phase of our social life has it not been driven, to the undue setting up of its false rival?

Are the police agricultural? The watchmen are. They wore woollen nightcaps to a man; they encouraged the growth of timber, by patriotically adhering to staves and rattles of immense size; they slept every night in boxes, which were but another form of the celebrated wooden walls of Old England; and they never woke up till it was too late – in which respect you might have thought them very farmers. How is it with the police? Their buttons are made at Birmingham; a dozen of their truncheons would poorly furnish forth a watchman's staff; they have no wooden walls to repose between; and the crowns of their hats are plated with cast-iron.

Are the doctors agricultural? Let Messrs MORISON and MOAT, of the Hygeian establishment at King's Cross, London, reply. Is it not, upon the constant showing of those gentlemen, an ascertained fact that the whole medical profession have united to depreciate the worth of the Universal Vegetable Medicines? And is this opposition to vegetables, and exaltation of steel and iron instead, on the part of the regular practitioners, capable of any interpretation but one? Is it not a distinct renouncement of the agricultural interest, and a setting up of the manufacturing interest instead?

Do the professors of the law at all fail in their truth to the beautiful maid whom they ought to adore? Inquire of the ATTORNEY-GENERAL for Ireland. Inquire of that honourable and learned gentleman, whose last public act was to cast aside the grey goose-quill, an article of agricultural produce, and take up the pistol, which, under the system of percussion-locks, has not even a flint to connect it with farming. Or put the question to a still higher legal functionary, who, on the same occasion, when he should have been a reed, inclining here and there, as adverse gales of evidence disposed him, was seen to be a manufactured image on the seat of Justice, cast by Power, in most impenetrable brass.

The world is too much with us in this manufacturing interest, early and late; that is the great complaint and the great truth. It is not so with the agricultural interest, or what passes by that name. It never thinks of the suffering world, or sees it, or cares to extend its knowledge of it; or, so long as it remains a world, cares anything about it. All those whom

DANTE placed in the first pit or circle of the doleful regions, might have represented the agricultural interest in the present Parliament, or at quarter sessions, or at meetings of the farmers' friends, or anywhere else.

But that is not the question now. It is conspired against; and we have given a few proofs of the conspiracy, as they shine out of various classes engaged in it. An indictment against the whole manufacturing interest need not be longer, surely, than the indictment in the case of the Crown against O'Connell and others. Mr Cobden may be taken as its representative – as indeed he is, by one consent already. There may be no evidence; but that is not required. A judge and jury are all that is needed. And the Government know where to find *them*, or they gain experience to little purpose.

20

Threatening Letter to Thomas Hood from an Ancient Gentleman By Favor of Charles Dickens

Hood's Magazine and Comic Miscellany, May 1844

Hood began publishing his monthly journal in January 1844 and, despite his continuing health and financial problems, it proved to be a successful venture (see J. Clubbe, *Victorian Forerunner: The Later Career of Thomas Hood* [1968], Ch. 5). Asked for help, Dickens contributed this satirical essay written as if by a reactionary old Tory lamenting the passing of the good old days, mocking the 'Young England' Tory splinter group led by Disraeli (see p. 243) and praising the savage sentence passed by Mr Justice Maule at the Old Bailey on 16 April on a woman called Mary Furley indicted for attempted suicide and the 'wilful murder' of her infant child. Driven desperate by brutal treatment in a workhouse and the struggle to keep herself and child alive by sweated labour and being robbed even of her meagre earnings, she had thrown herself and the child in the Thames. She was rescued, but the child drowned. After the jury had found her guilty, Maule told her, 'Your act, which would have been at any time cruel, is rendered more so by the fact of the crime being committed by you – the mother of the child' (*The Times*, 17 April), and sentenced her to death. As a result of a public outcry, the Home Secretary granted a stay of execution on 27 April and later commuted the sentence to seven years' transportation (this was, of course, after Dickens's article had appeared).

The main target of the satire in Dickens's 'Letter' is royal patronage of showbusiness phenomena and neglect of science and the arts. The American midget, General Tom Thumb, exhibited in England by Barnum 1844–6, was invited three times to perform before the Royal Family (thanking Dickens for his 'capital' paper, Hood wrote: 'I have been revolted myself by the royal running after the American mite' – see *Pilgrim*, Vol. IV, p. 87). Another American showman, Arthur Rankin, brought nine Ojibwa Indians to London in 1843 and they became for a few months an immensely popular sight at the Egyptian Hall, Piccadilly (see R.D. Altick, *The Shows of London* [1978], pp. 276–8), and were summoned to perform at Windsor Castle. One of the Ojibwas, their interpreter 'Strong Wind', married an English girl, hence Dickens's reference to 'the Ojibbeway Bride'. The 'Boy Jones' was William Jones, an apothecary's errand boy, who had a mania for getting into Buckingham Palace and was, after his third incursion, sent to the House of Correction (where Dickens went to see him) for three months in 1841. He was subsequently placed aboard an emigration ship bound for Brazil, as an apprentice seaman (see *Pilgrim*, Vol. II, p. 246).

Literary allusions (p. 70) 'train up his son in the way he should go': Proverbs 22: 6.

MS. Berg Collection, New York Public Library: shows no substantive variants from the printed text.

Mr Hood. Sir – The Constitution is going at last! You needn't laugh, Mr Hood. I am aware that it has been going, two or three times before; perhaps four times; but it is on the move now, sir, and no mistake.

I beg to say, that I use those last expressions advisedly, sir, and not in the sense in which they are now used by Jackanapeses. There were no Jackanapeses when I was a boy, Mr Hood. England was Old England when I was young. I little thought it would ever come to be Young England when I was old. But everything is going backward.

Ah! governments were governments, and judges were judges, in *my* day, Mr Hood. There was no nonsense then. Any of your seditious complainings, and we were ready with the military on the shortest notice. We should have charged Covent Garden Theatre, sir, on a Wednesday night: at the point of the bayonet. Then, the judges were full of dignity and firmness, and knew how to administer the law. There is only one judge who knows how to do his duty, now. He tried that revolutionary female the other day, who, though she was in full work (making shirts at three-halfpence a piece), had no pride in her country, but treasonably took it in her head, in the distraction of having been robbed of her easy earnings, to attempt to drown herself and her young child; and the

glorious man went out of his way, sir – out of his way – to call her up
for instant sentence of Death; and to tell her she had no hope of mercy
in this world – as you may see yourself if you look in the papers of
Wednesday the 17th of April. He won't be supported, sir, I know he
won't; but it is worth remembering that his words were carried into
every manufacturing town of this kingdom, and read aloud to crowds in
every political parlour, beer-shop, news-room, and secret or open place
of assembly, frequented by the discontented workingmen; and that no
milk-and-water weakness on the part of the executive can ever blot them
out. Great things like that, are caught up, and stored up, in these times,
and are not forgotten, Mr Hood. The public at large (especially those
who wish for peace and conciliation) are universally obliged to him. If it
is reserved for any man to set the Thames on fire, it is reserved for him;
and indeed I am told he very nearly did it, once.

But even he won't save the constitution, sir: it is mauled beyond the
power of preservation. Do you know in what foul weather it will be
sacrificed and shipwrecked, Mr Hood? Do you know on what rock it
will strike, sir? You don't, I am certain; for nobody does know, as yet,
but myself. I will tell you.

The constitution will go down, sir (nautically speaking), in the degener-
ation of the human species in England, and its reduction into a mingled
race of savages and pigmies.

That is my proposition. That is my prediction. That is the event of
which I give you warning. I am now going to prove it, sir.

You are a literary man, Mr Hood, and have written, I am told, some
things worth reading. I say I am told, because I never read what is
written in these days. You'll excuse me; but my principle is, that no man
ought to know anything about his own time, except that it is the worst
time that ever was, or is ever likely to be. That is the only way, sir, to
be truly wise and happy.

In your station, as a literary man, Mr Hood, you are frequently at the
Court of Her Gracious Majesty the Queen. God bless her! You have
reason to know that the three great keys to the royal palace (after rank
and politics) are Science, Literature, Art. I don't approve of this myself.
I think it ungenteel and barbarous, and quite un-English; the custom
having been a foreign one, ever since the reigns of the uncivilised sultans
in the Arabian Nights, who always called the wise men of their time
about them. But so it is. And when you don't dine at the royal table,
there is always a knife and fork for you at the equerries' table: where, I
understand, all gifted men are made particularly welcome.

But all men can't be gifted, Mr Hood. Neither scientific, literary, nor
artistical powers are any more to be inherited than the property arising
from scientific, literary, or artistic productions, which the law, with a

beautiful imitation of nature, declines to protect in the second generation. Very good, sir. Then, people are naturally very prone to cast about in their minds for other means of getting at Court Favour; and, watching the signs of the times, to hew out for themselves, or their descendants, the likeliest roads to that distinguished goal.

Mr Hood, it is pretty clear, from recent records in the Court Circular, that if a father wish to train up his son in the way he should go, to go to Court: and cannot indenture him to be a scientific man, an author, or an artist, three courses are open to him. He must endeavour by artificial means to make him a dwarf, a wild man, or a Boy Jones.

Now, sir, this is the shoal and quicksand on which the constitution will go to pieces.

I have made inquiry, Mr Hood, and find that in my neighbourhood two families and a fraction out of every four, in the lower and middle classes of society, are studying and practising all conceivable arts to keep their infant children down. Understand me. I do not mean down in their numbers, or down in their precocity, but down in their growth, sir. A destructive and subduing drink, compounded of gin and milk in equal quantities, such as is given to puppies to retard their growth: not something short, but something shortening: is administered to these young creatures many times a day. An unnatural and artificial thirst is first awakened in these infants by meals of salt beef, bacon, anchovies, sardines, red herrings, shrimps, olives, pea-soup, and that description of diet; and when they screech for drink, in accents that might melt a heart of stone, which they do constantly (I allude to screeching, not to melting), this liquid is introduced into their too confiding stomachs. At such an early age, and to so great an extent, is this custom of provoking thirst, then quenching it with a stunting drink, observed, that brine pap has already superseded the use of tops-and-bottoms; and wet-nurses, previously free from any kind of reproach, have been seen to stagger in the streets: owing, sir, to the quantity of gin introduced into their systems, with a view to its gradual and natural conversion into the fluid I have already mentioned.

Upon the best calculation I can make, this is going on, as I have said, in the proportion of about two families and a fraction in four. In one more family and a fraction out of the same number, efforts are being made to reduce the children to a state of nature; and to inculcate, at a tender age, the love of raw flesh, train oil, new rum, and the acquisition of scalps. Wild and outlandish dances are also in vogue (you will have observed the prevailing rage for the Polka); and savage cries and whoops are much indulged in (as you may discover, if you doubt it, in the House of Commons any night). Nay, some persons, Mr Hood; and persons of some figure and distinction too; have already succeeded in breeding wild sons; who have been publicly shown in the Courts of Bankruptcy, and in police-offices, and in other commodious exhibition-rooms, with great effect, but who have not yet found favour at court; in consequence, as I infer, of the impression made by Mr Rankin's wild men being too fresh and recent, to say nothing of Mr Rankin's wild men being foreigners.

I need not refer you, sir, to the late instance of the Ojibbeway Bride. But I am credibly informed, that she is on the eve of retiring into a savage fastness, where she may bring forth and educate a wild family, who shall in course of time, by the dexterous use of the popularity they are certain to acquire at Windsor and St James's, divide with dwarfs the principal offices of state, of patronage, and power, in the United Kingdom.

Consider the deplorable consequences, Mr Hood, which must result from these proceedings, and the encouragement they receive in the highest quarters.

The dwarf being the favourite, sir, it is certain that the public mind will run in a great and eminent degree upon the production of dwarfs. Perhaps the failure only will be brought up, wild. The imagination goes a long way in these cases; and all that the imagination *can* do, will be done, and is doing. You may convince yourself of this, by observing the condition of those ladies who take particular notice of General Tom Thumb at the Egyptian Hall, during his hours of performance.

The rapid increase of dwarfs, will be first felt in her Majesty's recruiting department. The standard will, of necessity, be lowered; the dwarfs will grow smaller and smaller; the vulgar expression 'a man of his inches' will become a figure of fact, instead of a figure of speech; crack regiments, household-troops especially, will pick the smallest men from all parts of the country; and in the two little porticoes at the Horse Guards, two Tom Thumbs will be daily seen, doing duty, mounted on a pair of Shetland ponies. Each of them will be relieved (as Tom Thumb is, at this moment, in the intervals of his performance) by a wild man; and a British Grenadier will either go into a quart pot, or be an Old Boy, or Blue Gull, or Flying Bull, or some other savage chief of that nature.

I will not expatiate upon the number of dwarfs who will be found representing Grecian statues in all parts of the metropolis; because I am inclined to think that this will be a change for the better; and that the engagement of two or three in Trafalgar Square will tend to the improvement of the public taste.

The various genteel employments at Court being held by dwarfs, sir, it will be necessary to alter, in some respects, the present regulations. It is quite clear that not even General Tom Thumb himself could preserve a becoming dignity on state occasions, if required to walk about with a scaffolding-pole under his arm; therefore the gold and silver sticks at present used, must be cut down into skewers of those precious metals; a twig of the black rod will be quite as much as can be conveniently preserved; the coral and bells of his Royal Highness the Prince of Wales, will be used in lieu of the mace at present in existence; and that bauble (as Oliver Cromwell called it, Mr Hood), its value being first calculated by Mr Finlayson, the government actuary, will be placed to the credit of the National Debt.

All this, sir, will be the death of the constitution. But this is not all. The constitution dies hard, perhaps; but there is enough disease impending, Mr Hood, to kill it three times over.

Wild men will get into the House of Commons. Imagine that, sir! Imagine Strong Wind in the House of Commons! It is not an easy matter to get through a debate now; but I say, imagine Strong Wind, speaking for the benefit of his constituents, upon the floor of the House of Commons! or imagine (which is pregnant with more awful consequences still) the ministry having an interpreter in the House of Commons, to tell the country, in English, what it really means!

Why, sir, that in itself would be blowing the constitution out of the mortar in St James's Park, and leaving nothing of it to be seen but smoke.

But this, I repeat it, is the state of things to which we are fast tending, Mr Hood; and I enclose my card for your private eye, that you may be quite certain of it. What the condition of this country will be, when its standing army is composed of dwarfs, with here and there a wild man to throw its ranks into confusion, like the elephants employed in war in former times, I leave you to imagine, sir. It may be objected by some hopeful jackanapeses, that the number of impressments in the navy, consequent upon the seizure of the Boy-Joneses, or remaining portion of the population ambitious of Court Favour, will be in itself sufficient to defend our Island from foreign invasion. But I tell those jackanapeses, sir, that, while I admit the wisdom of the Boy Jones precedent, of kidnapping such youths after the expiration of their several terms of imprisonment as vagabonds; hurrying them on board ship; and packing them off to sea again whenever they venture to take the air on shore; I deny the justice of the inference; inasmuch as it appears to me, that the inquiring minds of those young outlaws must naturally lead to their being hanged by the enemy as spies, early in their career: and before they shall have been rated on the books of our fleet as able seamen.

Such, Mr Hood, sir, is the prospect before us! And unless you, and some of your friends who have influence at Court, can get up a giant as a forlorn hope, it is all over with this ill-fated land.

In reference to your own affairs, sir, you will take whatever course may seem to you most prudent and advisable after this warning. It is not a warning to be slighted: that I happen to know. I am informed by the gentleman who favours this, that you have recently been making some changes and improvements in your Magazine, and are, in point of fact, starting afresh. If I be well informed, and this be really so, rely upon it that you cannot start too small, sir. Come down to the duodecimo size instantly, Mr Hood. Take time by the forelock; and, reducing the stature of your Magazine every month, bring it at last to the dimensions of the little almanack no longer issued, I regret to say, by the ingenious Mr Schloss: which was invisible to the naked eye until examined through a little eye-glass. You project, I am told, the publication of a new novel, by yourself, in the pages of your Magazine. A word in your ear. I am not a young man, sir, and have had some experience. Don't put your own name on the title-page; it would be suicide and madness. Treat with General Tom Thumb, Mr Hood, for the use of his name on any terms. If the gallant general should decline to treat with you, get Mr Barnum's name, which is the next best in the market. And when, through this politic course, you shall have received, in presents, a richly jewelled set of tablets from Buckingham Palace, and a gold watch and appendages from Marlborough House; and when those valuable trinkets shall be left under a glass case at your publisher's for inspection by your friends and the public in general; – then, sir, you will do me the justice of remembering this communication.

It is unnecessary for me to add, after what I have observed in the course of this letter, that I am not,

Sir,

ever

your

CONSTANT READER

TUESDAY, 23rd April 1844

P.S. – Impress it upon your contributors that they cannot be too short; and that if not dwarfish, they must be wild – or at all events not tame.

21

The Spirit of Chivalry in Westminster Hall

Douglas Jerrold's Shilling Magazine, August 1845

Dickens's close friend Daniel Maclise was one of six artists chosen by the Royal Commission of Fine Arts, chaired by Prince Albert, to produce cartoons for frescoes to be painted in the six arched compartments in the new House of Lords being built after the burning down of the Houses of Parliament in 1834. Three of the subjects were to be abstract – representations of Religion, Justice and the Spirit of Chivalry – and three were to be historical scenes exemplifying these concepts. The Commission also threw the project open to competition and all the resulting entries, together with the six invited artists' work, were shown in a series of exhibitions in Westminster Hall. The third such exhibition opened on 30 June 1845 and included Maclise's cartoon, which was criticised for being too cluttered. The *Illustrated London News* commented (Vol. 7, p. 10): 'Nothing can be finer in drawing, or more finished in execution than the individual portions of the Cartoon, nothing more ineffective, confused, and scattered than the general effect' (see further *Daniel Maclise 1806–1870*, 1972 exhibition catalogue, nos 91–3). Maclise subsequently simplified the design and the fresco, completed in 1847, is now on the wall behind the throne, next to another by him depicting the 'Spirit of Justice'.

Maclise read a proof of Dickens's article and was much gratified by his friend's superlative praise, but, as his work had not yet been officially chosen, he asked Forster to persuade Dickens to tone down the derogatory remarks about the Prince and the Commissioners: 'I certainly would not print what is contained *in the last page*, nor in any way allude to my not being employed to execute this cartoon …' (quoted in *Pilgrim*, Vol. IV, p. 304). Dickens complied and the passages that were omitted from the published version in *Douglas Jerrold's Shilling Magazine* are enclosed within square brackets in the text below. This text is that of the galley-proof now in the Forster Collection, Victoria and Albert Museum, which was the one printed by Matz, with several inaccuracies, in *MP*. It is headed 'Rough Proof' and annotated: 'Please to send corrected proof to Mr Forster.' Two changes were made, presumably by Forster, in addition to the deletions: 'allegorical bespeak' in paragraph 4 became 'allegorical order' in the published text; after 'ground-plan of a model cartoon' in the same paragraph, the published text continues: 'with all the commissioned proportions of height and breadth'. The last four paragraphs of the proof are replaced in the published version with two sentences: 'Let us hope so. We will contemplate no other possibility – at present.'

Literary allusions (p. 75) 'Of all the Cants …': Sterne, *Tristram Shandy*, Book 3, Ch. 12: 'Grant me patience, just Heaven! – Of all the cants which are canted in this canting world – though the cant of hypocrites may be the worst – the cant of criticism is the most tormenting!'; (p. 77) 'hewers and drawers': Joshua 9: 21; (p. 79) 'after what flourish his nature would': Shakespeare, *Hamlet*, Act 5, Sc. 2; (p. 79) 'Hath not a commissioner eyes?': Shakespeare, *The Merchant of Venice*, Act 3, Sc. 1.

'Of all the Cants that are canted in this canting world,' wrote Sterne, 'kind Heaven defend me from the cant of Art!' We have no intention of tapping our little cask of cant, soured by the thunder of great men's fame, for the refreshment of our readers: its freest draught would be unreasonably dear at a shilling, when the same small liquor may be had for nothing, at innumerable ready pipes and conduits[; and may even be drawn off, sparkling, from the fountain-head, on application to Mr Eastlake, secretary to the Fine Arts' Commission, who is obligingly ready to dispense it, *ex officio*, wholesale or retail, in any quantity].

But it is a main part of the design of this Magazine to sympathise with what is truly great and good; [to hail the bright nobility of genius, though it shine out through the clouds of Dilettanti lords and bargain-driving princes;] to scout the miserable discouragements that beset, especially in England, the upward path of men of high desert; and gladly to give honour where it is due, in right of Something achieved, tending to elevate the tastes and thoughts of all who contemplate it, and to prove a lasting credit to the country of its birth.

Upon the walls of Westminster Hall, there hangs, at this time, such a Something. A composition of such marvellous beauty, of such infinite variety, of such masterly design, of such vigorous and skilful drawing, of such thought and fancy, of such surprising and delicate accuracy of detail, subserving one grand harmony, and one plain purpose, that it may be questioned whether the Fine Arts in any period of their history have known a more remarkable performance.

It is the cartoon of Daniel Maclise, 'executed by order of the Commissioners,' and called The Spirit of Chivalry. [It is so many feet and inches high, by order of the Commissioners; and so many feet and inches broad, by order of the Commissioners. Its proportions are exceedingly difficult of management, by order of the Commissioners; and its subject and title were an order of the Commissioners.] It may be left an open question, whether or no this allegorical bespeak on the part of the Commissioners, displays any uncommon felicity of idea. We rather think not; and are free to confess that we should like to have seen the Commissioners' notion of the Spirit of Chivalry stated by themselves, in the first instance on a sheet of foolscap, as the ground-plan of a model cartoon. That the treatment of such an abstraction, for the purposes of Art, involves great and peculiar difficulties, no one who considers the subject for a moment can doubt. That nothing is easier than to render it absurd and monstrous, is a position as little capable of dispute by anybody who has beheld another cartoon on the same subject in the same Hall, representing a Ghoule in a state of raving madness, dancing on a Body in a very high wind, to the great astonishment of John the Baptist's head, which is looking on from a corner.

Cartoon for 'The Spirit of Chivalry' by Daniel Maclise, Illustrated London News, *9 August 1845.*

Mr Maclise's handling of the subject has by this time sunk into the hearts of thousands upon thousands of people. It is familiar knowledge among all classes and conditions of men. It is the great feature within the Hall, and the constant topic of discourse elsewhere. It has awakened in the great body of society a new interest in, and a new perception and a new love of, Art. Students of Art have sat before it, hour by hour, perusing in its many forms of Beauty, lessons to delight the world, and raise themselves, its future teachers, in its better estimation. Eyes well accustomed to the glories of the Vatican, the galleries of Florence, all the mightiest works of art in Europe, have grown dim before it with the strong emotions it inspires; ignorant, unlettered, drudging men, mere hewers and drawers, have gathered in a knot about it (as at our back a week ago), and read it, in their homely language, as it were a Book. In minds, the roughest and the most refined, it has alike found quick response; and will, and must, so long as it shall hold together.

For how can it be otherwise? Look up, upon the pressing throng who strive to win distinction from the Guardian Genius of all noble deeds and honourable renown: a gentle Spirit, holding her fair state for their reward and recognition (do not be alarmed, my Lord Chamberlain; this is only in a picture); and say what young and ardent heart may not find one to beat in unison with it − beat high with generous aspiration like its own − in following their onward course, as it is traced by this great pencil! Is it the Love of Woman, in its truth and deep devotion, that inspires you? See it here! Is it Glory, as the world has learned to call the pomp and circumstance of arms? Behold it at the summit of its exaltation, with its mailed hand resting on the altar where the Spirit ministers. The Poet's laurel-crown, which they who sit on thrones can neither twine or wither − is *that* the aim of thy ambition? It is there, upon his brow; it wreathes his stately forehead, as he walks apart and holds communion with himself. The Palmer and the Bard are there; no solitary wayfarers, now; but two of a great company of pilgrims, climbing up to honour by the different paths that lead to the great end. And sure, amidst the gravity and beauty of them all − unseen in his own form, but shining in his spirit, out of every gallant shape and earnest thought − the Painter goes triumphant!

Or say that you who look upon this work, be old, and bring to it grey hairs, a head bowed down, a mind on which the day of life has spent itself, and the calm evening closes gently in. Is its appeal to you confined to its presentment of the Past? Have you no share in this, but while the grace of youth and the strong resolve of maturity are yours to aid you? Look up again. Look up to where the Spirit is enthroned, and see about her, reverend men, whose task is done; whose struggle is no more; who cluster round her as her train and council; who have lost no share or interest in that great rising up and progress, but, true in Autumn to the purposes of Spring, are there to stimulate the race who follow in their steps; to contemplate, with hearts grown serious, not cold or sad, the striving in which they once had part; to die in that great Presence, which is Truth and Bravery, and Mercy to the Weak, beyond all power of separation.

It would be idle to observe of this last group that, both in execution and idea, they are of the very highest order of Art, and wonderfully serve the purpose of the picture. There is not one among its three and twenty heads of which the same remark might not be made. Neither will we treat of great effects produced by means quite powerless in other hands for such an end, or of the prodigious force and *colour* which so separate this work from all the rest exhibited, that it would scarcely appear to be produced upon the same kind of surface by the same description of instrument. The bricks and stones and timbers of the Hall itself are not facts more indisputable than these.

It has been objected to this extraordinary work that it is too elaborately finished; too complete in its several parts. And Heaven knows, if it be judged in this respect by any standard in the Hall about it, it will find no parallel, nor anything approaching it. But it is a design, intended to be afterwards copied and painted in fresco; and certain finish must be had at last, if not at first. It is very well to take it for granted in a Cartoon that a series of cross-lines, almost as rough and far apart as the lattice-work of a garden summer-house, represents the texture of the human face; but the face cannot be *painted* so. A smear upon the paper may be understood, by virtue of the context gained from what surrounds it, to stand for a limb, or a body, or a cuirass, or a hat and feathers, or a flag, or a boot, or an angel. But when the time arrives for rendering these things in colours on a wall, they must be grappled with, and cannot be slurred over in this wise. Great misapprehension on this head seems to have been engendered in the minds of some observers by the famous Cartoons of Raphael; but they forget that these were never intended as designs for fresco painting. They were designs for tapestry-work, which is susceptible of only certain broad and general effects, as no one better knew than the Great Master. Utterly detestable and vile as the tapestry is, compared with the immortal Cartoons from which it is worked, it is impossible for any man who casts his eyes upon it where it hangs at Rome, not to see immediately the special adaptation of the drawings to that end, and for that purpose. The aim of these Cartoons being wholly different, Mr Maclise's object, if we understand it, was to show precisely what he meant to do, and knew he could perform, in fresco, on a wall. And here his meaning is; worked out; without a compromise of any difficulty; without the avoidance of any disconcerting truth; expressed in all its beauty, strength, and power.

To what end? To be perpetuated hereafter in the high place of the chief Senate-House of England? To be wrought, as it were, into the very elements of which that Temple is composed; to co-endure with it, and still present, perhaps, some lingering traces of its ancient Beauty, when London shall have sunk into a grave of grass-grown ruin; and the whole circle of the Arts, another revolution of the mighty wheel completed, shall be wrecked and broken?

[Let us suppose no such reward in store for the great English artist who has set his genius on this English stake. Let us go further; and putting a hypothetical case founded on certain rumours, which have already made their way into print, or into pretty general discussion with some aspect of authority, endeavour to explain to two or three of the Commissioners our own idea of what the spirit of chivalry in *them* would be. We do not exactly contemplate the likelihood of the manifestation of their own subject in all of them; that were mere midsummer madness as Commissioners go; but we have heard of there being among them men of letters: men devoted to pursuits and tastes not altogether removed from, nay, somewhat closely leading to, the just appreciation and the manly championship of such a Work; as Poets, Writers of History, Orators and Scholars, who have words enough at their command when they see fit to use them. Now, we should deem it no inappropriate illustration of the Spirit of Chivalry in one of these, if, rising in his place among the rest, he told them a few wholesome truths, and, speaking after what flourish his nature would, shaped out this matter thus: —

'What, my Lords and Gentlemen! Reserve for another, the Post of Honour, the conspicuous place behind the Throne; and offer to the man who has set this before you, an inferior place in an inferior room; an ante-chamber of the House of Commons, where he may try his hand like some poor journeyman in Art! Is this the true performance of your trust? Is this the British recognition of a claim which any little sovereign in Europe would have been proud to honour and reward? Hath not a commissioner eyes? Hath not a commissioner hands, organs, dimensions, senses, affections, passions? Does he lose them all in the Commission Room, and dwindle down into a mere polite machine: a deferential and obsequious instrument?

'Oh, your royal Highness, look upon this work again! Have some regard for its originality: its execution, its design, its combination of high qualities so rare, that any One of them has often furnished forth a Painter! I do not question the ability of the artist whom you raise above this lofty head: I have ever done it justice, and I do so now. Nor do I venture to dispute that it is natural and amiable in you to love the German school of art, even at second-hand. But there is Justice to be done! The object of this competition was encouragement and exaltation of English art; and in this work, albeit done on paper which soon rots, the Art of England will survive, assert itself, and triumph, when the stronger seeming bones and sinews of your royal Highness and the rest, shall be but so much Dust. A breath from princely lungs may blow it, light as thistle-down, into a disregarded corner of the pile now rearing, but when that breath has been puffed out, and stopped for scores upon scores of years, the frail thing now discouraged, will wax strong against you!'

In the hypothetical case we have put, this is our notion of the Spirit of Chivalry in any one of the Commissioners. In the same hypothetical case, we will conclude by observing that anything short of this, is the exact realisation of our notion of the innermost Spirit of Meanness and Injustice.]

22

Review: *The Night Side of Nature; or, Ghosts and Ghost Seers* by Catherine Crowe

The Examiner, 26 February 1848

As Dickens's opening words show, Mrs Crowe had an established reputation as a novelist when she published *The Night Side of Nature*. Her object was, according to her Preface, 'to suggest inquiry and stimulate observation, in order ... to discover something regarding our psychical nature, as it exists here in the flesh, and as it is to exist hereafter, out of it'. The book was widely read and reached a third edition in 1852. Dickens's authorship of *The Examiner* review is established by his reference to it in a letter (*Pilgrim*, Vol. v, p. 255) to the Swiss banker Emile de la Rue with whom he had become friendly in Genoa four years before, and was first noted by Philip Collins ('Dickens on Ghosts: An Uncollected Article, with Introduction and Notes', *The Dickensian*, Vol. 59 [1963], pp. 5–14). The promised follow-up article (para. 3) in which Dickens proposed to put the other, anti-sceptical, side of the case, unfortunately never appeared, *The Examiner*'s columns being full of the political news from France following the Revolution there. Mrs Crowe later contributed three articles to *HW*.

The story of the Ghostly Soldier (p. 89) appears in Ch. 11 ('The Power of Will') of Crowe's book. Dickens's satirical allusion to Lord Londonderry (para. 5) refers back to his scathing review of Londonderry's *A Letter to Lord Ashley* ... (see p. 49). The 'patient' referred to in paragraph 10 is Mme de la Rue, Emile's English wife (called 'our patient' in Dickens's letter to Emile cited above), whose nervous and mental sufferings Dickens had relieved by the exercise of his mesmeric powers ('animal magnetism') during his residence in Italy 1844–5 (see *Pilgrim*, Vol. IV, p. 243 *et seq.*).

All his life Dickens was passionately interested in the subject of psychic phenomena, but he had also a keen dislike of spiritual fraud and humbug; in February 1858, for example, he ridiculed Spiritualist mediums in an article in *HW* entitled 'Well-authenticated Rappings'. Eleven years after writing his review of Mrs Crowe's book, he became embroiled in controversy over ghosts with one of the star witnesses of her chapter on 'Haunted Houses', William Howitt. Howitt was a miscellaneous writer, much valued by Dickens as a contributor to *HW*, who objected to some sceptical articles about alleged ghosts appearing in *ATYR*. Dickens wrote to him (6 September 1859; *Nonesuch*, Vol. III, p. 121): 'I have always had a strong interest in the subject, and never knowingly lose an opportunity of pursuing it', but added that he needed to be 'reasonably sure that [ghost-seers] were not suffering under a disordered condition of the nerves or senses'. He continued the theme in the 1859 Christmas number of *ATYR* called 'A Haunted House' (see further Harry Stone, 'The Unknown Dickens', *Dickens Studies Annual*, Vol. I [1970], pp. 1–22). In a 'Note by the Conductor' in *ATYR* (22 June 1867), he referred again to the Lady Beresford case (para. 9), saying that he had 'some years ago' suggested 'a state of sleep-walking or half-consciousness' as the true explanation of the affair.

Literary allusions (p. 82) 'solemn bourne': Shakespeare, *Hamlet*, Act 3, Sc. 1; (p. 84) Dr Johnson: *Rasselas*, Ch. 31; (p. 84) 'Fielding holds that if a certain number of young men ...': 'An Essay in the Knowledge of the Characters of Men', *Miscellanies*, Vol. I (1743); (p. 85) 'the Kilmarnock weaver's prayer ...': see Burns's poem 'To a Louse'; (p. 85) 'thick and slab': Shakespeare, *Macbeth*, Act 4, Sc. 3; (p. 88): Defoe *A System of Magic; or, a History of the Black Art* (1728), Ch. 2 (Collins notes that the italics are Dickens's); (p. 89) 'Doubting Castle': Bunyan's *The Pilgrim's Progress* (1684).

The authoress of 'Susan Hopley' and 'Lilly Dawson' has established her title to a hearing whenever she chooses to claim one. She can never be read without pleasure and profit, and can never write otherwise than sensibly and well.

The 'night side of nature' is a German phrase derived from the astronomers, who term that side of a planet which is turned from the sun, its night side. Analogy between the substantial and spiritual worlds has led to the adoption of this phrase by German writers on subjects akin to those of Mrs Crowe's book; and hence Mrs Crowe has chosen it for the title of one of the most extraordinary collections of 'Ghost Stories' that has ever been published.

We propose, in the present notice of this very curious book, to glance at a few obvious heads of objection that may be ranged against the ghosts; and, resuming the subject next week, to sum up what may be said in their favour.

Disclaiming all intention 'of teaching, or enforcing opinions,' and desiring only to induce people to inquire into such stories and reflect upon them, instead of laughing at them and dismissing them – and with the further object of making the English public acquainted with the sentiments of German writers of undoubted ability in reference to the probability of an occasional return of travellers from that solemn bourne to which all living things are always tending – Mrs Crowe, without enforcing any particular theory or construction of her own, but apparently with an implicit belief in everything she narrates, and a purpose of communicating the same belief to her readers, shrinks neither from dreams, presentiments, warnings, wraiths, witches, doubles, apparitions, troubled spirits, haunted houses, spectral lights, apparitions attached to certain families, nor even from the tricksy spirit, Robin Goodfellow himself; but calls credible witnesses into court on behalf of each and all, and accumulates testimony on testimony until the Jury's hair stands on end, and going to bed becomes uncomfortable.

We think that, in this, there is the common fault of seeking to prove too much. As no witness to character at the Old Bailey ever heard of a better man than the prisoner at the bar; and as that sage statesman, Lord Londonderry, when it was suggested that the occupation of a trapper (a little child who sits alone in the dark, at the bottom of a mine, all day, opening and shutting a door) had something dreary in it, could conceive nothing jollier than 'a jolly little trapper,' and could, in fact, recognise the existence of no greater jollity in this imperfect state of existence than that which was inseparable from a trapper's occupation; so Mrs Crowe stands by her weakest ghost at least as manfully as by her strongest. She even champions the celebrated Stockwell Ghost of 1772, admitting that there is some vague and unfounded contradiction afloat, but appearing not to know that the late Mr Hone (as he relates in the first volume of the *Every-Day Book*, page 68) did, in 1817, obtain the whole solution of that famous mystery from one Mr Brayfield, to whom the whole imposition had been confessed, years after it was practised, by the sole contriver of it, Ann Robinson, the servant in the haunted house, who was present in all the haunted scenes.

Mrs Crowe submits that if we believe in any history at all, and are content to receive anything as true, on the relation of other people, we are bound to believe in spectres and apparitions; their appearance in all times being handed down to us on that kind of testimony. But it is perfectly reasonable, we can conceive, to believe in Caesar, and not to believe in the ghost of Caesar. Caesar left his mark upon the world, and was seen of hundreds and thousands of people, in hundreds of thousands of places, and left an enormous mass of testimony to the fact of his having existed; whereas Caesar's ghost,* appearing in a tent at night to but one troubled mind, contented itself with uttering a prediction, which, it is rational to suppose, was quite unnecessary and no news at all to that troubled mind, even if it had been one of common instead of uncommon sagacity. So, with all history. Past events that we receive on the faith of historians, have confirmation of their likelihood in our own times and within our own knowledge. Troublesome priests, venal politicians, glozing lawyers, sensual kings, jaunty young gentlemen, who are very maggots from the graves of feudal barons, have been, within our own experience, to attest that there is no social nuisance and no social enormity in past times, whereof we may not find some reflection in the present. Mr Newman, on his way to Rome, writing pamphlets against Dr Hampden, and jesuitically perverting his text, is the shadow of any past Father Newman aloft in a temporary pulpit in the open air, piously exhorting any past Dr Hampden, while the fire was bringing to consume him. But the ghosts don't give us this sort of satisfaction. They always elude us. Doubtful and scant of proof at first, doubtful and scant of proof still, all mankind's experience of *them* is, that their alleged appearances have been, in all ages, marvellous, exceptional, and resting on imperfect grounds of proof; that in vast numbers of cases they are known to be delusions superinduced by a well-understood, and by no means uncommon disease; and that, in a multitude of others, they are often asserted to be seen, even on Mrs Crowe's own showing, in that imperfect state of perception, between sleeping and waking, than which there is hardly any less reliable incidental to our nature. 'I'll swear that I was not asleep,' is very easily and conscientiously said; but there is a middle state between sleeping and waking, and which is not either, when impressions, though false, are extraordinarily strong, and when the individual not asleep, is, most distinctly, not awake. In some countries, there is no twilight, and no gradual break of day. In some constitutions, and in many conditions, this middle state does not prevail; and it is not sufficiently allowed for, or considered, when it does.

* Assuming for our purpose, Shakespeare to be historical in this respect, which he is not. Plutarch, in his Life of Brutus, calls the apparition 'a horrible and monstrous spectre, standing stilly, by his side;' and in his Life of Caesar, describes it as 'a terrible appearance, in the human form, but of a prodigious stature, and the most hideous aspect'.

Mrs Crowe quotes Addison in favour of the re-appearance of departed spirits; referring, we presume, to No. 110 of the *Spectator*, where he recites a story of a dream from Josephus and unquestionably does express belief; although it is to be remarked, by the way, that in No. 419 of the same *Spectator*, he treats of 'ghosts, fairies, witches, and the like imaginary persons,' and holds that almost the whole substance of that kind of literature 'owes its original to the darkness and superstition of later ages, when pious frauds were made use of to amuse mankind, and frighten them into a sense of their duty.' Dr Johnson might, likewise, be cited, thus: ' "That the dead are seen no more," said Imlac, "I will not undertake to maintain, against the concurrent testimony of all ages, and of all nations. There is no people, rude or learned, among whom apparitions of the dead are not related and believed. This opinion, which perhaps prevails as far as human nature is diffused, could become universal only by its truth." ' But is this a wise deduction? *Could* it only become universal by its truth? May not this belief, or perhaps it would be better to say, the distrust upon the subject which is not disbelief, be thus widely spread, because, 'as far as human nature is diffused,' there is that dread uncertainty in reference to what ensues upon the awful change from life to death — that instinctive avoidance of death, which is one of the hardest conditions on which we hold our being — that attraction of repulsion to the awful veil that hangs so heavily and inexorably over the grave — engendering a curiosity and proneness to imagine and believe in such things, which proves nothing but the universality of death, and human speculation on its spiritual nature? Many men of strong minds are unable to satisfy themselves that they altogether disbelieve in supernatural appearances; very few men perhaps, placed in the dead of night in circumstances particularly lonely, terrifying, and mysterious, would be able to shake off this vague alarm of something not belonging to the world in which we live. But all this is no evidence of there being any other ground for the misgiving, than the universal mystery surrounding universal death. It carries us no farther than Imlac's premises. Fielding holds that if a certain number of young men had been bred from their cradles to believe the Royal Exchange (closely shut up for the purpose of this their education) a sacred place, they would, one and all, be hewn down at the gate in its defence, believing that they maintained a mighty cause, and won a glorious passport to Paradise. The same devoted body would naturally invest the mystery of the Royal Exchange with wild and fantastic solemnities and properties, born of their own fancies. Sacred groves, chambers of oracles, druidical temples, miraculous shrines, and the whole paraphernalia of imposture and superstition, have been so invested by their votaries in all times. Who then shall say, of the one, real, profound, tremendous mystery affecting all mankind, past, present and to come, that it is not sufficient, of itself, to engender and maintain, through all ages and in all countries, one obvious, groundless belief, taking many shapes according to the diverse lives, habits, and modes of education, of the believers?

And it may be fairly urged that this influence of habit and education on the kind of spirit that is popular in this place, or in that, is hardly taken into fair consideration by Mrs Crowe, with reference to the general probabilities. For example, here is the Doppelgänger, or Double, or Fetch, of Germany. This Doppelgänger, it appears, is so common among learned professors and studious men in Germany, that they have no need of the Kilmarnock weaver's prayer for grace to see themselves as others see them, but enjoy that privilege commonly. Here is one good man who sees himself knock at his own door, take a tangible tallow candle from his own maid, and go upstairs to his own bed: he himself looking on, very much disconcerted from over the way. But, how does it happen that one little spot of earth is famous for these particular appearances? If there is no immediate contagion of imagination, and no influence of education, in the case, why not more Doubles, in England, France, India, Sarawak? Mrs Crowe lays some stress on the evidence that fasting is favourable to the perception of spirits, but the Germans are not fasters – they are heavy feeders; their gravies are thick and slab, as visitors amongst them can avouch; and their meat is sodden, and they eat a great deal of it, with store of vinegar, sweet cherries, and sharp pickles. We have heard it suggested that the use of immoderately hot stoves, which often have an uneasy influence upon the head, and seem to make the sight waver, as if there were water between it and the object seen, may have something to do with the abundance of phantoms perceived in Germany; and we think it a reasonable suggestion, especially when the stove is in a sleeping room. Perhaps the Double, if not a result of taking double allowance, is attached to such chambers. It certainly is difficult to believe that spirits, like wines, are of so peculiar a growth as to become indigenous to certain patches of soil, and that the Doppelgänger and the Hockheimer necessarily flourish together.

Although Mrs Crowe cannot admit that an excited imagination is to be received as the solution of some of these ghost stories, she has faith enough in the strong-working of imagination to believe in the three ecstatica of the Tyrol, who all exhibited the stigmata. Now, although of all kinds of marvels this particular class is to be received with the greatest caution, and only to be admitted on the strongest evidence and the most careful inquiry, by reason of the suspicion that fairly attaches to the attendant priests, who have attempted imposition in such cases before today or yesterday – witness the exposure of an exactly parallel miracle, in the case of the novice Yetser, at Berne, three hundred years ago, whose side and hands and feet were pierced, after he was made drunk with wine and opium, by the monks of his own convent, of whom the sub-prior had previously enacted the Virgin Mary in a celestial appearance to him – there would seem reason to believe that the force of a strongly excited and concentrated imagination, in some ecstatic cases, has actually produced these marks upon the patient's body. Nor is it unworthy of notice that, in the best accredited cases, the subjects are women; as if the operating influence were some fantastic and distorted perversion of the power a mother has, of marking the body of her unborn child, with the visible stamp of any image strongly impressed on her imagination. But, surely, if we are to admit the force of strong imagination in one case, we cannot reasonably refuse to make great allowance for it in another. Mrs Crowe maintains the renowned Lady Beresford ghost story, to be a real ghost story. Its facts, we believe, are these. That Lady Beresford, lying in bed, by the side of her husband, who was asleep, held a certain confidential communication with a certain apparition of a person deceased. That she required of the apparition that it would leave some sign of its having really been there. That the apparition, thereupon, hoisted up the curtains of the bed, over a very high tester, not easily within Lady Beresford's reach. That Lady Beresford replied (very rationally, as Mrs Crowe will admit, for she is well acquainted with the strange powers possessed by somnambulists, except in supposing them to be generally exercised with closed eyes, which is not the case), that although she could not do this waking, she might be able to do it sleeping, and so required another sign. That the apparition, thereupon, put its autograph in her pocket book. That Lady Beresford again urged that she herself might be able to imitate its living hand exactly, when asleep, though not in her waking moments, and so required another sign. That the apparition, thereupon, clutched her by the wrist, which she found, on waking, shrivelled up in a remarkable manner, and which she covered with a bandage ever afterwards. Now, to say nothing of the lady being so much wiser, in respect of the infallibility of these tokens, than the apparition – which, however, is worthy of remark, as a genuine spirit might be naturally supposed to be infinitely the wiser of the two, – is there anything more remarkable or ghostly in Lady Beresford having a shrivelled wrist, than in the three ecstatica of the Tyrol having bleeding wounds in their feet, hands, and sides? Is it greatly straining a point to suppose, that when she suggested the possibility of her doing these other acts in her sleep, she not only knew that she could do them, but was, then and there, actually doing them, with that disturbed, imperfect consciousness of doing them which is not uncommon in cases of somnambulism, or even in common dreams; when the sleeper, lying on his own arm, or throwing off his own bedclothes, makes his own act the act of an imaginary person, and elaborately constructs a story in his sleep, out of which such incidents seem to arise?

The exact coincidence, in cases not very dissimilar, between real effects and imaginary causes, is indisputable. It has happened to ourselves to be closely acquainted with a case, in which the patient was afflicted with a violent and acute disorder of the nerves, and was, besides, continually troubled with horrible spectral illusions – not so numerous as those which beset Nicolai the Berlin bookseller, but not so harmless either, and much more hostile and vigilant. In this instance, the patient, a lady, perfectly acquainted with the nature and origin of the phantoms by which she was haunted, was sometimes threatened and beaten by them: and the beating, which was generally upon the arm, left an actual soreness and local affection there. But, experience had taught her, that the approaching real effect suggested the imaginary cause; and she never became a ghost-seer from otherwise connecting the two.

Again, as to witches. Mrs Crowe attributes the self-accusation of supposed witches, to delusions produced by animal magnetism, if not to certain ointments, compounded for the purpose of engendering such fancies. But, surely this is to make animal magnetism, in which she is a believer, a very stupid, dull affair – a very miserable and swinish influence. A power that can heal the sick, and give the sleepless rest, and carry the *clairvoyante* girl among the stars, produce nothing better, in the minds even of the wretched women who were drowned, and burned, and hanged all over England, to the everlasting disgrace of those good old times, than a stereotyped absurdity of a lecherous old man giving indecent supper parties! Frisking about, after supper, full-dressed with the popular appendages of horns and tail, in an infernal Sir Roger de Coverley of fifty couples; becoming a great baby at the breasts of withered old beldames; or literally making a beast of himself, and maundering up and down, as a blundering old goat, or a dog, or a cat! There is no class of deplorable absurdities in which the absurdity is of so uniform a character, as in the pretended disclosures about witchcraft; and none in which the fancy – if one may apply the term to such pauperism of the intellect – is so low, and mean, and grovelling. Mrs Crowe says: 'It is difficult to imagine that all the unfortunate wretches who suffered death at the stake in the middle ages for having attended the unholy assemblies they described, had no faith in their own stories;' and asks, 'how, then, are we to account for the pertinacity of their confessions, but by supposing them to be the victims of some extraordinary delusion?' De Foe, in his system of magic, thus forestals one answer to the question. 'It is very strange, men should be so fond of being thought wickeder than they are; that they cannot forbear, but that they must abuse the very Devil, whether he has any knowledge of them or no; but thus it is, *and we need not go to Egypt for examples, when we have so many pieces of dull witchcraft among ourselves.'* Further, vast numbers of these cases involved accusations by ignorant malicious people against their enemies. Thus, they not only aspired, in this strange wickedness of which De Foe treats, to the dignity of being supposed to be diabolically connected themselves, but to the gratification of destroying those whom they hated. Further, there is no greater contagion than the contagion of folly, mixed with horror. Further, there was in those days (which Mrs Crowe seems, for the moment, to have forgotten) a certain institution, very powerful in eliciting confession, but not always powerful in eliciting truth, called the Torture: and she may rely upon it that if that fragment of ancestorial wisdom were restored tomorrow by Mr Pugin, and incorporated, with the statutes against witches, into the law of the land; and that if witchcraft, as a theme for the vulgar, were again disseminated on the four winds of heaven into every lurking-place of ignorance, diseased and morbid fancy, and dormant wickedness, in this kingdom; she would find, despite the advance of the times, any amount of monstrous testimony to the Devil's still doing a great stroke of business in this line, on record in a twelvemonth. Our life upon it, that we should have good pattern witches rising up among the inmates of our metropolitan workhouses, before half the period was out.

In treating of the general subject, we do not think it taking strong ground to lay any great stress on the repute in which magicians were held in old times. The word did not then express what it is understood to express in modern days. They were wise men and scholars, students of astronomy, observers of nature, versed in natural and experimental philosophy. They engrossed, in short, the knowledge and foresight of their time. Hence Pharaoh, or Nebuchadnezzar, or Belshazzar, or any the like ancient monarch, being in a difficulty, sent for his soothsayers and magicians, as his wisest subjects, and best-informed and longest-headed advisers, both as to facts and probable consequences. Just as Queen Victoria, wishing to be resolved of her doubts on the subject of fever and other infectious diseases, applies to Dr Southwood Smith – in reference to her foreign relations, consults Lord Palmerston – refers the coming comet to the Astronomer-Royal – or bespeaks, towards the happy introduction of another approaching body, the services of Dr Locock, and Professor Simson of Edinburgh – none of whom are magicians in these days, because of the division of labour, and the application of each of them to some distinct branch of knowledge, and the general knowledge that goes abroad.

Mrs Crowe's idea that the predictions of soothsayers, and their oracular solutions of dreams, and so forth, must have been true, because the craft did not lose ground by failure, would make the almanack of Francis

Moore, Physician, at its sale of twenty years ago, one of the lost books of the Sybil.

Without observing on the cases of ghosts in fustian jackets, who come express from the other world to order a family's coals (as one of Mrs Crowe's ghosts does), further than to remark that it is a proof of an obliging disposition, which would be greatly enhanced if they paid for them also (which does not appear to be the case), we will roof in our Doubting Castle, before proceeding to reconnoitre it from the opposite camp, with this position; that it is the peculiarity of almost all ghost stories, as contradistinguished from all other kinds of narratives purporting to be true, to depend, *as* ghost stories, on some one little link in the chain of evidence, and that supposing that link to be destructible, the whole supernatural character is gone. We have been strongly impressed by this consideration, in reading Mrs Crowe's remarkable collection. In history, in biography, in voyages and travels, in criminal records, in any narrative connected with the visible world, this peculiarity does not, and cannot obtain; for, take away one link, however important, the rest of the chain is substantial, and remains. Supposing Lord Nelson not to have been killed by a shot from the mizzen top of the *Redoubtable* in the action of Trafalgar, there would still be no doubt that he *was* killed in that engagement, or that the engagement took place, and was a fight; or supposing the hero not to have fallen on the spot that was marked with his secretary's blood, or supposing there to have been no blood at all on that part of the *Victory's* deck, or supposing him not to have been carried below, by this man or by that, the great event of that bloody day would still remain indisputable; so, under whatever circumstances Captain Bligh was dispossessed of his ship the *Bounty*, and put into an open boat, dispossessed of his ship he was, and in an open boat he sailed and suffered. But, almost invariably, the alteration of some slight incident in the narrative, the removal of some one little figure from the group, shatters a ghost story, and reduces it to no very remarkable affair of common life.

As a slight instance of what we mean, we will give this case of

THE GHOSTLY SOLDIER

'A very remarkable circumstance occurred some years ago, at Kirkcaldy, when a person, for whose truth and respectability I can vouch, was living in the family of a Colonel M., at that place. The house they inhabited was at one extremity of the town, and stood in a sort of paddock. One evening, when Colonel M. had dined out, and there was nobody at home but Mrs M., her son (a boy about twelve years old), and Ann, the maid (my informant). Mrs M. called the latter and directed her attention to a soldier, who was walking backwards and forwards in the drying ground, behind the house, where some linen was hanging on the lines. She said, she wondered what he could be doing there, and bade Ann fetch in the linen, lest he should purloin any of it. The girl, fearing he might be some ill-disposed person, felt afraid; Mrs M., however, promising to watch from the window, that nothing happened to her, she went; but still apprehensive of the man's intentions, she turned her back towards him, and hastily pulling down the linen, she carried it into the house; he, continuing his walk the while, as before, taking no notice of her, whatever. Ere long, the Colonel returned, and Mrs M. lost no time in taking him to the window to look at the man, saying, she could not conceive what he could mean by walking backwards and forwards there all that time; whereupon, Ann added, jestingly, "I think it's a ghost, for my part!" Colonel M. said "he would soon see that," and calling a large dog that was lying in the room, and accompanied by the little boy, who begged to be permitted to go also, he stepped out and approached the stranger; when, to his surprise, the dog, which was an animal of high courage, instantly flew back, and sprung through the glass door, which the Colonel had closed behind him, shivering the panes all around.

'The Colonel, meantime, advanced and challenged the man, repeatedly, without obtaining any answer or notice whatever; till, at length, getting irritated, he raised a weapon with which he had armed himself, telling him he "must speak, or take the consequences," when just as he was preparing to strike, lo! there was nobody there! The soldier had disappeared, and the child sunk senseless to the ground. Colonel M. lifted the boy in his arms, and as he brought him into the house, he said to the girl, "You are right, Ann. It *was* a ghost!" He was exceedingly impressed with this circumstance, and much regretted his own behaviour, and also the having taken the child with him, which he thought had probably prevented some communication that was intended. In order to repair, if possible, these errors, he went out every night, and walked on that spot for some time, in hopes the apparition would return. At length, he said, that he had seen and had conversed with it; but the purport of the conversation he would never communicate to any human being; not even to his wife. The effect of this occurrence on his own character was perceptible to everybody that knew him. He became grave and thoughtful, and appeared like one who had passed through some strange experience.'

There is something vaguely terrible in the opening of this story. But, take away the dog, or the implied occasion of the dog's terror, and, as a ghost story, the whole tumbles down like a house of cards. That a soldier, having a pistol presented at him, with a warning that he was going to be shot, should be disposed to retreat, is strictly in accordance with the military tactics of flesh and blood. That he was likely to have the means of retreating quickly, in a yard behind a house where clothes lines were hanging, and, possibly, where some large piece of linen, not easily removable by one girl in a hurry, was still left drying, is highly probable. Nobody appears to have wondered how he got in. That a child should be alarmed, and swoon, when he supposed a man was going to be shot dead before his eyes, is the likeliest thing in the world. That this soldier may have known of some secret affecting Colonel M., which Colonel M. may have desired to treat with him about, and to hush up, is at least more probable than the apparition which disappeared when it was going to be fired at – exactly the time, of all others, when it could have given a singularly awful proof of its supernatural nature, by remaining.

23

Ignorance and Crime

The Examiner, 22 April 1848

This article appeared as the third item in 'The Political Examiner' on the front page of the issue for 22 April, continuing over to p. 2. The connection between crime and the absence of provision for meaningful education among the poorest classes was something that Dickens always felt strongly about and often alluded to, both in his journalism and his fiction (in the *Christmas Carol* [1843] Scrooge, for example, is warned by the Ghost of Christmas Present to beware especially of the boy Ignorance 'for on his brow I see that written which is Doom, unless the writing be erased'). In the late 1840s he was actively engaged in trying to do something about the matter with the help of the wealthy philanthropist Angela Burdett-Coutts and others. In October 1847 Miss Burdett-Coutts's 'Home' for women from the streets or discharged from prison opened under Dickens's direction, and he would have had this very much in mind when commenting in this piece on the utter ignorance of domestic matters shown by female offenders (para. 4). As he was to explain in a later article for *HW*, 'Home for Homeless Women' (23 April 1853; see Vol. 3 of this edition), the regime at the Home was organised to ensure that every inmate might 'become acquainted with the whole routine of household duties'. Dickens had also in 1846 visited and greatly admired the Limehouse Schools of Industry, established for pauper children by the local Board of Poor Law Guardians, and was doubtless thinking of them when he wrote the penultimate paragraph of this piece (many years later he returned to the Limehouse Schools as 'the Uncommercial Traveller' and wrote in their praise in an essay called 'The Short Timers' – see Vol. 4 of this edition).

The scornful reference to the belief that 'a parrot-acquaintance with the church catechism' (see p. 94) was an adequate moral education for the young relates to a vigorous campaign, to which Dickens may have contributed, that *The Examiner* was running against the use of knowledge of the catechism as a legal test as to whether or not a child witness's testimony could be received (see K.J. Fielding and Alec W. Brice, 'Charles Dickens on "The Exclusion of Evidence"', *The Dickensian*, Vols. 64 [1968], pp. 131–40, and 65 [1969] pp. 35–41). Dickens ridicules the notion both in *David Copperfield* (Ch. 1: Ham Peggotty being 'a very dragon at his catechism' must be a 'credible witness') and in *Bleak House* (Ch. 11, where the coroner rejects Jo's testimony). See also next article.

Dickens's reference to 'pot-valiant' tailors might remind us of the 'little tailor' in the *Carol* 'fined five shillings ... for being drunk and blood-thirsty in the streets' (Stave 1); and the jibe at Sir Peter Laurie recalls another of Dickens's Christmas Books. In *The Chimes* (1844) he pilloried Laurie as 'Alderman Cute', a brutally unfeeling magistrate whose campaign to 'put down' suicide and severely punish all who attempted it, regardless of the desperation to which they might have been reduced by poverty and distress, was clearly based on Laurie's activities on the bench.

Literary allusions (p. 94) 'the Slough of Despond ... Giants Slay-Good and Despair': Bunyan's *The Pilgrim's Progress*; (p. 95) 'Let the State prevent vices ...': Sir Thomas More's *Utopia* (CUP edn [1989], p. 34).

MS. Forster Collection, Victoria and Albert Museum, headed 'London Crime'. Matz reprinted this MS. version (with many inaccuracies) in *MP*. The text printed here is from *The Examiner*. One MS. cancellation is worth noting: after 'pot-valiant' (para. 2) Dickens originally wrote, 'smiths would seem to have a weakness in respect of dog-stealing'.

A remarkable document, and one suggesting many weighty considerations and supplying much important evidence in reference to the alliance of crime with ignorance, has been recently published by the Government. It is a statement of the number of persons taken into custody by the Metropolitan Police, summarily disposed of, and tried and convicted in the year 1847; to which are appended certain comparative statements from the year 1831 to 1847 inclusive.

In one part of this return, the trades and professions of the various persons taken into custody in the course of the year, are set forth in detail. Although this information is necessarily imperfect, in the absence of an accurate statistical return, set forth side by side with it, of the gross number of persons pursuing each of such trades or professions in the metropolis, it is very curious. Out of a total of between forty-one and forty-two thousand male offenders distributed over seventy-nine trades, twelve thousand four hundred and ten are labourers, of whom one-twelfth offend against the vagrant laws. Next, in point of number, come the sailors, who exceed eighteen hundred. Next, the carpenters, who are about a hundred below the sailors. Next, the shoemakers, who muster some six hundred weaker than the carpenters. Next, the tailors, who are about a hundred in the rear of the shoemakers. Next, the bricklayers, who are again about a hundred below the tailors. And so on down to four sheriff's officers, three clergymen, and one umbrella-maker. Nor are the offences of each class less notable. Thus, of the three clergymen, one is drunk, one disorderly, and one pugilistic; which is exactly the case with the sheriffs' officers. The solitary umbrella-maker, figures as a murderer. Of five parish officers, one is a suspicious character, one a horse stealer, and three commit assaults. Of sixteen postmen, seven steal money from letters, and six get drunk. Butchers are more disposed to common assaults than to any other class of offence. The chief weakness of carpenters is drunkenness; after that, a disposition to assault the lieges: after that, a tendency to petty larceny. Tailors, as we all know, are disorderly in their drink, and pot-valiant. Female servants are greatly tempted into theft. Ill-paid milliners and dressmakers would seem to lapse the most into such offences as may be supposed to arise from, or to lead to, prostitution.

One extraordinary feature of these tables, is the immense number of persons who have no trade or occupation, which may be stated, in round numbers, as amounting to eleven thousand one hundred out of forty-one thousand men, and to *seventeen thousand one hundred out of twenty thousand five hundred women*. Of this last-mentioned number of women, nine thousand can neither read nor write; eleven thousand can only read, or read and write imperfectly; and only fourteen can read and write well! The proportion of total ignorance, among the men, is as thirteen thousand out of forty-one thousand; only one hundred and fifty out of all that forty-one thousand can read and write well; and no more knowledge than the mere ability to blunder over a book like a little child, or to read and write imperfectly, is possessed by the rest. This state of mental confusion is what has been commonly called 'education' in England for a good many years. And that ill-used word might, quite as reasonably, be employed to express a teapot.

It should be remembered that the very best aspect of this widely diffused ignorance among criminals, is presented through the medium of these returns, and that they are, probably, unduly favourable to the attainments of these wretched persons. It is one of the properties of ignorance to believe itself wiser than it is. Striking instances are within our knowledge in which this alleged ability to read well, and write a little – appearing to be claimed by offenders in perfect faith – has proved, on examination, scarcely to include the lowest rudiments of a child's first primer. Of this vast number of women who have no trade or occupation (seventeen thousand out of twenty thousand), it is pretty certain that an immense majority have never been instructed in the commonest house-hold duties, or the plainest use of needle and thread. Every day's experience in our great prisons shows the prevailing ignorance in these respects among the women who are constantly passing and repassing through them, to be scarcely less than their real ignorance of the arts of reading and writing and the moral ends to which they conduce. And in the face of such prodigious facts, sects and denominations of Christians quarrel with each other, and leave the prisons full of, and ever filling with, people who begin to be educated within the prison walls!

The notion that education for the general people is comprised in the faculty of tumbling over words, letter by letter, and syllable by syllable, like the learned pig, or of making staggering pothooks and hangers inclining to the right, has surely had its day by this time, and a long day too. The comfortable conviction that a parrot-acquaintance with the church catechism and the ten commandments, is enough shoe-leather for poor pilgrims by the Slough of Despond, sufficient armour against the great giants Slay-Good and Despair, and a sort of parliamentary train for third-class passengers to the Beautiful Gate of the City, must be pulled up by the roots, or its growth will overshadow this land. Side by side with crime, disease, and misery in England, ignorance is always brooding, and is always certain to be found. The union of night with darkness is not more certain and indisputable. Schools of industry, schools where the simple knowledge learned from books is made pointedly *useful*, and immediately applicable to the duties and business of life, directly conducive to order, cleanliness, punctuality, and economy; – schools where the sublime lessons of the New Testament are made the super-structure to be reared enduringly on such foundations; not frittered away piece-meal into harassing unintelligibilities, and associated with weariness, languor, and distaste, by the use of the Gospel as a dog's-eared spelling-book, than which nothing in what is called instruction is more common, and nothing more to be condemned; – schools on such principles, deep as the lowest depth of society, and leaving none of its dregs untouched, are the only means of removing the scandal and the danger that beset us in this nineteenth century of our Lord. Their motto they may take from MORE: 'Let the State prevent vices, and take away the occasions for offences by well ordering its subjects, and not by suffering wickedness to increase, afterward to be punished.'

Even Sir Peter Laurie's sagacity does not appear by these returns to have quite 'put down' suicide yet. It has remained almost as steady, indeed, as if the world rejoiced in no such magnate. Four years ago, the number of metropolitan suicides committed in a twelvemonth was one hundred and fifty-five; and last year it was one hundred and fifty-two; not to mention two thousand persons reported last year to the police as lost or missing, of whom only half were found again.

24

Ignorance and Its Victims

The Examiner, 29 April 1848

This piece was clearly written as a follow-up to the preceding article, the opportunity provided by the Hammersmith magistrate being too good to be missed. It was first identified by Alec W. Brice, who printed it with a commentary in *The Dickensian*, Vol. 63 (1967), pp. 143–7.

The National Schools were those run by the Church of England with some financial assistance from the Government. Unsurprisingly, much emphasis was placed on knowledge of the catechism, the Church's question-and-answer method of instructing a child in the basic tenets of Anglican Christianity. The third question asks what the catechist's godparents did for him or her at baptism and part of the answer is that they promised on the catechist's behalf renunciation of 'the pomps and vanities of this wicked world'; later, a definition of the word 'sacrament' is required and the answer is 'an outward and visible sign of an inward and spiritual grace'.

Brice points out a somewhat ironic echo in *Hard Times* eight years later of Dickens's comments here about the desirability of children being 'helped out of [the] state of wonderment' depicted in the nursery rhyme 'Twinkle, twinkle, little star'. In Book 1, Ch. 3 of the novel, attacking the Gradgrind theory of 'factual' education, Dickens writes: 'No little Gradgrind had ever learnt the silly jingle, Twinkle, twinkle, little star; how I wonder what you are! No little Gradgrind had ever known wonder on the subject, each little Gradgrind having at five years old dissected the Great Bear like a Professor Owen...'

An apt illustration of the shortcomings and inefficiency of what is called 'education' for the general people – on which we offered a few words of comment last week – has since been presented in the newspapers.

'HAMMERSMITH. – Alice Lee, a pretty-looking young gipsy, with a child in her arms, was charged with fortune-telling.

'Susan Grant, a simple-looking young woman, about 24 years of age, stated that the prisoner came, on the 7th of February last, to her master's house in Ladbroke square, and after a little conversation offered to read her fortune. Prisoner told complainant that she must first cross her hand with a piece of silver. Witness then gave her half-a-crown, when the prisoner left, saying she would go and look at the book; afterwards she returned and said witness must cross her hand with a piece of gold. She gave her a sovereign; and the prisoner told her she must put another piece of gold, with a card, into her bosom, and keep it there until she saw her again. When she called again, she said she must have the piece of gold that was in her bosom, and she would go and "rule the planets." She took the second sovereign away with her, but came again, and said she must have witness's best gown, which she also took away with her. She afterwards had another gown, a shawl, several new articles of body linen, stockings, &c., all of which she said were absolutely necessary for properly ruling the planets, and she promised to return them the next day. She, however, never set eyes on her again until she happened to meet her that day in Kensington, with one of the gowns on, and the shawls wrapped round the child.

'The prisoner said the young woman had given her the money and things for telling her fortune and finding her a sweetheart.

'The magistrate, *having elicited that the complainant had been educated at the Kensington National School, expressed his surprise at her credulity.*

'The prisoner was committed to the House of Correction, with hard labour, for three months.'

'The magistrate having elicited that the complainant had been *educated!*' As if any kind of instruction possessing the faintest claim to that designation in its lowest and most limited acceptance, could have left the complainant in the belief that a pretty-looking young gipsy with a child in her arms, could 'rule the planets' with a half-crown, a sovereign, two gowns, a shawl, and several new articles of body linen!

It is popularly said of any very ignorant person, that he or she has only to be told that the moon is made of green cheese to accept it as an astronomical fact. But surely, if the complainant in this case had left the Kensington National School with a religious belief that the moon was an immense agglomeration of green cheese, and the whole solar system so many myriads of small stiltons, the results of her 'education' need not have been more surprising to the good magistrate. Such a belief would not have involved a more enormous absurdity, and it would probably have saved her money and her wardrobe.

This is one of the effects of teaching by rote certain pet abstractions, most weary of acquirement and of doubtful service when acquired confusedly, and leaving plain, interesting, solid knowledge quite out of the question. The complainant in this case could repeat her catechism to-morrow very likely, with parrot-like precision; and could gabble on about pomps and vanities, and outward and visible signs, with no greater amount of stumbling over it than of comprehension of what she was talking about. But suppose she had been told what a planet was; suppose the scholars at the Kensington National School had looked out of window sometimes, up at the night sky, and had heard meanwhile in a very few clear words something concerning the architecture of the heavens, and how and why they declare themselves the work of an Almighty hand; might not the ruling of the stars by means of gowns and body-linen have afterwards presented itself to her mind as something not exactly possible? Might not her reverence for the Creator and creation have been somewhat exalted above that possibility? And would not her education have been a little more complete?

When Aladdin went down into the cave leading to the gardens where the wonderful lamp was burning, the magician, keeping watch over the entrance, charged him not to touch the walls about him by so much as the skirt of his garment, or he would die. Some of the magicians who keep watch over the wonderful lamp of knowledge in the nineteenth century, still proceed on the same plan; and taboo all approach on the part of their pupils to an acquaintance with the commonest objects that surround them in the blind dark journey, from which they never grope their way into the light.

There is a certain piece of poetry to be said or sung by children, beginning

> Twinkle, twinkle, little star,
> How I wonder what you are!

It is a pity National School children are not helped out of this state of wonderment, and shown what a star is, and how, among all the stars that philosophers have catalogued, there is not one shining yet which is known to be materially influenced by any young gipsy with a child in her arms.

A *National* School! The time is coming when we shall begin to feel the sarcasm and reproach conveyed in that association of words, and our experience, past and present, of the National ignorance.

25

The Chinese Junk

The Examiner, 24 June 1848

The three-masted *Keying*, built of teakwood, 160 feet long and 33 feet maximum breadth, arrived in the East India Docks in March, having left Hong Kong on 6 December 1846 with a crew of thirty Chinese and twelve English. She had been bought, reported the *Illustrated London News* (1 April 1848), 'by a few enterprising Englishmen, who experienced the greatest difficulty in obtaining her ... Chinese laws strictly prohibiting, under pain of death, the sale of Chinese vessels to foreigners'. She was the first Chinese ship to round the Cape of Good Hope and arrived safely at St Helena, whence she sailed for England but was driven out of her course towards America. 'The crew becoming discontented ... at the length of the voyage', the captain made for New York, where the ship became a huge tourist attraction and subsequently visited Boston also. She left for England on 17 February 1848 and crossed the Atlantic in twenty-one days despite running into 'tempestuous weather'. The *Illustrated London News* published a full description of the vessel on 20 May and reported that it had already been visited by the Duke of Wellington, the Queen and Prince Albert, and the Queen Dowager; it concluded: 'this promises to be one of the most popular exhibitions of our metropolis for some time to come; it is certainly one of the most rational objects of curiosity which has ever been brought to our shores'. The Chinese 'doctrine of finality' and superstitious idol-worship provide Dickens with a fine opportunity for ironic reflections on reactionary British politicians and sectarian squabbles among the various Christian denominations (the reference to standing out on 'points of silver paper and tinfoil [and] the lighting of joss-sticks upon altars' is clearly a hit at the Oxford Movement – see p. 102).

The Chinese Junk, Keying, Illustrated London News, *1 April 1848*.

Literary allusions (p. 101) 'the bull with the china shop on St Patrick's day in the morning': a comic song sung by Grimaldi as Clown in *Harlequin Highflyer* at Sadler's Wells 1808 (*Memoirs of Grimaldi*, new edn. [1846], note to Ch. 15).

MS. Forster Collection, Victoria and Albert Museum. In his *Life of Dickens* (Book 6, Ch. 3) Forster prints two long passages from this item as having been first sent to him in private letters by Dickens, commenting that it was 'so good a description that [as editor of *The Examiner*] I could not resist the temptation of using some parts of it at the time'. His quoted passages exhibit several variants from both the Forster Collection MS. and the *Examiner* text (e.g., 'preposterous tissue-paper umbrella', para. 4), whilst at other points agreeing with the MS. against *The Examiner*, e.g., after 'marvel.' (para. 2) the MS. has 'Aladdin's palace was transported hither and thither by the rubbing of a lamp', and Forster reads the same except for 'As' before 'Aladdin' and 'so' after 'lamp' and both the MS. and Forster read 'Punch's Show' for 'Puppet Show' in the same paragraph. This suggests that Dickens did originally describe the *Keying* in letters to Forster, as the latter claims, and then, at his friend's request, rewrote the description, with a few minor alterations, as an article. Forster's dating of the alleged letters is clearly erroneous, however, as the *Pilgrim* editors point out (*Pilgrim*, Vol.

v, p. xiii) when explaining their reason for not accepting Forster's account of the genesis of this piece.

The shortest road to the Celestial Empire is by the Blackwall railway. You may take a ticket, through and back, for a matter of eighteen pence. With every carriage that is cast off on the road – at Stepney, Limehouse, Poplar, West India Docks – thousands of miles of space are cast off too. The flying dream of tiles and chimney-pots, backs of squalid houses, frowzy pieces of waste ground, narrow courts and streets, swamps, ditches, masts of ships, gardens of dock-weed, and unwholesome little bowers of scarlet beans, whirls away in half a score of minutes. Nothing is left but China.

How the flowery region ever got, in the form of the junk *Keying*, into the latitude and longitude where it is now to be found, is not the least part of the marvel. The crew of Chinamen aboard the *Keying* devoutly believed that their good ship would arrive quite safe, at the desired port, if they only tied red rags enough upon the mast, rudder, and cable. Perhaps they ran short of rag, through bad provision of stores; certain it is, that they had not enough on board to keep them from the bottom, and would most indubitably have gone there, but for such poor aid as could be rendered by the skill and coolness of a dozen English sailors, who brought this extraordinary craft in safety over the wide ocean.

If there be any one thing in the world that it is not at all like, that thing is a ship of any kind. So narrow, so long, so grotesque, so low in the middle, so high at each end (like a China pen-tray), with no rigging, with nowhere to go to aloft, with mats for sails, great warped cigars for masts, gaudy dragons and sea monsters disporting themselves from stem to stern, and, on the stern, a gigantic cock of impossible aspect, defying the world (as well he may) to produce his equal – it would look more at home at the top of a public building, at the top of a mountain, in an avenue of trees, or down in a mine, than afloat on the water. Of all unlikely callings with which imagination could connect the Chinese lounging on the deck, the most unlikely and the last would be the mariner's craft. Imagine a ship's crew, without a profile among them, in gauze pinafores and plaited hair; wearing stiff clogs, a quarter of a foot thick in the sole; and lying at night in little scented boxes, like backgammon men or chess pieces, or mother-of-pearl counters!

The most perplexing considerations obtrude themselves on your mind when you go down in the cabin. As, what became of all those lanterns hanging to the roof, when the junk was out at sea? Whether they dangled there, banging and beating against each other, like so many jesters' baubles? Whether the idol, Chin Tee, of the eighteen arms, enshrined in a celestial Puppet Show, in the place of honour, ever tumbled out in heavy weather? Whether the incense and the joss-stick still burnt before her with a faint perfume and a little thread of smoke, while the mighty waves were roaring all around? Whether that preposterous umbrella in the corner was always spread, as being a convenient maritime instrument for walking about the decks with, in a storm? Whether all the cool and shiny little chairs and tables were continually sliding about and bruising each other, and if not, why not? Whether anybody, on the voyage, ever read those two books printed in characters like bird-cages and fly-traps? Whether the Mandarin passenger, He Sing, who had never been ten miles from home in his life before, lying sick on a bamboo couch in a private China closet of his own (where he is now perpetually writing autographs for inquisitive barbarians), ever began to doubt the potency of the goddess of the sea, whose counterfeit presentment, like a flowery monthly nurse, occupies the sailors' joss-house in the second gallery? Whether it is possible that the said Mandarin, or the artist of the ship, Sam Sing, Esquire, R.A., of Canton, *can* ever go ashore without a walking-staff of cinnamon, agreeably to the usage of their likenesses in British tea-shops? Above all, whether the hoarse old ocean can ever have been seriously in earnest with this floating toyshop, or merely played with it in lightness of spirit – roughly, but meaning no harm – as the bull did with the china-shop, on St Patrick's day in the morning?

Here, at any rate, is the doctrine of finality beautifully worked out, and shut up in a corner of a dock near the Whitebait-house at Blackwall, for the edification of men. Thousands of years have passed away, since the first Chinese junk was constructed on this model; and the last Chinese junk that was ever launched was none the better for that waste and desert of time. In all that interval, through all the immense extent of the strange kingdom of China – in the midst of its patient and ingenious, but never advancing art, and its diligent agricultural cultivation – not one new twist or curve has been given to a ball of ivory; not one blade of experience has been grown. The general eye has opened no wider, and seen no farther, than the mimic eye upon this vessel's prow, by means of which she is supposed to find her way. It has been set in the flowery-head to as little purpose, for thousands of years. Sir Robert Inglis, member for the University of Oxford, ought to become Ty Kong or managing man of the *Keying*, and nail the red rag of his party to the mast for ever.

There is no doubt, it appears, that if any alteration took place, in this junk, or any other, the Chinese form of government would be destroyed. It has been clearly ascertained by the wise men and lawgivers that to make the cock upon the stern (the Grand Falcon of China) by a feather's breadth a less startling phenomenon, or to bring him within the remotest verge of ornithological possibility, would be to endanger the noblest institutions of the country. For it is a remarkable circumstance in China (which is found to obtain nowhere else), that although its institutions are the perfection of human wisdom, and are the wonder and envy of the world by reason of their stability, they are constantly imperilled in the last degree by very slight occurrences. So, such wonderful contradictions as the neatness of the *Keying*'s cups and saucers, and the ridiculous rudeness of her guns and rudder, continue to exist. If any Chinese maritime generation were the wiser for the wisdom of the generation gone before, it is agreed upon by all the Ty Kongs in the navy that the Chinese constitution would immediately go by the board, and that the church of the Chinese Bonzes would be effectually done for.

It is pleasant, coming out from behind the wooden screen that encloses this interesting and remarkable sight (which all who can, should see) to glance upon the mighty signs of life, enterprise, and progress, that the great river and its busy banks present. It is pleasant, coming back from China by the Blackwall railway, to think that WE trust no red rags in storms, and burn no joss-sticks before idols; that WE never grope our way by the aid of conventional eyes which have no sight in them; and that, in our civilisation, we sacrifice absurd forms to substantial facts. The ignorant crew of the *Keying* refused to enter on the ship's books, until 'a considerable amount of silvered paper, tinfoil, and joss-sticks' had been laid in, by the owners, for the purposes of their worship; but OUR seamen – far less our bishops, priests, and deacons – never stand out upon points of silvered paper and tin-foil, or the lighting up of joss-sticks upon altars! Christianity is not Chin-Teeism; and therein all insignificant quarrels as to means, are lost sight of in remembrance of the end.

There is matter for reflection aboard the *Keying* to last the voyage home to England again.

26

Review: *The Drunkard's Children. A Sequel to the Bottle.* In Eight Plates, by George Cruikshank

The Examiner, 8 July 1848

In 1847 Cruikshank had published *The Bottle*, a series of eight large plates depicting the ruin of an artisan-class family through drink, a ruin that begins with the husband offering his wife a glass of spirits in a comfortable domestic setting and ends in the total desolation of the home, wife-murder and the confinement of the man in a madhouse. It was hugely popular, selling 'by tens of thousands' according to Cruikshank's biographer, Blanchard Jerrold, and was also successfully presented as a stage melodrama. Dickens wrote to Forster that he thought the work 'very powerful indeed' with touches worthy of Hogarth, but that the 'philosophy of the thing, as a great lesson' was 'all wrong': 'the drinking should have begun in sorrow, or poverty, or ignorance – the three things in which, in its awful aspect, it *does* begin', but this would have been 'too "radical" for good old George, I suppose' (*Pilgrim*, Vol. v, p. 156). After producing *The Bottle*, Cruikshank became, shortly after his fifty-fifth birthday, a fervent advocate of teetotalism and remained so for the rest of his long life. Dickens was always strongly critical of the excesses of the Temperance Movement (see article 35 and his *HW* article 'Whole Hogs', 23 August 1851, reprinted in *MP*) and a few months before publishing this piece in *The Examiner* had written to Cruikshank in connection with the use made of his name by Temperance campaigners: 'I think those Temperance Societies (always remarkable for their indiscretion) are doing a very indiscreet thing in reference to you – and that they will keep many of your friends, away from your side when they would most desire to stand there' (15 February 1848; *Pilgrim*, Vol. v, p. 247). In 1853 he was to mock Cruikshank's importation of Temperance propaganda into fairy tales ('Frauds on the Fairies', *HW*, 1 October 1853, reprinted in *MP*).

Dickens had a lifelong admiration for the work of Hogarth and the range and detail of his references in this review attest to his intimate knowledge of it. The 'most neglected, wretched neighbourhood' depicted in 'Gin Lane' (1751) was the notorious slum of St Giles's, which in 1847 was cleared to facilitate the building of New Oxford Street (connecting Oxford Street with Holborn). Dickens quotes from Charles Lamb's discussion of 'Gin Lane' in his 1811 essay (*The Reflector*, No. 3) 'On the Genius and Character of Hogarth': 'the very houses, tumbling all about in various directions, seem drunk – seem absolutely reeling from the effect of that diabolical spirit of phrenzy which goes forth over the whole composition'. The 'prominent and handsome church' that Hogarth features in his print is Hawksmoor's St George's, Bloomsbury.

The Bishop of London in 1848 was Charles James Blomfield, to whom Dickens had challengingly dedicated his 1836 pamphlet *Sunday Under Three Heads* (see Vol. 1 of this edition, p. 476).

Literary allusions (p. 107) 'like the figures in the pictures of which the Spanish Friar spoke to Wilkie': this alludes to an anecdote recorded by

Wordsworth in his 'Lines suggested by a Portrait from the Pencil of F. Stone', ll. 95–117.

MS. Forster Collection, Victoria and Albert Museum. This shows no variants from the *Examiner* text. In his *Life of Dickens* (Book 6, Ch. 3) Forster prints most of the article but with the paragraphs in a different order and with a few variant readings (none of any great significance), stating that he is quoting from letters received from Dickens holidaying in Broadstairs. Although, as in the case of the Chinese Junk letter, his dating may be out (see p. 99), we may presume that this *Examiner* review had a similar genesis.

A 'Sequel to the Bottle' seems to us to demand a few words by way of gentle protest. Few men have a better right to erect themselves into teachers of the people than Mr George Cruikshank. Few men have observed the people as he has done, or know them better; few are more earnestly and honestly disposed to teach them for their good; and there are very, very few artists, in England or abroad, who can approach him in his peculiar and remarkable power.

But this teaching, to last, must be fairly conducted. It must not be all on one side. When Mr Cruikshank shows us, and shows us so forcibly and vigorously, that side of the medal on which the people in their crimes and faults are stamped, he is bound to help us to a glance at that other side on which the government that forms the people, with all *its* faults and vices, is no less plainly impressed. Drunkenness, as a national horror, is the effect of many causes. Foul smells, disgusting habitations, bad workshops and workshop customs, want of light, air, and water, the absence of all easy means of decency and health, are commonest among its common, everyday, physical causes. The mental weariness and languor so induced, the want of wholesome relaxation, the craving for *some* stimulus and excitement, which is as much a part of such lives as the sun is; and, last and inclusive of all the rest, ignorance, and the need there is amongst the English people of reasonable, rational training, in lieu of mere parrot-education, or none at all; are its most obvious moral causes. It would be as sound philosophy to issue a series of plates under the title of The Physic Bottle, or The Saline Mixture, and, tracing the history of typhus fever by such means, to refer it all to the gin-shop, as it is to refer drunkenness thither and to stop there. Drunkenness does not begin there. It has a teeming and reproachful history anterior to that stage; and at the remediable evil in that history, it is the duty of the moralist, if he strikes at all, to strike deep and spare not.

HOGARTH avoided the Drunkard's Progress, we conceive, precisely because the causes of drunkenness among the poor were so numerous and widely spread, and lurked so sorrowfully deep and far down in all human misery, neglect and despair, that even *his* pencil could not bring them fairly and justly into the light. That he was never contented with beginning at the effect, witness the Miser (his shoe new-soled with the binding of his Bible) dead before the Young Rake begins his career; the worldly father, listless daughter, impoverished nobleman, and crafty lawyer, in the first plate of the *Mariage à la Mode*; the detestable advances in the Stages of Cruelty; and the progress downward of Thomas Idle! That he did not spare that kind of drunkenness which was of more 'respectable' engenderment, his midnight modern conversation, the election plates, and a crowd of stupid aldermen and other guzzlers, amply testify. But after one immortal journey down Gin Lane, he turned away in grief and sorrow – perhaps in hope of better things one day, from better laws, and schools, and poor men's homes – and went back no more. It is remarkable of that picture, that while it exhibits drunkenness in its most appalling forms, it forces on the attention of the spectator a most neglected, wretched neighbourhood (the same that is only just now cleared away for the extension of Oxford Street), and an unwholesome, indecent, abject condition of life, worthy to be a Frontispiece to the late Report of the Sanitary Commissioners, made nearly one hundred years afterwards. We have always been inclined to think the purpose of this piece not adequately stated, even by Charles Lamb. 'The very houses seem absolutely reeling,' it is true; but they quite as powerfully indicate some of the more prominent causes of intoxication among the neglected orders of society, as any of its effects. There is no evidence that any of the actors in the dreary scene have ever been much better off than we find them. The best are pawning the commonest necessaries, and tools of their trades, and the worst are homeless vagrants who give us no clue to their having been otherwise in bygone days. All are living and dying miserably. Nobody is interfering for prevention or for cure in the generation going out before us, or the generation coming in. The beadle (the only sober man in the composition except the pawnbroker), is mightily indifferent to the orphan-child crying beside its parent's coffin. The little charity-girls are not so well taught or looked after, but that they can take to dram-drinking already. The church is very prominent and handsome, but coldly surveys these things, in progress underneath the shadow of its tower (it was in the year of grace eighteen hundred and forty-eight that a Bishop of London first came out respecting something wrong in poor men's social accommodations), and is passive in the picture. We take all this to have a meaning, and to the best of our knowledge it has not grown obsolete in a century.

Whereas, to all such considerations Mr Cruikshank gives the go-by.

The hero of the Bottle, and father of these children, lived in undoubted comfort and good esteem until he was some five-and-thirty years of age, when, happening, unluckily, to have a goose for dinner one day, in the bosom of his thriving family, he jocularly sent out for a bottle of gin, and persuaded his wife (until then a pattern of neatness and good housewifery) to take a little drop, after the stuffing; from which moment the family never left off drinking gin, and rushed downhill to destruction, very fast.

Entertaining the highest respect for Mr Cruikshank's great genius, and no less respect for his motives in these publications, we deem it right, on the appearance of a sequel to the Bottle, to protest against this. First, because it is a compromising of a very serious and pressing truth; secondly, because it will, in time, defeat the end these pictures are designed to bring about. There is no class of society so certain to find out their weak place, as the class to which they are especially addressed. It is particularly within their knowledge and experience.

In the present series we trace the brother and sister whom we left in that terrible representation of the father's madness with which the first series closed, through the career of vice and crime then lowering before them. The gin-shop, beer-shop, and dancing-rooms receive them in turn. They are tried for a robbery. The boy is convicted, and sentenced to transportation; the girl acquitted. He dies, prematurely, on board the hulks; and she, desolate and mad, flings herself from London Bridge into the night-darkened river.

The power of this closing scene is extraordinary. It haunts the remembrance, like an awful reality. It is full of passion and terror, and we question whether any other hand could so have rendered it. Nor, although far exceeding all that has gone before, as such a catastrophe should, is it without the strongest support all through the story. The death-bed scene on board the hulks – the convict who is composing the face – and the other who is drawing the screen round the bed's head – are masterpieces, worthy of the greatest painter. The reality of the place, and the fidelity with which every minute object illustrative of it is presented, are quite surprising. But the same feature is remarkable throughout. In the trial scene at the Old Bailey the eye may wander round the court, and observe everything that is a part of the place. The very light and atmosphere of the reality are reproduced with astonishing truth. So in the gin-shop and the beer-shop; no fragment of the fact is indicated and slurred over, but every shred of it is honestly made out. It is curious, in closing the book, to recall the number of faces we have seen that have as much individual character and identity in our remembrance as if we had been looking at so many living people of flesh and blood. The man behind the bar in the gin-shop, the barristers round

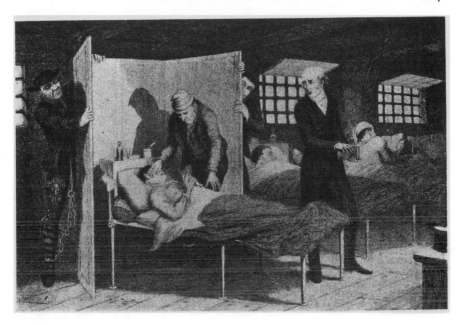

'The Wretched Convict Droops and Dies' by George Cruikshank. From The Drunkard's Children. A Sequel to the Bottle *(1848).*

the table in court, the convicts already mentioned, will be, like the figures in the pictures of which the Spanish Friar spoke to Wilkie, realities, when thousands of living shadows shall have passed away. May Mr Cruikshank linger long behind to give us many more of such realities, and to do with simple means, such as are used here, what the whole paraphernalia and resources of Art could not effect, without a master hand!

The sequel to the Bottle is published at the same price as its predecessor. The eight large plates may be bought for a shilling!

27

Review: *Narrative of the Expedition sent by her Majesty's Government to the river Niger in 1841, under the command of Captain H.D. Trotter, RN.* By Captain William Allen, RN, Commander of HMS Wilberforce, and T.R.H. Thomson, M.D., one of the medical officers of the Expedition. Published with the sanction of the Colonial Office and the Admiralty.

The Examiner, 19 August 1848

Dickens was all his life a passionately keen reader of books of travels and voyages: 'Such books', he wrote in 1853 ('The Long Voyage', *RP*), 'have had a strong fascination for my mind from my earliest childhood.' Forster records (Book 6, Ch. 3) that Dickens was reading in the summer of 1848 a 'surprising number of books of African and other travel for which he had an insatiable relish' and they are recalled later in 'The Long Voyage': 'All the African travellers, wayworn, solitary and sad [who] submit themselves ... to drunken, murderous, man-selling despots' (alluding, no doubt, among others, to explorer Richard Lander and the Obi of Aboh – see p. 109). Allen's *Narrative* would clearly have been of great interest to Dickens simply as an African travel-book, but the Exeter Hall connection would have made it doubly compelling, given his general hostility to overseas missionary activity, which he was so memorably to express in *Bleak House* (1853).

The 1841 expedition had, as Dickens explains in his third paragraph, both a commercial and a missionary purpose and it was fervently sponsored by the Society for the Extinction of the Slave Trade and for Civilisation of Africa, of which Sir Thomas Fowell Buxton, a philanthropic brewer, was a leading light. Humphry House quotes (*The Dickens World* [1942], Ch. 4) Harriet Martineau's description 'of public meetings, with Prince Albert in the Chair, so crowded that persons were carried out fainting; of the congratulations and mutual praises of statesmen and prelates, of grand subscriptions and yet grander hopes'. The resultant fiasco, exulted over by *The Times* and the *Edinburgh Review*, 'set back the growth of commercial enterprise ten years', according to Michael Crowder (*The Story of Nigeria* [1962], p. 126), though it does also mark the beginning of missionary penetration of what is now Nigeria. For Dickens, the expedition's failure focused many strongly felt concerns about the grotesque imbalance, as he saw it, between the money and energy poured into overseas missionary work and the scant attention paid to the appallingly benighted condition of the poorest classes in England. The result is a piece of writing which

House rightly hailed as 'remarkable even today for its vigour, eloquence and even, in places, enlightenment.'

The route taken by the expedition, after calling at Sierra Leone, a Crown Colony since 1808, and Cape Coast, one of the trading forts established by the British on the coast of what is now Ghana, was up the Nun branch of the Niger to the top of the Niger Delta. This traversed three African states. The first was the coastal one of Nembe, called Brass by the Europeans and ruled by King Amain Kulo, known as King Boy. The second was the Ibo city-state of Aboh, which controlled trade on the Niger for about fifty miles and the ruler of which was called the Obi. Obi Asai was already in power when the Landers reached Aboh in the early 1830s. Their favourable first impressions ('a sprightly young man with a mild open countenance, and an eye which indicates quickness, intelligence and good nature, rather than the ferocity we had been told he possesses' – *The Niger Journal of Richard and John Lander*, ed. Robin Hallett [1965], p. 251) was gradually replaced as he insisted on a substantial ransom before letting them go. The third, and most northerly, state reached by the expedition was that of Igara, the capital of which was called Idah, the ruler being known as the Attah of Idah. It was here that the ill-fated Model Farm was established, near Lokoja close to the confluence of the Benue and the Niger. As the crews were hit by fever, each ship returned down the Niger (Crowder notes, *op. cit.*, p. 126, that the ships carried plenty of quinine, the only cure for malaria, but it was used only when patients already showed signs of recovery and were in the healthier climate of the island of Fernando Po, leased to Britain by Spain 1827–58).

Memories of the expedition would have been fresh in the minds of Dickens's readers when in *Bleak House* he satirised the preference of many contemporary philanthropical organisations for saving African souls rather than the less glamorous alternative of caring for the domestic poor. His portrait of Mrs Jellyby certainly owes something to his experience of Caroline Chisholm and her Family Colonisation Loan Society, but Mrs Jellyby's African project (Chisholm was concerned with emigration to Australia) is clearly meant to recall the grandiose hopes of the 1841 expedition. The Model Farm project becomes Mrs Jellyby's scheme 'to have from a hundred and fifty to two hundred healthy families cultivating coffee and educating the natives of Borrioboola-Gha, on the left bank of the Niger' and her coadjutor Mr Quale's scheme 'for teaching the coffee colonists to teach the natives to turn pianoforte legs and establish an export trade', schemes that eventually fail 'in consequence of the King of Borrioboola wanting to sell everybody – who survived the climate – for Rum'.

Literary allusions (p. 110) 'gruel ... thick and slab': Shakespeare, *Macbeth*, Act 4, Sc. 1; (p. 119) 'Master Slender ... not altogether an ass': Shakespeare,

The Merry Wives of Windsor, Act 1, Sc. 1; (p. 120) 'a wilderness of Africans':
Shakespeare, *The Merchant of Venice*, Act 3, Sc. 1; (p. 125) 'great gulf set':
Luke 16:26; (p. 125) 'a girdle round the earth': Shakespeare, *A Midsummer
Night's Dream*, Act 2, Sc. 1; (p. 125) 'To your tents, O Israel!': 1 Kings 12:16.

MS. Forster Collection, Victoria and Albert Museum. Thirty pages, 1–8
in dark ink, 9–30 in light blue. Dickens gives instructions for the insertion
of the extracts from the *Narrative*. These are taken from Vol. 1, pp. 216–21,
222–5, 226–7, 252–3, 362–4, and Vol. 2, pp. 12–13 and 78. The paragraph
beginning 'Mr Schön recapitulated ...' (p. 118) is misprinted as part of
Dickens's text in *The Examiner*. The stage-directions in the first long extract
are italicised in the *Narrative*, but the italicisation of the indirect and direct
speech on p. 118 would appear to be Dickens's own. Between MS. and
publication he evidently corrected a factual error: 'the very mistake with
which Denham so astonished' became 'the self-same error with which
Clapperton so astonished' (p. 118). Dixon Denham accompanied Hugh
Clapperton on his Nigerian exploration in the mid-1820s and wrote an
account of it. The 'mistake' attributed to him was therefore merely reported
by him and Dickens takes care to get this right.

THE NIGER EXPEDITION

It might be laid down as a very good general rule of social and political
guidance, that whatever Exeter Hall champions, is the thing by no means
to be done. If it were harmless on a cursory view, if it even appeared to
have some latent grain of commonsense at the bottom of it – which is a
very rare ingredient in any of the varieties of gruel that are made thick
and slab by the weird old women who go about, and exceedingly
roundabout, on the Exeter Hall platform – such advocacy might be held
to be a final and fatal objection to it, and to any project capable of
origination in the wisdom or folly of man.

The African Expedition, of which these volumes contain the melancholy history, is in no respect an exception to the rule. Exeter Hall
was hot in its behalf, and it failed. Exeter Hall was hottest on its weakest
and most hopeless objects, and in those it failed (of course) most signally.
Not, as Captain Allen justly claims for himself and his gallant comrades,
not through any want of courage and self-devotion on the part of those
to whom it was entrusted; – the sufferings of all, the deaths of many, the
dismal wear and tear of stout frames and brave spirits, sadly attest the
fact; – but because, if the ends sought to be attained are to be won, they
must be won by other means than the exposure of inestimable British
lives to certain destruction by an enemy against which no gallantry can

contend, and the enactment of a few broad farces for the entertainment of a King Obi, King Boy, and other such potentates, whose respect for the British force is, doubtless, likely to be very much enhanced by their relishing experiences of British credulity in such representations, and our perfect impotency in opposition to their climate, their falsehood, and deceit.

The main ends to be attained by the Expedition were these: The abolition, in great part, of the Slave Trade, by means of treaties with native chiefs, to whom were to be explained the immense advantages of general unrestricted commerce with Great Britain in lieu thereof; the substitution of free for Slave labour in the dominions of those chiefs; the introduction into Africa of an improved system of agricultural cultivation; the abolition of human sacrifices; the diffusion among those Pagans of the true doctrines of Christianity; and a few other trifling points, no less easy of attainment. A glance at this short list, and a retrospective glance at the great number of generations during which they have all been comfortably settled in our own civilized land, never more to be the subjects of dispute, will tend materially to remove any aspect of slight difficulty they may present. To make the treaties, certain officers of the Expedition were constituted her Majesty's Commissioners. To render them attractive to the native chiefs, a store of presents was provided. And to enforce them, 'one or more small forts' were to be built, on land to be bought for the purpose on the banks of the Niger; which forts were 'to assist in the abolition of the Slave Trade', and further the innocent trade of her Majesty's subjects. The Niger was to be explored, the resources and productions of the country were to be inquired into and reported on, and various important and scientific observations, astronomical, geographical, and otherwise, were to be made; but these were by the way. A Model-Farm was to be established by an agricultural society at home; and besides allowing stowage-room on board the ships for its various stores, implements, etc., the Admiralty granted a free passage to Mr Alfred Carr, a West Indian gentleman of colour, engaged as its superintendent. By all these means combined, as Dr Lushington and Sir Thomas Fowell Buxton wrote to Lord John Russell, who was then Colonial Secretary, the people of Africa were 'to be awakened to a proper sense of their own degradation.'

On this awakening mission three vessels were appointed. They were flat-bottomed iron steam vessels, built for the purpose. The *Albert* and the *Wilberforce,* each 139 feet 4 inches in length, and 27 feet in breadth of beam, and drawing 6 feet water, were in all respects exactly alike. The *Soudan,* intended for detached service, was much smaller, and drew a foot and a half less water. They were very ingeniously conceived, with certain rudder-tails and sliding keels for sea service; but they performed most unaccountable antics in bad weather, and had a perverse tendency to go to leeward, which nothing would conquer. Dr Reid fitted them up with what 'My Lords' describe as 'an ingenious and costly' ventilating apparatus, the preparation of which occasioned a loss of much valuable time, and the practical effect of which was to suffocate the crews. 'That truly amiable Prince,' the Prince Consort, came on board at Woolwich, and gave a handsome gold chronometer to each of the three captains. The African Civilisation Society came down with a thousand pounds. The Church of England Missionary Society provided a missionary and a catechist. Exeter Hall, in a ferment, was for ever blocking up the gangway. At last, on the 12th of May 1841, at half-past six in the morning, the line-of-battle ships anchored in Plymouth Sound gave three cheers to the Expedition as it steamed away, unknowing, for 'the Gate of the Cemetery.' Such was the sailors' name, thereafter, for the entrance to the fatal river whither they were bound.

At Sierra Leone, in the middle of June following, the interpreters were taken on board, together with some liberated Africans, their wives and children, who were engaged there by Mr Carr as labourers on the Model Farm. Also, a large gang of Krumen to assist in working the vessels, and to save the white men as much as possible from exposure to the sun and heavy rains. Of these negroes – a faithful, cheerful, active, affectionate race – a very interesting account is given; which seems to render it clear that they, under civilized direction, are the only hopeful human agents to whom recourse can ultimately be had for aid in working out the slow and gradual raising up of Africa. Those eminent Krumen, Jack Frying Pan, King George, Prince Albert, Jack Sprat, Bottle-of-Beer, Tom Tea Kettle, the Prince of Wales, the Duke of York, and some four-score others, enrolled themselves on the ships' books, here, under Jack Andrews, their head man; and these being joined, at Cape Palmas, by Jack Smoke, Captain Allen's faithful servant and attendant in sickness in his former African expedition, the complement was complete. Thence the Expedition made for Cape Coast Castle, where much valuable assistance was derived from Governor MacLean; and thence for the Nun branch of the Niger – the Gate of the Cemetery*.

After a fortnight's voyage up the river the royal residence of King Obi was reached. A solemn conference with this sovereign was soon afterwards held on board the *Albert*. His Majesty was dressed 'in a sergeant-major's

* Most English readers will be as unwilling as the manly writers of these volumes, to leave one spot at Cape Coast Castle, without a word of remembrance.

'In passing across the square within the walls, an object of deep interest presents itself in the little space containing all that was mortal of the late Mrs McLean; the once well-known, amiable, and accomplished L. E. L. A plain marble slab, bearing the following inscription, is placed over the spot:

coat, given him by Lander, and a loose pair of scarlet trousers, presented to him on the same occasion,' and 'a conical black velvet cap was stuck on his head in a slanting manner.' The following extracts describe the process of

TREATY-MAKING WITH OBI

On being shown to the after-part of the quarter-deck, where seats were provided for himself and the Commissioners, he sat down to collect his scattered ideas, which appeared to be somewhat bewildered; and after a few complimentary remarks from Captain Trotter and the other Commissioners, the conference was opened.

Captain Trotter, Senior Commissioner, explained to Obi Osaï, that her Majesty the Queen of Great Britain had sent him and the three other gentlemen composing the Commission, to endeavour to enter into treaties with African Chiefs for the abolition of the trade in human beings, which her Majesty and all the British nation held to be an injustice to their fellow-creatures, and repugnant to the laws of God; that the vessels which he saw were not trading ships, but belonging to our Queen, and were sent, at great expense, expressly to convey the Commissioners appointed by her Majesty, for the purpose of carrying out her benevolent intentions, for the benefit of Africa. Captain Trotter therefore requested the King to give a patient hearing to what the Commissioners had to say to him on the subject.

Obi expressed himself through his interpreter, or 'mouth,' much gratified at our visit; that he understood what was said, and would pay attention.

The Commissioners then explained that the principal object in inviting him to a conference was, to point out the injurious effects to himself and to his people of the practice of selling their slaves, thus depriving themselves of their services for ever, for a trifling sum; whereas, if these slaves were kept at

---

Hic jacet sepultum,
Omne quod mortale fuit
LETITIÆ ELIZABETHÆ McLEAN,
Quam egregia ornatam indole, Musis
Unice amatam. Omniumque amores
Secum trahentem; in ipso etatis flore,
Mors immatura rapuit.
Die Octobris xv., MDCCCXXXVIII. Ætatis XXXVI.
Quod spectas viator marmor vanum
Heu doloris monumentum
Conjux mærens erexit.

'The beams of the setting sun throw a rich but subdued colouring over the place, and as we stood in sad reflection on the fate of the gifted poetess, some fine specimens of the *Hirundo Senegalensis,* or African swallow, fluttered gracefully about, as if to keep watch over a spot sacred indeed to the Muses; while the noise of the surf, breaking on the not distant shore, seemed to murmur a requiem over departed genius.'

King Obi and some of his Womenfolk. From Allen's Narrative of an
Expedition ... to the River Niger *(1848).*

home, and employed in the cultivation of the land, in collecting palm oil, or
other productions of the country for commerce, they would prove a permanent
source of revenue. Obi replied, that he was very willing to do away with the
slave-trade *if a better traffic could be substituted.*

COMMISSIONERS – Does Obi sell slaves from his own dominions?

OBI – No; they come from countries far away.

COMMISSIONERS – Does Obi make war to procure slaves?

OBI – When other chiefs quarrel with me and make war, I take all I can
as slaves.

COMMISSIONERS – What articles of trade are best suited to your people,
or what would you like to be brought to your country?

OBI – Cowries, cloth, muskets, powder, handkerchiefs, coral beads, hats –
anything from the white man's country will please.

COMMISSIONERS – You are the King of this country, as our Queen is the
sovereign of Great Britain; but she does not wish to trade with you; she only
desires that her subjects may trade fairly with yours. Would they buy salt?

OBI – Yes.

COMMISSIONERS – The Queen of England's subjects would be glad to trade for raw cotton, indigo, ivory, gums, camwood. Now have your people these things to offer in return for English trade-goods?

OBI – Yes.

COMMISSIONERS – Englishmen will bring everything to trade but rum or spirits, which are injurious. If you induce your subjects to cultivate the ground, you will all become rich; but if you sell slaves, the land will not be cultivated, and you will become poorer by the traffic. If you do all these things which we advise you for your own benefit, our Queen will grant you, for your own profit and revenue, one out of every twenty articles sold by British subjects in the Abòh territory; so that the more you persuade your people to exchange native produce for British goods, the richer you will become. You will then have a regular profit, enforced by treaty, instead of trusting to a 'dash' or present, which depends on the willingness of the traders.

OBI – I will agree to discontinue the slave-trade, but I expect the English to bring goods for traffic.

COMMISSIONERS – The Queen's subjects cannot come here to trade, unless they are certain of a proper supply of your produce.

OBI – I have plenty of palm-oil.

COMMISSIONERS – Mr Schön, missionary, will explain to you in the Ibu language what the Queen wishes; and if you do not understand, it shall be repeated.

Mr Schön began to read the address drawn up for the purpose of showing the different tribes what the views of the Expedition were; but Obi soon appeared to be tired of a palaver which lasted so much longer than those to which he was accustomed. He manifested some impatience, and at last said: 'I have made you a promise to drop this slave-trade, and do not wish to hear anything more about it.'

COMMISSIONERS – Our Queen will be much pleased if you do, and you will receive the presents which she sent for you. When people in the white man's country sign a treaty or agreement, they always abide by it. The Queen cannot come to speak to you, Obi Osaï, but she sends us to make the treaty for her.

OBI – I can only engage my word for my own country.

COMMISSIONERS – You cannot sell your slaves if you wish, for our Queen has many warships at the mouth of the river, and Spaniards are afraid to come and buy there.

OBI – I understand.

He seemed to be highly amused on our describing the difficulties the slave-dealers have to encounter in the prosecution of the trade; and on one occasion he laughed immoderately when told that our cruisers often captured slave-ships, with the cargo on board. We suspected, however, that much of his amusement arose from his knowing that slaves were shipped off at parts of the coast little thought of by us. The abundance of Brazilian rum in Abòh showed that they often traded with nations who have avowedly no other object.

It is not difficult to imagine that Obi was 'highly amused' with the whole 'palaver,' except when the recollection of its interposing between him and the presents made him restless. For nobody knew better than Obi what a joke it all was, as the result very plainly showed.

Some of the presents were now brought in, which Obi looked at with evident pleasure. His anxiety to examine them completed his inattention to the rest of the palaver.

COMMISSIONERS – These are not all the presents that will be given to you. We wish to know if you are willing to stop boats carrying slaves through the waters of your dominions?

OBI – Yes, very willing; except those I do not see.

COMMISSIONERS – Also to prevent slaves being carried over your land?

OBI – Certainly; but the English must furnish me and my people with arms, as my doing so will involve me in war with my neighbours.

Obi then retired for a short time to consult with his headmen.

COMMISSIONERS (*on his return*) – Have you power to make an agreement with the Commissioners in the name of all your subjects?

OBI – I am the King. What I say is law. Are there two Kings in England? There is only one here.

COMMISSIONERS – Understanding you have sovereign power, can you seize slaves on the river?

OBI – Yes.

COMMISSIONERS – You must set them free.

OBI – Yes (*snapping his fingers several times*).

COMMISSIONERS – The boats must be destroyed.

OBI – I will break the canoe, but kill no one.

COMMISSIONERS – Suppose a man-of-war takes a canoe, and it is proved to be a slaver, the officer's word must be taken by the King. You, Obi, or some one for you, can be present to see justice done.

OBI – I understand.

COMMISSIONERS – Any new men coming henceforth to Abòh are not to be made slaves.

OBI – Very good.

COMMISSIONERS – If any King, or other person, sends down slaves, Obi must not buy them.

OBI – I will not go to market to sell slaves.

COMMISSIONERS – Any white men that are enslaved are to be made free.

The Commissioners here alluded to the case of the Landers; and asked Obi if he did not remember the circumstance of their being detained some time as slaves. Obi, turning round to his sons and headmen, appealed to them, and then denied all knowledge of Lander's detention.

COMMISSIONERS – British people who settle in Abòh must be treated as friends, in the same way as Obi's subjects would be if they were in England.

OBI – What you say to me I will hold fast, and perform.

COMMISSIONERS – People may come here, and follow their own religion without annoyance? Our countrymen will be happy to teach our religion, without which blessing we should not be prosperous, as a nation, as we now are.

OBI – Yes, let them come; we shall be glad to hear them.

COMMISSIONERS – British people may trade with your people; but whenever it may be in Abòh, one-twentieth part of the goods sold is to be given to the King. Are you pleased with this?

OBI – Yes – 'makka.' – It is good (*snapping his fingers*).

COMMISSIONERS – Is there any road from Abòh to Benin?

OBI – Yes.

COMMISSIONERS – They must all be open to the English.

OBI – Yes.

COMMISSIONERS – All the roads in England are open alike to all foreigners.

OBI – In this way of trade I am agreeable.

COMMISSIONERS – Will Obi let the English build, cultivate, buy and sell, without annoyance?

OBI – Certainly.

COMMISSIONERS – If your people do wrong to them, will you punish them?

OBI – They shall be judged, and if guilty, punished.

COMMISSIONERS – When the English do wrong, Obi must send word to an English officer, who will come and hold a palaver. You must not punish white people.

OBI – I assent to this. (*He now became restless and impatient.*)

COMMISSIONERS – If your people contract debts with the English, they must be made to pay them.

OBI – They shall be punished if they do not.

COMMISSIONERS – The Queen may send an agent?

OBI – If any Englishman comes to reside, I will show him the best place to build a house, and render him every assistance.

* * *

COMMISSIONERS – Obi must also give every facility for forwarding letters, etc., down the river, so that the English officer who receives them may give a receipt, and also a reward for sending them.

OBI – Very good (*snapping his fingers*).

COMMISSIONERS – Have you any opportunity of sending to Bonny?

OBI – I have some misunderstanding with the people intermediate between Abòh and Bonny; but I can do it through the Brass people.

Commissioners – Will you agree to supply men of war with firewood, provisions, etc. etc., at a fair and reasonable price?

Obi – Yes, certainly.

The Commissioners requested Mr Schön, the respected missionary, *to state to King Obi, in a concise manner, the difference between the Christian religion and heathenism*, together with some description of the settlement at Sierra Leone.

Mr Schön – There is but one God.

Obi – *I always understood there were two.**

Mr Schön recapitulated the Decalogue and the leading truths of the Christian faith, and then asked Obi if this was not a good religion, to which he replied, with a snap of his fingers, 'Yes, very good' (makka).

Obi concluded the conference by remarking very emphatically 'that he wanted this palaver settled; that he was tired of so much talking, and that he wished to go on shore.' He finally said, with great impatience, 'that this Slave Palaver was all over now, and he didn't wish to hear anything more of it.'

The upshot of the Slave Palaver was, that Obi agreed to every article of the proposed treaty, and plighted his troth to it then and there amidst a prodigious beating of tom-toms, which lasted all night. Of course he broke the treaty on the first opportunity (being one of the falsest rascals in Africa), and went on slave-dealing vigorously. When the Expedition became helpless and disabled, newly-captured slaves, chained down to the bottoms of canoes, were seen passing along the river in the heart of this same Obi's dominions.

The following is curious: –

OBI ON CAPITAL PUNISHMENT

28th. Agreeably to his promise, Obi Osaï went on board the *Albert* this morning, where he was received by Captain Trotter and the Commissioners, with whom he breakfasted. His dress was not so gay as on his visit of yesterday, being merely a cotton jacket and trousers, much in want of a laundress, a red cap on his head, and some strings of coral, and teeth of wild beasts, round his neck, wrists, and ankles. He entered frankly into the views previously explained to him, and assented unhesitatingly to all required from him. It was, however, necessary that the Treaty, which had been drawn up on the basis of the draft furnished by Lord John Russell, with the addition of some articles relating especially to the free navigation of the river, should be again read and explained to Obi and his principal headmen, especially the heir-presumptive and the chief Ju-juman, much to their annoyance; and as all this occupied a long while, apparently to very little purpose, he completely turned

* Some former traveller – Lander, perhaps – had possibly bewildered Obi with the Athanasian Creed.

against ourselves the charge we made against the black people – of not knowing the value of time. In agreeing to the additional article, binding the Chief and his people to the discontinuance of the horrid custom of sacrificing human beings, Obi very reasonably inquired what should be done with those who might deserve death as punishment for the commission of great crimes.

Something very like this question of Obi's has been asked, once or twice, by the very Government which sent out these 'devil-ships,' or steamers, to remodel his affairs for him; and the point has not been settled yet.

Now let us review this Diplomacy for a moment. Obi, though a savage in a sergeant-major's coat, may claim with Master Slender, and perhaps with better reason, to be not altogether an ass. Obi knows, to begin with, that the English Government maintains a blockade, the object of which is to prevent the exportation of slaves from his native coasts, and which is inefficient and absurd. The very mention of it sets him a-laughing. Obi, sitting on the quarter-deck of the *Albert*, looking slyly out from under his savage forehead and his conical cap, sees before him her Majesty's white Commissioners from the distant blockade-country gravely propounding, at one sitting, a change in the character of his people (formed, essentially, in the inscrutable wisdom of God, by the soil they work on and the air they breathe)   the substitution of a religion it is utterly impossible he can appreciate or understand, be the mutual interpretation never so exact and never so miraculously free from confusion, for that in which he has been bred, and with which his priest and jugglers subdue his subjects, the entire subversion of his whole barbarous system of trade and revenue – and the uprooting, in a word, of all his, and his nation's, preconceived ideas, methods, and customs. In return for this, the white men are to trade with him by means of ships that are to come there one day or other; and are to quell infractions of the treaty by means of other white men, who are to learn how to draw the breath of life there, by some strong charm they certainly have not discovered yet. Can it be supposed that on this earth there lives a man who better knows than Obi, leering round upon the river's banks, the dull dead mangrove trees, the slimy and decaying earth, the rotting vegetation, that these are shadowy promises and shadowy threats, which he may give to the hot winds? In any breast in the white group about him, is there a dark presentiment of death (the pestilential air is heavier already with such whispers, to some noble hearts) half so certain as this savage's foreknowledge of the fate fast closing in? In the mind's-eye of any officer or seaman looking on, is there a picture of the bones of white men bleaching in a pestilential land, and of the timbers of their poor, abandoned, pillaged ships, showing, on the shore, like gigantic skeletons,

The Court of the Attah of Igara. From Allen's Narrative of an Expedition....

half so vivid as Obi's? 'Too much palaver,' says Obi, with good reason. 'Give me the presents and let me go home, and beat my tom-toms all night long, for joy!'

Yet these were the means by which the African people were to be awakened to a proper sense of their own degradation. For the conclusion of such treaties with such powers, the useful lives of scholars, students, mariners, and officers – more precious than a wilderness of Africans – were thrown away!

There was another monarch at another place on the Niger, a certain Attàh of Iddàh, 'whose feet, enclosed in very large red leather boots, surrounded with little bells, dangled carelessly over the side of the throne,' who spoke through a state functionary, called the king's mouth, and who had this very orthodox notion of the Divine Right: 'God made me after his image; I am all the same as God; and he appointed me a king.' With this good old sovereign a similar scene was enacted; and he, too, promised everything that was asked, and was particularly importunate to see the presents. He also was very much amused by the missionary's spectacles, it was supposed; and as royalty in these parts must not smile in public, the fan-bearers found it necessary to hide his face very often. The Attàh dines alone – like the Pope – and is equally infallible. Some land for the Model Farm was purchased of him, and the settlement established. The reading of the deed was very patiently attended to, 'unless,' say the writers of these volumes, with the frankness which distinguishes them – 'unless we mistook apathy for such a laudable bearing.'

So much is done towards the great awakening of the African people. By this time the Expedition has been in the river five weeks; fever has appeared on board of all the ships in the river; for the last three days especially, it has progressed with terrible rapidity. On board the *Soudan* only six persons can move about. On board the *Albert* the assistant surgeon lies at the point of death. On board the *Wilberforce* several are nearly at the same pass. Another day, and sixty in all are sick, and thirteen dead. 'Nothing but muttering delirium or suppressed groans are heard on every side on board the vessels.' Energy of character and strength of hope are lost, even among those not yet attacked. One officer, remarkable for fortitude and resignation, bursts into tears on being addressed, and being asked the reason, replies that it is involuntary weakness produced by the climate; though it afterwards appears that, 'in addition to this cause, he has been disheartened, during a little repose snatched from his duties, by a feverish dream of home and family.' An anxious consultation is held. Captain Trotter decides to send the sick back to the sea, in the *Soudan,* but Captain Allen knows the river will begin to fall straightway, and that the most unhealthy season will set in, and places his opinion on record that the ships had better all return, and make no further effort at that time to ascend the river.

DEPARTURE OF THE SICK

The *Soudan* was accordingly got ready with the utmost possible despatch, to receive her melancholy cargo, and Commander W. Allen was directed to send his sick on board. That officer, however, feeling perfectly convinced from his former experience of the river, and the present condition of the crews that in a very short time HMS *Wilberforce* would be reduced to the necessity of following the *Soudan,* requested permission to send such only of the sick as might desire to go; especially as he considered – in which his surgeon, Dr Pritchett, concurred – that the removal of the men in the state in which some of them were, would be attended with great risk. Only six expressed a wish to leave, the others, sixteen in number, preferred to remain by their ship. One man, on being asked whether he would like to go, said he thought we had got into a very bad place, and the sooner we were out of it the better, but he would stay by his ship.

In order to have as much air as possible for the sufferers, and to keep them from the other men, Commander W. Allen had a large screened berth fitted on the upper deck, in the middle of the vessel, well protected from the sun and the dews at night, by thick awnings, from which was suspended a large punkah.

Sunday, 19th – The *Soudan* came alongside the *Wilberforce* to receive our invalids, who took a melancholy farewell of their officers and messmates.

Prayers were read to the crews of both vessels. It was an affecting scene. The whole of one side of the little vessel was covered with invalids, and the cabins were full of officers; there was, indeed, no room for more.

The separation from so many of our companions under such circumstances could not be otherwise than painful to all; – the only cheering feature was in the hope that the attenuated beings who now departed would soon be within the influence of a more favourable climate, and that we might meet under happier auspices.

In a short time the steam was got up, and our little consort – watched by many commiserating eyes – rapidly glided out of view.

Only two or three days have elapsed since this change was effected, and now the *Wilberforce* has thirty-two men sick of the fever, leaving only thirteen, officers and seamen, capable of duty. She, too, returns to the sea, on Captain Allen's renewed protest and another council; and the *Albert* goes on up the melancholy river alone.

THE WILBERFORCE ON HER RETURN

We proceeded through these narrow and winding reaches with feelings very different to those we experienced in ascending the river. Then the elasticity of health and hope gave to the scenery a colouring of exceeding loveliness. The very silence and solitude had a soothing influence which invited to meditation and pleasing anticipations for the future. Now it was the stillness of death, – broken only by the strokes and echoes of our paddle-wheels and the melancholy song of the leadsmen, which seemed the knell and dirge of our dying comrades. The palm-trees, erst so graceful in their drooping leaves, were now gigantic hearse-like plumes.

So she drops down to Fernando Po, where the *Soudan* is lying, on whose small and crowded decks death has been, and is still, busy. Commanding-officer, surgeons, seamen, engineers, marines, all sick, many dead. Captain Allen, with the sick on board the *Wilberforce*, sails for Ascension, as a last hope of restoring the sick; and the *Soudan* is sent back to assist the *Albert*. She meets her coming out at the Gate of the Cemetery; thus:

THE ALBERT ON HER RETURN

It was a lovely morning and the scenery about the river looked very beautiful, affording a sad contrast to the dingy and deserted look of the *Albert*.

Many were of course the painful surmises as to the fate of those on board. On approaching, however, the melancholy truth was soon told. The fever had been doing its direst work; several were dead, many dying, and of all the officers, but two, Drs McWilliam and Stanger, were able to move about. The former presented himself and waved his hand, and one emaciated figure was seen to be raised up for a second. This was Captain Trotter, who in his anxiety to look at the *Soudan* again, had been lifted out of his cot.

A spectacle more full of painful contemplation could scarcely have been witnessed. Slowly and portentously, like a plague-ship filled with its dead and dying, onwards she moved in charge of her generous pilot, Mr Beecroft. Who would have thought that little more than two months previously she had entered that same river with an enterprising crew, full of life, and buoyant with bright hopes of accomplishing the objects on which all had so ardently entered?

The narrative of the *Albert's* solitary voyage, which occupied about a month, is given from the journal of Dr McWilliam, and furnishes, to our thinking, one of the most remarkable instances of quiet courage and unflinching constancy of purpose that is to be found in any book of travel ever written. The sickness spreading, Captain Trotter falling very ill, officers, engineers, and men lying alike disabled, and the *Albert's* head turned, in the necessity of despair, once more towards the sea, the two doctors on board, Dr McWilliam and Dr Stanger – names that should ever be memorable and honoured in the history of truly heroic enterprise – took upon themselves, in addition to the duty of attending the sick, the task of navigating the ship down the river. The former took charge of her, the latter worked the engines, and, both persevering by day and night – through all the horrors of such a voyage, with their friends raving and dying around them, and some, in the madness of the fever, leaping overboard – brought her in safety to the sea. We would fain hope this feat would live, in Dr McWilliam's few, plain, and modest words; and, better yet, in the grateful remembrance handed down by the survivors of this fatal expedition; when the desperate and cruel of whole generations of the world shall have fallen into oblivion.

Calling at the Model Farm as they came down the Niger, they found the superintendent, Mr Carr, and the schoolmaster and gardener – both Europeans – lying prostrate with fever. These were taken on board the *Albert* and brought away for the restoration of their health; and the settlement – now mustering about forty natives, in addition to the people brought from Sierra Leone – was left in the charge of one Ralph Moore, an American negro emigrant.

The rest of the sad story is soon told. The sea-breeze blew too late on many wasted forms, to shed its freshness on them for their restoration, and Death, Death, Death was aboard the *Albert* day and night. Captain Trotter, as the only means of saving his life, was with difficulty prevailed on to return to England; and after a long delay at Ascension and in the Bay of Amboises (in the absence of instructions from the Colonial Office), and when the Expedition, under Captain Allen, was on the eve of another hopeless attempt to ascend the Niger, it was ordered home. It being necessary to revisit the Model Farm, in obedience to orders, Lieutenant Webb, Captain Allen's first officer, immediately volunteered for that service; and with the requisite number of officers, and a black crew, took command of the *Wilberforce*, and once again went boldly up the fatal Niger. Disunion and dismay were rife at the Model Farm, on their arrival there; Mr Carr, who had returned from Fernando Po when restored to health, had been murdered – by direction of 'King Boy,' it would appear, and not without strong suspicion of co-operation on the part of our friend Obi – and the settlement was abandoned. Obi (though he is somewhat unaccountably complimented by Dr McWilliam) came out in his true colours on the *Wilberforce*'s return, and, not being by any means awakened to a proper sense of his own degradation, appears to have evinced an amiable intention of destroying the crew and seizing the ship. Being baffled in this design, however, by the coolness and promptitude of Lieutenant Webb and his officers, the white men happily left him behind in his own country, where he is no doubt ready at this moment, if still alive, to enter into any treaty that may be proposed to him, with presents to follow; and to be 'highly amused' again on the subject of the Slave Trade, and to beat his tom-toms all night long for joy.

The fever, which wrought such terrible desolation on this and the preceding Expedition, becomes a subject of painful interest to the readers of these volumes. The length to which our notice has already extended, prevents our extracting, as we had purposed, the account of it which is given in the present narrative. Of the predisposing causes, little can be positively stated; for the most delicate chemical tests failed to detect, in the air or water, the presence of those deleterious gases which were very confidently supposed to exist in both. It is preceded either by a state of great prostration, or great excitement, and unnatural indifference; it developes itself on board ship about the fifteenth day after the ascent of the river is commenced; a close and sultry atmosphere without any breeze stirring, is the atmosphere most unfavourable to it; it appears to yield to calomel in the first instance, and strong doses of quinine afterwards, more than to any other remedies; and it is remarkable that in cases of 'total abstinence' patients, it seems from the first to be hopelessly and surely fatal.

The history of this Expedition is the history of the Past, in reference to the heated visions of philanthropists for the railroad Christianisation of Africa and the abolition of the Slave Trade. May no popular cry, from Exeter Hall or elsewhere, ever make it, as to one single ship, the history of the Future! Such means are useless, futile, and we will venture to add – in despite of hats broad-brimmed or shovel-shaped, and coats of drab or black, with collars or without – wicked. No amount of philanthropy has a right to waste such valuable life as was squandered here, in the teeth of all experience and feasible pretence of hope. Between the civilized European and the barbarous African there is a great gulf set. The air that brings life to the latter brings death to the former. In the mighty revolutions of the wheel of time, some change in this regard may come about; but in this age of the world, all the white armies and white missionaries of the world would fall, as withered reeds, before the rolling of one African river. To change the customs even of civilized and educated men, and impress them with new ideas, is – we have good need to know it – a most difficult and slow proceeding; but to do this by ignorant and savage races, is a work which, like the progressive changes of the globe itself, requires a stretch of years that dazzles in the looking at. It is not, we conceive, within the likely providence of God, that Christianity shall start to the banks of the Niger, until it shall have overflowed all intervening space. The stone that is dropped into the ocean of ignorance at Exeter Hall, must make its widening circles, one beyond another, until they reach the negro's country in their natural expansion. There is a broad, dark sea between the Strand in London, and the Niger, where those rings are not yet shining; and through all that space they must appear, before the last one breaks upon the shore of Africa. Gently and imperceptibly the widening circle of enlightenment must stretch and stretch, from man to man, from people on to people, until there is a girdle round the earth; but no convulsive effort, or far-off aim, can make the last great outer circle first, and then come home at leisure to trace out the inner one. Believe it, African Civilisation, Church of England Missionary, and all other Missionary, Societies! The work at home must be completed thoroughly, or there is no hope abroad. To your tents, O Israel! but see they are your own tents! Set *them* in order; leave nothing to be done *there*; and outpost will convey your lesson on to outpost, until the naked armies of King Obi and King Boy are reached, and taught. Let a knowledge of the duty that man owes to man, and to his God, spread thus, by natural degrees and growth of example, to the outer shores of Africa, and it will float in safety up the rivers, never fear!

We will not do injustice to Captain Allen's scheme of future operations, by reproducing it, shorn of its fair proportions. As a most distinguished officer, and a highly accomplished gentleman, than whom there is no one living so well entitled to be heard, on all that relates to Africa, it merits, and assuredly will receive, great attention. We are not, on the ground we have just now indicated, so sanguine as he; but there is sound wisdom in his idea of approaching the black man through the black man, and in his conviction that he can only be successfully approached by a studied reference to the current of his own opinions and customs instead of ours. So true is this, that it is doubtful whether any European save Bruce – who had a perfectly marvellous genius for accommodating himself, not only to the African character, but to every variety of character with which he came in contact – has ever truly won to himself a mingled sentiment of confidence, respect, and fear in that country. So little has our Government profited by his example, that one of the foremost objects of this very Expedition is to repeat the self-same mistake with which Clapperton so astonished the King Boy and King Obi of his time, by running head-foremost at the abolition of the Slave Trade; which, of all possible objects, is the most inconceivable, unpalatable, and astounding to these barbarians!

Captain Allen need be under no apprehension that the failure of the Expedition will involve his readers in any confusion as to the sufferings and deserts of those who sacrificed themselves to achieve its unattainable objects. No generous mind can peruse this narrative without a glow of admiration and sympathy for himself and all concerned. The quiet spot by Lander's tomb, lying beyond the paths of guava and the dark-leaved trees, where old companions dear to his heart lie buried side by side beneath the sombre and almost impenetrable brushwood, is not to be ungratefully remembered, or lightly forgotten. Though the African is not yet awakened to a proper sense of his degradation, the resting-place of those brave men is sacred, and their history a solemn truth.

28

'A Truly British Judge'

(From a Correspondent) *The Examiner*, 19 August 1848

This piece is printed on the same page of *The Examiner* as the preceding article, in the political section of the paper (the Niger Expedition review is in the literary one). This is no direct evidence of Dickens's authorship, but a very persuasive case for the ascription is made out by Alec W. Brice in ' "A Truly British Judge". Another Article by Dickens', *The Dickensian*, Vol. 66 (1970), pp. 30–5. Brice reprints the article and supplies information about Sir

Thomas Platt, Baron of the Exchequer 1845–56, and notes that he was again attacked by Dickens in *The Examiner* over the Drouet case (see p. 156) on 21 April 1849; also that he appears as 'that truly British judge, Mr Baron Platt' in Dickens's *Household Narrative* (a monthly supplement to *HW*; August 1851, p. 170), when another judgment of his was ridiculed. Platt, educated at Harrow and Trinity College, Cambridge, was a strong Tory and hence, as Brice observes, 'fair game' for Dickens and his circle. Brice notes also that Gloucester Prison 'has a particularly grim reputation' at this time. Dickens may have heard about this case from Talfourd, who was counsel in another case at this Assizes. A report appeared in the *Gloucestershire Chronicle* on 12 August, but none has been found in the London papers.

The following scene is sketched, or rather copied *verbatim*, from nature; being the first scene of a melo-dramatic entertainment by a strolling company, with some Metropolitan stars, lately 'on circuit' at Gloucester.

It *was* a maxim of English jurisprudence that punishment should be proportioned to the crime, and that sentence and its execution should follow conviction with certainty. Verily! there is nothing more edifying than a morning at court with 'a thorough English Judge.' – *Reporter*.

CROWN COURT, GLOUCESTER, *Thursday*, 10th August, 1848 –
The Court is opened with all due solemnities.

RICHARD HOOPER, aged *ten* years (the first prisoner, peeping over the dock), is charged with stealing a purse with five shillings and threepence from Mrs Albinia Cooke on the Queen's highway, at Leckhampton. Verdict – Guilty.

Mr BARON PLATT (to the Gaoler) – 'How do they flog the boys here in your gaol? on the back, or the same as they do at school, *or how?*'

GAOLER – 'The same as they do at school, my Lord!'

The JUDGE – 'Richard Hooper! you have been convicted of stealing; you are very young: *the sentence of the Court* upon you is that you be *imprisoned* in the gaol or penitentiary of this county for the space of *one month*, and that during that period you—

[Mr HEMP, Clerk of Arraigns, interrupting by a whisper inaudible to the Judge.]

JUDGE (aloud to the Clerk of Arraigns) – 'What! is there *no gaol* in this county?'

[Clerk of Arraigns whispers again, that for *felony* there is no power *to flog*.]

JUDGE (to the prisoner) – 'I fear that if I send you to gaol you will come out a worse thief than you go in – I had better transport you. *The sentence of the Court*, therefore, is that you be *transported* beyond the seas for the space of *seven years*. (Aside to the prisoner) – This sentence will *not be carried into effect*, but you'll be sent to a place where you'll be taken care of, and taught better, and if you behave well you'll be discharged in a short time.'

CROWN COURT, *Friday Morning.* – Court opens.

Mr Baron Platt (to the Gaoler) – 'Put up Richard Hooper.' The urchin is accordingly 'put up.' There is breathless attention.

Judge (to prisoner) – 'Richard Hooper! I have bestowed a great deal of consideration upon your case, and I *revoke* the sentence of transportation which I passed upon you yesterday. *The sentence of the Court* upon you is that you be *imprisoned* in the Penitentiary of this county for the space of *two years*, to be limited to *one year* if you are well conducted and make progress in learning the trade which will be there taught you. In short, the duration of your punishment will entirely *depend upon yourself.*

Some comment upon this method of administering criminal justice may not be altogether impertinent. A boy of ten years – an infant of tender age – steals a purse. The Judge's first impression is that one month's privation of his liberty, in addition to the six weeks' imprisonment he had undergone since his commitment for trial, was a *punishment proportioned to the offence*, and accordingly awarded it. The Clerk of Arraigns intercepts the completion and recording of the sentence by reminding the Judge that he had *no power to flog*; and, from considerations to which no criminal judge who had a proper sense of the gravity of his office would pay the slightest attention, Justice then exhibits her caprices in awarding *seven years' transportation*, in revoking that sentence, and ultimately in falling back upon *two years'* imprisonment, as (upon consideration) the true measure of this urchin's iniquity. Of course one cannot irreverently assume that the learned Judge, in at last making up his mind, so agitated upon the fate of this little wicked boy, deprived him of his liberty – tore him from his rural home at the picturesque village of Leckhampton – separated him, at his tender years, from the sweet face of green and flowery nature, and the sweeter sympathies of kindred – and consigned him for two tedious years to the contamination, the stone cells and passages, the chilling damps, the rugged turnkeys, stolid chaplains, and staring red brick walls of the great Gloucester Penitentiary, out of a *tender regard* for the child's future morals.

To suppose this, would be to suspect Baron Platt of utter ignorance of human nature and total unfitness for the office of a criminal Judge; for he has no right to increase the punishment for the benefit of the offender.

Yet it is difficult to reconcile the vacillating conduct of the serio-comic functionary upon this occasion with any other theory. Whatever may have been the motive (good we doubt not), the exhibition before the people on this occasion is unfortunate; – Justice halts, reels, and finally stumbles over the moral difficulties presented by the case of this little boy, who probably might have returned to Leckhampton, and his parents' cottage, sufficiently corrected by the first sentence; and will be no better in heart, if improved in tuition, by even *one* year in that frightful Penitentiary. We cannot help thinking that the Judge who thus lightly deals out, recals, increases, revokes, and remodels such sentences, has no true sense of the value of human liberty, nor sympathies with human and erring nature.

29

Review: *The Poetry of Science, or Studies of the Physical Phenomena of Nature,* by Robert Hunt

The Examiner, 9 December 1848

Robert Hunt was Keeper of Mining Records at the Museum of Practical Geology 1843–83 and a lecturer on mechanical science and experimental physics at the Royal School of Mines. He was a prolific writer on scientific subjects, the author of *A Popular Treatise on the Art of Photography* (1841) and *Researches on Light* (1844). In 1856 he contributed an article, 'Gold in Great Britain', to *HW* (Vol. 13, pp. 541–3). *The Poetry of Science* was, Hunt's Preface announces, an attempt 'to link together those scientific facts which bear directly and visibly upon Natural Phenomena, and to show that they have a value superior to their mere economic applications, in their power of exalting the mind to the contemplation of the Universe'. The opening sentences of his Introduction read: 'The True is the Beautiful. Whenever this becomes evident to our senses, its influences are of a soul-elevating character.' Chapters follow on such subjects as Motion, Gravitation, Molecular Forces, Light, Electricity, Magnetism, Time-Geological Phenomena and Phenomena of Vegetable Life. Throughout, Hunt seeks, as Dickens explains, to demonstrate how fictions about the natural world (fables, poetic imaginings, ancient superstitions) often point us to scientific truths and how 'the task of wielding the wand of science ... is one which leads the mind through nature up to nature's God' (p. 398):

'Great Pan is dead,' but the mountains are not voiceless; they speak in a more convincing tone; and instead of the ear catching the dying echo of an obscure truth, it is gladdened with the full, clear note of nature in

the sweetest voice proclaiming secrets which superstition dared not even
seek for. (p. 387)

The publisher and amateur geologist Robert Chambers's immensely
popular, anonymously published *Vestiges of the Natural History of Creation*
(1844) put forward a pre-Darwinian evolutionary theory of 'Progressive
Development' involving the idea of the transmutation of species, resulting
from universal laws ordained by a Creator, but not postulating any theory
of natural selection. *Vestiges* was condemned by churchmen and fiercely
attacked as over-credulous by professional scientists like Hunt, but had a
huge impact on the public mind and had reached its sixth edition by 1847.
It is noteworthy that Dickens goes out of his way to praise the work in this
review, the only piece of writing of his that we have which is directly on
science.

Dickens's review closely follows Hunt's arguments and examples (the
astronomical observations leading to the discovery of the planet Neptune
are mentioned on p. 23 of the book). The passage on p. 307 about geological
speculation objected to by Dickens reads in part as follows:

A few observations are made over a limited area ... and at once the
mind, 'fancy free', penetrates the profound depths of the earth, and
imagination ... creates causes by which every effect is to be interpreted.
Such observers, generally ignorant of the first principles of physics,
knowing little of mineralogy, and less of chemistry, to say nothing of
palaeontology ... boldly assume premises which are untenable, and think
they have explained a phenomenon, given to the world a truth, when
they have merely promulgated an unsubstantiated speculation....

The tone of exclusive professionalism here would have irritated Dickens,
but his overall enthusiasm for Hunt's book is manifest in the review. There
is a clear parallel between Hunt's lament that 'as we progress from fable
to fact, much of the soul-sentiment which made the romantic holy ... is
too frequently merged in a cheerless philosophy which ... reduces the mind
to a mechanical condition, delighting in the accumulation of facts' (pp.
175–9) and Dickens's later satire on Gradgrindian utilitarianism in *Hard
Times* (1854), as well as his whole programme for *HW* as set forth in his
'Preliminary Word' (see p. 175).

MS. Forster Collection, Victoria and Albert Museum. This confirms that
Dickens excerpted several more passages from Hunt than are given in the
MP reprint of this review. He used Forster's copy of the book, which is
also in the Forster Collection and shows Dickens's markings. All the excerpts
are present in the *Examiner* text. They are as follows (Dickens's headings):
'The Electricity of a Tear': Hunt, p. xxiii, together with Hunt's long

footnote (p. 442) quoting Faraday's *Experimental Researches on Electricity*; 'Gravitation': Hunt, p. 21f.; 'Light': Hunt, p. 135: passage begins, 'Light is necessary to life; the world was a dead chaos before its creation and mute disorder would again be the consequence of its annihilation'; 'First knowledge of electricity': Hunt, p. 161f.; 'A Brown Stone': Hunt, p. 203f. (about magnetism). All these precede the extracts reprinted in the *MP* text.

Judging from certain indications scattered here and there in this book, we presume that its author would not consider himself complimented by the remark that we are perhaps indebted for the publication of such a work to the author of the *Vestiges of the Natural History of Creation*, who, by rendering the general subject popular, and awakening an interest and spirit of inquiry in many minds, where these had previously lain dormant, has created a reading public – not exclusively scientific or philosophical – to whom such offerings can be hopefully addressed. This, however, we believe to be the case; and in this, as we conceive, the writer of that remarkable and well-abused book has not rendered his least important service to his own time.

The design of Mr Hunt's volume is striking and good. To show that the facts of science are at least as full of poetry, as the most poetical fancies ever founded on an imperfect observation and a distant suspicion of them (as, for example, among the ancient Greeks); to show that if the Dryades no longer haunt the woods, there is, in every forest, in every tree, in every leaf, and in every ring on every sturdy trunk, a beautiful and wonderful creation, always changing, always going on, always bearing testimony to the stupendous workings of Almighty Wisdom, and always leading the student's mind from wonder on to wonder, until he is wrapt and lost in the vast worlds of wonder by which he is surrounded from his cradle to his grave; it is a purpose worthy of the natural philosopher, and salutary to the spirit of the age. To show that Science, truly expounding nature, can, like nature herself, restore in some new form whatever she destroys; that, instead of binding us, as some would have it, in stern utilitarian chains, when she has freed us from a harmless superstition, she offers to our contemplation something better and more beautiful, something which, rightly considered, is more elevating to the soul, nobler and more stimulating to the soaring fancy; is a sound, wise, wholesome object. If more of the learned men who have written on these themes had had it in their minds, they would have done more good, and gathered upon their track many followers on whom its feeblest and most distant trace has only now begun to shine.

Science has gone down into the mines and coal-pits, and before the safety-lamp the Gnomes and Genii of those dark regions have disappeared. But, in their stead, the process by which metals are engendered in the course of ages; the growth of plants which, hundreds of fathoms underground, and in black darkness, have still a sense of the sun's presence in the sky, and derive some portion of the subtle essence of their life from his influence; the histories of mighty forests and great tracts of land carried down into the sea, by the same process which is active in the Mississippi and such great rivers at this hour; are made familiar to us. Sirens, mermaids, shining cities glittering at the bottom of the quiet seas, and in deep lakes, exist no longer; but in their place, Science, their destroyer, shows us whole coasts of coral reef constructed by the labours of minute creatures; points to our own chalk cliffs and limestone rocks, as made of the dust of myriads of generations of infinitesimal beings that have passed away; reduces the very element of water into its constituent airs, and re-creates it at her pleasure. Caverns in rocks, choked with rich treasures shut up from all but the enchanted hand, Science has blown to atoms, as she can rend and rive the rocks themselves; but in those rocks she has found, and read aloud, the great stone book which is the history of the earth, even when darkness sat upon the face of the deep. Along their craggy sides she has traced the footprints of birds and beasts, whose shapes were never seen by man. From within them she has brought the bones, and pieced together the skeletons, of monsters that would have crushed the noted dragons of the fables at a blow. The stars that stud the firmament by night are watched no more from lonely towers by enthusiasts or impostors, believing, or feigning to believe, those great worlds to be charged with the small destinies of individual men down here; but two astronomers, far apart, each looking from his solitary study up into the sky, observe, in a known star, a trembling which forewarns them of the coming of some unknown body through the realms of space, whose attraction at a certain period of its mighty journey causes that disturbance. In due time it comes, and passes out of the disturbing path; the old star shines at peace again; and the new one, evermore to be associated with the honoured names of Le Verrier and Adams, is called Neptune! The astrologer has faded out of the castle turret-room (which overlooks a railroad now), and forebodes no longer that because the light of yonder planet is diminishing, my lord will shortly die; but the professor of an exact science has arisen in his stead, to *prove* that a ray of light must occupy a period of six years in travelling to the earth from the nearest of the fixed stars; and that if one of the remote fixed stars were 'blotted out of heaven' to-day, several generations of the mortal inhabitants of this earth must perish out of time, before the fact of its obliteration could be known to man!

This ample compensation, in respect of poetry alone, that Science has given us in return for what she has taken away, it is the main object of

Mr Hunt's book to elucidate. The subject is very ably dealt with, and the object very well attained. We might object to an occasional discursiveness, and sometimes we could have desired to be addressed in a plainer form of words. Nor do we quite perceive the force of Mr Hunt's objection (at p. 307) to certain geological speculations; which we must be permitted to believe many intelligent men to be capable of making, and reasonably sustaining, on a knowledge of certain geological facts; albeit they are neither practical chemists nor palæontologists. But the book displays a fund of knowledge, and is the work of an eloquent and earnest man; and, as such, we are too content and happy to receive it, to enlarge on these points.

We subjoin a few short extracts.

HOW WE 'COME LIKE SHADOWS, SO DEPART'

A plant exposed to the action of natural or artificial decomposition passes into air, leaving but a few grains of solid matter behind it. An animal, in like manner, is gradually resolved into 'thin air.' Muscle, and blood, and bones having undergone the change, are found to have escaped as gases, 'leaving only a pinch of dust,' which belongs to the more stable mineral world. Our dependency on the atmosphere is therefore evident. We derive our substance from it – we are, after death, resolved again into it. We are really but fleeting shadows. Animal and vegetable forms are little more than consolidated masses of the atmosphere. The sublime creations of the most gifted bard cannot rival the beauty of this, the highest and the truest poetry of science. Man has divined such changes by the unaided powers of reason, arguing from the phenomena which science reveals in unceasing action around him. The Grecian sage's doubts of his own identity was only an extension of a great truth beyond the limits of our reason. Romance and superstition resolve the spiritual man into a visible form of extreme ethereality in the spectral creations, 'clothed in their own horror,' by which their reigns have been perpetuated.

When Shakespeare made his charming Ariel sing –

> 'Full fathom five thy father lies,
> Of his bones are coral made,
> Those are pearls that were his eyes,
> Nothing of him that doth fade,
> But doth suffer a sea change,
> Into something rich and strange;'

he little thought how correctly he painted the chemical changes, by which decomposing animal matter is replaced by a siliceous or calcareous formation.

Why Mr Hunt should be of opinion that Shakespeare 'little thought' how wise he was, we do not altogether understand. Perhaps he founds the supposition on Shakespeare's not having been recognised as a practical chemist or palæontologist.

We conclude with the following passage, which seems to us strikingly suggestive of the shortness and hurry of our little life which is rounded with a sleep, and the calm majesty of Nature.

RELATIVE IMPORTANCE OF TIME TO MAN AND NATURE

All things on the earth are the result of chemical combination. The operation by which the commingling of molecules and the interchange of atoms take place, we can imitate in our laboratories; but in nature they proceed by slow degrees, and, in general, in our hands they are distinguished by suddenness of action. In nature chemical power is distributed over a long period of time, and the process of change is scarcely to be observed. By art we concentrate chemical force, and expend it in producing a change which occupies but a few hours at most.

30

The American Panorama

The Examiner, 16 December 1848

For the great popularity of Panoramas and Dioramas in early Victorian England, see p. 201; and for the New-York-born John Banvard and his career, see R.D. Altick, *The Shows of London* (1978), pp. 204–6. Altick suggests that the three-mile length claimed for the painting was probably an exaggeration, but the *Dictionary of American Biography* notes that 'the fidelity of the portrayal was testified by a number of Mississippi river captains and pilots' (see the testimonial, signed by the Mayor of Louisville, reproduced in Michael Slater, *Dickens on America and the Americans* [1979], p. 213). Dickens had his own 1842 experience of the Mississippi to compare Banvard's painting with and his one reservation about the colour of the water in the Panorama may be compared with his description of the river in *American Notes*, where he calls it 'an enormous ditch ... running liquid mud'. On the same day that the *Examiner* notice was published, Dickens wrote to Banvard (who had invited him to a private view) saying that he was 'in the highest degree interested and pleased by your picture – by its truthfulness – ... – by the striking and original manner in which the scenes it represents, are plainly presented to the spectator' (*Pilgrim*, Vol. v, p. 458). The 'odd original humour' of Banvard's commentary, replete, according to the *Illustrated London News* (quoted by Altick), 'with Jonathanisms and jokes, poetry and patter, which delight his audience mightily', did not give universal pleasure. The *Pilgrim* editors quote Henry Crabb Robinson's diary: 'It is an execrable daub of a picture. And the intense vulgarity of the Yankee explainer actually excited disgust.'

In his second paragraph Dickens is referring to the exquisite Dioramas (of the Alps, Venice, etc.) painted by his much-loved older friend Clarkson Stanfield for the Christmas pantomimes at Drury Lane in the early 1830s (for details, see P.T. van der Merwe, *The Spectacular Career of Clarkson Stanfield*, Tyne and Wear County Council Museums [1979], pp. 87–92).

MS. Forster Collection, Victoria and Albert Museum. The opening of the second sentence in the *Examiner* text, 'With one or two exceptions', does not appear in the MS.

A very extraordinary exhibition is open at the Egyptian Hall, Piccadilly, under the title of 'Banvard's Geographical Panorama of the Mississippi and Missouri Rivers.' With one or two exceptions, its remarkable claims to public notice seem scarcely to have been recognised as they deserve. We recommend them to the consideration of all holiday-makers and sight-seers this Christmas.

It may be well to say what the panorama is *not*. It is not a refined work of art (nor does it claim to be, in Mr Banvard's modest description); it is not remarkable for accuracy of drawing, or for brilliancy of colour, or for subtle effects of light and shade, or for any approach to any of the qualities of those delicate and beautiful pictures by Mr Stanfield which used, once upon a time, to pass before our eyes in like manner. It is not very skilfully set off by the disposition of the artificial light; it is not assisted by anything but a pianoforte and a seraphine.

But it is a picture three miles long, which occupies two hours in its passage before the audience. It is a picture of one of the greatest streams in the known world, whose course it follows for upwards of three thousand miles. It is a picture irresistibly impressing the spectator with a conviction of its plain and simple truthfulness, even though that were not guaranteed by the best testimonials. It is an easy means of travelling, night and day, without any inconvenience from climate, steamboat company, or fatigue, from New Orleans to the Yellow Stone Bluffs (or from the Yellow Stone Bluffs to New Orleans, as the case may be), and seeing every town and settlement upon the river's banks, and all the strange wild ways of life that are afloat upon its waters. To see this painting is, in a word, to have a thorough understanding of what the great American river is – except, we believe, in the colour of its water – and to acquire a new power of testing the descriptive accuracy of its best describers.

These three miles of canvas have been painted by one man, and there he is, present, pointing out what he deems most worthy of notice. This is his history. Poor, untaught, wholly unassisted, he conceives the idea – a truly American idea – of painting 'the largest picture in the world.' Some capital must be got for the materials, and the acquisition of that is his primary object. First, he starts 'a floating diorama' on the Wabash river, which topples over when people come to see it, and keeps all the company at the pumps for dear life. This entertainment drawing more water than money, and being set upon, besides, by robbers armed with bowie-knives and rifles, is abandoned. Then, he paints a panorama of Venice, and exhibits it in the West successfully, until it goes down in a steamer on the Western waters. Then he sets up a museum at St Louis, which fails. Then he comes down to Cincinnati, where he does no better. Then, without a farthing, he rows away on the Ohio in a small boat, and lives, like a wild man, upon nuts; until he sells a revolving pistol which cost him twelve dollars, for five-and-twenty. With the proceeds of this commercial transaction he buys a larger boat, lays in a little store of calicoes and cottons, and rows away again among the solitary settlers along-shore, bartering his goods for bee's-wax. Thus, in course of time, he earns enough to buy a little skiff, and go to work upon the largest picture in the world!

In his little skiff he travels thousands of miles, with no companions but his pencil, rifle, and dog, making the preparatory sketches for the largest picture in the world. Those completed, he erects a temporary building at Louisville, Kentucky, in which to paint the largest picture in the world. Without the least help, even in the grinding of his colours or the splitting of the wood for his machinery, he falls to work, and keeps at work; maintaining himself meanwhile, and buying more colours, wood, and canvas, by doing odd jobs in the decorative way. At last he finishes the largest picture in the world, and opens it for exhibition on a stormy night, when not a single 'human' comes to see it. Not discouraged yet, he goes about among the boatmen, who are well acquainted with the river, and gives them free admissions to the largest picture in the world. The boatmen come to see it, are astonished at it, talk about it. 'Our country' wakes up from a rather sullen doze at Louisville, and comes to see it too. The upshot is, that it succeeds; and here it is in London, with its painter standing on a little platform by its side explaining it; and probably, by this time next year, it and he may be in Timbuctoo.

Few can fail to have some interest in such an adventure and in such an adventurer, and they will both repay it amply. There is a mixture of shrewdness and simplicity in the latter, which is very prepossessing; a modesty, and honesty, and an odd original humour, in his manner of telling what he has to tell, that give it a peculiar relish. The picture itself, as an indisputably true and faithful representation of a wonderful region – wood and water, river and prairie, lonely log hut and clustered city rising in the forest – is replete with interest throughout. Its incidental revelations of the different states of society, yet in transition, prevailing at different points of these three thousand miles – slaves and free republicans, French and Southerners; immigrants from abroad, and restless Yankees and Down-Easters ever steaming somewhere; alligators, store-boats, show-boats, theatre-boats, Indians, buffaloes, deserted tents of extinct tribes, and bodies of dead Braves, with their pale faces turned up to the night-sky, lying still and solitary in the wilderness, nearer and nearer to which the outposts of civilisation are approaching with gigantic strides to tread their people down, and erase their very track from the earth's face teem with suggestive matter. We are not disposed to think less kindly of a country when we see so much of it, although our sense of its immense responsibility may be increased.

It would be well to have a panorama, three miles long, of England. There might be places in it worth looking at, a little closer than we see them now; and worth the thinking of, a little more profoundly. It would be hopeful, too, to see some things in England, part and parcel of a *moving* panorama: and not of one that stood still, or had a disposition to go backward.

31

Judicial Special Pleading

The Examiner, 23 December 1848

During the winter and spring of 1847–8 the great pro-democratic movement known as Chartism had been causing alarm in the British Government and the property-owning classes. Fears of imminent revolution were heightened by the toppling of King Louis-Philippe in France in February. As the time drew nearer for the mass demonstration planned for 10 April, when huge numbers of Chartists were due to assemble on Kennington Common, south London, and to march from there to Parliament to petition for the third time for the passing of the People's Charter, tension continued to mount and thousands of special constables were sworn in as auxiliaries to the regular police. The event turned out to be a fiasco, but the ruling classes had been seriously disturbed, especially by the fiery speeches of the so-called 'physical force' Chartists, advocates of what we should today call 'direct action'. There were many arrests and a series of political trials began in July in London and elsewhere. In his *1848: The British State and the Chartist Movement* (1987) J. Savile notes that all the judges involved responded similarly to the situation. Their fear of the threat to property and the dangerous state of Ireland (the Chartist leader Feargus O'Connor had sought to link the movement with agitation for Irish political reform) led to the 'jettisoning of any element of judicial impartiality': the trials were 'exercises in the miscarriage of justice; the obliteration of reason by prejudice and the subversion of legal principles by partisanship of a virulent order' (p. 174). Sir Edward Alderson, Baron of the Exchequer since 1834, was no exception. He was a conservative and a strong churchman and his charge to the Chester jury, printed in full in *The Times* on 8 December 1848, was 'a lengthy, highly political speech, delivered with the purpose of convincing the jury that their political instincts condemning the accused radicals were properly founded in history and contemporary fact' (Savile, p. 176). He ended his charge by urging jurors to help the poor as much as possible, adding the sublime comment that 'affording an opportunity of exercising virtue in this manner might be one reason why Providence permitted so much suffering'.

Dickens drew on the French historian Louis Adolphe Thiers to controvert Alderson's interpretation of history. A copy of Thiers's *History of the French Revolution*, translated by F. Shoberl (5 vols, 1838), was in Dickens's library (*Pilgrim*, Vol IV, p. 712). The anecdote about the Duke of Orléans (nicknamed Égalité on account of his siding with the people against his cousin Louis XVI) spreading public tables in the streets for the paupers of Paris in 1788–9 appears in a footnote on p. 10 of Vol. I and the long quotation is on p. 20 of the same volume (Dickens slightly alters the last sentence, which reads in the original: 'It subsisted therefore by the sweat of the brow; it defended with its blood the upper classes of society, without being able to subsist itself'). Dickens's Carlyle-inspired view of the French Revolution as the inevitable consequence of extreme oppression, 'demonising' the people, was later given memorable expression in *A Tale of Two Cities* (1859): 'Crush humanity out of shape once more, under similar hammers, and it will twist itself into the same tortured forms' (Book II, Ch. 15).

The Bickerstaff reference in paragraph 3 is to Sir Richard Steele's *Tatler*, no. 220 (5 September 1710; see *The Tatler*, ed. D.F. Bond [1987], Vol III, p. 150). Isaac Bickerstaff was a fictitious personage invented by Swift for satirical purposes and taken over by Steele as the supposed author of his periodical.

MS. Forster Collection, Victoria and Albert Museum, marked 'Leader'. There are one or two very minor variants from the *Examiner* text, e.g., capital letters for 'Wrath' and 'Persecution' (para. 3).

It is unnecessary for us to observe that we have not the least sympathy with physical-force chartism in the abstract, or with the tried and convicted physical-force chartists in particular. Apart from the atrocious designs to which these men, beyond all question, willingly and easily subscribed, even if it be granted that such extremes of wickedness were mainly suggested by the spies in whom their dense ignorance confided, they have done too much damage to the cause of rational liberty and freedom all over the world to be regarded in any other light than as enemies of the common weal, and the worst foes of the common people.

But, for all this, we would have the language of common-sense and knowledge addressed to these offenders – especially from the Bench. They need it very much; and besides that the truth should be spoken at all times, it is desirable that it should always appear in conjunction with the gravity and authority of the judicial ermine.

Mr Baron Alderson, we regret to observe, opened the late special commission for the county of Chester with a kind of judicial special-constableism by no means edifying. In sporting phrase, he 'went in' upon the general subject of Revolution with a determination to win; and as nothing is easier than for a man, wigged or unwigged, to say what he pleases when he has all the talk to himself and there is nobody to answer him, he improved the occasion after a somewhat startling manner. It is important that it should not be left wholly unnoticed. On Mr Isaac Bickerstaff's magic thermometer, at his apartment in Shoe Lane, the Church was placed between zeal and moderation; and Mr Bickerstaff observed that if the enchanted liquor rose from the central point, Church, too high in zeal, it was in danger of going up to wrath, and from wrath to persecution. The substitution of 'Bench' for 'Church' by the wise old censor of Great Britain, would no doubt have been attended with the same result.

Mr Baron Alderson informed the grand jury, for their edification, that 'previous to the Revolution in France, of 1790, the physical comforts possessed by the poor greatly exceeded those possessed by them subsequent to that event.' Before we pass to Mr Baron Alderson's proof in support of this allegation, we would inquire whether, at this time of day, any rational man supposes that the first Revolution in France was an event that could have been avoided, or that is difficult to be accounted for, on looking back? Whether it was not the horrible catastrophe of a drama, which had already passed through every scene and shade of progress, inevitably leading on to that fearful conclusion? Whether there is any record, in the world's history, of a people among whom the arts and sciences, and the refinements of civilised life existed, so oppressed, degraded, and utterly miserable, as the mass of the French population were before that Revolution? Physical comforts! No such thing was known among the French people – among *the people* – for years before the Revolution. They had died of sheer want and famine, in numbers. The hunting-trains of their kings had ridden over their bodies in the Royal Forests. Multitudes had gone about, crying and howling for bread, in the streets of Paris. The line of road from Versailles to the capital had been blocked up by starvation and nakedness pouring in from the departments. The tables spread by Égalité Orléans in the public streets had been besieged by the foremost stragglers of a whole nation of paupers, on the face of every one of whom the shadow of the coming guillotine was black. An infamous feudality and a corrupt government had plundered and ground them down, year after year, until they were reduced to a condition of distress which has no parallel. As their wretchedness deepened, the wantonness and luxury of their oppressors heightened, until the very fashions and customs of the upper classes ran mad from being unrestrained, and became monstrous.

'All,' says Thiers, 'was monopolised by a few hands, and the burdens bore upon a single class. The nobility and the clergy possessed nearly two-thirds of the landed property. The other third, belonging to the people, paid taxes to the king, a multitude of feudal dues to the nobility, the tithe to the clergy, and was, moreover, liable to the devastations of noble sportsmen and their game. The taxes on consumption weighed heavily on the great mass, and consequently on the people. The mode in which they were levied was vexatious. The gentry might be in arrear with impunity; the people, on the other hand, ill-treated and imprisoned, were doomed to suffer in body, in default of goods. They defended with their blood the upper classes of society, without being able to subsist themselves.'

Bad as the state of things was which succeeded to the Revolution, and must always follow any such dire convulsion, if there be anything in history that is certain, it is certain that the French people had NO physical comforts when the Revolution occurred. And when Mr Baron Alderson talks to the grand jury of that Revolution being a mere struggle for 'political rights,' he talks (with due submission to him) nonsense, and loses an opportunity of pointing his discourse to the instruction of the chartists. It was a struggle on the part of the people for social recognition and existence. It was a struggle for vengeance against intolerable oppressors. It was a struggle for the overthrow of a system of oppression, which in its contempt of all humanity, decency, and natural rights, and in its systematic degradation of the people, had trained them to be the demons that they showed themselves, when they rose up and cast it down for ever.

Mr Baron Alderson's proof of his position would be a strange one, by whomsoever adduced, but is an especially strange one to be put forward by a high functionary, one of whose most important duties is the examination and sifting of evidence, with a view to its being the better understood by minds unaccustomed to such investigations.

It had been assumed, on very competent authority, that the physical comforts of the poor might be safely judged of by the quantity of meat consumed by the population; and, taking this as the criterion, the statistics of Paris gave the following results: In 1789, during the period of the old monarchy, the quantity of meat consumed was 147 lb. per man; in 1817, after the Bourbon dynasty had been restored to the throne, subsequent to the Revolution, it was 110 lb. 2 oz. per man; and in 1827, the medium period between the restoration of the Bourbons and the present time, the average was still about 110 lb.; while, after the Revolution of 1830, it fell to 98 lb. 11 oz., and at this period it was in all probability still less.'

The statistics, *of Paris*, in 1789! When the Court, displaying extraordinary magnificence, was in Paris; when the three orders, all the great dignitaries of the state, and all their immense train of followers and dependants, were in Paris; when the aristocracy, making their last effort at accommodation with the king, were in Paris, and remained there until the close of the year; when there was the great procession to the church of Notre Dame, in Paris; when the opening of the States-General took place, in Paris; when the Commons constituted themselves the National Assembly, in Paris; when the electors, assembled from sixty districts, refused to depart from Paris; when the garden of the Palais Royal was the scene of the nightly assemblage of more foreigners, debauchees, and loungers, than had ever been seen in Paris; when people came into Paris from all parts of France; when there was all the agitation, uproar, revelling, banquetting, and delirium in Paris, which distinguished that year of great events; – when, in short, the meat-eating classes were all in Paris, and all at high-feasting in the whirl and fury of such a time!

Mr Baron Alderson takes this very year of 1789, and dividing the quantity of meat consumed by the population of Paris, sets before the grand jury the childish absurdity of there having been 147 lb. of meat per man, as a proof of the physical comforts of the people! This year of 1789 being on record as the hardest ever known by the French people since the disasters of Louis XIV and the immortal charity of Fénélon! This year of

1789 being the year when Mirabeau was speaking in the Assembly of 'famished Paris'; when the king was forced to receive deputations of women who demanded bread; and when they rang out to all Paris, 'Bread! rise up for bread!' with the great bell of the Hôtel de Ville!

It would be idle to dissect such evidence more minutely. It is too gross and palpable. We will conclude with a final and grave reason, as it seems to us, for noticing this serious mistake on the part of Mr Baron Alderson.

That learned judge is much deceived if he imagines that there are not, among the chartists, men possessed of sufficient information to detect such juggling, and make the most of it. Those active and mischievous agents of the chartists who live by lecturing, will do more with such a charge as this, than they could do with all the misery in England for the next twelve months. In any common history of the French Revolution, they have the proof against Mr Baron Alderson under their hands. The grade of education and intellect they address is particularly prone to accept a brick as a specimen of a house, and its ready conclusion from such an exposition is, that the whole system which rules and restrains it is a falsehood and a cheat.

It was but the other day that Mr Baron Alderson stated to some chartist prisoners, as a fact which everybody knew, that any man in England who was industrious and persevering could obtain political power. Are there no industrious and persevering men in England on whom this comfortable doctrine casts a slur? We rather think the chartist lecturers might find out some.

32

Review: *The Rising Generation, a series of twelve Drawings on Stone*. By John Leech. From his Original Designs in the Gallery of Mr Punch

The Examiner, 30 December 1848

John Leech was by this time a good friend of Dickens's, having worked with him as illustrator of *A Christmas Carol* and chief illustrator of the succeeding Christmas Books (1843–8). Born in London of cultured but not wealthy parents, Leech had been educated at the Charterhouse School, where he began a lifelong friendship with Thackeray; he subsequently abandoned the study of medicine for an artistic career, which did not really take off until he began to draw for *Punch* in 1841. From March 1843 he was the paper's chief cartoonist and his comic sketches of contemporary middle-class life and manners were particularly popular. M.H. Spielmann comments on Leech's 'exceptional love of beauty ... those dainty backgrounds in which the loveliest scenery is so skilfully reproduced' (*The History of 'Punch'* [1895], p. 429) and the 'pretty woman' figure ('short in stature ... with big eyes and rounded chin, with bewitching dimples and pretty ringlets') that is so ubiquitous in his cartoons, a figure based on Leech's adored little wife. Among the various cartoon-series Leech did for *Punch* was the one showing middle-class children behaving in a precocious manner, sometimes using a catch-phrase of the day, 'the rising generation'.

The 'old caricature' of the farmer's daughter at the harpsichord that Dickens refers to is by Gillray: 'Farmer Giles and his Wife shewing off their daughter Betty to their Neighbours ...' (1809). The Leech cartoon on p. 9 of the *Punch* Almanack for 1849, 'Autumnal Fashions for the Ladies', shows several of his 'pretty women' (two shown smoking cigars, intended to underline the wilful unfemininity of their behaviour) dressed in masculine-looking fitted overcoats outside a shop advertising 'the Lady's Slap-up Paletot'.

The phrase 'Virgil, dog's-eared and defaced' in paragraph 5 alludes to the use of Virgil as a public school textbook, perhaps meaning that the boy will deface his copy by scribbling her name over it. The allusion to lecturing on 'the Concrete in connection with the Will' would seem to be a joke about the contemporary vogue for Transcendentalist philosophy. The reference (p. 147) to mention of Cruikshank in the *Quarterly Review* concerns a review of *Oliver Twist* by Richard Ford which appeared in the *Quarterly* in June 1839 (Vol. 64). In it Ford wrote:

> Long before Boz was heard of, George Cruikshank had captured a snug niche in the Temple of Fame – one far more secure than ninety-nine Royal Academicians in a hundred ever get possession of ... We are really surprised that such judges as Wilkie, Landseer, Leslie, Allan, &c., have not ere now insisted on breaking through all puny laws, and giving this man of undoubted genius his diploma.

Literary allusions (p. 146) the 'Barnwell case': allusion to *The London Merchant* by George Lillo (1731), that stock item of the eighteenth- and nineteenth-centuries' theatrical repertoire, in which the apprentice George Barnwell robs his master and murders his well-to-do uncle in the latter's garden in Camberwell.

MS. Forster Collection, Victoria and Albert Museum. No significant variations from the *Examiner* text. Forster reprints most of it in his *Life* (Book 6, Ch. 3), with some slight alterations of wording, and notes that the 'little essay' was written at his request. Introducing it, he remarks that Dickens believed Leech had 'turned caricature into character; and

would leave behind him not a little of the history of his time and its
follies, sketched with inimitable grace'.

These are not stray crumbs that have fallen from Mr Punch's well-
provided table, but a careful reproduction by Mr Leech, in a very graceful and cheerful manner, of one of his best series of designs. Admirable
as the 'Rising Generation' is in Mr Punch's gallery, it shows to infinitely
greater advantage in the present enlarged and separate form of publication.

It is to be remarked of Mr Leech that he is the very first English
caricaturist (we use the word for want of a better) who has considered
beauty as being perfectly compatible with art. He almost always introduces into his graphic sketches some beautiful faces or agreeable forms;
and in striking out this course and setting this example, we really believe
he does a great deal to refine and elevate that popular branch of art
which the facilities of steam-printing and wood-engraving are rendering
more popular every day.

If we turn back to a collection of the works of Rowlandson or Gillray,
we shall find, in spite of the great humour displayed in many of them,
that they are rendered wearisome and unpleasant by a vast amount of
personal ugliness. Now, besides that it is a poor device to represent what
is satirised as being necessarily ugly – which is but the resource of an
angry child or a jealous woman – it serves no purpose but to produce a
disagreeable result. There is no reason why the farmer's daughter in the
old caricature who is squalling at the harpsichord (to the intense delight,
by-the-bye, of her worthy father, the farmer, whom it is her duty to
please) should be squab and hideous. The satire on the manner of her
education, if there be any in the thing at all, would be just as good if
she were pretty. Mr Leech would have made her so. The average of
farmers' daughters in England are not impossible bumps of fat. One is
quite as likely to find a pretty girl in a farm-house as to find an ugly
one; and we think, with Mr Leech, that the business of this style of art
is with the pretty one. She is not only a pleasanter object in our portfolio,
but we have more interest in her. We care more about what does become
her, and does not become her. In Mr Punch's *Almanack* for the new year,
there is one illustration by Mr Leech representing certain delicate
creatures with bewitching countenances, encased in several varieties of
that amazing garment, the ladies' paletot. Formerly these fair creatures
would have been made as ugly and ungainly as possible, and there the
point would have been lost, and the spectator, with a laugh at the absurdity of the whole group, would not have cared one farthing how such
uncouth creatures disguised themselves, or how ridiculous they became.

But to represent female beauty as Mr Leech represents it, an artist
must have a most delicate perception of it, and the gift of being able to

realise it to us with two or three slight, sure touches of his pencil. This power Mr Leech possesses in an extraordinary degree.

For this reason, we enter our protest against those of the 'rising generation' who are precociously in love, being made the subject of merriment by a pitiless and unsympathising world. We never saw a boy more distinctly in the right than the young gentleman kneeling on the chair to beg a lock of hair from his pretty cousin, to take back to school. Madness is in her apron, and Virgil, dog's-eared and defaced, is in her ringlets. Doubts may suggest themselves of the perfect disinterestedness of this other young gentleman contemplating the fair girl at the piano – doubts engendered by his worldly allusion to 'tin' (though even that may arise in his modest consciousness of his own inability to support an establishment); but that he should be 'deucedly inclined to go and cut that fellow out,' appears to us one of the most natural emotions of the human breast. The young gentleman with the dishevelled hair and clasped hands, who loves the transcendent beauty with the bouquet, and can't be happy without her, is, to us, a withering and desolate spectacle. Who *could* be happy without her?

The growing boys, or the rising generation, are not less happily observed and agreeably depicted than the grown women. The languid little creature who 'hasn't danced since he was quite a boy,' is perfect; and the eagerness of the little girl whom he declines to receive for a partner at the hands of the glorious old lady of the house – her feet quite ready for the first position – her whole heart projected into the quadrille – and her glance peeping timidly at him out of her flutter of hope and doubt – is quite delightful to look at. The intellectual juvenile who awakens the tremendous wrath of a Norma of private life, by considering woman an inferior animal, is lecturing, this present Christmas, we understand, on the Concrete in connection with the Will. We recognised the legs of the philosopher who considers Shakespeare an over-rated man, dangling over the side of an omnibus last Tuesday. The scowling young gentleman who is clear that 'if his governor don't like the way he goes on in, why, he must have chambers and so much a week,' is not of our acquaintance; but we trust he is by this time in Van Diemen's Land, or he will certainly come to Newgate. We should be exceedingly unwilling to stand possessed of personal property in a strong box, and be in the relation of bachelor-uncle to that youth. We would on no account reside at that suburb of ill omen, Camberwell, under such circumstances, remembering the Barnwell case.

In all his drawings, whatever Mr Leech desires to do, he does. The expression indicated, though indicated by the simplest means, is exactly the natural expression, and is recognised as such immediately. His wit is good-natured, and always the wit of a true gentleman. He has a becoming

Juvenile: 'I tell you what it is, governor, the sooner we come to some understanding the better. You can't expect a young Feller to be always at home, and if you don't like the way I go on – why I must have chambers, and so much a week.'

Plate from The Rising Generation *by John Leech.*

sense of responsibility and self-restraint; he delights in pleasant things; he imparts some pleasant air of his own to things not pleasant in themselves; he is suggestive and full of matter, and he is always improving. Into the tone, as well as into the execution of what he does, he has brought a certain elegance which is altogether new, without involving any compromise of what is true. He is an acquisition to popular art in England who has already done great service, and will, we doubt not, do a great deal more. Our best wishes for the future, and our cordial feeling towards him for the past, attend him in his career.

It is eight or ten years ago since a writer in the *Quarterly Review*, making mention of Mr George Cruikshank, commented, in a few words, on the absurdity of excluding such a man from the Royal Academy, because his works were not produced in certain materials, and did not occupy a certain space annually on its walls. Will no Members and Associates be found upon its books, one of these days, the labours of whose oils and brushes will have sunk into the profoundest obscurity, when the many pencil-marks of Mr Cruikshank and of Mr Leech will still be fresh in half the houses in the land?

33

The Paradise at Tooting

The Examiner, 20 January 1849

Dickens had shown himself aware of the scandal of pauper baby-farms in *Oliver Twist* (1837), where he describes (Ch. 2) the infant Oliver being 'farmed' by the workhouse authorities 'to a branch-workhouse some three miles off, where twenty or thirty other juvenile offenders against the poor-laws rolled about the floor all day, without the inconvenience of too much food or too much clothing'. The atrocious conduct of Bartholomew Drouet at his 'Infant Pauper Asylum' in Tooting, about eight miles south-west of central London, makes the comparatively small-scale brutality of Mrs Mann in *Oliver Twist* seem positively humane, however.

Drouet contracted with a number of London Boards of Guardians (workhouse authorities) to feed, clothe and keep children for four shillings and sixpence per head per week. There were over 1,300 children in the Asylum when cholera broke out there at the end of 1848. The Board of Health, a newly established government body, of which Dickens's brother-in-law, Henry Austin, was General Secretary, had, three months earlier, issued a very widely publicised official warning about a possible outbreak of cholera, describing its symptoms and the best means of combating it, all completely ignored by Drouet. By 12 January 126 children had died and a damning report (quoted by Dickens in this article) of the appalling conditions at the Asylum by Dr Grainger, an inspector sent there by the Board of Health, had received extensive press coverage. Arguments began about who was responsible for the scandal, whether the local Boards of Guardians who sent the children to Drouet, the Poor Law Commissioners, who oversaw the whole system nationwide, or merely Drouet himself. Meanwhile, the Surrey coroner, in whose jurisdiction Tooting lay, did not see fit to hold an inquest on any of the eighty children buried in Tooting churchyard, and it was not until some of the victims who had been removed from the Asylum began dying in the area of West Middlesex that the law intervened. The coroner for that region was Thomas Wakley, founder of *The Lancet* and a very active medical and social reformer. Dickens greatly admired him, having in 1840 served on a jury at an inquest presided over by Wakley. The case involved a wretched pauper girl suspected of killing an illegitimate baby and Dickens later described Wakley's conduct of the inquest as 'nobly patient and humane' ('Some Recollections of Mortality', *The Uncommercial Traveller*, Cheap Edition [1865]).

On 14 January Wakley opened an inquest at Chelsea Workhouse on five children who had died after being returned from Tooting, followed by similar inquests at the Free Hospital and Kensington Workhouse. In their comprehensive article, 'Dickens and the Tooting Disaster' (*Victorian Studies*, Vol. 12, December 1968, pp. 227–44), Alec W. Brice and K.J. Fielding comment (p. 231): 'Wakley's conduct of the inquests was wonderfully thorough and controlled. He was determined to get at the truth with complete fairness, and to establish as far as he could where the responsibility lay ...' Dickens's article, which, like the three follow-up ones he wrote (see pp. 155–6), appeared on the front page of *The Examiner*, was published before the inquest juries had reached their verdicts, but, as can be seen, he does not pull his punches and ends with a vigorous swipe at the 'so-much vaunted self-government' of London, which was specifically exempted from the Board of Health's remit.

Literary allusions (p. 149) 'Sydney Smith's admirable description ...': in his review of Jeremy Bentham's *Book of Fallacies* for the *Edinburgh Review* (Vol. 42 [August 1825], pp. 367–89) Smith called one of Bentham's fallacies 'the self-trumpeter's fallacy' and remarked of certain office-holders, 'If you expose any abuse ... they set up a cry of surprise' and assert that everything is working splendidly ('All are honourable and delightful men. The person who opens the door of the office is a person of approved fidelity ...'): this review was reprinted in Vol. 2 of *The Works of the Reverend Sydney Smith* (1840), a copy of which was in Dickens's library; (p. 149) 'the innocent Candide': hero of Voltaire's great satire on human complacency, *Candide* (1759).

MS. Forster Collection, Victoria and Albert Museum. This shows a number of variants from the *Examiner* text, e.g., after 'for his own profit' (paragraph 4), the MS. has 'and (it may turn out) at his own peril'. In the same paragraph the sentence 'The dietary of the children ... hog-wash' reads in the MS.: 'The dietary of the children is injudicious, even if it be sufficient – of which there are grave doubts.' In paragraph 5 the whole passage beginning 'He has a pleasant brother' and ending '... amiably eccentric brother' is not present in the MS.

When it first became known that a virulent and fatal epidemic had broken out in Mr Drouet's farming establishment for pauper children at Tooting, the comfortable flourish of trumpets usual on such occasions (Sydney Smith's admirable description of it will be fresh in the minds of many of our readers) was performed as a matter of course. Of all similar establishments on earth, that at Tooting was the most admirable. Of all similar contractors on earth, Mr Drouet was the most disinterested, zealous, and unimpeachable. Of all the wonders ever wondered at, nothing perhaps had ever occurred more wonderful than the outbreak and rapid increase of a disorder so horrible, in a place so perfectly regulated. There was no warning of its approach. Nothing was less to be expected. The farmed children were slumbering in the lap of peace and plenty; Mr Drouet, the farmer, was slumbering with an easy conscience, but with one eye perpetually open, to keep watch upon the blessings he diffused, and upon the happy infants under his paternal charge; when, in a moment, the destroyer was upon them, and Tooting churchyard became too small for the piles of children's coffins that were carried out of this Elysium every day.

The learned coroner for the county of Surrey deemed it quite unnecessary to hold any inquests on these dead children, being as perfectly satisfied in his own mind that Mr Drouet's farm was the best of all possible farms, as ever the innocent Candide was that the chateau of the great Baron Thunder-ten Tronkh was the best of all possible chateaux. Presuming that this learned functionary is amenable to some authority or other, and that he will be duly complimented on his sagacity, we will refer to the proceedings before a very different kind of coroner, Mr Wakley, and his deputy Mr Mills. But that certain of the miserable little creatures removed from Tooting happened to die within Mr Wakley's jurisdiction, it is by no means unlikely that a committee might have sprung into existence, by this time, for presenting Mr Drouet with some magnificent testimonial, as a mark of public respect and sympathy.

Mr Wakley, however, being of little faith, holds inquests, and even manifests a disposition to institute a very searching inquiry into the causes of these horrors; rather thinking that such grievous effects must have some grievous causes. Remembering that there is a public institution called the 'Board of Health,' Mr Wakley summons before him Dr Grainger, an inspector acting under that board, who has examined Mr Drouet's Elysium, and has drawn up a report concerning it.

It then comes out – truth is so perverse – that Mr Drouet is not altogether that golden farmer he was supposed to be. It appears that there is a little alloy in his composition. The 'extreme closeness, oppression, and foulness of air' in that supposed heaven upon earth over which he presides, 'exceeds in offensiveness anything ever yet witnessed by the inspector, in apartments in hospitals, or elsewhere, occupied by the sick.' He has a bad habit of putting four cholera patients in one bed. He has a weakness in respect of leaving the sick to take care of themselves, surrounded by every offensive, indecent, and barbarous circumstance that can aggravate the horrors of their condition and increase the dangers of infection. He is so ignorant, or so criminally careless, that he has taken none of the easy precautions, and provided himself with none of the simple remedies, expressly enjoined by the Board of Health in their official announcement published in the *Gazette*, and distributed all over the country. The experience of all the medical observers of cholera, in all parts of the world, is not in an instant overthrown by Mr Drouet's purity, for he had unfortunately one fortnight's warning of the impending danger, which he utterly disregarded. He has been admonished by the authorities to take only a certain number of unfortunates into his farm, and he increases that number immensely at his own pleasure, for his own profit. His establishment is crammed. It is in no respect a fit place for the reception of the throng shut up in it. The dietary of the children is so unwholesome and insufficient, that they climb secretly over palings, and pick out scraps of sustenance from the tubs of hog-wash. Their clothing by day, and their covering by night, are shamefully defective. Their rooms are cold, damp, dirty, and rotten. In a word, the age of miracles is past, and of conceivable places in which pestilence might – or rather *must* – be expected to break out, and to make direful ravages, Mr Drouet's model farm stands foremost.

In addition to these various proofs of his mortal fallibility, Mr Drouet, even when he is told what to do to save life, has an awkward habit of prevaricating, and not doing it. He also bullies his assistants, in the inspector's presence, when they show an inclination to reveal disagreeable truths. He has a pleasant brother – a man of an amiable eccentricity – who besides being active, for all improper purposes, in the farm, is 'with difficulty restrained' from going to Kensington 'to thrash the Guardians' of that Union for proposing to remove their children! The boys under Mr Drouet's fostering protection are habitually knocked down, beaten, and brutally used. They are put on short diet if they complain. They are 'very lean and emaciated.' Mr Drouet's system is admirable, but it entails upon them such slight evils as 'wasting of the limbs, debility, boils, etc.,' and a more dreadful aggravation of the itch than a medical witness of great experience has ever beheld in thirty years' practice. A kick, which would be nothing to a child in sound health, becomes, under Mr Drouet's course of management, a serious wound. Boys who were intelligent before going to Mr Drouet, lose their animation afterwards (so swears a Guardian) and become fools. The surgeon of St Pancras reported, five months ago, of the excellent Mr Drouet, 'that a great deal of severity, not to use a harsh term,' – but why not a harsh term, surgeon, if the occasion require it? – 'has been exercised by the masters in authority, as well as some out of authority,' meaning, we presume, the amiably eccentric brother. Everything, in short, that Mr Drouet does, or causes to be done, or suffers to be done, is vile, vicious, and cruel. All this is distinctly in proof before the coroner's jury, and therefore we see no reason to abstain from summing it up.

But there is blame elsewhere; and though it cannot diminish the heavy amount of blame that rests on this sordid contractor's head, there is great blame elsewhere. The parish authorities who sent these children to such a place, and, seeing them in it, left them there, and showed no resolute determination to reform it altogether, are culpable in the highest degree. The Poor-Law Inspector who visited this place, and did not in the strongest terms condemn it, is not less culpable. The Poor-Law Commissioners, if they had the power to issue positive orders for its better management (a point which is, however, in question), were as culpable as any of the rest.

It is wonderful to see how those who, by slurring the matter when they should have been active in it, have become, in some sort, *participes criminis*, desire to make the best of it, even now. The Poor-Law Inspector thinks that the issuing of an order by the Poor-Law Commissioners, prohibiting boards of guardians from sending children to such an institution, would have been 'a very strong measure.' As if very strong cases required very weak measures, or there were no natural affinity between the measure and the case! He certainly did object to the children sleeping three in a bed, and Mr Drouet afterwards told him he had reduced the number to two – its increase to four when the disease was raging being, we suppose, a special sanitary arrangement. He did not make any recommendation as to ventilation. He did not call the children privately before him, to inquire how they were treated. He considers the dietary a fair dietary – If *proper quantities were given where no precise quantity is specified.* He thinks that, with care, the premises might have been occupied without injury to health, If *all the accommodation on the premises had been judiciously applied.* As though a man should say he felt convinced he could live pretty comfortably on the top of the Monument, If a handsome suite of furnished apartments were constructed there expressly for him, and a select circle came up to dinner every day!

These children were farmed to Mr Drouet at four shillings and sixpence a week each; and some of the officials seem to set store by its being a great deal of money, and to think exoneration lies in that. It may be a very sufficient sum, considering that Mr Drouet was entitled to the profits of the children's work besides; but this seems to us to be no part of the question. If the payment had been fourteen and sixpence a week each, the blame of leaving the children to Mr Drouet's tender mercies without sufficient protection, and of leaving Mr Drouet to make his utmost profit without sufficient check, would have been exactly the same. When a man keeps his horse at livery, he does not take the corn for granted, because he pays five-and-twenty shillings a week. In the history of this calamity, one undoubted predisposing cause was insufficient clothing. What says Mr William Robert James, solicitor and clerk to the Board of Guardians of the Holborn Union, on that head? Mr Drouet '*told him in conversation* (!) that the four and sixpence a week would include clothing. *No particular description of clothing was mentioned.*' Is it any wonder that the flannel petticoats worn by the miserable female children, in the severest weather of this winter, could be – as was publicly stated in another metropolitan union a few days ago – 'read through'?

This same Mr James produces minutes of visits made by deputations of guardians to the Tooting Paradise. Thus: –

'As regards the complaint of Hannah Sleight, as to the insufficiency of food, we believe it to be unfounded. Elizabeth Male having complained that on her recent visit she found her children in a dirty state, her children had our particular attention, and we beg to state that there was no just cause of complaint on her part.'

It being clear to the meanest capacity that Elizabeth Male's children not being dirty then, never could by possibility have been dirty at any antecedent time.

But it appears that this identical James, solicitor and clerk to the Board of Guardians of the Holborn Union, had a valuable system of his own for eliciting the truth, which was, to ask the boys in Mr Drouet's presence if they had anything to complain of, and when they answered 'Yes,' to recommend that they should be instantly horsewhipped. We learn this from the following extraordinary minute of one of these official visits: –

'We beg to report to the board our having on Tuesday, the 9th of May, visited Mr Drouet's establishment to ascertain the state of the children, belonging to this union. We were there at the time of dinner being supplied, and in our opinion the meat provided was good, but the potatoes were bad. We visited the schoolrooms, dormitories, and workshops. *Everything appeared clean and comfortable, yet we are of opinion that the new sleeping rooms for infants on the ground floor have a very unhealthy smell.* The girls belonging to the union looked very well. *The boys appeared sickly,* which induced us to question them as to whether they had any cause of complaint as to supply of food or otherwise. About forty of them held up their hands to intimate their dissatisfaction, upon which Mr Drouet's conduct became violent. He called the boys liars, described some that had held up their hands as the worst boys in the school, and said that if he had done them justice, he would have followed out the suggestion of Mr James, and well thrashed them. (Laughter.) We then began to question the boys individually, and some of them complained of not having sufficient bread at their breakfast. Whilst pressing the inquiry, Mr Drouet's conduct became more violent. He said we were acting unfairly in the mode of inquiry, that we ought to be satisfied of his character without such proceedings, and that we had no right to pursue the inquiry in the way we were doing, and that he would be glad to get rid of the children. To avoid further altercation we left, not having fully completed the object of our visit.'

If Mr Drouet was sincere in saying he would be glad to get rid of the children, he must be in a very complacent frame of mind at present when he has succeeded in getting rid, for ever, of so many. But the general complacency, on the occasions of these visits, is marvellous. Hear Mr Winch, one of the guardians of the poor for the Holborn Union, who was one of the visiting party at the Tooting Paradise on this 9th of May: –

'I was in company with Mr Mayes and Mr Rebbeck. The children were at dinner. They were all standing; I was informed they never sit at their meals. I tasted the meat, and I cut open about 100 potatoes at different tables, *none of which were fit to eat.* They were black and diseased. I told Mr Drouet the potatoes were very bad. He replied that they cost him £7 a ton. The children had no other vegetables. *I told Mr Drouet I should give them other food. He made no reply. I also told Mr Drouet I thought the newly erected rooms smelt unhealthy.* Mr Mayes said it was a pity when he was building he had not made the rooms higher; when *Mr Drouet said he would have enough to do if he paid attention to everybody.* We went through some of the sleeping-rooms, which appeared very clean. The girls looked well; but the boys, who were mustered in the schoolroom, appeared very sickly and unhealthy. *Mr Drouet, his brother, and the schoolmaster were present.* Mr Rebbeck said to the boys: "Now, if you have anything to complain of – want of food, or anything else – hold up your hands"; and from thirty to forty held up their hands. *Mr Drouet became very violent,* and said we were treating him in an ungentlemanly manner; he said that some of the boys who had held up their hands were liars, and scoundrels, and rascals. He said we were using him very unfairly; *that his character was at stake;* and if we had anything to complain of, that was not the way to proceed. *One of the boys whom I questioned told me they had not bread enough either for breakfast or supper; and, on comparing their dietary with that in our workhouse, I think such is the case.* In consequence of the confusion, we left Mr Drouet's without signing the visitors' book. I did not make any motion in the Board of Guardians for the removal of the children. I again visited Mr Drouet's establishment on the 30th of May. The potatoes were then of excellent quality. *I went into the pantry, and was surprised to find the bread was not weighed out. We weigh it out in the union, as we find that is the only way to give satisfaction.* The loaves at Mr Drouet's were cut into sixteen pieces without being weighed. I saw no supply of salt in the dining-room, but some of the boys who had salt in bags were bartering their salt for potatoes. *I did not ask the children whether they had been punished in consequence of what had taken place at my previous visit.* We were in the establishment for an hour and a half or two hours on the 30th. *We then expressed our satisfaction at what we witnessed.* We made no further inquiry as to what had occurred on our previous visit. I made no suggestion to the board for the improvement of the dietary. *We had no means of ascertaining that the children received the amount of food mentioned in the diet-table.'*

But we expressed our satisfaction at what we witnessed. Oh dear yes. Our unanimity was delightful. Nobody complained. The boys had had ample encouragement to complain. They had seen Mr Drouet standing glowering by, on the previous occasion. They had heard him break out about liars, and scoundrels, and rascals. They had understood that his precious character – immeasurably more precious than the existence of any number of pauper children – was at stake. They had had the benefit of a little fatherly advice and caution from him, in the interval. They were in a position, moral and physical, to be high-spirited, bold and open. Yet not a boy complained. We went home to our Holborn Union, rejoicing. Our clerk was in tip-top spirits about the thrashing joke. Everything was comfortable and pleasant. Of all places in the world, how could the cholera ever break out, after this, in Mr Drouet's Paradise at Tooting!

If we had been left to the so-much vaunted self-government, the question might have been unanswered still, and the Drouet testimonial might have been in full vigour. But the Board of Health – an institution of which every day's experience attests in some new form the value and importance – has settled the question. Plainly thus: – The cholera, or some unusually malignant form of typhus assimilating itself to that disease, broke out in Mr Drouet's farm for children, because it was brutally conducted, vilely kept, preposterously inspected, dishonestly defended, a disgrace to a Christian community, and a stain upon a civilised land.

Dickens followed up this article a week later with another on the subject, entitled 'The Tooting Farm' (*The Examiner*, 27 January, reprinted in *MP*), after the Holborn jury had reached a verdict of manslaughter against Drouet, also criticising the local Board of Guardians for negligence and 'regretting' the inadequacy of the Poor Law in the matter of infant paupers. Dickens wrote that he had 'no intention of prejudging a case which is now to be brought to issue before a criminal court', but wanted to say why the case 'should be rigidly dealt with upon its own merits' without 'that vague disposition to smooth over the things that be, which sometimes creeps into the most important English proceedings'. Alluding to the recent Chartist trials, he argues as he had done in 'Judicial Special Pleading' (p. 142) that the state must be perceived by the poor as 'unfeignedly mindful of them, and truly anxious to redress their tangible and obvious wrongs', otherwise they will be easily led astray by Chartist agitators fomenting discontent among them. Dickens sees the Drouet case, involving the terrible fate of so many children of the poor, as a particularly vital one in this respect – 'there are probably very few poor working-men who have not thought "this might be my child's case, tomorrow"'. It must not be wasted 'in play with foolscap and red tape [bewildering] all those listening ears with mere official gabble about Boards, and Inspectors, and Guardians . . . and powers, and clauses, and sections and chapters, until the remedy is crushed to pieces in a mill of words'.

The case came before the Central Criminal Court, and the Recorder of the City of London, Charles Ewan Law, a staunch Conservative, appeared in his address to the Grand Jury (26 February) to be so biased in Drouet's favour (see Brice and Fielding, *op. cit.*, p. 234) that Dickens was provoked into writing another article, 'A Recorder's Charge', which appeared in *The Examiner* on 3 March 1849 and is reprinted in full by Brice and Fielding (pp. 235–9). It is a trenchant demolition of Law's highly specious reasoning (in order to convict Drouet of manslaughter the jury had to determine that some *particular* act of his had caused the children to die of cholera). Dickens compares the Recorder to an Indian Medicine Man dancing round the jury in a 'wild manner': 'In law, we have a solemn jingling of words and phrases which is the most bewildering and unmeaning Medicine of all.' (Brice and Fielding note that Dickens re-used this idea in 1863, in his 'Medicine Men of Civilisation' reprinted in *The Uncommercial Traveller*, Cheap Edition [1865].) Drouet was finally brought to trial on 13 April and charged with the manslaughter of one child (representative of all the 150 dead children), but the prosecution could not, of course, prove that it was wholly on account of Drouet's negligence that this particular child had died of cholera. The judge, Baron Platt (see p. 127), directed the jury to acquit him. Dickens's last article on the subject, 'The Verdict for Drouet', appeared in *The Examiner* on 21 April and is reprinted in *MP*. It is surprisingly restrained in tone, though sharply critical of Platt's behaviour ('The prosecution being less strongly represented than the defence, he took the first opportunity of siding with the stronger. Witnesses that required encouragement he brow-beated; and witnesses that could do without it he insulted and ridiculed'). Dickens rightly pointed out that Drouet had got off on a legal technicality, but was 'certainly not released ... from the guilt of the charge', and concludes that the child-farming system must end as a result of the case: 'everyone must recognise that a trade which derived its profits from the deliberate torture and neglect of a class the most innocent on earth, as well as the most wretched and defenceless, can never on any pretence be resumed'.

Dickens remained haunted by the Drouet case as can be seen from the several subsequent references he makes to it, most famously in *Bleak House* (1852) where Mrs Snagsby's much-put-upon slavey, Guster, a workhouse child, is subject to fits, 'although she was farmed or contracted for during her growing time by an amiable benefactor of his species resident at Tooting, and cannot fail to have been developed under the most favourable circumstances' (Ch. 10). He refers back to Drouet in 'Pet Prisoners', 'The Begging-Letter Writer' and 'A Walk in a Workhouse' (see pp. 218, 233 and 238); and in 'A Home for Homeless Women' (*HW*, 23 April 1853; *MP*) describes the mental torpor of a girl who had been brought up 'in the establishment of that amiable victim of popular prejudice, the late Mr Drouet, of Tooting'. Also, among the dummy book-backs he devised during the 1850s for his study first at Tavistock House and subsequently at Gad's Hill we find a grim joke: *Drouet's Farming. Vols.* I–V.

34

Theatre Review: *Virginia* by John Oxenford and *Black-eyed Susan* by Douglas Jerrold at the Royal Marylebone Theatre

The Examiner, 12 May 1849

Oxenford, for many years the dramatic critic of *The Times*, was a prolific manufacturer of plays, especially farces. James A. Davies notes that he helped Forster with theatre reviews on the *Examiner* (*John Forster: A literary life* [1983], p. 223), which perhaps accounts for the *Examiner*'s later (13 October 1849, p. 646) remarks on 'the remarkable skill with which Mr Oxenford translates and adapts from the French. He selects the higher class of drama, and in transforming does not lower it ... He is not only the expert dramatist, but the man of literature and poetry.' Here he has translated *Virginie*, a tragedy by Isidore Latour de St Ybars, which had been produced at the Théâtre-Français in 1845 with Rachel in the title role.

The ancient Roman legend of Virginius had already been the subject of three native British dramas – *Appius and Virginia* by John Webster (early seventeenth century), a second play of the same name by John Dennis (1709) and *Virginius* by James Sheridan Knowles. This last, first produced at Covent Garden in 1820, was regarded as one of the greatest plays of the age by early Victorian critics, and Virginius was one of Macready's most celebrated roles. The story had also been the subject of one of Macaulay's *Lays of Ancient Rome* (1842).

The legend, first recorded in Livy's Roman History, describes the plot of a corrupt decemvir, Appius Claudius, to obtain possession of Virginia, betrothed to Icilius, by allowing one of his followers to claim her as a slave. Her centurion father, Virginius, stabs her to death to save her from dishonour and then (in Knowle's version) runs mad and also kills Appius.

Anna Mowatt and Edward Loomis Davenport were Americans who came to act in England at the end of 1847. Davenport's portrayal of the sailor-hero William in Douglas Jerrold's endlessly popular nautical melodrama *Black-eyed Susan* (first produced at the Surrey Theatre in 1829) almost rivalled in popularity that of the legendary creator of the role, T.P. Cooke (who continued to play it into the 1850s). Jerrold, dramatist and Radical satirist, was a close friend of Dickens's. His *Susan* tells the story of a gallant sailor condemned to execution for striking his superior officer when defending his wife's honour; he is reprieved at the last minute.

Fanny Vining (born in London in 1829, daughter of a leading actor) had married Davenport in January 1849 and accompanied him on his return to America in 1854. The Marylebone Theatre, built in 1831 to serve the West London neighbourhood of Paddington, became the Royal Marylebone in 1837. H. Barton Baker notes (*The London Stage* [1889], Vol. II, p. 260f.) that it was for some time 'little better than a show'. In 1847, however, 'an attempt was made ... to regenerate the house, when ... it was directed by the celebrated tragic actress, Mrs Warner', but 'her efforts were unsuccessful' and in the 1850s it became 'the western home of East-end melodrama'.

Literary allusions (p. 158) 'Mr Puff's Tragedy': refers to Puff's ludicrous play *The Armada*, which is rehearsed in Sheridan's *The Critic* (1779), and in which Queen Elizabeth never appears; (para. 3) 'o'ersteps the modesty of nature': Shakespeare, *Hamlet*, Act 3, Sc. 2.

MS. Forster Collection, Victoria and Albert Museum. Reprinted with several inaccuracies ('Virginie' for 'Virginia', 'the Oxenford' for 'Mr Oxenford', 'Norman' for 'Roman', etc., in *MP*).

A play in five acts by Mr Oxenford, founded on the French *Virginie*, by M. Latour de St Ybars, was produced here on Monday night to a crowded house, with very great success, thoroughly deserved in all respects. The English version of the play is most spirited, scholarly, and elegant; the principal characters were sustained with great power; and the getting-up of the piece was quite extraordinary in respect of the care, good sense, and good taste bestowed upon it.

There is sufficient novelty in this version of the great Roman story, to which Mr Oxenford has done delicate poetical justice, to attract and interest even that portion of the play-going public who are familiar with the fine tragedy by Mr Knowles. A much larger share of the interest is thrown upon the heroine. *Icilius*, like *Queen Elizabeth* in Mr Puff's tragedy, is kept in the green-room all night, until he is slain through the treachery of *Appius Claudius*. And the curtain falls upon the death of *Virginia*, and the slaying of *Appius Claudius* by *Virginius* on the judgment seat.

Virginia was acted by Mrs Mowatt. Throughout it, and especially in the more quiet scenes, as in the appeal to the household gods before leaving home on the bridal morning, the character was rendered in a touching, truthful, womanly manner, that might have furnished a good lesson to some actresses of high pretensions we could name. There is great merit in all this lady does. She very rarely o'ersteps the modesty of nature. She is not a conventional performer. She has a true feeling for nature, and for her art; and we question whether any one now upon the stage could have acted this part better, or have acted it so well. Mr Davenport also, as *Virginius*, played admirably; with a great deal of pathos, passion, and dignity. Both were loudly called for at the close of the play, and heartily greeted.

We have already spoken, in general terms, of the manner in which the piece was put upon the stage. It would be unjust not to particularise the last scene of the Roman Forum, which exhibits quite a wonderful use of the space and resources of the Theatre, and is a most complete and beautiful thing. The same spirit pervades all that is brought forward here. A fortnight since, we saw *Romeo and Juliet* on this stage, really presented in a way that would do credit to any theatre in the world.

The tragedy was followed by Mr Jerrold's *Black-eyed Susan*, at which the audience laughed and wept with all their hearts, and which is a remarkable illustration of what a man of genius may do with a common-enough theme, and how what he does will remain a thing apart from all imitation. Of the many nautical dramas that have come and gone like showers (and not very wholesome showers either) since *Black-eyed Susan* was first produced, there is probably not one but has had this piece for its model, and has pillaged and rifled it, according to its (Dramatic) Author's taste. And the whole run of them are as like it, at last, as the Marylebone Theatre is like St Paul's or St Peter's. Acted as it is here, it should be seen again. Nothing can be better, in all respects, than Mr Davenport's *William*; Miss Vining, a very clever actress, is excellent in *Susan*; and neither the court-martial nor the execution scene were ever half so well presented in our remembrance.

It is a pleasant duty to point out the deserts of this theatre as it is now conducted, and to recommend it. We know what some minor theatres in London are, and we know what this was before it became a refuge for the proscribed drama. The influence of such a place cannot but be beneficial and salutary. It richly deserves support, and we hope it will be supported.

35

Demoralisation and Total Abstinence

The Examiner, 27 October 1849

This leading article, which occupies the first one-and-a-half pages of this number of *The Examiner*, was first identified as Dickens's by Alec W. Brice and K.J. Fielding in 'A New Article by Dickens: "Demoralisation and Total Abstinence"' (*Dickens Studies Annual*, Vol. IX [1981], pp. 1–19). They consider it, with some justice, 'perhaps the clearest and the most complete statement of his social philosophy that he was to write outside his fiction', and set it very fully in its historical context. They note also the 'whiff of radical Carlylism' detectable in the piece. I am indebted to Brice and Fielding for much of the background information in this headnote.

Elihu Burritt was an American pacifist who founded an international peace society, the 'League of Universal Brotherhood'. He was in Britain in 1846, and organised Peace Congresses in Brussels and Paris in 1848 and 1849. Dickens referred to him again, as 'the Dove Delegate from America', in 'Whole Hogs' (*HW*, 23 August 1851; *MP*). The phrase about Austria's 'murdering noble men' refers to the brutal suppression, by combined Habsburg and Russian forces, of the newly declared Hungarian state in the summer of 1849, and the hanging and shooting of its political and military leaders. An *Examiner* leader of 20 October condemned the 'judicial murder' of Count Batthyany ('Language fails us when we would speak of such barbarities') and there was another leader on 'The Austrian Cruelties' in the same issue as this piece by Dickens.

Thomas Beggs was Secretary of the National Temperance Association 1846–8 and Secretary of the Health of Towns Association in 1848. Benjamin Rotch was a former MP and Middlesex magistrate, very active in committee work connected with prisons, and a zealous Temperance advocate. He had caused much trouble to the Governor of Coldbath Fields Prison, Captain George Chesterton, by his activities in the prison. He 'wanted all prisoners to sign the pledge (in circumstances where the pledge was virtually meaningless), and he displayed notable favouritism towards those prisoners and officers who, at least nominally, supported his campaign' (P. Collins, *Dickens and Crime* [1962], p. 68). He also attempted to introduce some vocational training with sheep-shearing classes for male prisoners (to encourage them to emigrate to a farming life in Australia after their release). As a result of all this, he became 'Drinkwater Rotch, the Sheep-shearing Magistrate', a figure of fun in the popular press (Collins, p. 69). Chesterton was much respected by Dickens and was advising him and Miss Burdett-Coutts on disciplinary matters connected with the Home for Fallen Women they were establishing, so it was not surprising that Dickens would take his side against Rotch. The latter had already been mocked in an article 'Prison and Convict Discipline' in *The Examiner* on 10 March 1849 to which Dickens refers (p. 164; Brice and Fielding comment that he is 'presumably using the editorial first person' or possibly indicating that he might have had a hand in the earlier article).

Dickens was immersed in the writing of *David Copperfield*, serialisation of which had begun in May 1849, when he wrote this article. He returned to the theme of the foolish encouragement of hypocritical protestations of reformation among prisoners in an *HW* article, 'Pet Prisoners' (p. 212), and in *Copperfield* itself, Ch. 61 (pub. November 1850), where the visiting magistrate Mr Creakle is clearly intended for a satirical portrait of Rotch (see Collins, *op. cit.*, p. 163).

Literary allusions (p. 162) 'all the ills that flesh is heir to': Shakespeare, *Hamlet*, Act 3, Sc. 1; (p. 165) 'that because they are *not* virtuous, there shall be no cakes and ale': Shakespeare, *Twelfth Night*, Act 2, Sc. 3 ('Dost thou think because thou art virtuous there shall be no more cakes and ale?');

(p. 167) 'known by their fruits': Matthew 7: 20; (p. 169) Longfellow, 'The Warning' (*Poems of Slavery*, 1842).

It is a characteristic of the age that it comprehends a large class of minds apparently unable to distinguish between use and abuse. Because war is costly, because the horrors inseparable from it are great, because its triumphs and successes are of very little worth when balanced against the immense price, moral and physical, at which they are purchased, a number of well-meaning men spring up who would disarm England. And this too, at a time when a deplorable reaction towards tyranny is visible throughout Europe, and when it is, of all times, most important for the hopes of the world that a free country, abhorrent of the detestable cruelties practised by absolute government, should be in a bold and strong position. We can imagine nothing more agreeable to Austria (unless it be the murdering of noble men) than the abandonment of all the barracks and arsenals of this kingdom to statues of Mr Elihu Burritt; but, precisely because Austria is not agreeable to us, we are not agreeable to this, and, as a choice of two evils, would infinitely prefer a fleet and an army to any amount of Mr Elihu Burritt – though we have no doubt he is a very honest man in his way.

So, because drunkenness is, for the most part, inseparably associated with crime and misery, a leap is made at the conclusion that there must be no drinking. Because Bill Brute, the robber in Newgate, and Mr Brallaghan of Killalloo, resident down the next court, make wild beasts of themselves under the influence of strong liquor, therefore Jones, the decent and industrious mechanic, going to Hampton Court for a summer day with his wife and family, is not to have his pint of beer and his glass of gin and water – a proposition which we make bold to say is simply ridiculous. So, because certain zealots take it into their hot heads that there is going to be a Post-office delivery of letters in London on a Sunday – which none but themselves have ever dreamed of – straightway there is to be an agitation for putting a stop to the delivery of any letters, anywhere, under any circumstances, on a Sunday. And so on, to the end of a long chapter.

All these wrong conclusions, from premises that are to a certain extent right, have a strong family likeness in the manner of their enforcement. The members of a Peace Society proclaim, as an original discovery, that war is a mighty evil. The members of a Tee-total Society proclaim, as an original discovery, that a drunken man or woman is a degraded object. Nobody has ever arrived at either of these advanced stages of enlightenment before; nobody ever can arrive at either of them without being a member of the Peace Society or the Tee-total Society. The one thing wanting in this world is the one Society, whose claims chance at the moment to be thrust upon us. Thus, in reading the newspaper advertisements, we find that Morison's pills are the only cure for every disease to which human nature is liable, until we stumble on Professor Holloway, and find that his is the only nostrum for all the ills that flesh is heir to!

The same strong family likeness, among the misbegotten children of Cant, is to be observed in the illogical, irrational, unscrupulous, and wanton way, in which facts are perverted, sweeping assertions hazarded, and motives wrongfully attributed, to support the one idea. Quack society, quack medicine, or quack Post-office opposition, it is all the same! Down goes poor truth, at the first charge, into the dust, and away ride the whole field, whooping, pell mell, over her!

Mr Beggs, who has just written an elaborate treatise on what he calls the 'Extent and Causes of Juvenile Depravity,' gives us two good instances of sweeping assertion. In 1839, when an official inquiry showed the number of known prostitutes in London to be 7,000, a voluntary association, multiplying them by nearly twelve, manfully stated them at 80,000! No assertion is more common in 'Temperance Literature' than the assertion that 60,000 drunkards die annually in this kingdom. Now, the fact is, says Mr Beggs, that 10,000 – one-sixth of this amount – is a high estimate, for which there is no warrant in any known data. The favourite temperance statement of the sixty thousand, 'making deductions for children under fifteen, and aged persons above eighty, as well as for the smaller proportion of female than male inebriates, gives us *every fourth or fifth person dying a drunkard!* Is it not almost time that we had a Temperance Society in strong statements as well as strong drinks?

But Mr Beggs, while he repudiates these exaggerated falsehoods, still pleads the total abstinence (miscalled, in a similar want of honesty, the temperance cause), and calls upon the women of England – not the drunken women, as one might suppose, but the women who do not get drunk – to 'dash down the cup,' and upon the men – again, not the drunken men, but the sober – to 'banish the social glass,' &c. &c., occasionally in an excited strain which is more like the Temperance Literature whose assertions he holds in such just estimation, than the patient pursuer of facts he generally shows himself to be. Premising that his elaborate treatise is, in a revised and improved form, an essay written by him in competition for a Hundred Pound prize recently offered for the best essay on Juvenile Depravity; that the adjudicators awarded it the second prize; and that without making any pretensions to novelty of reflection or suggestion on the momentous subject of which it treats, it contains a mass of important and well-arranged facts, – we propose to reason a little on this total abstinence question, and to investigate one or two main positions of its advocates, sustained by Mr Beggs.

Now, we will begin by expressing our opinion that Total Abstinence Societies beg the whole question, and that drunkenness, in this country, is already made disgraceful. It is regarded as a low, abandoned, miserable vice. While it is the vice of the poor and wretched, and the guilty, it is not the vice of the upper classes, or of the middle classes (whose improvement within the last hundred years is in no respect more remarkable than in this); and it is not, generally speaking, the vice of the great body of respectable mechanics, or of servants, or of small tradesmen. We hold that it is quite as often the consequence as the cause of the condition in which the poor and wretched are found; and that it prevails in the low depths of society, as an evil of vast extent, because those depths have been too long unfathomed and unsunned, and because, while all above them has been undergoing some improvement, their moral condition has got worse and worse, until it is as bad as bad can be. If every motherly, good woman in England were to dash down her cup, in compliance with the invocation of Mr Beggs (which we seem to have heard before), and if every well-conducted man were to banish his social glass and fly with enthusiasm to the pump, there would not be, we sincerely believe, one drunken man or woman the less, within the compass of the United Kingdom – why should there be? But, if the women of England could dash down the window tax, and the water monopoly, and the stifling walls and roofs that keep out air; and could dash open the doors of some new schools for poor people's children – emphatically poor people's children – where common sense and common duty should be taught in common terms; and if the men of England could banish the social filth, indecency, and degradation in which scores upon scores of thousands are forced to wear out life, – they might just leave their cups and their social glasses alone, and keep their whole little possession of crockery exactly in its present state.

We object, altogether, to the evidence of confirmed criminals in prisons, about the cup and the social glass. We have no doubt of their having been drunkards; we have no doubt of their having abused everything they should have used; but we believe that they lied, deceived, and violated the whole table of the law, through many causes. Mr Beggs supplies us with a return of the answers made by certain prisoners to the question, What did they assign as the first cause of their falling into error? One might reasonably suppose that some few people lapsed into crime by reason of a want of control over their passions, through the disregard of truth, from not holding theft in abhorrence, from indulgence in other sensual pleasures than drink, from cupidity, from greed of many kinds. Not at all. These are not the answers. Drink is the favourite, and there is a run upon the favourite. Now it is, or it may be, within the observation of every man, that these people constantly think there is an excuse for what they have done in drink. Nothing is more common in the police reports than for a prisoner to say he was drunk when he committed the offence with which he is charged; and for the assertion, on the magistrate's referring to the inspector who took the charge, turning out to be wholly untrue. Besides this, we will engage that ninety out of a hundred of all the prisoners in all the gaols in the United Kingdom would, without the least reference to fact, return exactly such an answer to such a question as they thought would be agreeable to the questioner; and that if a notion arose that the wearing of brass buttons led to crime, and they were questioned to elucidate that point, we should have such answers as, 'I was happy till I wore brass buttons,' 'Brass buttons did it,' 'Buttons is the cause of my being here,' all down long columns of a grave return.

One Mr Rotch – we had almost written Mr Botch, remembering his sheep-shearing, to which we referred some time ago – who is a magnate among prisoners, writes a pathetic letter to Mr Beggs, printed in the appendix to his volume, in which he says:

> So true is what you say (that while the more respectable of our countrymen alone have the power to change this drinking system, it is they who give respectability to it), that the moment my term of office as a visiting justice of Coldbath Fields expired, and I went out of the committee by rotation, a wicked crusade was immediately commenced against all the warders and sub-warders who had signed the temperance pledge. The governor insulted them; the subordinates designated them as 'Rotch's Saints.'

We notice this, not because the chief of these saints was discharged from his office for drunkenness (which we, however, know to be the fact), nor to comment on the honest use of the term drinking customs in the sense of drunken customs, and the calumnious accusation against the respectable portion of the community of countenancing them, but to point out the monstrous absurdity and impropriety of an indiscriminate administration of this pledge to common London thieves and vagabonds *in prison* – to such of them, in short, as chose to take it from the hands of Mr Rotch, in the palmy days of his superseded visitation. Any one in the least degree acquainted with the habits of these persons, knows that there is nothing the generality of them would not profess, when at that disadvantage, to curry favour with a man in power. In the monotony and restraint of their prison life, any opportunity of 'doing' such a man, with a solemn face, would be esteemed, besides, as a joke of the first magnitude. The fun of taking the pledge where there was nothing but water to be got, with the prospect of breaking it the moment the prison gate should open on the gin-shops, can only have been equalled by their delicate enjoyment of the jest of being supposed to hold that solemn promise in the least regard, when lying was known to be the trade and business of their lives. Nevertheless we are uncharitable enough to begrudge them this hypocritical relaxation, on the ground of its having a most demoralising and pernicious tendency. We contend that a prison-yard is not fit pasturage for Mr Rotch's hobby, or Mr anybody else's; and we believe that the last state of those men was worse than the first.

Here is a case against strong drink from Mr Beggs' book. The subject is a girl:

> It appears that she had been indulgently and well brought up, that she had obtained at a very early age an excellent situation as nursery-maid in a family which had been known to her widowed mother in more prosperous days. All went on smoothly until, in one of her holidays, she fell in with some female companions and went with them to the tea-gardens. At this place she met with a gentleman who paid her polite and particular attention. The acquaintanceship was continued for some time. She was flattered by his addresses, – she was frequently invited to accompany him to amusements for which she had every inclination; but as she could not accept them on account of the rules of the family in which she lived, she began to feel her situation irksome. One evening she obtained leave of absence on some pretence until a later hour, and went with her admirer to a ball, from which she was hurried away, after having in a moment of excessive fatigue swallowed a small glass of wine-negus. She scarcely recollected what took place afterwards, but found herself in the morning away from her kind friends in a strange place, and at the mercy of him who had wronged her.

We do not quite understand what share the 'small glass of wine-negus' is supposed to have had in this melancholy history. If it were drugged, we presume a cup of tea might have been drugged too. If the poor girl was stupified by the unassisted fumes of the negus (which we must beg to be excused for not believing), we suppose that a total abstinence from the negus on the part of Clapham and Stoke Newington would not have prevented the negus from being in those tea-gardens, or the poor girl from drinking it. If it be contended that, for the sake of all poor girls in the like peril, there must be no tea-gardens and no negus – that because they are *not* virtuous, there shall be no cakes and ale – then we cannot stop there. There must be no liberty, no holiday, no breathing of fresh air. There must be an immense procession of police-vans in connexion with the churches, on Sundays, carrying young people to and from the services closeted up from temptation. If those who do not misuse opportunities of innocent enjoyment, are to suffer for those who do, we must come to this complexion. We must put the whole world in mourning, and give up social life as a bad job.

The number of uneducated children in London, according to the first annual report of the Ragged School Union, considerably exceeds 100,000, of which number it has since been ascertained, by an examination from house to house, that 16,000 are to be found in Spitalfields and Bethnal-green alone. Says Mr Beggs in one place, 'the causes of juvenile immorality must be sought not only in the want of education, but in the drinking habits of the community.' Says Mr Beggs in another place, 'could we lose our familiarity with the scenes of misery drink produces, and after a temporary forgetfulness, awaken up to a sight of what one single gin-shop could disclose, would it not be banished from our tables and renounced by all good men?' Why should it be banished from our tables and renounced by all good men? What would be the use of its being banished from our tables, and renounced by all good men? Most of us know perfectly well what heartrending sights of misery and woe a single gin-shop can disclose, without being put under the influence of chloroform, and waking up again, for the purpose. But what *we* drink has no part in that; and the draining of all the rivers of the earth for our drink, would not quench a spark of that baleful fire. We abstain from bad language, from horrible oaths, from filthy and profane conversation, from fighting and kicking. Our abstinence is no example to the lowest orders. And why? Because their lives are lives of ignorance, indecency, squalor, filth, neglect, and desolate wretchedness. Every incident in every such life, every minute of every day of every year of every such life, is a provocation to drunkenness; and while such lives are led by scores of thousands of people in the capital of the world alone, drunkenness will flourish, though the sober people were to drink the sea dry.

'The causes of juvenile depravity must be sought, not only in the want of education, but in the drinking habits of the community.' For 'drinking' read 'drunken,' and for 'community' read 'lowest orders,' – to be plain and honest, for once, in this kind of statement, – and we assent to the proposition. But Mr Beggs knows (he states that he knows, over and over again, afterwards) that drunkenness is the inseparable companion of ignorance. Drunkenness, dirt, and ignorance, are the three Fates of the wretched. And are we to be told, being out of Bedlam, that the removal of the ignorance, and the removal of the dirt, would not remove the drunkenness, because the middle and the upper classes choose to set the example of moderation instead of abstinence? If the lowest classes were brought within the influence of any wholesome example at all, which they are not now, is there no example in that quality of moderation which Tee-Total Societies so sorely need?

'Among the institutions which are the glory and the pride of our time,' says Mr Beggs, 'we place Sabbath-schools.' We are not quite so enthusiastic as Mr Beggs on this point, though we give great credit to that 'noble band' of whom he speaks, the teachers in the Sunday-schools.

But we consider that a system of education infinitely more judiciously administered, and taking a wider worldly range, than any which obtains in any Sunday-school, is necessary for these miserable people whom the Sunday-schools have hitherto addressed in vain; and we consider that for all young people it is very dangerous to make the Sunday (as it is the tendency of the existing schools to do) too restrictive and severe. Let us turn to Mr Beggs on Sunday-schools.

Mr T.B. Smithies, of York, a zealous Sabbath-school teacher, informs us, that he recently visited one of the prisons in York Castle, in which were fourteen convicts, principally youths under fourteen years of age. On conversing with them, he found *that thirteen of them had been Sunday-scholars*, and ten out of the thirteen acknowledged that drink had brought them there. A medical gentleman connected with a public institution had been curious enough to inquire into the moral condition of a number of unfortunate women who had been brought under his care. His inquiries were made in relation to their previous modes of life, education, cause of fall, &c. Out of thirty cases, where he felt he might rely upon the statements, he found that twenty-four were under twenty years of age, and eighteen had commenced a vicious course of life before they were seventeen; *fourteen had been educated in Sunday-schools*, the remainder had received no education of any kind. One had been a governess, and another a publican's daughter. A warm friend of Sunday-schools and the temperance cause states, that in a town in Lancashire no less than *four unfortunate females were seen together in the street, every one of whom had been a teacher in a Sabbath-school.* In a large proportion of the cases, drink or drinking establishments was the first cause of their fall. The Committee of the Rochdale Temperance Society commenced, a short time back, a most important inquiry in relation to Sabbath-school children. 'A few months ago a member of the Committee visited one of the singing saloons in Rochdale, and on a Saturday evening, about eleven o'clock, he observed sixteen boys and girls seated at a table in front of the stage; several of the lads had long pipes each, with a glass or jug containing intoxicating liquor, and *no less than fourteen of the number were members of the Bible classes in different Sunday-schools.* There they sat, listening to the most obscene songs, witnessing scenes of the most immoral kind, and swallowing liquid fire.' It is added, '*These sinks of iniquity are thronged with old Sunday scholars, especially on Sunday evenings,* and not infrequently until twelve o'clock.' Still further, '*The appalling results of the drinking system are not wholly confined to the scholars; many a promising teacher has fallen a victim.*'

This is all owing to drink, of course, and particularly to the sober women who have not dashed down their cups, and the sober men who have not banished their social glasses. But, there are minds so constituted, perhaps, as to infer from these premises that there must be something a little amiss in the Sunday-schools themselves – unless they have a special dispensation from being known by their fruits, like all other institutions.

It is a good instance of the confusion of ideas which prevails among the declaimers about total abstinence, that the strongest piece of evidence in all this volume goes directly to the advantages of moderation, and has nothing in the world to do with total abstinence. In certain coal, copper, tin, and chemical works in Glamorganshire, employing, of men, women, and children, about 4,500, it appears that a most just and humane system of society has been established by the employers. 'The sanitary condition of their dwellings is of the most favourable kind, with suitable accommodation for the wants of families.' There are churches and chapels. There are schools. There are lectures on useful and entertaining subjects. There is singing in classes. There are innocent and healthful sports. Is there anything more? A little more.

> *The temptation of the public-house is as far as possible removed.* THERE ARE ONLY TWO allowed upon the property of the Company, *which are also kept under strict regulations, and are never open after ten o'clock at night.* Mr Vigurs adds the remarkable testimony (in most striking contrast with the degraded sensuality of the people of the great works 'on the hills' of Monmouthshire and Brecon), *that he does not remember to have seen, during his long residence, a drunken man wandering about, or that a case, arising out of drunkenness, was once brought before the magistrates.*

It does not appear that these good employers have done any damage to their own cups and social glasses. It does not appear that they have got upon platforms to deliver statements 'cooked' like Mr Hudson's accounts, or sought to make a braggart reputation by administering pledges, to be broken like the same honourable gentleman's iron diadem. But they have bestirred themselves, like men of energy and sense – like good, practical, earnest, honest, faithful, resolute men – to raise their work-people to a condition of cleanliness, comfort, steady industry, instruction, relaxation, self-respect. And the condition of their work-people is in startling contrast with the degraded sensuality of other work-people similarly employed, and there is no drunkenness among them! And this it is that is needful to be done, on a great scale, for the moral redemption of the prostrate thousands in this kingdom. Drunkenness is rife among the very poor and wretched, as every other low and sensual vice is rife among them, because, for years, they have been left behind in the march of civilisation, and have been sinking deeper and deeper down into the mire, left in the track of the advancing forces. Where drunkenness obtains among workmen who receive good wages, as among the miners, and the iron-workers in the North, it is bred in similar causes. Their occupation is of an exhausting kind; a state of lassitude succeeds, demanding some relief, and having none; their ignorance is dense, their little towns and villages are miserable, and their only refuge is in that accursed vice, born as naturally of such a state of things as fire and smoke of lighted gunpowder. No such attempt as that made at the Glamorganshire works, has ever been discreetly made, and failed. The time is close at hand, when the Government, in imitation of such gallant individuals, must cope with the great evil and great danger of this country, or there is no hope left in us.

But, before such an effort can be made with any chance of success, a deep conviction of its necessity, and a full determination on the part of all classes of society to co-operate for such an end, must spread throughout the length and breadth of England. Now, we tell the total abstinence declaimers plainly, that the association of this great question with the emphatic, homely English phrase of humbug; with Jesuitical perversions of all fact, and truth, and fair deduction; with slanderous aspersions of the industrious and well-conducted parts of the community; with visitations of their own failure on the rational and reasonable home-enjoyments of honest men, who are capable of self-control; is fatal to that state of union and preparation. If they would rest their case on the fair ground of temperance for those who can be temperate, and total abstinence for those who cannot be temperate, and would be content to parade the good they have done (which we do not dispute) in the exceptional cases where persons having no excuse for such misconduct, have yielded to a depraved passion for strong liquor and fallen into a gulf of misery, we should regard them as a good example and a public benefit. But, running a-muck like mad Malays, we look upon them as a bad example, and a public evil, only less intolerable than drunkenness itself.

For, the condition of the lowest classes in this country, and the ever-rising, ever-increasing generation of unhappy beings included under that denomination, is a question far too momentous to be trifled with, by the weakness or the unscrupulous devotion to one idea, of any order of men.

'There is a poor blind Samson in this land,'

writes Mr Longfellow of slavery in America; but there is a poor blind Samson in *this* land, as dangerous as he. Like the strong man of old, he is led by a child – an ignorant child. Like him, he has his sinewy arms – one branded Pauperism, and the other Crime – already round the pillars whereupon the house standeth. Let us beware of him in time, before he makes his awful prayer to be avenged upon us for his blindness, and brings the edifice upon himself, and us – a heap of ruins!

36

Theatre Review: Macready as King Lear

The Examiner, 27 October 1849

Since 1681 the version of *King Lear* played in the English theatre had been that of Nahum Tate. This gave the play a happy ending, restoring Lear to his kingdom and marrying Cordelia to Edgar; it also omitted the Fool. In an 1834 production Macready returned to Shakespeare's text, but still left out the Fool. During his management of Covent Garden 1837–9, however, he did restore the Fool to the cast, the part being played by a young actress-singer, Priscilla Horton. The production opened on 25 January 1838 and was a triumphant success. Illness prevented Forster from attending, but he wrote enthusiastically in *The Examiner* on 28 January citing at length the opinion of 'a friend on whose judgment we have thorough reliance' ('... the character [of the Fool] was exquisitely played by Miss P. Horton; the face, gait, voice, and manner were alike in perfect keeping with the part; the attachment and fidelity of the poor *Fool* to the houseless, broken-hearted King were most affectionately and beautifully portrayed ...'). W.J. Carlton convincingly argues, in the article cited below, that this friend was most probably Dickens and that Dickens is referring back to this in his 1849 review.

This review was first identified as Dickens's by L.C. Staples in *The Dickensian* in 1948 (Vol. 44, pp. 78–80). Staples discovered the MS. of the review in the Forster Collection and printed it. Previously, and indeed for a long time after Staples's reprinting of the 1849 review, a long *Examiner* review of the 1838 production (4 February 1838), entitled 'The Restoration of Shakespeare's Lear to the Stage', had been attributed to Dickens on the strength of its having been included in *MP* by Matz. Carlton decisively demonstrates, however, that it was the work of Forster; see 'Dickens or Forster?' Some *King Lear* Criticisms Re-examined', *The Dickensian*, Vol. 61 (1965), pp. 133–40.

Literary allusions (p. 171) ' "The greatness of Lear," writes Charles Lamb ...': from the essay 'On the Tragedies of Shakespeare considered with reference to their fitness for stage representation', published in *The Reflector* (1811).

MS. Forster Collection, Victoria and Albert Museum.

HAYMARKET THEATRE

Mr Macready appeared on Wednesday Evening in *King Lear.* The House
was crowded in every part before the rising of the curtain and he was
received with deafening enthusiasm. The emotions awakened in the
audience by his magnificent performance, and often demonstrated during
its progress, did not exhaust their spirits. At the close of the tragedy, they
rose in a mass to greet him with a burst of applause that made the
building ring.

Of the many great impersonations with which Mr Macready is
associated and which he is now, unhappily for dramatic art in England,
presenting for the last time, perhaps his *Lear* is the finest. The deep and
subtle consideration he has given to the whole noble play, is visible in
all he says and does. From his rash renunciation of the gentle daughter
who can only love him and be silent, to his falling dead beside her,
unbound from the rack of this tough world, a more affecting, truthful
and awful picture never surely was presented on the stage.

'The greatness of Lear,' writes Charles Lamb, 'is not in corporal
dimension, but in intellectual; the explosions of his passion are terrible
as a volcano: they are storms, turning up and disclosing to the bottom
that sea – his mind, with all its vast riches. It is his mind which is laid
bare. This case of flesh and blood seems too insignificant to be thought
on; even as he himself neglects it. On the stage we see nothing but
corporal infirmities and weakness, the impotence of rage.'

Not so in the performance of Wednesday night. It was the mind of
Lear on which we looked. The heart, soul and brain of the ruin'd piece
of nature, in all the stages of its ruining, were bare before us. What Lamb
writes of the character might have been written of this representation of
it and been a faithful description.

To say of such a performance that this or that point is most observable
in it for its excellence, is hardly to do justice to a piece of art so complete
and beautiful. The tenderness, the rage, the madness, the remorse and
sorrow, all come of one another and are linked together in a chain. Only
of such tenderness, could come such rage; of both combined, such
madness; of such a strife of passions and affections, the pathetic cry:

> Do not laugh at me;
> For, as I am a man, I think this lady
> To be my child Cordelia;

only of such recognition and its sequel, such a broken heart.

Some years have elapsed since we first noticed Miss Horton's acting
of the *Fool,* restored to the play, as one of its most affecting and necessary
features, under Mr Macready's management at Covent Garden. It has

lost nothing in the interval. It would be difficult indeed to praise so exquisite and delicate an assumption too highly.

Miss Reynolds appeared as *Cordelia* for the first time, and was not (except in her appearance) very effective. Mr Stuart played *Kent*, and, but for fully justifying his banishment by his very uproarious demeanour towards his sovereign, played it well. Mr Wallack was a highly meritorious *Edgar*. We have never seen the part so well played. His manner of delivering the description of Dover cliff – watching his blind father the while, and not looking as if he really saw the scene he describes, as it is the manner of most *Edgars* to do – was particularly sensible and good. Mr Howe played with great spirit and Mrs Warner was most wickedly beautiful in *Goneril*. The play was carefully and well presented, and its effect upon the audience hardly to be conceived from this brief description.

37

Court Ceremonies

The Examiner, 15 December 1849

The pious Dowager Queen Adelaide, widow of William IV, whom she had urged to veto the Reform Bill, died on 2 December 1849; 'a person of no character – latterly harmless, except in the annual prodigious sum she received from us who labour for what we get', Macready noted in his diary (*Diaries of William Charles Macready*, ed. William Toynbee [1912], Vol. II, p. 436). Her request for as little funeral pomp as possible would have caught Dickens's attention, given his lifelong horror of elaborate funeral ceremonies (see p. 193 for example; also *Martin Chuzzlewit*, Ch. 19, and *Great Expectations*, Ch. 35). His piece appeared as the second leader in the 'Political Examiner'. On p. 792 of the same issue appears a very full account (nearly three columns, framed in a black border) of the progress of the funeral cortège from the Queen's home at Stanmore to Windsor and an elaborate description of the funeral itself. The Queen's directions, quoted by Dickens, are given again and the reporter comments, 'The mortal remains of Royalty have seldom been conveyed to their resting-place with so little pomp and vanity.'

Literary allusions (p. 174) '*Tom Thumb*': Henry Fielding's mock-heroic farce, *The Tragedy of Tragedies, or, The Life and Death of Tom Thumb the Great* (1731), which features a ludicrous royal Court; (p. 175) 'My good Lord Chamberlain ...': Shakespeare, *Richard III*, Act 1, Sc. 1.

The late Queen Dowager, whose death has given occasion for many public tributes to exalted worth, often formally and falsely rendered on similar occasions, and rarely, if ever, better deserved than on this, committed to writing eight years ago her wishes in reference to her funeral. This truly religious and most unaffected document has been published by her Majesty the Queen's directions. It is more honourable to the memory of the noble lady deceased than broadsides upon broadsides of fulsome panegyric, and is full of good example to all persons in this empire, but particularly, as we think, to the highest persons of all.

I die in all humility, knowing well that we are all alike before the Throne of God, and I request, therefore, that my mortal remains be conveyed to the grave without any pomp or state. They are to be moved to St George's Chapel, Windsor, where I request to have as private and quiet a funeral as possible.

I particularly desire not to be laid out in state, and the funeral to take place by daylight; no procession; the coffin to be carried by sailors to the chapel.

All those of my friends and relations, to a limited number, who wish to attend may do so. My nephew, Prince Edward of Saxe Weimar, Lords Howe, and Denbigh, the Hon. William Ashley, Mr Wood, Sir Andrew Barnard, and Sir D. Davies, with my dressers, and those of my Ladies who may wish to attend.

I die in peace, and wish to be carried to the tomb in peace, and free from the vanities and the pomp of this world.

I request not to be dissected, nor embalmed; and desire to give as little trouble as possible.

November 1841.   ADELAIDE R.

It may be questionable whether the 'Ceremonial for the private interment of her late Most Excellent Majesty, Adelaide the Queen Dowager, in the Royal Chapel of St George at Windsor,' published at the same time as this affecting paper, be quite in unison with the feelings it expresses. Uneasy doubts obtrude themselves upon the mind whether 'her late Majesty's state carriage drawn by six horses, in which will be the crown of her late Majesty, borne on a velvet cushion,' would not have been more in keeping with the funeral requests of the late Mr Ducrow. The programme setting forth in four lines,

THE CHIEF MOURNER,
the Duchess of Norfolk
(veiled)
Attended by a Lady,

is like a bad play-bill. The announcement how 'the Archbishop having concluded the service, Garter will pronounce near the grave the style of Her late Majesty; after which the Lord Chamberlain and the Vice Chamberlain of Her late Majesty's household will break their staves of office, and, kneeling, deposit the same in the Royal Vault,' is more like the announcement outside a booth at a fair, respecting what the elephant or the conjurer will do within, by-and-bye, than consists with the simple solemnity of that last Christian service which is entered upon with the words, 'We brought nothing into this world, and it is certain we can carry nothing out. The Lord gave, and the Lord hath taken away; blessed be the name of the Lord.'

We would not be misunderstood on this point, and we wish distinctly to express our full belief that the funeral of the good Dowager Queen was conducted with proper absence of conventional absurdity. We are persuaded that the highest personages in the country respected the last wishes so modestly expressed, and were earnest in impressing upon all concerned a desire for their exact fulfilment. It is not so much because of any inconsistencies on this particular occasion, as because the Lord Chamberlain's office is the last stronghold of an enormous amount of tomfoolery, which is infinitely better done upon the stage in *Tom Thumb*, which is cumbrous and burdensome to all outside the office itself, and which is negative for any good purpose and often positive for much harm, as making things ridiculous or repulsive which can only exist beneficially in the general love and respect, that we take this occasion of hoping that it is fast on the decline.

This is not the first occasion on which we have observed upon the preposterous constraints and forms that set a mark upon the English Court among the nations of Europe, and amaze European Sovereigns when they first become its guests. In times that are marked beyond all others by rapidity of change, and by the condensation of centuries into years in respect of great advances, it is in the nature of things that these constraints and forms should yearly, daily, hourly, become more preposterous. What was obsolete at first, is rendered in such circumstances, a thousand times more obsolete by every new stride that is made in the onward road. A Court that does not keep pace with a People will look smaller, through the tube which Mr Stephenson is throwing across the Menai Straits, than it looked before.

It is typical of the English Court that its state dresses, though greatly in advance of its ceremonies, are always behind the time. We would bring it up to the time, that it may have the greater share in, and the stronger hold upon, the affections of the time. The spectacle of a Court going down to Windsor by the Great Western Railway, to do, from morning to night, what is five hundred years out of date; or sending such messages to Garter by electric telegraph, as Garter might have received in the lists, in the days of King Richard the First; is not a good one. The example of the Dowager Queen, reviving and improving on the example of the late Duke of Sussex, makes the present no unfit occasion for the utterance of a hope that these things are at last progressing, changing, and resolving themselves into harmony with all other things around them. It is particularly important that this should be the case when a new line of Sovereigns is stretching out before us. It is particularly important that this should be the case when the hopes, the happiness, the property, the liberties, the lives of innumerable people may, and in great measure must, depend on Royal childhood not being too thickly hedged in, or loftily walled round, from a great range of human sympathy, access, and knowledge. Therefore we could desire to have the words of their departed relative, 'We are all alike before the throne of God,' commended to the earliest understanding of our rising Princes and Princesses. Therefore we could desire to bring the chief of the Court ceremonies a little more into the outer world, and cordially to give him the greeting.

My good Lord Chamberlain,
Well are you welcome to this open air!

38

A Preliminary Word

Household Words, 30 March 1850

In this editorial manifesto for his new journal Dickens is concerned to position it among the many already existing weekly publications that were aimed at a mass market. Outstandingly successful among those was *Chambers's Journal*, founded as *Chambers's Edinburgh Journal* in 1832, published at three half-pennies, with a circulation of over 50,000. It was intended to provide 'a meal of healthful, useful and agreeable mental instruction' for all classes and conditions of readers, and mingled informative articles with poetry and some fiction (see L. James, *Fiction for the Working Man* [1974 edn.], pp. 16–17). John Sutherland calls *Chambers's* 'the direct inspiration' for *HW* (*The Longman Companion to Victorian Fiction* [1988], p. 113) and W.H. Wills, Dickens's *HW* sub-editor, had worked on it 1842–5. For Dickens, however, *Chambers's* was 'a somewhat cast-iron and utilitarian publication (as congenial to me, generally, as the brown paper packages in which Ironmongers keep Nails)' (*Pilgrim*, Vol. IV, p. 110), and he here announces how different the editorial emphasis in his own journal will be.

As Harry Stone has pointed out (Stone, Vol. I, p. 13), 'A Preliminary Word' expresses 'some of Dickens's most deeply held beliefs' which appear again and again in his writing, not least in the two novels that came next after the founding of *HW*. The idea of the 'Romance' to be found in 'all familiar things' is a major part of the inspiration for *Bleak House* (1853–4), as the Preface to that novel states, and the need to 'cherish that light of Fancy which is inherent in the human breast' and the dire consequences of society's failing to do so is absolutely central to *Hard Times* (1854).

If Dickens is concerned to distinguish *HW* from *Chambers's*, he is even more concerned to distance it from the publications of G.W.M. Reynolds, whose sensational *feuilletons*, *The Mysteries of London* (1846–8) and *The Mysteries of the Court of London* (1849–56), were published in weekly penny numbers and had a huge circulation. Reynolds started his penny weekly, *Reynolds Miscellany*, in 1846, writing its first serial, *Wagner: The Werewolf*, and featuring in every issue an address 'to the industrial classes' in which (as in his *Reynolds's Weekly Newspaper* begun in 1850) he expounded his strong Chartist and republican views (he had emerged as an active Chartist leader in 1848). The extremity of his political views was abhorrent to Dickens, as was his sensationalist fiction. Hence the double denunciation of him as a 'bastard of the Mountain' ('the Mountain' was the name given to the Robespierre/Danton party, which sat high up in the 1790's French National Assembly; in 1848 the term was revived to denote the extreme republican party in France) and as a 'pander to the basest passions of the lowest natures'. In *Household Narrative* for April 1851 Reynolds was described (p. 73) as 'a person notorious for his attempts to degrade the working men of England by circulating among them books of a debasing tendency'. No doubt an extra edge was given to Dickens's detestation of Reynolds by the fact that the letter had impudently and profitably plagiarised *Pickwick Papers* in his *Pickwick Abroad: or the Tour in France* (1837–8), in which the Pickwickians are plunged into 'the sensualities of the Paris underworld' (James, *op. cit.*, p. 61).

Literary allusions (p. 178) 'Slaves of the Lamp': alludes to the story of Aladdin and the wonderful lamp in *The Arabian Nights*; (p. 178) 'shapes "that give delight and hurt not" ': from Shakespeare, *The Tempest*, Act 3, Sc. 2; (p. 178) 'the old fairy story': the story in *The Arabian Nights*, called 'The Sisters who envied their Younger Sister', in which those climbing a stone-strewn mountain in quest of a magical singing bird 'hear on all sides a confusion of voices … a thousand injurious abuses' meant to alarm and discourage them; any climber who stops to look behind him is at once turned into stone (*The Arabian Nights*, trans. E.W. Lane [1901], Vol. 6, p. 277); (p. 178) 'the stones have sermons in them … good in everything': Shakespeare, *As You Like It*, Act 2, Sc. 1.

The name that we have chosen for this publication expresses, generally, the desire we have at heart in originating it.

We aspire to live in the Household affections, and to be numbered among the Household thoughts, of our readers. We hope to be the comrade and friend of many thousands of people, of both sexes, and of all ages and conditions, on whose faces we may never look. We seek to bring into innumerable homes, from the stirring world around us, the knowledge of many social wonders, good and evil, that are not calculated to render any of us less ardently persevering in ourselves, less tolerant of one another, less faithful in the progress of mankind, less thankful for the privilege of living in this summer-dawn of time.

No mere utilitarian spirit, no iron binding of the mind to grim realities, will give a harsh tone to our Household Words. In the bosoms of the young and old, of the well-to-do and of the poor, we would tenderly cherish that light of Fancy which is inherent in the human breast; which, according to its nurture, burns with an inspiring flame, or sinks into a sullen glare, but which (or woe betide the day!) can never be extinguished. To show to all, that in all familiar things, even in those which are repellent on the surface, there is Romance enough, if we will find it out: – to teach the hardest workers at this whirling wheel of toil, that their lot is not necessarily a moody, brutal fact, excluded from the sympathies and graces of imagination; to bring the greater and the lesser in degree, together, upon that wide field, and mutually dispose them to a better acquaintance and a kinder understanding – is one main object of our Household Words.

The mightier inventions of this age are not, to our thinking, all material, but have a kind of souls in their stupendous bodies which may find expression in Household Words. The traveller whom we accompany on his railroad or his steamboat journey, may gain, we hope, some compensation for incidents which these later generations have outlived, in new associations with the Power that bears him onward; with the habitations and the ways of life of crowds of his fellow creatures among whom he passes like the wind; even with the towering chimneys he may see, spirting out fire and smoke upon the prospect. The swart giants, Slaves of the Lamp of Knowledge, have their thousand and one tales, no less than the Genii of the East; and these, in all their wild, grotesque, and fanciful aspects, in all their many phases of endurance, in all their many moving lessons of compassion and consideration, we design to tell.

Our Household Words will not be echoes of the present time alone, but of the past too. Neither will they treat of the hopes, the enterprises, triumphs, joys, and sorrows, of this country only, but, in some degree, of those of every nation upon earth. For nothing can be a source of real interest in one of them, without concerning all the rest.

We have considered what an ambition it is to be admitted into many homes with affection and confidence; to be regarded as a friend by children and old people; to be thought of in affliction and in happiness; to people the sick room with airy shapes 'that give delight and hurt not,' and to be associated with the harmless laughter and the gentle tears of many hearths. We know the great responsibility of such a privilege; its vast reward; the pictures that it conjures up, in hours of solitary labour, of a multitude moved by one sympathy; the solemn hopes which it awakens in the labourer's breast, that he may be free from self-reproach in looking back at last upon his work, and that his name may be remembered in his race in time to come, and borne by the dear objects of his love with pride. The hand that writes these faltering lines, happily associated with *some* Household Words before today, has known enough of such experiences to enter in an earnest spirit upon this new task, and with an awakened sense of all that it involves.

Some tillers of the field into which we now come, have been before us, and some are here whose high usefulness we readily acknowledge, and whose company it is an honour to join. But, there are others here – Bastards of the Mountain, draggled fringe on the Red Cap, Panders to the basest passions of the lowest natures – whose existence is a national reproach. And these, we should consider it our highest service to displace.

Thus, we begin our career! The adventurer in the old fairy story, climbing towards the summit of a steep eminence on which the object of his search was stationed, was surrounded by a roar of voices, crying to him, from the stones in the way, to turn back. All the voices *we* hear, cry Go on! The stones that call to us have sermons in them, as the trees have tongues, as there are books in the running brooks, as there is good in everything! They, and the Time, cry out to us Go on! With a fresh heart, a light step, and a hopeful courage, we begin the journey. The road is not so rough that it need daunt our feet: the way is not so steep that we need stop for breath, and looking faintly down, be stricken motionless. Go on, is all we hear, Go on! In a glow already, with the air from yonder height upon us, and the inspiriting voices joining in this acclamation, we echo back the cry, and go on cheerily!

39

The Amusements of the People (1)

Household Words, 30 March 1850

Dickens wrote or co-wrote three pieces for the first number of his new journal. For the co-authored piece, 'Valentine's Day at the Post-Office', written with his sub-editor W.H. Wills, and another article, 'A Bundle of Emigrants' Letters', in which Dickens presented some letters home from emigrants to Australia, see Stone. 'The Amusements of the People' is the first instalment of a two-part polemical report on the kind of entertainment available to working-class audiences at two well-known popular theatres. It relates directly to one aspect of the editorial project announced in Dickens's 'Preliminary Word' in that it is concerned with the cultivation of the imagination, cherishing 'that light of Fancy which is inherent in the human breast'. For Dickens, one of the supreme sites for imaginative experience was the theatre and here he directs his middle-class readers' attention to the kind of dramatic entertainment provided at his neighbourhood theatre for the generically named Joe Whelks (whelks, like oysters, were a favourite delicacy of the Victorian poor).

The theatre visited in this piece is the one now called the Old Vic, which is located south of the river in Lambeth, near Waterloo Station (the New Cut, now simply the Cut, connects Waterloo and Blackfriars Roads; it was cut across Lambeth Marsh around 1812). Opened as the Royal Coburg in 1818 and renamed the Royal Victoria in 1833 in compliment to the young Princess, the theatre held over 3,000 people and drew on a mainly local audience. From 1841 it had been under the management of David Osbaldiston, an actor celebrated in 'heavy' melodramatic roles, and his leading lady Eliza Vincent, who was also his mistress. The Theatre Reform Act of 1843 extended the Lord Chamberlain's licensing powers, previously restricted to the patent theatres and Westminster, to all London theatres and the play Dickens saw had been licensed under the title *May Morning;*

or the Mendicant Heir. It was first produced on 26 January 1850 and, George
Rowell notes (*The Old Vic Theatre: A History* [1993], p. 37), 'was withdrawn
after a respectable run' at the end of February. The 'cheerful sailor, with
very loose legs' had been an immensely popular stage figure since the great
success of Jerrold's *Black-eyed Susan* (see article 34) and invariably danced a
hornpipe at some point in whatever play he appeared in. See Rowell, *op.
cit.*, for a good account of the Royal Victoria at this time (when it was
described by Henry Mayhew and – very hostilely – by Charles Kingsley,
as well as by Dickens). *Red Riven* was a stock melodrama first produced at
the Coburg in 1825.

Literary allusions (p. 181) *The Maid and the Magpie* and *The Dog of
Montargis; or the Forest of Bondy* were stock items in the repertoire of the early
nineteenth-century popular theatre; (p. 181) 'Those who would live to please
...': Johnson's 'Prologue at the Opening of Drury Lane' – 'The drama's
laws the drama's patrons give,/For we that live to please, must please to
live'; (p. 181) 'hold the Mirror up to Nature': Shakespeare, *Hamlet*, Act 3,
Sc. 2; 'like the dyer's hand': Shakespeare, Sonnet No. 111.

MS. Corrected proof in Forster Collection, Victoria and Albert Museum.

As one half of the world is said not to know how the other half lives, so
it may be affirmed that the upper half of the world neither knows nor
greatly cares how the lower half amuses itself. Believing that it does not
care, mainly because it does not know, we purpose occasionally recording
a few facts on the subject.

The general character of the lower class of dramatic amusements is a
very significant sign of a people, and a very good test of their intellectual
condition. We design to make our readers acquainted in the first place
with a few of our experiences under this head in the metropolis.

It is probable that nothing will ever root out from among the common
people an innate love they have for dramatic entertainment in some
form or other. It would be a very doubtful benefit to society, we think,
if it could be rooted out. The Polytechnic Institution in Regent Street,
where an infinite variety of ingenious models are exhibited and explained,
and where lectures comprising a quantity of useful information on many
practical subjects are delivered, is a great public benefit and a wonderful
place, but we think a people formed *entirely* in their hours of leisure by
Polytechnic Institutions would be an uncomfortable community. We
would rather not have to appeal to the generous sympathies of a man of
five-and-twenty, in respect of some affliction of which he had had no
personal experience, who had passed all his holidays, when a boy, among

cranks and cogwheels. We should be more disposed to trust him if he had been brought into occasional contact with a Maid and a Magpie; if he had made one or two diversions into the Forest of Bondy; or had even gone the length of a Christmas Pantomime. There is a range of imagination in most of us, which no amount of steam-engines will satisfy; and which The-great-exhibition-of-the-works-of-industry-of-all-nations, itself, will probably leave unappeased. The lower we go, the more natural it is that the best-relished provision for this should be found in dramatic entertainments; as at once the most obvious, the least troublesome, and the most real, of all escapes out of the literal world. Joe Whelks, of the New Cut, Lambeth, is not much of a reader, has no great store of books, no very commodious room to read in, no very decided inclination to read, and no power at all of presenting vividly before his mind's eye what he reads about. But put Joe in the gallery of the Victoria Theatre; show him doors and windows in the scene that will open and shut, and that people can get in and out of; tell him a story with these aids, and by the help of live men and women dressed up, confiding to him their innermost secrets, in voices audible half a mile off; and Joe will unravel a story through all its entanglements, and sit there as long after midnight as you have anything left to show him. Accordingly the Theatres to which Mr Whelks resorts, are always full; and whatever changes of fashion the drama knows elsewhere, it is always fashionable in the New Cut.

The question, then, might not unnaturally arise, one would suppose, whether Mr Whelks's education is at all susceptible of improvement, through the agency of his theatrical tastes. How far it is improved at present, our readers shall judge for themselves.

In affording them the means of doing so, we wish to disclaim any grave imputation on those who are concerned in ministering to the dramatic gratification of Mr Whelks. Heavily taxed, wholly unassisted by the State, deserted by the gentry, and quite unrecognised as a means of public instruction, the higher English Drama has declined. Those who would live to please Mr Whelks, must please Mr Whelks to live. It is not the Manager's province to hold the Mirror up to Nature, but to Mr Whelks – the only person who acknowledges him. If, in like manner, the actor's nature, like the dyer's hand, becomes subdued to what he works in, the actor can hardly be blamed for it. He grinds hard at his vocation, is often steeped in direful poverty, and lives, at the best, in a little world of mockeries. It is bad enough to give away a great estate six nights a-week, and want a shilling; to preside at imaginary banquets, hungry for a mutton chop; to smack the lips over a tankard of toast and water, and declaim about the mellow produce of the sunny vineyard on the banks of the Rhine; to be a rattling young lover, with the measles at home;

and to paint sorrow over with burnt cork and rouge; without being called upon to despise his vocation too. If he can utter the trash to which he is condemned, with any relish, so much the better for him, Heaven knows; and peace be with him!

A few weeks ago, we went to one of Mr Whelks's favourite Theatres, to see an attractive Melo-Drama called *May Morning, or The Mystery of 1715, and the Murder*! We had an idea that the former of these titles might refer to the month in which either the mystery or the murder happened, but we found it to be the name of the heroine, the pride of Keswick Vale; who was 'called May Morning' (after a common custom among the English Peasantry) 'from her bright eyes and merry laugh.' Of this young lady, it may be observed, in passing, that she subsequently sustained every possible calamity of human existence, in a white muslin gown with blue tucks; and that she did every conceivable and inconceivable thing with a pistol, that could anyhow be effected by that description of fire-arms.

The Theatre was extremely full. The prices of admission were, to the boxes, a shilling; to the pit, sixpence; to the gallery, threepence. The gallery was of enormous dimensions (among the company, in the front row, we observed Mr Whelks); and overflowing with occupants. It required no close observation of the attentive faces, rising one above another, to the very door in the roof, and squeezed and jammed in, regardless of all discomforts, even there, to impress a stranger with a sense of its being highly desirable to lose no possible chance of effecting any mental improvement in that great audience.

The company in the pit were not very clean or sweet-savoured, but there were some good-humoured young mechanics among them, with their wives. These were generally accompanied by 'the baby,' insomuch that the pit was a perfect nursery. No effect made on the stage was so curious, as the looking down on the quiet faces of these babies fast asleep, after looking up at the staring sea of heads in the gallery. There were a good many cold fried soles in the pit, besides; and a variety of flat stone bottles, of all portable sizes.

The audience in the boxes was of much the same character (babies and fish excepted) as the audience in the pit. A private in the Foot Guards sat in the next box; and a personage who wore pins on his coat instead of buttons, and was in such a damp habit of living as to be quite mouldy, was our nearest neighbour. In several parts of the house we noticed some young pickpockets of our acquaintance; but as they were evidently there as private individuals, and not in their public capacity, we were little disturbed by their presence. For we consider the hours of idleness passed by this class of society as so much gain to society at large; and we do not join in a whimsical sort of lamentation that is generally made over them, when they are found to be unoccupied.

As we made these observations the curtain rose, and we were presently in possession of the following particulars.

Sir George Elmore, a melancholy Baronet with every appearance of being in that advanced stage of indigestion in which Mr Morison's patients usually are, when they happen to hear through Mr Moat, of the surprising effects of his Vegetable Pills, was found to be living in a very large castle, in the society of one round table, two chairs, and Captain George Elmore, 'his supposed son, the Child of Mystery, and the Man of Crime.' The Captain, in addition to an undutiful habit of bullying his father on all occasions, was a prey to many vices: foremost among which may be mentioned his desertion of his wife, 'Estella de Neva, a Spanish lady,' and his determination unlawfully to possess himself of May Morning; M. M. being then on the eve of marriage to Will Stanmore, a cheerful sailor, with very loose legs.

The strongest evidence, at first, of the Captain's being the Child of Mystery and the Man of Crime was deducible from his boots, which, being very high and wide, and apparently made of sticking-plaster, justified the worst theatrical suspicions to his disadvantage. And indeed he presently turned out as ill as could be desired: getting into May Morning's Cottage by the window after dark; refusing to 'unhand' May Morning when required to do so by that lady; waking May Morning's only surviving parent, a blind old gentleman with a black ribbon over his eyes, whom we shall call Mr Stars, as his name was stated in the bill thus *** and showing himself desperately bent on carrying off May Morning by force of arms. Even this was not the worst of the Captain; for, being foiled in his diabolical purpose – temporarily by means of knives and pistols, providentially caught up and directed at him by May Morning, and finally, for the time being, by the advent of Will Stanmore – he caused one Slink, his adherent, to denounce Will Stanmore as a rebel, and got that cheerful mariner carried off, and shut up in prison. At about the same period of the Captain's career, there suddenly appeared in his father's castle, a dark complexioned lady of the name of Manuella, 'a Zingara Woman from the Pyrenean Mountains; the Wild Wanderer of the Heath, and the Pronouncer of the Prophecy,' who threw the melancholy baronet, his supposed father, into the greatest confusion by asking him what he had upon his conscience, and by pronouncing mysterious rhymes concerning the Child of Mystery and the Man of Crime, to a low trembling of fiddles. Matters were in this state when the Theatre resounded with applause, and Mr Whelks fell into a fit of unbounded enthusiasm, consequent on the entrance of 'Michael the Mendicant.'

At first we referred something of the cordiality with which Michael the Mendicant was greeted, to the fact of his being 'made up' with an excessively dirty face, which might create a bond of union between himself and a large majority of the audience. But it soon came out that Michael the Mendicant had been hired in old time by Sir George Elmore to murder his (Sir George Elmore's) elder brother – which he had done; notwithstanding which little affair of honour, Michael was in reality a very good fellow; quite a tender-hearted man; who, on hearing of the Captain's determination to settle Will Stanmore, cried out, 'What! more bel-ood!' and fell flat – overpowered by his nice sense of humanity. In like manner, in describing that small error of judgment into which he had allowed himself to be tempted by money, this gentleman exclaimed, 'I ster-ruck him down, and fel-ed in er-orror!' and further he remarked, with honest pride, 'I have liveder as a beggar – a roadsider vaigerant, but no ker-rime since then has stained these hands!' All these sentiments of the worthy man were hailed with showers of applause; and when, in the excitement of his feelings on one occasion, after a soliloquy, he 'went off' *on his back*, kicking and shuffling along the ground, after the manner of bold spirits in trouble, who object to be taken to the station-house, the cheering was tremendous.

And to see how little harm he had done, after all! Sir George Elmore's elder brother was NOT dead. Not he! He recovered, after this sensitive creature had 'fel-ed in er-orror,' and, putting a black ribbon over his eyes to disguise himself, went and lived in a modest retirement with his only child. In short, Mr Stars was the identical individual! When Will Stanmore turned out to be the wrongful Sir George Elmore's son, instead of the Child of Mystery and the Man of Crime, who turned out to be Michael's son (a change having been effected, in revenge, by the lady from the Pyrenean Mountains, who became the Wild Wanderer of the Heath, in consequence of the wrongful Sir George Elmore's perfidy to her and desertion of her), Mr Stars went up to the Castle, and mentioned to his murdering brother how it was. Mr Stars said it was all right; he bore no malice; he had kept out of the way in order that his murdering brother (to whose numerous virtues he was no stranger) might enjoy the property; and now he would propose that they should make it up and dine together. The murdering brother immediately consented, embraced the Wild Wanderer, and it is supposed sent instructions to Doctors' Commons for a licence to marry her. After which, they were all very comfortable indeed. For it is not much to try to murder your brother for the sake of his property, if you only suborn such a delicate assassin as Michael the Mendicant?

All this did not tend to the satisfaction of the Child of Mystery and Man of Crime, who was so little pleased by the general happiness, that he shot Will Stanmore, now joyfully out of prison and going to be married directly to May Morning, and carried off the body, and May Morning to boot, to a lone hut. Here, Will Stanmore, laid out for dead at fifteen minutes past twelve, P.M., arose at seventeen minutes past, infinitely fresher than most daisies, and fought two strong men single-handed. However, the Wild Wanderer, arriving with a party of male wild wanderers, who were always at her disposal – and the murdering brother arriving arm-in-arm with Mr Stars – stopped the combat, confounded the Child of Mystery and Man of Crime, and blessed the lovers.

The adventures of '*Red Riven the Bandit*' concluded the moral lesson of the evening. But, feeling by this time a little fatigued, and believing that we already discerned in the countenance of Mr Whelks a sufficient confusion between right and wrong to last him for one night, we retired: the rather as we intended to meet him, shortly, at another place of dramatic entertainment for the people.

40

A Child's Dream of a Star

Household Words, 6 April 1850 (leading article) (*RP*)

Dickens wrote to Forster on 14 March that he had felt, when reviewing the proposed contents for the second number of *HW*, 'an uneasy sense of there being a want of something tender, which would apply to some universal household knowledge'; looking at the stars during a journey on the railway ('always a wonderfully suggestive place to me when I am alone'), he found himself 'revolving a little idea about them' and, putting the two things together, wrote this piece 'straightway' (*Pilgrim*, Vol. VI, p. 65). It was given pride of place in the new number.

Forster notes (Book 6, Ch. 4) apropos of this piece that Dickens told him he and his much-loved sister Fanny 'used to wander at night about a churchyard near their house [in Chatham] looking up at the stars', and that Fanny's early death in the summer of 1848 'had vividly reawakened all the childish associations which made her memory dear to him'. There seems to be a clear reference to his childhood companionship with Fanny in the opening paragraph of 'A Child's Dream', but, as I have argued elsewhere, the presence of his idolised sister-in-law Mary Hogarth (whose sudden death at the age of seventeen had been such a terrible blow to him in 1837) can also be strongly felt in the piece (see Slater, *Dickens and Women* [1983], p. 92).

The form and style of this 'Child's Dream' echoes that of Carové's *Das Märchen Ohne Ende* ('The Story without an End'), which Dickens had drawn on many years earlier for the purposes of political satire (see p. 10).

MS. John Rylands Library, University of Manchester. The MS. variants mainly concern accidentals (Dickens consistently wrote Angel with a capital A, for example) apart from three places: for 'the man who had been a child saw his daughter,' the MS. reads 'he saw his child'; for 'old man', the MS. reads 'old old man'; for 'I thank thee', the MS. reads 'I thank thee humbly'.

There was once a child, and he strolled about a good deal, and thought of a number of things. He had a sister, who was a child too, and his constant companion. These two used to wonder all day long. They wondered at the beauty of the flowers; they wondered at the height and blueness of the sky; they wondered at the depth of the bright water; they wondered at the goodness and the power of GOD who made the lovely world.

They used to say to one another, sometimes, Supposing all the children upon earth were to die, would the flowers, and the water, and the sky, be sorry? They believed they would be sorry. For, said they, the buds are the children of the flowers, and the little playful streams that gambol down the hill-sides are the children of the water; and the smallest bright specks, playing at hide and seek in the sky all night, must surely be the children of the stars; and they would all be grieved to see their playmates, the children of men, no more.

There was one clear-shining star that used to come out in the sky before the rest, near the church spire, above the graves. It was larger and more beautiful, they thought, than all the others, and every night they watched for it, standing hand in hand at a window. Whoever saw it first, cried out, 'I see the star!' And often they cried out both together, knowing so well when it would rise, and where. So they grew to be such friends with it, that, before lying down in their beds, they always looked out once again, to bid it good night; and when they were turning round to sleep, they used to say, 'God bless the star!'

But while she was still very young, oh very very young, the sister drooped, and came to be so weak that she could no longer stand in the window at night; and then the child looked sadly out by himself, and when he saw the star, turned round and said to the patient pale face on the bed, 'I see the star!' and then a smile would come upon the face, and a little weak voice used to say, 'God bless my brother and the star!'

And so the time came, all too soon! when the child looked out alone, and when there was no face on the bed; and when there was a little grave among the graves, not there before, and when the star made long rays down towards him, as he saw it through his tears.

Now, these rays were so bright, and they seemed to make such a shining way from earth to Heaven, that when the child went to his solitary bed, he dreamed about the star; and dreamed that, lying where he was, he saw a train of people taken up that sparkling road by angels. And the star, opening, showed him a great world of light, where many more such angels waited to receive them.

All these angels, who were waiting, turned their beaming eyes upon the people who were carried up into the star; and some came out from the long rows in which they stood, and fell upon the people's necks, and kissed them tenderly, and went away with them down avenues of light, and were so happy in their company, that lying in his bed he wept for joy.

But, there were many angels who did not go with them, and among them one he knew. The patient face that once had lain upon the bed was glorified and radiant, but his heart found out his sister among all the host.

His sister's angel lingered near the entrance of the star, and said to the leader among those who had brought the people thither:

'Is my brother come?'

And he said 'No.'

She was turning hopefully away, when the child stretched out his arms, and cried 'O, sister, I am here! Take me!' and then she turned her beaming eyes upon him, and it was night; and the star was shining into the room, making long rays down towards him as he saw it through his tears.

From that hour forth, the child looked out upon the star as on the Home he was to go to, when his time should come; and he thought that he did not belong to the earth alone, but to the star too, because of his sister's angel gone before.

There was a baby born to be a brother to the child; and while he was so little that he never yet had spoken word, he stretched his tiny form out on his bed, and died.

Again the child dreamed of the opened star, and of the company of angels, and the train of people, and the rows of angels with their beaming eyes all turned upon those people's faces.

Said his sister's angel to the leader:

'Is my brother come?'

And he said 'Not that one, but another.'

As the child beheld his brother's angel in her arms, he cried, 'O, sister, I am here! Take me!' And she turned and smiled upon him, and the star was shining.

He grew to be a young man, and was busy at his books, when an old servant came to him, and said:

'Thy mother is no more. I bring her blessing on her darling son!'

Again at night he saw the star, and all that former company. Said his sister's angel to the leader:

'Is my brother come?'

And he said, 'Thy mother!'

A mighty cry of joy went forth through all the star, because the mother was re-united to her two children. And he stretched out his arms and cried, 'O, mother, sister, and brother, I am here! Take me!' And they answered him 'Not yet,' and the star was shining.

He grew to be a man, whose hair was turning grey, and he was sitting in his chair by the fireside, heavy with grief, and with his face bedewed with tears, when the star opened once again.

Said his sister's angel to the leader, 'Is my brother come?'

And he said, 'Nay, but his maiden daughter.'

And the man who had been the child saw his daughter, newly lost to him, a celestial creature among those three, and he said, 'My daughter's head is on my sister's bosom, and her arm is round my mother's neck, and at her feet there is the baby of old time, and I can bear the parting from her, GOD be praised!'

And the star was shining.

Thus the child came to be an old man, and his once smooth face was wrinkled, and his steps were slow and feeble, and his back was bent. And one night as he lay upon his bed, his children standing round, he cried, as he had cried so long ago:

'I see the star!'

They whispered one another 'He is dying.'

And he said, 'I am. My age is falling from me like a garment, and I move towards the star as a child. And O, my Father, now I thank thee that it has so often opened, to receive those dear ones who await me!'

And the star was shining; and it shines upon his grave.

41

Perfect Felicity in a Bird's-Eye View

Household Words, 6 April 1850

'Happy Families', or collections of small animals and birds who were natural enemies shown living peaceably together in the same cage, were a popular form of street entertainment in the mid-Victorian period, one such show being elaborately described by Mayhew (*London Labour and the London Poor* [1861–2], Vol. iii, pp. 214–19). This provides Dickens with a fine device for a general satire on contemporary squabbling over such matters as national education (bedevilled by sectarian rivalry) and ecclesiastical affairs, dubious social experiments such as the Pentonville Prison 'solitary system' (see p. 213), Parliamentary conventions (more extensively ridiculed in 'A Few Conventionalities', *HW*, 28 June 1851; *MP*), and the organised hypocrisy of 'Society'. Sir Peter Laurie, whom Dickens had already satirised as 'Alderman Cute' in *The Chimes* (1844) following the former Lord Mayor's notorious campaign to 'put down' suicide, is again singled out for special attack. He had just made himself ridiculous by declaring at a meeting of the Marylebone Vestry in March that the slum area of Jacob's Island did not really exist, but was 'only' an invention of Dickens's in *Oliver Twist*. Dickens had seized the opportunity of the issue of the Cheap Edition of *Oliver* in that same month to write a whole new Preface mocking Laurie's absurdity ('when Fielding described Newgate, the prison immediately ceased to exist . . .') and gives him the *coup de grâce* here.

For the other detailed allusions in this piece, see the Index and Glossary.

The device of this piece also gives Dickens an opportunity to express his delight in the nature of ravens. He had kept two successively as pets and took great pleasure in studying their behaviour. The first died in March 1841 and Dickens wrote a marvellous comic lament for him in a letter to Maclise (*Pilgrim*, Vol ii, pp. 230–2); the second, 'older and more gifted', was soon afterwards found for Dickens at a village pub in Yorkshire and survived till 1845. Both birds contributed to the character of Grip in *Barnaby Rudge* (1841) and were celebrated by Dickens in the Preface to the Cheap Edition of that novel (March 1849).

Literary allusions (p. 190) 'his quiddits, his quillets . . .' Shakespeare, *Hamlet*, Act 5, Sc. 1; (p. 191) 'sham': a favourite word of Carlyle's.

I am the Raven in the Happy Family – and nobody knows what a life of misery I lead!

The dog informs me (he was a puppy about town before he joined us; which was lately) that there is more than one Happy Family on view in London. Mine, I beg to say, may be known by being the Family which contains a splendid Raven.

I want to know why I am to be called upon to accommodate myself to a cat, a mouse, a pigeon, a ringdove, an owl (who is the greatest ass I have ever known), a guinea-pig, a sparrow, and a variety of other creatures with whom I have no opinion in common. Is this national education? Because, if it is, I object to it. Is our cage what they call neutral ground, on which all parties may agree? If so, war to the beak I consider preferable.

What right has any man to require me to look complacently at a cat on a shelf all day? It may be all very well for the owl. My opinion of *him* is that he blinks and stares himself into a state of such dense stupidity that he has no idea what company he is in. I have seen him, with my own eyes, blink himself, for hours, into the conviction that he was alone in a belfry. But *I* am not the owl. It would have been better for me, if I had been born in that station of life.

I am a Raven. I am, by nature, a sort of collector, or antiquarian. If I contributed, in my natural state, to any Periodical, it would be The Gentleman's Magazine. I have a passion for amassing things that are of no use to me, and burying them. Supposing such a thing – I don't wish it to be known to our proprietor that I put this case, but I say, supposing such a thing – as that I took out one of the Guinea-Pig's eyes; how could I bury it here? The floor of the cage is not an inch thick. To be sure, I could dig through it with my bill (if I dared), but what would be the comfort of dropping Guinea-Pig's eye into Regent Street?

What *I* want, is privacy. I want to make a collection. I desire to get a little property together. How can I do it here? Mr Hudson couldn't have done it, under corresponding circumstances.

I want to live by my own abilities, instead of being provided for in this way. I am stuck in a cage with these incongruous companions, and called a member of the Happy Family; but suppose you took a Queen's Counsel out of Westminster Hall, and settled him board and lodging free, in Utopia, where there would be no excuse for 'his quiddits, his quillets, his cases, his tenures, and his tricks,' how do you think *he*'d like it? Not at all. Then why do you expect *me* to like it, and add insult to injury by calling me a 'Happy' Raven!

This is what *I* say: I want to see men do it. I should like to get up a Happy Family of men, and show 'em. I should like to put the Rajah Brooke, the Peace Society, Captain Aaron Smith, several Malay Pirates,

Dr Wiseman, the Reverend Hugh Stowell, Mr Fox of Oldham, the Board of Health, all the London undertakers, some of the Common (very common *I* think) Council, and all the vested interests in the filth and misery of the poor into a good-sized cage, and see how *they*'d get on. I should like to look in at 'em through the bars, after they had undergone the training I have undergone. You wouldn't find Sir Peter Laurie 'putting down' Sanitary Reform then, or getting up in *that* vestry, and pledging his word and honour to the non-existence of Saint Paul's Cathedral, I expect! And very happy *he*'d be, wouldn't he, when he couldn't do that sort of thing?

I have no idea of you lords of the creation coming staring at me in this false position. Why don't you look at home? If you think I'm fond of the dove, you're very much mistaken. If you imagine there is the least goodwill between me and the pigeon, you never were more deceived in your lives. If you suppose I wouldn't demolish the whole Family (myself excepted), and the cage too, if I had my own way, you don't know what a real Raven is. But if you *do* know this, why am *I* to be picked out as a curiosity? Why don't you go and stare at the Bishop of Exeter? 'Ecod, he's one of our breed, if anybody is!

Do you make me lead this public life because I seem to be what I ain't? Why, I don't make half the pretences that are common among you men! You never heard *me* call the sparrow my noble friend. When did *I* ever tell the Guinea-Pig that he was my Christian brother? Name the occasion of my making myself a party to the 'sham' (my friend Mr Carlyle will lend me his favourite word for the occasion) that the cat hadn't really her eye upon the mouse! Can *you* say as much? What about the last Court Ball, the next Debate in the Lords, the last great Ecclesiastical Suit, the next long assembly in the Court Circular? I wonder you are not ashamed to look me in the eye! I am an independent Member – of the Happy Family; and I ought to be let out.

I have only one consolation in my inability to damage anything, and that is that I hope I am instrumental in propagating a delusion as to the character of Ravens. I have a strong impression that the sparrows on our beat are beginning to think they may trust a Raven. Let 'em try! There's an uncle of mine in a stable-yard down in Yorkshire who will very soon undeceive any small bird that may favour him with a call.

The dogs too. Ha, ha! As they go by, they look at me and this dog, in a quite friendly way. They never suspect how I should hold on to the tip of his tail, if I consulted my own feelings instead of our proprietor's. It's almost worth being here, to think of some confiding dog who has seen me, going too near a friend of mine who lives at a hackney-coach stand in Oxford Street. You wouldn't stop *his* squeaking in a hurry, if my friend got a chance at him.

It's the same with the children. There's a young gentleman with a hat and feathers, resident in Portland Place, who brings a penny to our proprietor, twice a week. He wears very short white drawers, and has mottled legs above his socks. He hasn't the least idea what I should do to his legs, if I consulted my own inclinations. He never imagines what I am thinking of, when we look at one another. May he only take those legs, in their present juicy state, close to the cage of my brother-in-law of the Zoological Gardens, Regent's Park!

Call yourselves rational beings, and talk about our being reclaimed? Why, there isn't one of us who wouldn't astonish you, if we could only get out. Let *me* out, and see whether I should be meek or not. But this is the way you always go on in – you know you do. Up at Pentonville, the sparrow says – and he ought to know, for he was born in a stack of chimneys in that prison – you are spending I am afraid to say how much, every year out of the rates, to keep men in solitude, where they CAN'T do any harm (that you know of), and then you sing all sorts of choruses about their being good. So am I what you call good – here. Why? Because I can't help it. Try me outside!

You ought to be ashamed of yourselves, the Magpie says; and I agree with him. If you are determined to pet only those who take things and hide them, why don't you pet the Magpie and me? We are interesting enough for you, ain't we? The Mouse says you are not half so particular about the honest people. He is not a bad authority. He was almost starved when he lived in a workhouse, wasn't he? He didn't get much fatter, I suppose, when he moved to a labourer's cottage? He was thin enough when he came from that place, here – I know that. And what does the Mouse (whose word is his bond) declare? He declares that you don't take half the care you ought of your own young, and don't teach 'em half enough. Why don't you then? You might give our proprietor something to do, I should think, in twisting miserable boys and girls *into* their proper nature, instead of twisting us out of ours. You are a nice set of fellows, certainly, to come and look at Happy Families, as if you had nothing else to look after!

I take the opportunity of our proprietor's pen and ink in the evening to write this. I shall put it away in a corner – quite sure, as it's intended for the Post Office, of Mr Rowland Hill's getting hold of it somehow, and sending it to somebody. I understand he can do anything with a letter. Though the Owl says (but I don't believe him), that the present prevalence of measles and chicken-pox among infants in all parts of this country, has been caused by Mr Rowland Hill. I hope I needn't add that we Ravens are all good scholars, but that we keep our secret (as the Indians believe the Monkeys do, according to a Parrot of my acquaintance) lest our abilities should be imposed upon. As nothing

—

worse than my present degradation as a member of the Happy Family can happen to me, however, I desert the General Freemason's Lodge of Ravens, and express my disgust in writing.

Dickens used the Raven for three more satirical pieces in *HW*: a general satire on human failings (11 May 1850), in which the Raven threatens to write a book about human beings as Buffon had about animals, exposing their vices and follies as experienced by various domestic animals; a satire on one of Dickens's perennial *bêtes noires*, elaborate funeral ceremonies (8 June 1850), topicality being given to the piece by the fact of a 'General Interment Bill' being before Parliament; and a third piece (24 August 1850) in which the Raven mocks gawping sight-seers constantly seeking novelty and presents his friend the Horse's unflattering view of humanity. In similar vein is 'The "Good" Hippopotamus' (12 October 1850), which develops the Raven's suggestion in the previous piece that a statue should be put up to the Hippopotamus, currently the star turn at the Zoological Gardens in Regent's Park (this is Dickens's response to the proposal to erect by public subscription a statue to the recently dead Duke of Cambridge, who would seem to have done nothing whatever to deserve such an honour). The texts of all four pieces may be found in *MP*.

42

The Amusements of the People (II)

Household Words, 13 April 1850

The theatre described in this piece is the Britannia Saloon, which was located in Hoxton in the East End of London. A theatre was first built in the grounds of the Britannia Tavern in 1841 and reopened as the Britannia Saloon in 1843 after all London theatres had been brought under the jurisdiction of the Lord Chamberlain by the Theatre Regulations Act. For an excellent detailed history of the place, see the Introduction to Jim Davis's edition of *The Britannia Diaries 1863–1875* (pub. Society for Theatre Research, 1992), in which he cites (pp. 16–17) Dickens's later description of the Britannia in 'Two Views of a Cheap Theatre' (*The Uncommercial Traveller*). Davis notes (p. 5) that theatres were designated saloons, where 'access was only possible to the theatre buildings through the taverns to which they were attached'. The other saloon mentioned by Dickens, the Eagle (later called the Grecian Theatre), was, according to H. Barton Baker (*The London Stage* [1889], Vol. II, p. 254), opened in 1832. It was devoted mainly to musical entertainment and was the setting for Dickens's 'Miss Evans and the Eagle' (1835) in *Sketches by Boz* (see Vol. I of this edition, pp. 226–30).

Davis states (p. 8) that the Britannia 'established a strong repertory, an excellent company and an ever-increasing reputation during the later 1840s and 1850s', with the writer Dibdin Pitt providing 'a constant succession of Gothic and domestic melodramas'.

It is interesting to note that Dickens here attacks the system of official licensing of plays not on the grounds of artistic freedom but because it is connected with a royal official. The Examiner of Plays acted under the authority of the Lord Chamberlain and until 1968 could prevent the performance of any or all parts of a play. The case Dickens refers to was that of the *Athenaeum* music critic H.F. Chorley's play, *Old Love and New Fortune*, which opened triumphantly at the Surrey on 18 February 1850 and had to close the following night because the Lord Chamberlain's licence had not been obtained ('the difficulty was soon got over, and the piece enjoyed a favourable tenure of public favour', H.G. Hewlett, *Henry Fothergill Chorley: Autobiography, Memoirs and Letters* [1873], Vol. II, p. 20). What Dickens seems to be advocating here as regards state regulation of the drama is something resembling Lord Reith's control of the early BBC, 'a real, responsible, educational trust'. Compare his use of the word 'dandy' here to express aristocratic privilege and perks with his satire on 'Dandyism' in *Bleak House* (Ch. 12), especially the passage about the Fine Arts 'attending in powder and walking backward like the Lord Chamberlain' before the ladies and gentlemen who want to keep all art merely 'languid and pretty'.

Dickens's argument that 'people have a right to be amused', and that if the Britannia were closed 'the people who now resort here, *will* be amused somewhere', looks forward four years to the lisping circus-owner Mr Sleary's famous words to Mr Gradgrind in *Hard Times* (Book I, Ch. 6): 'People must be amuthed, Thquire, thomehow ... Make the betht of uth; not the wortht.'

Literary allusions (p. 195) 'All the queen's horses ...': the nursery rhyme 'Humpty Dumpty'; (p. 197) 'theme of Thomas Ingoldsby': refers to R.H. Barham's *Ingoldsby Legends*, 3rd Series (1847), 'The House-Warming!! A legend of Bleeding-Heart Yard', which describes an Elizabethan Lady Hatton selling her soul to the devil in return for his getting her husband advancement at Court and eventually having to fulfil her part of the bargain.

MS. Forster Collection, Victoria and Albert Museum. This shows that the

phrase 'except at a public execution' (para. 4) must have been added at
proof stage and that 'In most conditions of life ...' (para. 5) originally read:
'In all conditions of life ...'. After '... improving the character of their
amusement' (p. 198), the MS. reads: 'and with it the character of those
who are amused'.

MR WHELKS being much in the habit of recreating himself at a class of
theatres called 'Saloons,' we repaired to one of these, not long ago, on
a Monday evening; Monday being a great holiday-night with MR
WHELKS and his friends.

The Saloon in question is the largest in London (that which is known
as the Eagle, in the City Road, should be excepted from the generic
term, as not presenting by any means the same class of entertainment),
and is situate not far from Shoreditch Church. It announces 'The People's
Theatre' as its second name. The prices of admission are, to the boxes,
a shilling; to the pit, sixpence; to the lower gallery, fourpence; to the
upper gallery and back seats, threepence. There is no half-price. The
opening piece on this occasion was described in the bills as 'the greatest
hit of the season, the grand new legendary and traditionary drama,
combining supernatural agencies with historical facts, and identifying
extraordinary superhuman causes with material, terrific, and powerful
effects.' All the queen's horses and all the queen's men could not have
drawn MR WHELKS into the place like this description. Strengthened by
lithographic representations of the principal superhuman causes, combined with the most popular of the material, terrific, and powerful effects,
it became irresistible. Consequently, we had already failed, once, in
finding six square inches of room within the walls, to stand upon; and
when we now paid our money for a little stage box, like a dry shower-
bath, we did so in the midst of a stream of people who persisted on
paying theirs for other parts of the house, in despite of the representations
of the Money-taker that it was 'very full, everywhere.'

The outer avenues and passages of the People's Theatre bore abundant
testimony to the fact of its being frequented by very dirty people. Within,
the atmosphere was far from odoriferous.

The place was crammed to excess, in all parts. Among the audience
were a large number of boys and youths, and a great many very young
girls grown into bold women before they had well ceased to be children.
These last were the worst features of the whole crowd, and were more
prominent there than in any other sort of public assembly that we know
of, except at a public execution. There was no drink supplied, beyond
the contents of the porter-can (magnified in its dimensions, perhaps),
which may be usually seen traversing the galleries of the largest Theatres

as well as the least, and which was here seen everywhere. Huge ham sandwiches, piled on trays like deals in a timber-yard, were handed about for sale to the hungry; and there was no stint of oranges, cakes, brandy-balls, or other similar refreshments. The Theatre was capacious, with a very large capable stage, well lighted, well appointed, and managed in a business-like, orderly manner in all respects; the performances had begun so early as a quarter past six, and had been then in progress for three-quarters of an hour.

It was apparent here, as in the theatre we had previously visited, that one of the reasons of its great attraction was its being directly addressed to the common people, in the provision made for their seeing and hearing. Instead of being put away in a dark gap in the roof of an immense building, as in our once National Theatres, they were here in possession of eligible points of view, and thoroughly able to take in the whole performance. Instead of being at a great disadvantage in comparison with the mass of the audience, they were here *the* audience, for whose accommodation the place was made. We believe this to be one great cause of the success of these speculations. In whatever way the common people are addressed, whether in churches, chapels, schools, lecture-rooms, or theatres, to be successfully addressed they must be directly appealed to. No matter how good the feast, they will not come to it on mere sufferance. If, on looking round us, we find that the only things plainly and personally addressed to them, from quack medicines upwards, be bad or very defective things, – so much the worse for them and for all of us, and so much the more unjust and absurd the system which has haughtily abandoned a strong ground to such occupation.

We will add that we believe these people have a right to be amused. A great deal that we consider to be unreasonable, is written and talked about not licensing these places of entertainment. We have already intimated that we believe a love of dramatic representations to be an inherent principle in human nature. In most conditions of human life of which we have any knowledge, from the Greeks to the Bosjesmen, some form of dramatic representation has always obtained.* We have a vast respect for county magistrates, and for the lord chamberlain; but we render greater deference to such extensive and immutable experience, and think it will outlive the whole existing court and commission. We

---

* In the remote interior of Africa, and among the North American Indians, this truth is exemplified in an equally striking manner. Who that saw the four grim, stunted, abject Bush-people at the Egyptian Hall – with two natural actors among them out of that number, one a male and the other a female – can forget how something human and imaginative gradually broke out in the little ugly man, when he was roused from crouching over the charcoal fire, into giving a dramatic representation of the tracking of a beast, the shooting of it with poisoned arrows, and the creature's death?

would assuredly not bear harder on the fourpenny theatre than on the four shilling theatre or the four guinea theatre; but we would decidedly interpose to turn to some wholesome account the means of instruction which it has at command, and we would make that office of Dramatic Licenser, which, like many other offices, has become a mere piece of Court favour and dandy conventionality, a real, responsible, educational trust. We would have it exercise a sound supervision over the lower drama, instead of stopping the career of a real work of art, as it did in the case of Mr Chorley's play at the Surrey Theatre, but a few weeks since, for a sickly point of form.

To return to MR WHELKS. The audience, being able to see and hear, were very attentive. They were so closely packed that they took a little time in settling down after any pause; but otherwise the general disposition was to lose nothing, and to check (in no choice language) any disturber of the business of the scene.

On our arrival, MR WHELKS had already followed Lady Hatton the Heroine (whom we faintly recognised as a mutilated theme of the late THOMAS INGOLDSBY) to the 'Gloomy Dell and Suicide's Tree,' where Lady H. had encountered the 'apparition of the dark man of doom,' and heard the 'fearful story of the Suicide.' She had also 'signed the compact in her own Blood;' beheld 'the Tombs rent asunder;' seen 'skeletons start from their graves, and gibber Mine, mine, for ever!' and undergone all these little experiences (each set forth in a separate line in the bill) in the compass of one act. It was not yet over, indeed, for we found a remote king of England of the name of 'Enerry,' refreshing himself with the spectacle of a dance in a Garden, which was interrupted by the 'thrilling appearance of the Demon.' This 'superhuman cause' (with black eyebrows slanting up into his temples, and red-foil cheekbones) brought the Drop-Curtain down as we took possession of our Shower-Bath.

It seemed, on the curtain's going up again, that Lady Hatton had sold herself to the Powers of Darkness, on very high terms, and was now overtaken by remorse, and by jealousy too; the latter passion being excited by the beautiful Lady Rodolpha, ward to the king. It was to urge Lady Hatton on to the murder of this young female (as well as we could make out, but both we and MR WHELKS found the incidents complicated) that the Demon appeared 'once again in all his terrors.' Lady Hatton had been leading a life of piety, but the Demon was not to have his bargain declared off, in right of any such artifices, and now offered a dagger for the destruction of Rodolpha. Lady Hatton hesitating to accept this trifle from Tartarus, the Demon, for certain subtle reasons of his own, proceeded to entertain her with a view of the 'gloomy court-yard of a convent,' and the apparitions of the 'Skeleton Monk,' and the 'King of Terrors.' Against these superhuman causes, another superhuman cause, to wit the ghost of Lady H.'s mother, came into play, and greatly confounded the Powers of Darkness, by waving the 'sacred emblem' over the head of the else devoted Rodolpha, and causing her to sink unto the earth. Upon this the Demon, losing his temper, fiercely invited Lady Hatton to 'Be-old the tortures of the damned!' and straightway conveyed her to a 'grand and awful view of Pandemonium, and Lake of Transparent Rolling Fire,' whereof, and also of 'Prometheus chained, and the Vulture gnawing at his liver,' MR WHELKS was exceedingly derisive.

The Demon still failing, even there, and still finding the ghost of the old lady greatly in his way, exclaimed that these vexations had such a remarkable effect upon his spirit as to 'sear his eyeballs,' and that he must go 'deeper down,' which he accordingly did. Hereupon it appeared that it was all a dream on Lady Hatton's part, and that she was newly married and uncommonly happy. This put an end to the incongruous heap of nonsense, and set MR WHELKS applauding mightily; for, except with the lake of transparent rolling fire (which was not half infernal enough for him), MR WHELKS was infinitely contented with the whole of the proceedings.

Ten thousand people, every week, all the year round, are estimated to attend this place of amusement. If it were closed tomorrow – if there were fifty such, and they were all closed tomorrow – the only result would be to cause that to be privately and evasively done which is now publicly done; to render the harm of it much greater, and to exhibit the suppressive power of the law in an oppressive and partial light. The people who now resort here, *will be* amused somewhere. It is of no use to blink that fact, or to make pretences to the contrary. We had far better apply ourselves to improving the character of their amusement. It would not be exacting much, or exacting anything very difficult, to require that the pieces represented in these Theatres should have, at least, a good, plain, healthy purpose in them.

To the end that our experiences might not be supposed to be partial or unfortunate, we went, the very next night, to the Theatre where we saw *May Morning*, and found MR WHELKS engaged in the study of an 'Original old English Domestic and Romantic Drama,' called '*Eva the Betrayed, or The Ladye of Lambythe.*' We proceed to develop the incidents which gradually unfolded themselves to MR WHELKS's understanding.

One Geoffrey Thornley the younger, on a certain fine morning, married his father's ward, Eva the Betrayed, the Ladye of Lambythe. She had become the betrayed, in right – or in wrong – of designing Geoffrey's machinations; for that corrupt individual, knowing her to be under promise of marriage to Walter More, a young mariner (of whom he was accustomed to make slighting mention as 'a minion'), represented the said More to be no more, and obtained the consent of the too trusting Eva to their immediate union.

Now, it came to pass, by a singular coincidence, that on the identical morning of the marriage More came home, and was taking a walk about the scenes of his boyhood – a little faded since that time – when he rescued 'Wilbert the Hunchback' from some very rough treatment. This misguided person, in return, immediately fell to abusing his preserver in round terms, giving him to understand that he (the preserved) hated 'manerkind, wither two eckerceptions,' one of them being the deceiving Geoffrey, whose retainer he was, and for whom he felt an unconquerable attachment; the other, a relative, whom, in a similar redundancy of emphasis, adapted to the requirements of MR WHELKS, he called his 'assister.' This misanthrope also made the cold-blooded declaration, 'There was a time when I loved my fellow keretures, till they deserpised me. Now, I live only to witness man's disergherace and woman's misery!' In furtherance of this amiable purpose of existence, he directed More to where the bridal procession was coming home from church, and Eva recognised More, and More reproached Eva, and there was a great to-do, and a violent struggling, before certain social villagers who were celebrating the event with morris-dances. Eva was borne off in a tearing condition, and the bill very truly observed that the end of that part of the business was 'despair and madness.'

Geoffrey, Geoffrey, why were you already married to another! Why could you not be true to your lawful wife Katherine, instead of deserting her, and leaving her to come tumbling into public-houses (on account of weakness) in search of you! You might have known what it would end in, Geoffrey Thornley! You might have known that she would come up to your house on your wedding day with her marriage-certificate in her pocket, determined to expose you. You might have known beforehand, as you now very composedly observe, that you would have 'but one course to pursue.' That course clearly is to wind your right hand in Katherine's long hair, wrestle with her, stab her, throw down the body behind the door (cheers from MR WHELKS), and tell the devoted Hunchback to get rid of it. On the devoted Hunchback's finding that it is the body of his 'assister,' and taking her marriage-certificate from her pocket and denouncing you, of course you have still but one course to pursue, and that is to charge the crime upon him, and have him carried off with all speed into the 'deep and massive dungeons beneath Thornley Hall.'

More having, as he was rather given to boast, 'a goodly vessel on the lordly Thames,' had better have gone away with it, weather permitting, than gone after Eva. Naturally, he got carried down to the dungeons too, for lurking about, and got put into the next dungeon to the

Hunchback, then expiring from poison. And there they were, hard and fast, like two wild beasts in dens, trying to get glimpses of each other through the bars, to the unutterable interest of MR WHELKS.

But when the Hunchback made himself known, and when More did the same; and when the Hunchback said he had got the certificate which rendered Eva's marriage illegal; and when More raved to have it given to him, and when the Hunchback (as having some grains of misanthropy in him to the last) persisted in going into his dying agonies in a remote corner of his cage, and took unheard-of trouble not to die anywhere near the bars that were within More's reach; MR WHELKS applauded to the echo. At last the Hunchback was persuaded to stick the certificate on the point of a dagger, and hand it in; and that done, died extremely hard, knocking himself violently about, to the very last gasp, and certainly making the most of all the life that was in him.

Still, More had yet to get out of his den before he could turn this certificate to any account. His first step was to make such a violent uproar as to bring into his presence a certain 'Norman Free Lance' who kept watch and ward over him. His second, to inform this warrior, in the style of the Polite Letter-Writer, that 'circumstances had occurred' rendering it necessary that he should be immediately let out. The warrior declining to submit himself to the force of these circumstances, Mr More proposed to him, as a gentleman and a man of honour, to allow him to step out into the gallery, and there adjust an old feud subsisting between them, by single combat. The unwary Free Lance, consenting to this reasonable proposal, was shot from behind by the comic man, whom he bitterly designated as 'a snipe' for that action, and then died exceedingly game.

All this occurred in one day – the bridal day of the Ladye of Lambythe; and now MR WHELKS concentrated all his energies into a focus, bent forward, looked straight in front of him, and held his breath. For, the night of the eventful day being come, MR WHELKS was admitted to the 'bridal chamber of the Ladye of Lambythe,' where he beheld a toilet table, and a particularly large and desolate four-post bedstead. Here the Ladye, having dismissed her bridesmaids, was interrupted in deploring her unhappy fate, by the entrance of her husband; and matters, under these circumstances, were proceeding to very desperate extremities, when the Ladye (by this time aware of the existence of the certificate) found a dagger on the dressing-table, and said, 'Attempt to enfold me in thy pernicious embrace, and this poignard—!' &c. He did attempt it, however, for all that, and he and the Ladye were dragging one another about like wrestlers, when Mr More broke open the door, and entering with the whole domestic establishment and a Middlesex magistrate, took him into custody and claimed his bride.

It is but fair to MR WHELKS to remark on one curious fact in this entertainment. When the situations were very strong indeed, they were very like what some favourite situations in the Italian Opera would be to a profoundly deaf spectator. The despair and madness at the end of the first act, the business of the long hair, and the struggle in the bridal chamber, were as like the conventional passion of the Italian singers, as the orchestra was unlike the opera band, or its 'hurries' unlike the music of the great composers. So do extremes meet; and so is there some hopeful congeniality between what will excite MR WHELKS, and what will rouse a Duchess.

43

Some Account of an Extraordinary Traveller

Household Words, 20 April 1850 (leading article)

The germ of this article can be found in a letter of Dickens to Charles Knight of 26 March 1850 (*Pilgrim*, Vol. VI, p. 73) in which he describes watching a globe-maker at work and revolving in his mind 'some faint idea of describing him as a traveller who was for ever going round the world without stirring out of that small street'. In the event he applied the idea to the current rage for Panoramas and Dioramas, which had been given fresh impetus in 1849 by the great success of Banvard's Panorama of the Mississippi, already publicly praised by Dickens (see p. 135f.). For a detailed account of the Panorama/Diorama phenomenon, see Chs 10–15 of R.D. Altick's *The Shows of London* (1978), and R. Hyde, *Panoramania! The Art and Entertainment of the 'All-Embracing' View*, the catalogue of an exhibition at the Barbican Art Gallery, London (1988–9). Citing Dickens's essay in his Introduction to the Barbican catalogue, Scott B. Wilcox notes (p. 39): 'The educational value of the panorama, recognised from the outset, had become, by the time of Booley's travels … its fundamental merit. The nouns "panorama" and "diorama" were commonly joined with the adjective "instructive".' Hence the presence of Miss Creeble and her young charges in this piece. As to Mr Booley, the Panorama enables him to become a kind of globe-trotting (instead of England-touring) Mr Pickwick, and his speech to the Social Oysters at the end of the piece recalls Mr Pickwick's comments on *his* travels to his club before retiring to Dulwich: 'Nearly the

whole of my previous life having been devoted to business and the pursuit
of wealth, numerous scenes of which I had no previous conception have
dawned upon me – I hope to the enlargement of my mind, and the
improvement of my understanding' (*The Pickwick Papers*, Ch. 57).

   The Panoramas viewed by Mr Booley begin with Banvard's Mississippi
one, followed by the same artist's Ohio River one (Altick, *op. cit.*, p. 207)
and S.C. Brees's 'Colonial Panorama' of New Zealand at the Linwood
Gallery in Leicester Square. Brees was the principal surveyor and engineer
of the New Zealand Company and the Panorama, based on his own
drawings but painted by others, was designed to encourage emigration (*The
Times* thought it 'would do more to promote emigration than a thousand
speeches and resolutions'). Both Altick and Hyde reproduce a charming
handbill advertising Brees's Panorama (Altick, p. 426, Hyde, p. 143): it
shows him rubbing noses and exchanging friendly noises with a feathered
and painted Maori warrior. Mr Booley continues his 'travels' with attendance at a Panorama of the Queen's August 1849 visit to Ireland (Cork,
Waterford, Dublin and Belfast) and another of Australia, before going, as
Dickens himself had done on 22 February (see *Pilgrim*, Vol. VI, p. 42), to
Bonomi, Fahey and Warren's Nile Panorama, showing at the Egyptian
Hall since July 1849. This was a transparency not a painting and Altick
notes (p. 206) that 'two of the most admired scenes were a tableau of the
interior of the Abu Simbel temple, seen by torchlight, and a representation
of a sandstorm overtaking a caravan in the Libyan desert'. Mr Booley then
attends the 'Overland Route to India' Panorama, which had just opened
at the Gallery of Illustration (see Altick, p. 207f., and Hyde, p. 143) to
universal praise (*Punch* hailed it as 'a most lovely work of art ... radiant
with beauty, and sparkling with costly Indian gems'), and finally Burford's
Leicester Square double bill on the subject of Ross's Arctic expedition of
1848–9 (Altick, p. 177).

   Dickens's ironic remarks (p. 209) about a 'Queen and country always
eager to distinguish peaceful merit' look forward to Esther Summerson in
uncharacteristically satiric vein in *Bleak House*, Ch. 35: 'I said it was not the
custom in England to confer titles on men distinguished by peaceful services,
however good and great; unless occasionally, when they consisted of the
accumulation of some very large amount of money.'

Literary allusions (p. 204) 'the magic skein in the story': allusion to one
of Grimm's fairy tales; 'The Story of the Three Swans'; (p. 208) 'like an
opium-eater in a mighty dream': Dickens probably has De Quincey's
Confessions of an English Opium Eater (1821) in mind here; (p. 210) 'increase of
appetite ... feeds on': Shakespeare, *Hamlet*, Act 2, Sc. 1.

No longer ago than this Easter time last past, we became acquainted with the subject of the present notice. Our knowledge of him is not by any means an intimate one, and is only of a public nature. We have never interchanged any conversation with him, except on one occasion when he asked us to have the goodness to take off our hat, to which we replied 'Certainly.'

MR BOOLEY was born (we believe) in Rood Lane, in the City of London. He is now a gentleman advanced in life, and has for some years resided in the neighbourhood of Islington. His father was a wholesale grocer (perhaps) and he was (possibly) in the same way of business; or he may, at an early age, have become a clerk in the Bank of England, or in a private bank, or in the India House. It will be observed that we make no pretence of having any information in reference to the private history of this remarkable man, and that our account of it might be received as rather speculative than authentic.

In person MR BOOLEY is below the middle size, and corpulent. His countenance is florid, he is perfectly bald, and soon hot; and there is a composure in his gait and manner, calculated to impress a stranger with the idea of his being, on the whole, an unwieldy man. It is only in his eye that the adventurous character of MR BOOLEY is seen to shine. It is a moist, bright eye, of a cheerful expression, and indicative of keen and eager curiosity.

It was not until late in life that MR BOOLEY conceived the idea of entering on the extraordinary amount of travel he has since accomplished. He had attained the age of sixty-five before he left England for the first time. In all the immense journeys he has since performed, he has never laid aside the English dress, nor departed in the slightest degree from English customs. Neither does he speak a word of any language but his own.

MR BOOLEY's powers of endurance are wonderful. All climates are alike to him. Nothing exhausts him; no alternations of heat and cold appear to have the least effect upon his hardy frame. His capacity of travelling, day and night, for thousands of miles, has never been approached by any traveller of whom we have any knowledge through the help of books. An intelligent Englishman may have occasionally pointed out to him objects and scenes of interest; but otherwise he has travelled alone, and unattended. Though remarkable for personal cleanliness, he has carried no luggage; and his diet has been of the simplest kind. He has often found a biscuit, or a bun, sufficient for his support over a vast tract of country. Frequently he has travelled hundreds of miles, fasting, without the least abatement of his natural spirits. It says much for the Total Abstinence causes, that MR BOOLEY has never had recourse to the artificial stimulus of alcohol, to sustain him under his fatigues.

His first departure from the sedentary and monotonous life he had hitherto led, strikingly exemplifies, we think, the energetic character, long suppressed by that unchanging routine. Without any communication with any member of his family – MR BOOLEY has never been married, but has many relations – without announcing his intention to his solicitor, or banker, or any person entrusted with the management of his affairs, he closed the door of his house behind him at one o'clock in the afternoon of a certain day, and immediately proceeded to New Orleans, in the United States of America.

His intention was to ascend the Mississippi and Missouri rivers, to the base of the Rocky Mountains. Taking his passage in a steamboat without loss of time, he was soon upon the bosom of the Father of Waters, as the Indians call the mighty stream which, night and day, is always carrying huge instalments of the vast continent of the New World down into the sea.

MR BOOLEY found it singularly interesting to observe the various stages of civilisation obtaining on the banks of these mighty rivers. Leaving the luxury and brightness of New Orleans – a somewhat feverish luxury and brightness, he observed, as if the swampy soil were too much enriched in the hot sun with the bodies of dead slaves – and passing various towns in every stage of progress, it was very curious to observe the changes of civilisation and of vegetation too. Here, while the doomed negro race were working in the plantations, while the republican overseer looked on, whip in hand, tropical trees were growing, beautiful flowers in bloom; the alligator, with his horribly sly face, and his jaws like two great saws, was basking on the mud; and the strange moss of the country was hanging in wreaths and garlands on the trees, like votive offerings. A little farther towards the west, and the trees and flowers were changed, the moss was gone, younger infant towns were rising, forests were slowly disappearing, and the trees, obliged to aid in the destruction of their kind, fed the heavily-breathing monster that came clanking up those solitudes laden with the pioneers of the advancing human army. The river itself, that moving highway, showed him every kind of floating contrivance, from the lumbering flat-bottomed boat, and the raft of logs, upward to the steamboat, and downward to the poor Indian's frail canoe. A winding thread through the enormous range of country, unrolling itself before the wanderer like the magic skein in the story, he saw it tracked by wanderers of every kind, roaming from the more settled world, to those first nests of men. The floating theatre, dwelling-house, hotel, museum, shop; the floating mechanism for screwing the trunks of mighty trees out of the mud, like antediluvian teeth; the rapidly-flowing river, and the blazing woods; he left them all behind – town, city, and log-cabin, too; and floated up into the prairies and savannahs, among the deserted lodges of tribes of savages, and among their dead, lying alone on little wooden stages with their stark faces upwards towards the sky. Among the blazing grass, and herds of buffaloes and wild horses, and among the wigwams of the fast-declining Indians, he began to consider how, in the eternal current of progress setting across this globe in one unchangeable direction, like the unseen agency that points the needle to the Pole, the Chiefs who only dance the dances of their fathers, and will never have a new figure for a new tune, and the Medicine men who know no Medicine but what was Medicine a hundred years ago, must be surely and inevitably swept from the earth, whether they be Choctawas, Mandans, Britons, Austrians, or Chinese.

He was struck, too, by the reflection that savage nature was not by any means such a fine and noble spectacle as some delight to represent it. He found it a poor, greasy, paint-plastered, miserable thing enough; but a very little way above the beasts in most respects; in many customs a long way below them. It occurred to him that the 'Big Bird,' or the 'Blue Fish,' or any of the other braves, was but a troublesome braggart after all; making a mighty whooping and halloaing about nothing particular, doing very little for science, not much more than the monkeys for art, scarcely anything worth mentioning for letters, and not often making the world greatly better than he found it. Civilisation, MR BOOLEY concluded, was, on the whole, with all its blemishes, a more imposing sight, and a far better thing to stand by.

MR BOOLEY's observations of the celestial bodies, on this voyage, were principally confined to the discovery of the alarming fact, that light had altogether departed from the moon; which presented the appearance of a white dinner-plate. The clouds, too, conducted themselves in an extraordinary manner, and assumed the most eccentric forms, while the sun rose and set in a very reckless way. On his return to his native country, however, he had the satisfaction of finding all these things as usual.

It might have been expected that at his advanced age, retired from the active duties of life, blessed with a competency, and happy in the affections of his numerous relations, MR BOOLEY would now have settled himself down, to muse for the remainder of his days, over the new stock of experience thus acquired. But travel had whetted, not satisfied, his appetite; and remembering that he had not seen the Ohio River, except at the point of its junction with the Mississippi, he returned to the United States, after a short interval of repose, and appearing suddenly at Cincinnati, the queen City of the West, traversed the clear waters of the Ohio to its Falls. In this expedition he had the pleasure of encountering a party of intelligent workmen from Birmingham who were making the same tour. Also his nephew Septimus, aged only thirteen. This intrepid boy had started from Peckham, in the old country, with two and sixpence sterling in his pocket; and had, when he encountered his uncle at a point of the Ohio River, called Snaggy Bar, still one shilling of that sum remaining!

Again at home, MR BOOLEY was so pressed by his appetite for knowledge as to remain at home only one day. At the expiration of that short period, he actually started for New Zealand.

It is almost incredible that a man in MR BOOLEY's station of life, however adventurous his nature, and however few his artificial wants, should cast himself on a voyage of thirteen thousand miles from Great Britain with no other outfit than his watch and purse, and no arms but his walking-stick. We are, however, assured on the best authority, that thus he made the passage out, and thus appeared, in the act of wiping his smoking head with his pocket-handkerchief, at the entrance to Port Nicholson in Cook's Straits: with the very spot within his range of vision, where his illustrious predecessor, Captain Cook, so unhappily slain at Otaheite, once anchored.

After contemplating the swarms of cattle maintained on the hills in this neighbourhood, and always to be found by the stockmen when they are wanted, though nobody takes any care of them – which MR BOOLEY considered the more remarkable, as their natural objection to be killed might be supposed to be augmented by the beauty of the climate – MR BOOLEY proceeded to the town of Wellington. Having minutely examined it in every point, and made himself perfect master of the whole natural history and process of manufacture of the flax-plant, with its splendid yellow blossoms, he repaired to a Native Pa, which, unlike the Native Pa to which he was accustomed, he found to be a town, and not a parent. Here he observed a chief with a long spear, making every demonstration of spitting a visitor, but really giving him the Maori or welcome – a word MR BOOLEY is inclined to derive from the known hospitality of our English Mayors – and here also he observed some Europeans rubbing noses, by way of shaking hands, with the aboriginal inhabitants. After participating in an affray between the natives and the English soldiery, in which the former were defeated with great loss, he plunged into the Bush, and there camped out for some months, until he made a survey of the whole country.

While leading this wild life, encamped by night near a stream for the convenience of water, in a Ware, or hut, built open in the front, with a roof sloping backward to the ground, and made of poles, covered and enclosed with bark or fern, it was MR BOOLEY's singular fortune to encounter Miss Creeble, of The Misses Creebles' Boarding and Day Establishment for Young Ladies, Kennington Oval, who, accompanied by three of her young ladies in search of information, had achieved this marvellous journey, and was then also in the Bush. Miss Creeble having very unsettled opinions on the subject of gunpowder, was afraid that it entered into the composition of the fire before the tent, and that something would presently blow up or go off. MR BOOLEY, as a more experienced traveller, assuring her that there was no danger; and calming the fears of the young ladies, an acquaintance commenced between them. They accomplished the rest of their travels in New Zealand together, and the best understanding prevailed among the little party. They took notice of the trees, as the Kaikatea, the Kauri, the Ruta, the Pukatea, the Hinau, and the Tanakaka – names which Miss Creeble had a bland relish in pronouncing. They admired the beautiful, arborescent, palm-like fern, abounding everywhere, and frequently exceeding thirty feet in height. They wondered at the curious owl, who is supposed to demand 'More Pork!' wherever he flies, and whom Miss Creeble termed 'an admonition of Nature's against greediness!' And they contemplated some very rampant natives of cannibal propensities. After many pleasing and instructive vicissitudes, they returned to England in company, where the ladies were safely put into a hackney cabriolet by MR BOOLEY, in Leicester Square, London.

And now, indeed, it might have been imagined that that roving spirit, tired of rambling about the world, would have settled down at home in peace and honour. Not so. After repairing to the tubular bridge across the Menai Straits, and accompanying Her Majesty on her visit to Ireland (which he characterised as 'a magnificent Exhibition'), MR BOOLEY, with his usual absence of preparation, departed for Australia.

Here again, he lived out in the Bush, passing his time chiefly among the working-gangs of convicts who were carrying timber. He was much impressed by the ferocious mastiffs chained to barrels, who assist the sentries in keeping guard over those misdoers. But he observed that the atmosphere in this part of the world, unlike the descriptions he had read of it, was extremely thick, and that objects were misty, and difficult to be discerned. From a certain unsteadiness and trembling, too, which he frequently remarked on the face of Nature, he was led to conclude that this part of the globe was subject to convulsive heavings and earthquakes. This caused him to return with some precipitation.

Again at home, and probably reflecting that the countries he had hitherto visited were new in the history of man, this extraordinary traveller resolved to proceed up the Nile to the second cataract. At the next performance of the great ceremony of 'opening the Nile,' at Cairo, MR BOOLEY was present.

Along that wonderful river, associated with such stupendous fables, and with a history more prodigious than any fancy of man, in its vast and gorgeous facts; among temples, palaces, pyramids, colossal statues, crocodiles, tombs, obelisks, mummies, sand and ruin; he proceeded, like an opium-eater in a mighty dream. Thebes rose before him. An avenue of two hundred sphinxes, with not a head among them, – one of six or eight, or ten such avenues, all leading to a common centre – conducted to the Temple of Carnak: its walls, eighty feet high and twenty-five feet thick, a mile and three-quarters in circumference; the interior of its tremendous hall, occupying an area of forty-seven thousand square feet, large enough to hold four great Christian churches, and yet not more than one-seventh part of the entire ruin. Obelisks he saw, thousands of years of age, as sharp as if the chisel had cut their edges yesterday: colossal statues fifty-two feet high, with 'little' fingers five feet and a half long; a very world of ruins, that were marvellous old ruins in the days of Herodotus; tombs cut high up in the rock, where European travellers live solitary, as in stony crows' nests, burning mummied Thebans, gentle and simple, – of the dried blood-royal maybe, – for their daily fuel, and making articles of furniture of their dusty coffins. Upon the walls of temples, in colours fresh and bright as those of yesterday, he read the conquests of great Egyptian monarchs; upon the tombs of humbler people in the same blooming symbols, he saw their ancient way of working at their trades, of riding, driving, feasting, playing games; of marrying and burying, and performing on instruments, and singing songs, and healing by the power of animal magnetism, and performing all the occupations of life. He visited the quarries of Silsileh, whence nearly all the red stone used by the ancient Egyptian architects and sculptors came; and there beheld enormous single-stoned colossal figures, nearly finished – redly snowed up, as it were, and trying hard to break out – waiting for the finishing touches, never to be given by the mummied hands of thousands of years ago. In front of the temple of Abou Simbel, he saw gigantic figures sixty feet in height and twenty-one across the shoulders, dwarfing live men on camels down to pigmies. Elsewhere he beheld complacent monsters tumbled down like ill-used Dolls of a Titanic make, and staring with stupid benignity at the arid earth whereon their huge faces rested. His last look of that amazing land was at the Great Sphinx, buried in the sand – sand in its eyes, sand in its ears, sand drifted on its broken nose, sand lodging, feet deep, in the ledges of its head – struggling out of a wide sea of sand, as if to look hopelessly forth for the ancient glories once surrounding it.

In this expedition, MR BOOLEY acquired some curious information in reference to the language of hieroglyphics. He encountered the Simoon in the Desert, and lay down, with the rest of his caravan, until it had passed over. He also beheld on the horizon some of those stalking pillars of sand, apparently reaching from earth to heaven, which, with the red sun shining through them, so terrified the Arabs attendant on Bruce, that they fell prostrate, crying that the Day of Judgment was come. More

Copts, Turks, Arabs, Fellahs, Bedouins, Mosques, Mamelukes, and Moosulmen he saw, than we have space to tell. His days were all Arabian Nights, and he saw wonders without end.

This might have satiated any ordinary man, for a time at least. But MR BOOLEY, being no ordinary man, within twenty-four hours of his arrival at home was making the overland journey to India.

He has emphatically described this, as 'a beautiful piece of scenery,' and 'a perfect picture.' The appearance of Malta and Gibraltar he can never sufficiently commend. In crossing the desert from Grand Cairo to Suez, he was particularly struck by the undulations of the Sandscape (he preferred that word to Landscape, as more expressive of the region), and by the incident of beholding a caravan upon its line of march; a spectacle which in the remembrance always affords him the utmost pleasure. Of the stations on the Desert, and the cinnamon gardens of Ceylon, he likewise entertains a lively recollection. Calcutta he praises also; though he has been heard to observe that the British military at that seat of Government were not as well proportioned as he could desire the soldiers of his country to be; and that the breed of horses there in use was susceptible of some improvement.

Once more in his native land, with the vigour of his constitution unimpaired by the many toils and fatigues he had encountered, what had MR BOOLEY now to do, but, full of years and honour, to recline upon the grateful appreciation of his Queen and country, always eager to distinguish peaceful merit? What had he now to do, but to receive the decoration ever ready to be bestowed, in England, on men deservedly distinguished, and to take his place among the best? He had this to do. He had yet to achieve the most astonishing enterprise for which he was reserved. In all the countries he had yet visited, he had seen no frost and snow. He resolved to make a voyage to the ice-bound Arctic Regions.

In pursuance of this surprising determination, MR BOOLEY accompanied the expedition under Sir James Ross, consisting of Her Majesty's ships, the Enterprise and Investigator, which sailed from the River Thames on the 12th of May, 1848, and which, on the 11th of September, entered Port Leopold Harbour.

In this inhospitable region, surrounded by eternal ice, cheered by no glimpse of the sun, shrouded in gloom and darkness, MR BOOLEY passed the entire winter. The ships were covered in, and fortified all round with walls of ice and snow; the masts were frozen up; hoar frost settled on the yards, tops, shrouds, stays, and rigging; around, in every direction, lay an interminable waste, on which only the bright stars, the yellow moon, and the vivid Aurora Borealis looked, by night or day.

And yet the desolate sublimity of this astounding spectacle was broken in a pleasant and surprising manner. In the remote solitude to which he had penetrated, MR BOOLEY (who saw no Esquimaux during his stay, though he looked for them in every direction) had the happiness of encountering two Scotch gardeners; several English compositors, accompanied by their wives; three brass-founders from the neigh-bourhood of Long Acre, London; two coach-painters, a gold-beater and his only daughter, by trade a stay-maker; and several other working-people from sundry parts of Great Britain who had conceived the extraordinary idea of 'holiday-making' in the frozen wilderness. Hither too, had Miss Creeble and her three young ladies penetrated; the latter attired in braided peacoats of a comparatively light material; and Miss Creeble defended from the inclemency of a Polar Winter by no other outer garment than a wadded Polka-jacket. He found this courageous lady in the act of explaining, to the youthful sharers of her toils, the various phases of nature by which they were surrounded. Her explanations were principally wrong, but her intentions always admirable.

Cheered by the society of these fellow-adventurers, MR BOOLEY slowly glided on into the summer season. And now, at midnight, all was bright and shining. Mountains of ice, wedged and broken into the strangest forms – jagged points, spires, pinnacles, pyramids, turrets, columns in endless succession and in infinite variety, flashing and sparkling with ten thousand hues, as though the treasures of the earth were frozen up in all that water – appeared on every side. Masses of ice, floating and driving hither and thither, menaced the hardy voyagers with destruction; and threatened to crush their strong ships, like nutshells. But, below these ships was clear sea-water, now; the fortifying walls were gone; the yards, tops, shrouds and rigging, free from that hoary rust of long inaction, showed like themselves again; and the sails, bursting from the masts, like foliage which the welcome sun at length developed, spread themselves to the wind, and wafted the travellers away.

In the short interval that has elapsed since his safe return to the land of his birth, MR BOOLEY has decided on no new expedition; but he feels that he will yet be called upon to undertake one, perhaps of greater magnitude than any he has achieved, and frequently remarks, in his own easy way, that he wonders where the deuce he will be taken to next! Possessed of good health and good spirits, with powers unimpaired by all he has gone through, and with an increase of appetite still growing with what it feeds on, what may not be expected yet from this extra-ordinary man!

It was only at the close of Easter week that, sitting in an armchair, at a private club called the Social Oysters, assembling at Highbury Barn, where he is much respected, this indefatigable traveller expressed himself in the following terms:

'It is very gratifying to me,' said he, 'to have seen so much at my time of life, and to have acquired a knowledge of the countries I have visited, which I could not have derived from books alone. When I was a boy, such travelling would have been impossible, as the gigantic-moving-panorama or diorama mode of conveyance, which I have principally adopted (all my modes of conveyance have been pictorial), had then not been attempted. It is a delightful characteristic of these times, that new and cheap means are continually being devised for conveying the results of actual experience to those who are unable to obtain such experiences for themselves; and to bring them within the reach of the people – emphatically of the people; for it is they at large who are addressed in these endeavours, and not exclusive audiences. Hence,' said MR BOOLEY, 'even if I see a run on an idea, like the panorama one, it awakens no ill-humour within me, but gives me pleasant thoughts. Some of the best results of actual travel are suggested by such means to those whose lot it is to stay at home. New worlds open out to them, beyond their little worlds, and widen their range of reflection, information, sympathy, and interest. The more man knows of man, the better for the common brotherhood among us all. I shall, therefore,' said MR BOOLEY 'now propose to the Social Oysters, the healths of Mr Banvard, Mr Brees, Mr Phillips, Mr Allen, Mr Prout, Messrs Bonomi, Fahey, and Warren, Mr Thomas Grieve, and Mr Burford. Long life to them all, and more power to their pencils'!

The Social Oysters have drunk this toast with acclamation, MR BOOLEY proceeded to entertain them with anecdotes of his travels. This he is in the habit of doing after they have feasted together, according to the manner of Sinbad the Sailor – except that he does not bestow upon the Social Oysters the munificent reward of one hundred sequins per night, for listening.

Mr Booley appears twice more in *HW* during 1850. 'A Card from Mr Booley' (18 May) apologises for the omission from Mr Booley's toast at the end of 'An Extraordinary Traveller' of the names of three artists (Telbin, Absolon and Herring) who worked with Thomas Grieve on the Overland Route into India Panorama; and the lead article in the 30 November issue is 'Mr Booley's View of the Last Lord Mayor's Show'. This is a sustained exercise in ferocious irony (five-and-a-half columns in length) at the expense of the backwardness and stupidity of the City Corporation, especially with regard to matters of public health. The Corporation's unwillingness to do anything about the brutal and unhygienic squalor of Smithfield meat market is a particular target and is one that Dickens returns to in 'A Monument of French Folly' (see p. 327f.). The fact that the 1850 Lord Mayor's Procession was organised by Mr Batty of Astley's Amphitheatre provides Dickens with a fine opportunity, at the outset of his piece, to expatiate on a favourite theme, the delightful absurdities of contemporary popular theatre:

> Mr Booley remarked that into whatever region he extended his travels, and however wide the range of his experience became, he still found, on repairing to Astley's Amphitheatre, that he had much to learn. For, he always observed within those walls, some extraordinary costume or curious weapon, or some apparently unaccountable manners and customs, which he had previously associated with no nation upon earth. Thus, Mr Booley said, he had acquired a knowledge of Tartar Tribes, and also of Wild Indians, and Chinese, which had greatly enlightened him as to the habits of those singular races of men, in whom he observed, as peculiarities common to the whole, that they were always hoarse; that they took equestrian exercise in a most irrational manner, riding up staircases and precipices without the least necessity; that it was impossible for them to dance, on any joyful occasion, without keeping time with their forefingers, erect in the neighbourhood of their ears; and that whenever their castles were on fire (a calamity to which they were particularly subject) numbers of them immediately tumbled down dead, without receiving any wound or blow, while others, previously distinguished in war, fell an easy prey to the comic coward of the opposite faction, who was usually armed with a strange instrument resembling an enormous, supple cigar.

44

Pet Prisoners

Household Words, 27 April 1850 (leading article)

This article represents Dickens's second major intervention in the great Anglo–American penological debate of the mid-nineteenth century, the first being his powerful description of his visit to 'Philadelphia and its Solitary Prison' in Ch. 7 of *American Notes* (1842). For many details he draws, as he acknowledges, on W. Hepworth Dixon's *The London Prisons* (pub. December 1849), a copy of which Dixon had sent him (see Dickens's letter of thanks, *Pilgrim*, Vol. v, p. 686); no doubt he also made use of the 'prison facts' which he thanked Wills for supplying on 12 March (*Pilgrim*, Vol. VI, p. 62).

The debate was primarily between proponents of the so-called 'Associated Silent System' and those who favoured the 'Separate System'. Under the Silent System, vigorously implemented by Dickens's much-admired friend Captain George Chesterton, Governor of the Middlesex House of Correction at Coldbath Fields since 1829, prisoners 'associated' together but were prohibited from communicating with each other at any time, all infringements of this rule being strictly punished. This was an expensive system in that it necessitated twenty-four-hour surveillance of the prisoners. Under the Separate System, the one officially favoured by the British Government from the mid-1830s, prisoners were kept in solitary confinement, working at trades in their own cells and being encouraged to repent of their crimes through study of the Bible and regular visits from the prison chaplain. Both systems aimed at doing away with the corruption and brutal squalor of eighteenth-century prisons, but there was rather more emphasis on punishment under the Silent System (Chesterton was an enthusiastic proponent of the treadmill and Dickens, as the last paragraph of this article makes clear, strongly supported him) and more on reclamation under the Separate System.

A few weeks before this piece appeared, Carlyle had enlivened the debate by publishing, in his *Latter-Day Pamphlets* series, a characteristically over-the-top attack on 'Model Prisons', in which criminals ('base-natured beings, on whom in the course of a maleficent subterranean life of London Scoundrelism ... Satan ... had now visibly impressed his seal') were being, as he saw it, pampered and cosseted at the expense of 'poor craftsmen that pay rates and taxes from their day's wages ... the dim millions that toil and moil continually'. Given Dickens's fervent admiration for Carlyle, it is hard to believe that his 'Pet Prisoners' was not at least partly inspired by 'Model Prisons'. Sydney Smith, whom Dickens also greatly admired and whose works were in his library, was probably also a strong influence on Dickens's penological views. Smith argued, 'A jail should be a place of punishment, from which men recoil with horror ... but if men can live idly, and live luxuriously, in a clean, well-aired, well-warmed spacious habitation, is it any wonder they set the law at defiance? ... Where the happiness of the prisoner is so much consulted we should be much more apprehensive of a conspiracy to break into, rather than out of prison' (*Works* [1839–40], Vol. 4, pp. 71, 78).

Dickens's visit (8 March 1842) to the Philadelphia Eastern Penitentiary, where the Separate System was rigidly enforced and prisoners sometimes kept many years in total solitary confinement, had filled him with horror at the physical and psychological effects this had on some inmates. In 'Pet Prisoners', however, he is dealing, as he acknowledges, with the modified British version of the Separate System in use at the new, purpose-built

Pentonville Prison. He concentrates first on a Carlylean contrasting of comfortably lodged prisoners with the hardships of the honest poor in workhouses or their own homes, and then on the way in which Separate prisoners were encouraged to profess moral and spiritual reformation (he had already made a passing satirical reference to this latter aspect in his first 'Raven' piece, see p. 189).

Dickens's chapter on the Philadelphia prison in *American Notes* had infuriated supporters of the Separate System. One of the most fervent of these, Joseph Adshead, had in his *Prisons and Prisoners* (1848) called Dickens 'this fugacious prison inspector' and asserted that he spent only two hours in the jail: 'with an effrontery unwarranted by his age or experience [he] questions the judgement and practice of veterans, we say, in the cause of humanity and philanthropy'. Adshead's words were quoted by the Rev. John Field, Chaplain of Reading Gaol, in his *Prison Discipline: The Advantages of the Separate System of Imprisonment* (1846; 2nd edn, 2 vols, 1848), and it is this book that Dickens has particularly in his sights in this piece (his quotations are taken from the second edition). Field, comments Philip Collins (*Dickens and Crime* [1962], p. 119), 'combined lavender-water sanctimoniousness towards his flock with a holy combativeness towards his enemies', and Dickens has really only to quote from him to expose his fatuity.

In his footnote Dickens defends himself against Adshead's attack as mediated by Field, both as regards the length of his Philadelphia visit and as regards his description of some female prisoners (Field had quoted Adshead's comment on some young women whose beauty and distress had moved Dickens: 'They were of the inferior class of low women to whom the appellative "beautiful" was inappropriate and unworthy; *two of them were Mulattoes and one of them a Negress!*'). Dickens also retorts on Field for dismissing *American Notes* as 'a work of mere amusement'.

Harriet Martineau had praised the Philadelphia prison system in her *Society in America* (1837) and did so again in *Retrospect of Western Travel* (1838), but with some reservations, such as the one quoted by Dickens below (the passage appears in *Retrospect*, Vol. I, p. 223).

Dickens's final and most devastating satire on Field's 'model prisoners' appeared in the final monthly number of *David Copperfield* (November 1850). In Ch. 61 David, visiting a prison, is shown 'two interesting penitents' in the shape of two villains, Uriah Heep and Littimer, now vying with each other in expressions of regret for their past 'follies' and appreciation of the spiritual benefits of solitary confinement ('It would be better for everybody, if they got took up, and was brought here').

For a more detailed placing of Dickens's writings on prison reform in the context of the contemporary debate and an illuminating analysis of them, see Collins, *op. cit.*, Chs 3, 5 and 6.

Literary allusions (p. 219) 'hewers of wood ...': Joshua 9: 21; (p. 219) 'consummation much to be desired': allusion to Shakespeare, *Hamlet*, Act 3. Sc. 1; (p. 222) 'the fox and the grapes': *Aesop's Fables*; (p. 224) 'Mr Croker cogently observes ...': Goldsmith, *The Good-Natured Man* (1768), end of Act 4.

The system of separate confinement first experimented on in England at the model prison, Pentonville, London, and now spreading through the country, appears to us to require a little calm consideration and reflection on the part of the public. We purpose, in this paper, to suggest what we consider some grave objections to this system.

We shall do this temperately, and without considering it necessary to regard every one from whom we differ, as a scoundrel, actuated by base motives, to whom the most unprincipled conduct may be recklessly attributed. Our faith in most questions where the good men are represented to be all *pro*, and the bad men to be all *con*, is very small. There is a hot class of riders of hobby-horses in the field, in this century, who think they do nothing unless they make a steeple-chase of their object, throw a vast quantity of mud about, and spurn every sort of decent restraint and reasonable consideration under their horses' heels. This question has not escaped such championship. It has its steeple-chase riders, who hold the dangerous principle that the end justifies any means, and to whom no means, truth and fair-dealing usually excepted, come amiss.

Considering the separate system of imprisonment, here, solely in reference to England, we discard, for the purpose of this discussion, the objection founded on its extreme severity, which would immediately arise if we were considering it with any reference to the State of Pennsylvania in America. For whereas in that State it may be inflicted for a dozen years, the idea is quite abandoned at home of extending it usually, beyond a dozen months, or in any case beyond eighteen months. Besides which, the school and the chapel afford periods of comparative relief here, which are not afforded in America.

Though it has been represented by the steeple-chase riders as a most enormous heresy to contemplate the possibility of any prisoner going mad or idiotic, under the prolonged effects of separate confinement; and although any one who should have the temerity to maintain such a doubt in Pennsylvania would have a chance of becoming a profane St Stephen; Lord Grey, in his very last speech in the House of Lords on this subject, made in the present session of Parliament, in praise of this separate system, said of it: 'Wherever it has been fairly tried, one of its great defects has been discovered to be this, – that it cannot be continued for a sufficient length of time without danger to the individual, and that human nature cannot bear it beyond a limited period. The evidence of medical authorities proves beyond dispute that, if it is protracted beyond twelve months, the health of the convict, mental and physical, would require the most close and vigilant superintendence. Eighteen months is stated to be the *maximum* time for the continuance of its infliction, and, as a general rule, it is advised that it never be continued for more than twelve months.' This being conceded, and it being clear that the prisoner's mind, and all the apprehensions weighing upon it, must be influenced from the first hour of his imprisonment by the greater or less extent of its duration in perspective before him, we are content to regard the system as dissociated in England from the American objection of too great severity.

We shall consider it, first in the relation of the extraordinary contrast it presents, in a country circumstanced as England is, between the physical condition of the convict in prison, and that of the hard-working man outside, or the pauper outside. We shall then enquire and endeavour to lay before our readers some means of judging, whether its proved or probable efficiency in producing a real, trustworthy, practically repentant state of mind, is such as to justify the presentation of that extraordinary contrast. If, in the end, we indicate the conclusion that the associated silent system is less objectionable, it is not because we consider it in the abstract a good secondary punishment, but because it is a severe one, capable of judicious administration, much less expensive, not presenting the objectionable contrast so strongly, and not calculated to pet and pamper the mind of the prisoner and swell his sense of his own importance. We are not acquainted with any system of secondary punishment that we think reformatory, except the mark system of Captain Macconnochie, formerly governor of Norfolk Island, which proceeds upon the principle of obliging the convict to some exercise of self-denial and resolution in every act of his prison life, and which would condemn him to a sentence of so much labour and good conduct instead of so much time. There are details in Captain Macconnochie's scheme on which we have our doubts (rigid silence we consider indispensable); but, in the main, we regard it as embodying sound and wise principles. We infer from the writings of Archbishop Whateley, that those principles have presented themselves to his profound and acute mind in a similar light.

We will first contrast the dietary of The Model Prison at Pentonville, with the dietary of what we take to be the nearest workhouse, namely, that of Saint Pancras. In the prison, every man receives twenty-eight ounces of meat weekly. In the workhouse, every able-bodied adult receives eighteen. In the prison, every man receives one hundred and forty ounces of bread weekly. In the workhouse, every able-bodied adult receives ninety-six. In the prison, every man receives one hundred and twelve ounces of potatoes weekly. In the workhouse, every able-bodied adult receives thirty-six. In the prison, every man receives five pints and a quarter of liquid cocoa weekly, (made of flaked cocoa or cocoa-nibs), with fourteen ounces of milk and forty-two drams of molasses; also seven pints of gruel weekly, sweetened with forty-two drams of molasses. In the workhouse, every able-bodied adult receives fourteen pints and a half of milk-porridge weekly, and no cocoa, and no gruel. In the prison, every man receives three pints and a half of soup weekly. In the workhouse, every able-bodied adult male receives four pints and a half, and a pint of Irish stew. This, with seven pints of table-beer weekly, and six ounces of cheese, is all the man in the workhouse has to set off against the immensely superior advantages of the prisoner in all the other respects we have stated. His lodging is very inferior to the prisoner's, the costly nature of whose accommodation we shall presently show.

Let us reflect upon this contrast in another aspect. We beg the reader to glance once more at The Model Prison dietary, and consider its frightful disproportion to the dietary of the free labourer in any of the rural parts of England. What shall we take his wages at? Will twelve shillings a week do? It cannot be called a low average, at all events. Twelve shillings a week make thirty-one pounds four a year. The cost, in 1848, for the victualling and management of every prisoner in the Model Prison was within a little of thirty-six pounds. Consequently, that free labourer, with young children to support, with cottage-rent to pay, and clothes to buy, and no advantage of purchasing his food in large amounts by contract, has, for the whole subsistence of himself and family, between four and five pounds a year *less* than the cost of feeding and overlooking one man in the Model Prison. Surely to his enlightened mind, and sometimes low morality, this must be an extraordinary good reason for keeping out of it!

But we will not confine ourselves to the contrast between the labourer's scanty fare and the prisoner's 'flaked cocoa or cocoa-nibs,' and daily dinner of soup, meat, and potatoes. We will rise a little higher in the scale. Let us see what advertisers in the *Times* newspaper can board the middle classes at, and get a profit out of, too.

A LADY, residing in a cottage, with a large garden, in a pleasant and healthful locality, would be happy to receive one or two LADIES to BOARD with her. Two ladies occupying the same apartment may be accommodated for 12s. a week each. The cottage is within a quarter of an hour's walk of a good market town, 10 minutes' of a South-Western Railway Station, and an hour's distance from town.

These two ladies could not be so cheaply boarded in the Model Prison.

BOARD and RESIDENCE, at £70 per annum, for a married couple, or in proportion for a single gentleman or lady, with a respectable family. Rooms large and airy, in an eligible dwelling, at Islington, about 20 minutes' walk from the Bank. Dinner hour six o'clock. There are one or two vacancies to complete a small, cheerful, and agreeable circle.

Still cheaper than the Model Prison!

BOARD and RESIDENCE – A lady, keeping a select school, in a town, about 30 miles from London, would be happy to meet with a LADY to BOARD and RESIDE with her. She would have her own bed-room and a sitting-room. Any lady wishing for accomplishments would find this desirable. Terms £30 per annum. References will be expected and given.

Again, some six pounds a year less than the Model Prison! And if we were to pursue the contrast through the newspaper file for a month, or through the advertising pages of two or three numbers of Bradshaw's Railway Guide, we might probably fill the present number of this publication with similar examples, many of them including a decent education into the bargain.

This Model Prison had cost at the close of 1847, under the heads of 'building' and 'repairs' alone, the insignificant sum of ninety-three thousand pounds – within seven thousand pounds of the amount of the last Government grant for the Education of the whole people, and enough to pay for the emigration to Australia of four thousand, six hundred and fifty poor persons at twenty pounds per head. Upon the work done by five hundred prisoners in the Model Prison, in the year 1848, (we collate these figures from the Reports, and from Mr Hepworth Dixon's useful work on the London Prisons,) there was no profit, but an actual loss of upwards of eight hundred pounds. The cost of instruction, and the time occupied in instruction, when the labour is necessarily unskilled and unproductive, may be pleaded in explanation of this astonishing fact. We are ready to allow all due weight to such considerations, but we put it to our readers whether the whole system is right or wrong; whether the money ought or ought not rather to be spent in instructing the unskilled and neglected outside the prison walls. It will be urged that it is expended in preparing the convict for the exile to which he is doomed. We submit to our readers, who are the jury in this case, that all this should be done outside the prison, first; that the first persons to be prepared for emigration are the miserable children who are consigned to the tender mercies of a DROUET, or who disgrace our streets; and that in this beginning at the wrong end, a spectacle of monstrous inconsistency is presented, shocking to the mind. Where is our Model House of Youthful Industry, where is our Model Ragged School, costing for building and repairs, from ninety to a hundred thousand pounds, and for its annual maintenance upwards of twenty thousand pounds a year? Would it be a Christian act to build that, first? To breed our skilful labour there? To take the hewers of wood and drawers of water in a strange country from the convict ranks, until those men by earnest working, zeal, and perseverance, proved themselves, and raised themselves? Here are two sets of people in a densely populated land, always in the balance before the general eye. Is Crime forever to carry it against Poverty, and to have a manifest advantage? There are the scales before all men. Whirlwinds of dust scattered in men's eyes – and there is plenty flying about – cannot blind them to the real state of the balance.

We now come to enquire into the condition of mind produced by the seclusion (limited in duration as Lord Grey limits it) which is purchased at this great cost in money, and this greater cost in stupendous injustice. That it is a consummation much to be desired, that a respectable man, lapsing into crime, should expiate his offence without incurring the liability of being afterwards recognised by hardened offenders who were his fellow-prisoners, we most readily admit. But, that this object, howsoever desirable and benevolent, is in itself sufficient to outweigh such objections as we have set forth, we cannot for a moment concede. Nor have we any sufficient guarantee that even this solitary point is gained. Under how many apparently inseparable difficulties, men immured in solitary cells, will by some means obtain a knowledge of other men immured in other solitary cells, most of us know from all the accounts and anecdotes we have read of secret prisons and secret prisoners from our school-time upwards. That there is a fascination in the desire to know something of the hidden presence beyond the blank wall of the cell; that the listening ear is often laid against that wall; that there is an overpowering temptation to respond to the muffled knock, or any other signal which sharpened ingenuity pondering day after day on one idea can devise: is in that constitution of human nature which impels mankind to communication with one another, and makes solitude a false condition against which nature strives. That such communication within the Model Prison, is not only probable, but indisputably proved to be possible by its actual discovery, we have no hesitation in stating as a fact. Some pains have been taken to hush the matter, but the truth is, that when the Prisoners at Pentonville ceased to be selected Prisoners, especially picked out and chosen for the purposes of that experiment, an extensive conspiracy was found out among them, involving, it is needless to say, extensive communication. Small pieces of paper with writing upon them, had been crushed into balls, and shot into the apertures of cell doors, by prisoners passing along the passages; false responses had been made during Divine Service in the chapel, in which responses they addressed one another; and armed men were secretly dispersed by the Governor in various parts of the building, to prevent the general rising, which was anticipated as the consequence of this plot. Undiscovered communication, under this system, we assume to be frequent.

The state of mind into which a man is brought who is the lonely inhabitant of his own small world, and who is only visited by certain regular visitors, all addressing themselves to him individually and personally, as the object of their particular solicitude – we believe in most cases to have very little promise in it, and very little of solid foundation. A strange absorbing selfishness – a spiritual egotism and vanity, real or assumed – is the first result. It is most remarkable to observe, in the cases of murderers who become this kind of object of interest, when they are at last consigned to the condemned cell, how the rule is (of course there are exceptions,) that the murdered person disappears from the stage of their thoughts, except as a part of their own important story; and how they occupy the whole scene. *I* did this, *I* feel that, *I* confide in the mercy of Heaven being extended to *me*; this is the autograph of *me*, the unfortunate and unhappy; in my childhood I was so and so; in my youth I did such a thing, to which I attribute my downfall – not this thing of basely and barbarously defacing the image of my Creator, and sending an immortal soul into eternity without a moment's warning, but something else of a venial kind that many unpunished people do. I don't want the forgiveness of this foully murdered person's bereaved wife, husband, brother, sister, child, friend; I don't ask for it, I don't care for it. I make no enquiry of the clergyman concerning the salvation of that murdered person's soul; *mine* is the matter; and I am almost happy that I came here, as to the gate of Paradise. 'I never liked him,' said the repentant Mr Manning, false of heart to the last, calling a crowbar by a milder name, to lessen the cowardly horror of it, 'and I beat in his skull with the ripping chisel.' I am going to bliss, exclaims the same authority, in effect. Where my victim went to, is not my business at all. Now, GOD forbid that we, unworthily believing in the Redeemer, should shut out hope, or even humble trustfulness, from any criminal at that dread pass; but, it is not in us to call this state of mind repentance.

The present question is with a state of mind analogous to this (as we conceive) but with a far stronger tendency to hypocrisy; the dread of death not being present, and there being every possible inducement, either to feign contrition, or to set up an unreliable semblance of it. If I, John Styles, the prisoner, don't do my work, and outwardly conform to the rules of the prison, I am a mere fool. There is nothing here to tempt me to do anything else, and everything to tempt me to do that. The capital dietary (and every meal is a great event in this lonely life) depends upon it; the alternative is a pound of bread a day. I should be weary of myself without occupation. I should be much more dull if I didn't hold these dialogues with the gentlemen who are so anxious about me. I shouldn't be half the object of interest I am, if I didn't make the professions I do. Therefore, I John Styles go in for what is popular here, and I may mean it, or I may not.

There will always, under any decent system, be certain prisoners, betrayed into crime by a variety of circumstances, who will do well in exile, and offend against the laws no more. Upon this class, we think the Associated Silent System would have quite as good an influence as this expensive and anomalous one; and we cannot accept them as evidence of the efficiency of separate confinement. Assuming John Styles to mean what he professes, for the time being, we desire to track the workings of his mind, and to try to test the value of his professions. Where shall we find an account of John Styles, proceeding from no objector to this system, but from a staunch supporter of it? We will take it from a work called 'Prison Discipline, and the advantages of the separate system of imprisonment,' written by the Reverend Mr Field, chaplain of the new County Gaol at Reading; pointing out to Mr Field, in passing, that the question is not justly, as he would sometimes make it, a question between this system and the profligate abuses and customs of the old unreformed gaols, but between it and the improved gaols of this time, which are not constructed on his favourite principles.*

* As Mr Field condescends to quote some vapouring about the account given by Mr Charles Dickens in his 'American Notes,' of the Solitary Prison at Philadelphia, he may perhaps really wish for some few words of information on the subject. For this purpose, Mr Charles Dickens has referred to the entry in his Diary, made at the close of that day. He left his hotel for the Prison at twelve o'clock, being waited on, by appointment, by the gentlemen who showed it to him, and he returned between seven and eight at night; dining in the prison in the course of that time; which, according to his calculation, in despite of the Philadelphia Newspaper, rather exceeds two hours. He found the Prison admirably conducted, extremely clean, and the system administered in a most intelligent, kind, orderly, tender, and careful manner. He did not consider (nor should he, if he were to visit Pentonville tomorrow) that the book in which visitors were expected to record their observation of the place, was intended for the insertion of criticisms on the system, but for honest testimony to the manner of its administration; and to that, he bore, as an impartial visitor, the highest testimony in his power. In returning thanks for his health being drunk, at the dinner within the walls, he said that what he had seen that day was running in his mind; that he could not help reflecting on it; and that it was an awful punishment. If the American officer who rode back with him afterwards should ever see these words, he will perhaps recall his conversation with Mr Dickens on the road, as to Mr Dickens having said so, very plainly and strongly. In reference to the ridiculous assertion that Mr Dickens in his book termed a woman 'quite beautiful' who was a Negress, he positively believes that he was shown no Negress in the Prison, but one who was nursing a woman much diseased, and to whom no reference whatever is made in his published account. In describing three young women, 'all convicted at the same time of a conspiracy,' he may, *possibly*, among many cases, have substituted in his memory for one of them whom he did not see, some other prisoner, confined for some other crime,

Now, here is John Styles, twenty years of age, in prison for a felony. He has been there five months, and he writes to his sister, 'Don't fret my dear sister, about my being here. I cannot help fretting when I think about my usage to my father and mother: when I think about it, it makes me quite ill. I hope God will forgive me; I pray for it night and day from my heart. Instead of fretting about imprisonment, I ought to thank God for it, for before I came here, I was living quite a careless life; neither was God in all my thoughts; all I thought about was ways that led me towards destruction. Give my respects to my wretched companions, and I hope they will alter their wicked course, for they don't know for a day nor an hour but what they may be cut off. I have seen my folly, and I hope they may see their folly; but I shouldn't if I had not been in trouble. It is good for me that I have been in trouble. Go to church, my sister, every Sunday, and don't give your mind to going to playhouses and theatres, for that is no good to you. There are a great many temptations.'

Observe! John Styles, who has committed the felony has been 'living quite a careless life.' That is his worst opinion of it, whereas his companions who did not commit the felony are 'wretched companions.' John saw *his* 'folly,' and sees *their* 'wicked course.' It is playhouses and theatres which many unfelonious people go to, that prey upon John's mind – not felony. John is shut up in that pulpit to lecture his companions and his sister, about the wickedness of the unfelonious world. Always supposing him to be sincere, is there no exaggeration of himself in this? Go to church where I can go, and don't go to theatres where I can't! Is there any tinge of the fox and the grapes in it? Is this the kind of penitence that will wear outside! Put the case that he had written, of his own mind, 'My dear sister, I feel that I have disgraced you and all who should be dear to me, and if it please God that I live to be free, I will

whom he did see; but he has not the least doubt of having been guilty of the (American) enormity of detecting beauty in a pensive quadroon or mulatto girl, or of having seen exactly what he describes; and he remembers the girl more particularly described in this connexion, perfectly. Can Mr Field really suppose that Mr Dickens had any interest or purpose in misrepresenting the system, or that if he could be guilty of such unworthy conduct, or desire to do it anything but justice, he would have volunteered the narrative of a man's having, of his own choice, undergone it for two years?

We will not notice the objection of Mr Field (who strengthens the truth of Burns to nature, by the testimony of Mr Pitt!) to the discussion of such a topic as the present in a work of 'mere amusement;' though, we had thought we remembered in that book a word or two about slavery, which, although a very amusing, can scarcely be considered an unmitigatedly comic theme. We are quite content to believe, without seeking to make a convert of the Reverend Mr Field, that no work need be one of 'mere amusement;' and that some works to which he would apply that designation have done a little good in advancing principles to which, we hope, and will believe, for the credit of his Christian office, he is not indifferent.

try hard to repair that, and to be a credit to you. My dear sister, when I committed this felony, I stole something – and these pining five months have not put it back – and I will work my fingers to the bone to make restitution, and oh! my dear sister, seek out my late companions, and tell Tom Jones, that poor boy, who was younger and littler than me, that I am grieved I ever led him so wrong, and I am suffering for it now!' Would that be better? Would it be more like solid truth?

But no. This is not the pattern penitence. There would seem to be a pattern penitence, of a particular form, shape, limits, and dimensions, like the cells. While Mr Field is correcting his proof-sheets for the press, another letter is brought to him, and in that letter too, that man, also a felon, speaks of his 'past folly,' and lectures his mother about labouring under 'strong delusions of the devil.' Does this overweening readiness to lecture other people, suggest the suspicion of any parrot-like imitation of Mr Field, who lectures him, and any presumptuous confounding of their relative positions?

We venture altogether to protest against the citation, in support of this system, of assumed repentance which has stood no test or trial in the working world. We consider that it proves nothing, and is worth nothing, except as a discouraging sign of that spiritual egotism and presumption of which we have already spoken. It is not peculiar to the separate system at Reading; Miss Martineau, who was on the whole decidedly favourable to the separate prison at Philadelphia, observed it there. 'The cases I became acquainted with,' says she, 'were not all hopeful. Some of the convicts were so stupid as not to be relied upon, more or less. Others canted so detestably, and were (always in connexion with their cant) so certain that they should never sin more, that I have every expectation that they will find themselves in prison again some day. One fellow, a sailor, notorious for having taken more lives than probably any man in the United States, was quite confident that he should be perfectly virtuous henceforth. He should never touch anything stronger than tea, or lift his hand against money or life. I told him I thought he could not be sure of all this till he was within sight of money and the smell of strong liquors; and that he was more confident than I should like to be. He shook his shock of red hair at me, and glared with his one ferocious eye, as he said he knew all about it. He had been the worst of men, and Christ had had mercy on his poor soul.' (Observe again, as in the general case we have put, that he is not at all troubled about the souls of the people whom he had killed.)

Let us submit to our readers another instance from Mr Field, of the wholesome state of mind produced by the separate system. 'The 25th of March, in the last year, was the day appointed for a general fast, on account of the threatened famine. The following note is in my journal

of that day. "During the evening I visited many prisoners, and found
with much satisfaction that a large proportion of them had observed the
day in a manner becoming their own situation, and the purpose for
which it had been set apart. I think it right to record the following
remarkable proof of the effect of discipline. ***** They were all supplied
with their usual rations. I went first this evening to the cells of the
prisoners recently committed for trial (Ward A. 1.), and amongst these
(upwards of twenty) I found that but three had abstained from any
portion of their food. I then visited twenty-one convicted prisoners who
had spent some considerable time in the gaol (Ward C. 1.), and amongst
them I found that some had altogether abstained from food, and of the
whole number two-thirds had partially abstained."' We will take it for
granted that this was not because they had more than they could eat,
though we know that with such a dietary even that sometimes happens,
especially in the case of persons long confined. 'The remark of one
prisoner whom I questioned, concerning his abstinence was, I believe,
sincere, and was very pleasing. "Sir, I have not felt able to eat to-day,
whilst I have thought of those poor starving people; but I hope that I
have prayed a good deal that God will give *them* something to eat."'

If this were not pattern penitence, and the thought of those poor
starving people had honestly originated with that man, and were really
on his mind, we want to know why he was not uneasy, every day, in the
contemplation of his soup, meat, bread, potatoes, cocoa-nibs, milk,
molasses, and gruel, and its contrast to the fare of 'those poor starving
people' who, in some form or other, were taxed to pay for it?

We do not deem it necessary to comment on the authorities quoted
by Mr Field to show what a fine thing the separate system is, for the
health of the body; how it never affects the mind except for good; how
it is the true preventive of pulmonary disease; and so on. The deduction
we must draw from such things is, that Providence was quite mistaken
in making us gregarious, and that we had better all shut ourselves up
directly. Neither will we refer to that 'talented criminal,' Dr Dodd, whose
exceedingly indifferent verses applied to a system now extinct, in reference
to our penitentiaries for convicted prisoners. Neither, after what we have
quoted from Lord Grey, need we refer to the likewise quoted report of
the American authorities, who are perfectly sure that no extent of
confinement in the Philadelphia prison has ever affected the intellectual
powers of any prisoners. Mr Croker cogently observes, in the Good-
Natured Man, that either his hat must be on his head, or it must be off.
By a parity of reasoning, we conclude that both Lord Grey and the
American authorities cannot possibly be right – unless indeed the
notoriously settled habits of the American people, and the absence of
any approach to restlessness in the national character, render them

unusually good subjects for protracted seclusion, and an exception from the rest of mankind.

In using the term 'pattern penitence' we beg it to be understood that we do not apply it to Mr Field, or to any other chaplain, but to the system; which appears to us to make these doubtful converts all alike. Although Mr Field has not shown any remarkable courtesy in the instance we have set forth in a note, it is our wish to show all courtesy to him, and to his office, and to his sincerity in the discharge of its duties. In our desire to represent him with fairness and impartiality, we will not take leave of him without the following quotation from his book:

'Scarcely sufficient time has yet expired since the present system was introduced, for me to report much concerning discharged criminals. Out of a class so degraded – the very dregs of the community – it can be no wonder that some, of whose improvement I cherished the hope, should have relapsed. Disappointed in a few cases I have been, yet by no means discouraged, since I can with pleasure refer to many whose conduct is affording proof of reformation. Gratifying indeed have been some accounts received from liberated offenders themselves, as well as from clergymen of parishes to which they have returned. I have also myself visited the homes of some of our former prisoners, and have been cheered by the testimony given, and the evident signs of improved character which I have there observed. Although I do not venture at present to describe the particular cases of prisoners, concerning whose reformation I feel much confidence, because, as I have stated, the time of trial has hitherto been short; yet I can with pleasure refer to some public documents which prove the happy effects of similar discipline in other establishments.'

It should also be stated that the Reverend Mr Kingsmill, the chaplain of the Model Prison at Pentonville, in his calm and intelligent report made to the Commissioners on the first of February, 1849, expresses his belief 'that the effects produced here upon the character of prisoners, have been encouraging in a high degree.'

But, we entreat our readers once again to look at that Model Prison dietary (which is essential to the system, though the system is so very healthy of itself); to remember the other enormous expenses of the establishment; to consider the circumstances of this old country, with the inevitable anomalies and contrasts it must present; and to decide, on temperate reflection, whether there are any sufficient reasons for adding this monstrous contrast to the rest. Let us impress upon our readers that the existing question is, not between this system and the old abuses of the old profligate Gaols (with which, thank Heaven, we have nothing to do), but between this system and the associated silent system, where the dietary is much lower, where the annual cost of provision, management, repairs, clothing, &c., does not exceed, on a liberal average, £25 for each prisoner; where many prisoners are, and every prisoner would be (if due accommodation were provided in some over-crowded prisons), locked up alone, for twelve hours out of every twenty-four, and where, while preserved from contamination, he is still one of a society of men, and not an isolated being, filling his whole sphere of view with a diseased dilation of himself. We hear that the associated silent system is objectionable, because of the number of punishments it involves for breaches of the prison discipline; but how can we, in the same breath, be told that the resolutions of prisoners for the misty future are to be trusted, and that, on the least temptation, they are so little to be relied on, as to the solid present? How can I set the pattern penitence against the career that preceded it, when I am told that if I put that man with other men, and lay a solemn charge upon him not to address them by word or sign, there are such and such great chances that he will want the resolution to obey?

Remember that this separate system, though commended in the English Parliament and spreading in England, has not spread in America, despite of all the steeple-chase riders in the United States. Remember that it has never reached the State most distinguished for its learning, for its moderation, for its remarkable men of European reputation, for the excellence of its public Institutions. Let it be tried here, on a limited scale, if you will, with fair representatives of all classes of prisoners: let Captain Macconochie's system be tried: let anything with a ray of hope in it be tried: but, only as a part of some general system for raising up the prostrate portion of the people of this country, and not as an exhibition of such astonishing consideration for crime, in comparison with want and work. Any prison built, at a great expenditure, for this system, is comparatively useless for any other; and the ratepayers will do well to think of this, before they take it for granted that it is a proved boon to the country which will be enduring.

Under the separate system, the prisoners work at trades. Under the associated silent system, the Magistrates of Middlesex have almost abolished the treadmill. Is it no part of the legitimate consideration of this important point of work, to discover what kind of work the people always filtering through the gaols of large towns – the pickpocket, the sturdy vagrant, the habitual drunkard, and the begging-letter impostor – like least, and to give them that work to do in preference to any other? It is out of fashion with the steeple-chase riders we know; but we would have, for all such characters, a kind of work in gaols, badged and degraded as belonging to gaols only, and never done elsewhere. And we must avow that, in a country circumstanced as England is, with respect to labour and labourers, we have strong doubts of the propriety of bringing the results of prison labour into the over-stocked market. On this subject some public remonstrances have recently been made by tradesmen; and we cannot shut our eyes to the fact that they are well-founded.

45

The Begging-Letter Writer

Household Words, 18 May 1850 (leading article) (*RP*)

From his rise to fame with *The Pickwick Papers*, Dickens was plagued by begging-letter writers. Forster comments (Book 2, Ch. 8) that there is not 'a particle of exaggeration' in Dickens's description of his victimisation here, but adds, 'for much of what he suffered he was himself responsible, by giving so largely, as at first he did, to almost everyone who applied to him'. Among the most persistent of these corresponding beggars was an old school-friend Daniel Tobin, who became 'an intolerable nuisance' (Forster, Book 1, Ch. 3), and he it was who finally made the bizarre request for a donkey, described here by Dickens (p. 230). In the paragraph immediately following this Dickens describes another case, that of John Walker, whom Dickens had given money to several times in 1844, sending his brother Fred to check that he really was in distress. Walker continued to write begging letters, which Dickens ceased to answer until he got one telling him that Walker's wife had died and begging 'a few crumbs from your table' to feed the children. When Dickens found that Mrs Walker was not dead, he referred the case to the Mendicity Society, which brought a prosecution against Walker at Marylebone Police Court, charging him with attempting to get money from Dickens 'by means of false and fraudulent representation'. He had been arrested without a warrant, however, and was shown to be really in a state of dire poverty, so he was discharged, much sympathy having been aroused by his very distressed behaviour in the dock and his wife's appeal to the court. Dickens, Forster tells us (Book 2, Ch. 8), 'broke down in his character of prosecutor' and got the Mendicity officers to suppress some of the evidence against the man. Although it was 'an exceedingly bad case', Dickens wrote to Forster, 'I was not sorry that the creature found the loophole for escape' (see *Pilgrim*, Vol. IV, pp. 129–30, for a fuller account of the affair).

Pecksniff in *Martin Chuzzlewit* (1844) is (somewhat improbably) degraded at the end of the novel to become 'a drunken, squalid, begging-letter-writing man', and the endless ingenuity of begging-letter writers forms the subject of a bravura passage at the end of Ch. 17 of Book 1 of *Our Mutual Friend* (1865). See also article 63.

Literary allusions (p. 232) 'Sydney Smith ... "the dangerous luxury of dishonesty" ': untraced; (p. 232) 'Angels' visits' refers to Robert Blair's poem *The Grave* (1743): '... visits/Like those of angels, short, and far between'.

MS. and (meticulously) corrected proofs in the Forster Collection, Victoria and Albert Museum.

He is a 'Household Word.' We all know something of him. The amount of money he annually diverts from wholesome and useful purposes in the United Kingdom, would be a set-off against the Window Tax. He is one of the most shameless frauds and impositions of this time. In his idleness, his mendacity, and the immeasurable harm he does to the deserving, – dirtying the stream of true benevolence, and muddling the brains of foolish justices, with inability to distinguish between the base coin of distress, and the true currency we have always among us, – he is more worthy of Norfolk Island than three-fourths of the worst characters who are sent there. Under any rational system, he would have been sent there long ago.

I, the writer of this paper, have been, for some time, a chosen receiver of Begging Letters. For fourteen years, my house has been made as regular a Receiving House for such communications as any one of the great branch Post-Offices is for general correspondence. I ought to know something of the Begging-Letter Writer. He has besieged my door, at all hours of the day and night; he has fought my servant; he has lain in ambush for me, going out and coming in; he has followed me out of town into the country; he has appeared at provincial hotels, where I have been staying for only a few hours; he has written to me from immense distances, when I have been out of England. He has fallen sick; he has died, and been buried; he has come to life again, and again departed from this transitory scene; he has been his own son, his own mother, his own baby, his idiot brother, his uncle, his aunt, his aged grandfather. He has wanted a great coat, to go to India in; a pound, to set him up in life for ever; a pair of boots, to take him to the coast of China; a hat, to get him into a permanent situation under Government. He has frequently been exactly seven-and-sixpence short of independence. He has had such openings at Liverpool – posts of great trust and confidence in merchants' houses, which nothing but seven-and-sixpence was wanting to him to secure – that I wonder he is not Mayor of that flourishing town at the present moment.

The natural phenomena of which he has been the victim, are of a most astounding nature. He has had two children, who have never grown up; who have never had anything to cover them at night; who have been continually driving him mad, by asking in vain for food; who have never come out of fevers and measles (which, I suppose, has accounted for his fuming his letters with tobacco smoke, as a disinfectant); who have never changed in the least degree, through fourteen long revolving years. As to his wife, what that suffering woman has undergone, nobody knows. She has always been in an interesting situation through the same long period, and has never been confined yet. His devotion to her has been unceasing. He has never cared for himself; *he* could have perished – he would rather, in short – but was it not his Christian duty as a man, a husband, and a father, to write begging-letters when he looked at her? (He has usually remarked that he would call in the evening for an answer to this question.)

He has been the sport of the strangest misfortunes. What his brother has done to him would have broken anybody else's heart. His brother went into business with him, and ran away with the money; his brother got him to be security for an immense sum, and left him to pay it; his brother would have given him employment to the tune of hundreds a-year, if he would have consented to write letters on a Sunday; his brother enunciated principles incompatible with his religious views, and he could not (in consequence) permit his brother to provide for him. His landlord has never shown a spark of human feeling. When he put in that execution I don't know, but he has never taken it out. The broker's man has grown grey in possession. They will have to bury him some day.

He has been attached to every conceivable pursuit. He has been in the army, in the navy, in the church, in the law; connected with the press, the fine arts, public institutions, every description and grade of business. He has been brought up as a gentleman; he has been at every college in Oxford and Cambridge; he can quote Latin in his letters (but generally mis-spells some minor English word); he can tell you what Shakespeare says about begging, better than you know it. It is to be observed, that in the midst of his afflictions he always reads the news-papers; and rounds off his appeals with some allusion, that may be supposed to be in my way, to the popular subject of the hour.

His life presents a series of inconsistencies. Sometimes he has never written such a letter before. He blushes with shame. That is the first time; that shall be the last. Don't answer it, and let it be understood that, then, he will kill himself quietly. Sometimes (and more frequently) he *has* written a few such letters. Then he encloses the answers, with an intimation that they are of inestimable value to him, and a request that they may be carefully returned. He is fond of enclosing something – verses, letters, pawnbrokers' duplicates, anything to necessitate an answer. He is very severe upon 'the pampered minion of fortune,' who refused him the half-sovereign referred to in the enclosure number two – but he knows me better.

He writes in a variety of styles; sometimes in low spirits; sometimes quite jocosely. When he is in low spirits, he writes down-hill, and repeats words – these little indications being expressive of the perturbation of his mind. When he is more vivacious, he is frank with me; he is quite the agreeable rattle. I know what human nature is, – who better? Well! He had a little money once, and he ran through it – as many men have done before him. He finds his old friends turn away from him now – many men have done that before him, too. Shall he tell me why he writes to me? Because he has no kind of claim upon me. He puts it on that ground, plainly; and begs to ask for the loan (as I know human nature) of two sovereigns, to be repaid, next Tuesday six weeks, before twelve at noon.

Sometimes, when he is sure that I have found him out, and that there is no chance of money, he writes to inform me that I have got rid of him at last. He has enlisted into the Company's service, and is off directly – but he wants a cheese. He is informed by the serjeant that it is essential to his prospects in the regiment that he should take out a single-Gloucester cheese, weighing from twelve to fifteen pounds. Eight or nine shillings would buy it. He does not ask for money, after what has passed; but if he calls at nine tomorrow morning, may he hope to find a cheese? And is there anything he can do to show his gratitude in Bengal?

Once, he wrote me rather a special letter proposing relief in kind. He had got into a little trouble by leaving parcels of mud done up in brown paper, at people's houses, on pretence of being a Railway-Porter, in which character he received carriage money. This sportive fancy he expiated in the House of Correction. Not long after his release, and on a Sunday morning, he called with a letter (having first dusted himself all over), in which he gave me to understand that, being resolved to earn an honest livelihood, he had been travelling about the country with a cart of crockery. That he had been doing pretty well, until the day before, when his horse had dropped down dead near Chatham, in Kent. That this had reduced him to the unpleasant necessity of getting into the shafts himself, and drawing the cart of crockery to London – a somewhat exhausting pull of thirty miles. That he did not venture to ask again for money; but that if I would have the goodness *to leave him out a donkey*, he would call for the animal before breakfast!

At another time, my friend (I am describing actual experiences) introduced himself as a literary gentleman in the last extremity of distress. He had had a play accepted at a certain Theatre – which was really open; its representation was delayed by the indisposition of a leading actor – who was really ill; and he and his were in a state of absolute starvation. If he made his necessities known to the Manager of the Theatre, he put it to me to say what kind of treatment he might expect? Well! we got over that difficulty to our mutual satisfaction. A little while afterwards he was in some other strait – I think Mrs Southcote, his wife, was in extremity – and we adjusted that point too. A little while afterwards, he had taken a new house, and was going headlong to ruin for want of a water-butt. I had my misgivings about the water-butt, and did not reply to that epistle. But, a little while afterwards, I had reason to feel penitent for my neglect. He wrote me a few broken-hearted lines, informing me that the dear partner of his sorrows died in his arms last night at nine o'clock!

I dispatched a trusty messenger to comfort the bereaved mourner and his poor children: but the messenger went so soon, that the play was not ready to be played out; my friend was not at home, and his wife was in a most delightful state of health. He was taken up by the Mendicity Society (informally it afterwards appeared), and I presented myself at a London Police-Office with my testimony against him. The Magistrate was wonderfully struck by his educational acquirements, deeply impressed by the excellence of his letters, exceedingly sorry to see a man of his attainments there, complimented him highly on his powers of composition, and was quite charmed to have the agreeable duty of discharging him. A collection was made for the 'poor fellow,' as he was called in the reports, and I left the court with a comfortable sense of being universally regarded as a sort of monster. Next day, comes to me a friend of mine, the governor of a large prison, 'Why did you ever go to the Police-Office against that man,' says he, 'without coming to me first? I know all about him and his frauds. He lodged in the house of one of my warders, at the very time when he first wrote to you; and then he was eating spring-lamb at eighteen-pence a pound, and early asparagus at I don't know how much a bundle!' On that very same day, and in that very same hour, my injured gentleman wrote a solemn address to me, demanding to know what compensation I proposed to make him for his having passed the night in a 'loathsome dungeon.' And next morning, an Irish gentleman, a member of the same fraternity, who had read the case, and was very well persuaded I should be chary of going to that Police-Office again, positively refused to leave my door for less than a sovereign, and, resolved to besiege me into compliance, literally 'sat down' before it for ten mortal hours. The garrison being well provisioned, I remained within the walls; and he raised the siege at midnight, with a prodigious alarum on the bell.

The Begging-Letter Writer often has an extensive circle of acquaintance. Whole pages of the Court Guide are ready to be references for him. Noblemen and gentlemen write to say there never was such a man for probity and virtue. They have known him, time out of mind, and there is nothing they wouldn't do for him. Somehow, they don't give him that one pound ten he stands in need of; but perhaps it is not enough – they want to do more, and his modesty will not allow it. It is to be remarked of his trade that it is a very fascinating one. He never leaves it; and those who are near to him become smitten with a love of it, too, and sooner or later set up for themselves. He employs a messenger – man, woman, or child. That messenger is certain ultimately to become an independent Begging-Letter Writer. His sons and daughters succeed to his calling, and write begging-letters when he is no more. He throws off the infection of begging-letter writing, like the contagion of disease. What Sydney Smith so happily called 'the dangerous luxury of dishonesty' is more tempting, and more catching, it would seem, in this instance than in any other.

He always belongs to a Corresponding Society of Begging-Letter Writers. Any one who will, may ascertain this fact. Give money today, in recognition of a begging-letter, – no matter how unlike a common begging-letter, – and for the next fortnight you will have a rush of such communications. Steadily refuse to give; and the begging-letters become Angels' visits, until the Society is from some cause or other in a dull way of business, and may as well try you as anybody else. It is of little use enquiring into the Begging-Letter Writer's circumstances. He may be sometimes accidentally found out, as in the case already mentioned (though that was not the first enquiry made); but apparent misery is always a part of his trade, and real misery very often is, in the intervals of spring-lamb and early asparagus. It is naturally an incident of his dissipated and dishonest life.

That the calling is a successful one, and that large sums of money are gained by it, must be evident to anybody who reads the Police Reports of such cases. But, prosecutions are of rare occurrence, relatively to the extent to which the trade is carried on. The cause of this, is to be found (as no one knows better than the Begging-Letter Writer, for it is a part of his speculation) in the aversion people feel to exhibit themselves as having been imposed on, or as having weakly gratified their consciences with a lazy, flimsy substitute for the noblest of all virtues. There is a man at large, at the moment when this paper is preparing for the press (on the 29th of April), and never once taken up yet, who, within these twelvemonths, has been probably the most audacious and the most successful swindler that even this trade has ever known. There has been something singularly base in this fellow's proceedings: it has been his business to write to all sorts and conditions of people, in the names of persons of high reputation and unblemished honor, professing to be in distress – the general admiration and respect for whom, has ensured a ready and generous reply.

Now, in the hope that the results of the real experience of a real person may do something more to induce reflection on this subject than any abstract treatise – and with a personal knowledge of the extent to which the Begging-Letter Trade has been carried on for some time, and has been for some time constantly increasing – the writer of this paper entreats the attention of his readers to a few concluding words. His experience is a type of the experience of many; some on a smaller; some on an infinitely larger scale. All may judge of the soundness or unsoundness of his conclusions from it.

Long doubtful of the efficacy of such assistance in any case whatever, and able to recal but one, within his whole individual knowledge, in which he had the least after-reason to suppose that any good was done by it, he was led, last autumn, into some serious considerations. The begging-letters flying about by every post, made it perfectly manifest, That a set of lazy vagabonds were interposed between the general desire to do something to relieve the sickness and misery under which the poor were suffering; and the suffering poor themselves. That many who sought to do some little to repair the social wrongs, inflicted in the way of preventible sickness and death upon the poor, were strengthening those wrongs, however innocently, by wasting money on pestilent knaves cumbering society. That imagination, – soberly following one of these knaves into his life of punishment in jail, and comparing it with the life of one of these poor in a cholera-stricken alley, or one of the children of one of these poor, soothed in its dying hour by the late lamented Mr Drouet, – contemplated a grim farce, impossible to be presented very much longer before God or man. That the crowning miracle of all the miracles summed up in the New Testament, after the miracle of the blind seeing, and the lame walking, and the restoration of the dead to life, was the miracle that the poor had the Gospel preached to them. That while the poor were unnaturally and unnecessarily cut off by the thousand, in the prematurity of their age, or in the rottenness of their youth – for of flower or blossom such youth has none – the Gospel was NOT preached to them, saving in hollow and unmeaning voices. That of all wrongs, this was the first mighty wrong the Pestilence warned us to set right. And that no Post-Office Order to any amount, given to a Begging-Letter Writer for the quieting of an uneasy breast, would be presentable on the Last Great Day as anything towards it.

The poor never write these letters. Nothing could be more unlike their habits. The writers are public robbers; and we who support them are parties to their depredations. They trade upon every circumstance within their knowledge that affects us, public or private, joyful or sorrowful; they pervert the lessons of our lives; they change what ought to be our strength and virtue, into weakness, and encouragement of vice. There is a plain remedy, and it is in our own hands. We must resolve, at any sacrifice of feeling, to be deaf to such appeals, and crush the trade.

There are degrees in murder. Life must be held sacred among us in more ways than one – sacred, not merely from the murderous weapon, or the subtle poison, or the cruel blow, but sacred from preventible diseases, distortions, and pains. That is the first great end we have to set against this miserable imposition. Physical life respected, moral life comes next. What will not content a Begging-Letter Writer for a week, would educate a score of children for a year. Let us give all we can; let us give more than ever. Let us do all we can; let us do more than ever. But let us give, and do, with a high purpose; not to endow the scum of the earth, to its own greater corruption, with the offals of our duty.

46

A Walk in a Workhouse

Household Words, 25 May 1850 (*RP*)

Dickens took this walk on Sunday, 5 May, with the chemist and philanthropist Jacob Bell, the founder of the Pharmaceutical Society, who was shortly to enter Parliament as MP for St Albans. He wrote to Bell on 12 May:

> I have thought a great deal about that woman, the Wardswoman in the Itch Ward, who was crying about the dead child. If anything useful can be done for her, I should like to do it. Will you bear this in mind, in confidence, and if you can put me in the way of helping her, do me the kindness of telling me how it can be best done? ...
>
> Without identifying the Workhouse, I have written a fanciful kind of description of our Walk, which you will find at page 204 of the enclosed proof.... [*Pilgrim*, Vol. VI, p. 99]

Dickens wrote again to Bell on 13 May explaining that it was too late for him to make a suggested alteration ('I purposely forebore sending you the Proof until the Number was at View, because I thought it delicate and right to abstain from making you in any way a party to the article'). He adds that he omitted describing 'Miss Bridges ... and the two blind men' because it might lead people to identify the workhouse in question; he clearly wished his description to be read as generic rather than a particular one. We can, however, identify the workhouse from Dickens's working notes (Forster Collection, Victoria and Albert Museum) for Ch. 31 of the ninth monthly number of *Little Dorrit* (July 1856). This chapter introduces a workhouse inmate Old Nandy enjoying a brief outing away from the place where he must live 'in a grove of two score and nineteen more old men, every one of whom smells of all the others'. Dickens's notes read:

Open with old Pauper out for the day —

Picture

Groves of old men in Marylebone Workhouse

(Cf. the old pauper overcome by drink on his day out, p. 360.)

N. Philip and V. Neuburg note (*Charles Dickens: A December Vision* [1986], p. 104) that in February 1849 the Marylebone Workhouse 'had 1,715 inmates ... plus a further 345 in the infirmary, including 79 lunatics'. The 'Itch Ward' would be used to segregate inmates suffering from 'the itch', i.e., scabies, a highly contagious disease resulting from mites burrowing under the skin.

Dickens's account of the Marylebone Workhouse makes an interesting comparison with his later description of Wapping Workhouse in *The Uncommercial Traveller*, first published in *ATYR* on 18 February 1860.

Literary allusions (p. 236) 'for the fatherless children and widows ... tribulation': these supplications are from the Litany in *The Book of Common Prayer*, but are there found in a different order from Dickens's here.

Textual note The *RP* text begins 'On a certain Sunday ...', and omits 'I do not hesitate to say she would ... it must be once more distinctly set before the reader that ...' (p. 237).

A few Sundays ago, I formed one of the congregation assembled in the chapel of a large metropolitan Workhouse. With the exception of the clergyman and clerk, and a very few officials, there were none but paupers present. The children sat in the galleries; the women in the body of the chapel, and in one of the side aisles; the men in the remaining aisle. The service was decorously performed, though the sermon might have been much better adapted to the comprehension and to the

circumstances of the hearers. The usual supplications were offered, with
more than the usual significancy in such a place, for the fatherless
children and widows, for all sick persons and young children, for all that
were desolate and oppressed, for the comforting and helping of the weak-
hearted, for the raising up of them that had fallen; for all that were in
danger, necessity, and tribulation. The prayers of the congregation were
desired 'for several persons in the various wards, dangerously ill;' and
others who were recovering returned their thanks to Heaven.

Among this congregation, were some evil-looking young women, and
beetle-browed young men; but not many – perhaps that kind of character
kept away. Generally, the faces (those of the children, excepted) were
depressed and subdued, and wanted colour. Aged people were there, in
every variety. Mumbling, blear-eyed, spectacled, stupid, deaf, lame;
vacantly winking in the gleams of sun that now and then crept in through
the open doors, from the paved yard; shading their listening ears, or
blinking eyes, with their withered hands; poring over their books, leering
at nothing, going to sleep, crouching and drooping in corners. There
were weird old women, all skeleton within, all bonnet and cloak without,
continually wiping their eyes with dirty dusters of pocket-handkerchiefs;
and there were ugly old crones, both male and female, with a ghastly
kind of contentment upon them which was not at all comforting to see.
Upon the whole, it was the dragon, Pauperism, in a very weak and
impotent condition; toothless, fangless, drawing his breath heavily enough,
and hardly worth chaining up.

When the service was over, I walked with the humane and conscientious
gentleman whose duty it was to take that walk, that Sunday morning,
through the little world of poverty enclosed within the workhouse walls.
It was inhabited by a population of some fifteen hundred or two thousand
paupers, ranging from the infant newly born or not yet come into the
pauper world, to the old man dying on his bed.

In a room opening from a squalid yard, where a number of listless
women were lounging to and fro, trying to get warm in the ineffectual
sunshine of the tardy May morning – in the 'Itch Ward,' not to
compromise the truth – a woman such as HOGARTH has often drawn,
was hurriedly getting on her gown, before a dusty fire. She was the
nurse, or wardswoman, of that insalubrious department – herself a
pauper – flabby, raw-boned, untidy – unpromising and coarse of aspect
as need be. But, on being spoken to about the patients whom she had
in charge, she turned round, with her shabby gown half on, half off, and
fell a-crying with all her might. Not for show, not querulously, not in
any mawkish sentiment, but in the deep grief and affliction of her heart;
turning away her dishevelled head: sobbing most bitterly, wringing her
hands, and letting fall abundance of great tears, that choked her utterance.

What was the matter with the nurse of the itch-ward? Oh, 'the dropped child' was dead! Oh, the child that was found in the street, and she had brought up ever since, had died an hour ago, and see where the little creature lay, beneath this cloth! The dear, the pretty dear!

The dropped child seemed too small and poor a thing for Death to be in earnest with, but Death had taken it; and already its diminutive form was neatly washed, composed, and stretched as if in sleep upon a box. I thought I heard a voice from Heaven saying, It shall be well for thee, O nurse of the itch-ward, when some less gentle pauper does those offices to thy cold form, that such as the dropped child are the angels who behold my Father's face!

In another room, were several ugly old women crouching, witch-like, round a hearth, and chattering and nodding, after the manner of the monkies. 'All well here? And enough to eat?' A general chattering and chuckling; at last an answer from a volunteer. 'Oh yes gentleman! Bless you gentleman! Lord bless the parish of St So-and-So! It feed the hungry, Sir, and give drink to the thusty, and it warm them which is cold, so it do, and good luck to the parish of St So-and-So, and thankee gentleman!' Elsewhere, a party of pauper nurses were at dinner. 'How do *you* get on?' 'Oh pretty well Sir! We works hard, and we lives hard – like the sodgers!'

In another room, a kind of purgatory or place of transition, six or eight noisy mad-women were gathered together, under the superintendence of one sane attendant. Among them was a girl of two or three and twenty, very prettily dressed, of most respectable appearance, and good manners, who had been brought in from the house where she had lived as domestic servant (having, I suppose, no friends), on account of being subject to epileptic fits, and requiring to be removed under the influence of a very bad one. She was by no means of the same stuff, or the same breeding, or the same experience, or in the same state of mind, as those by whom she was surrounded; and she pathetically complained that the daily association and the nightly noise made her worse, and was driving her mad – which was perfectly evident. The case was noted for enquiry and redress, but she said she had already been there for some weeks.

If this girl had stolen her mistress's watch, I do not hesitate to say she would, in all probability, have been infinitely better off. Bearing in mind, in the present brief description of this walk, not only the facts already stated in this Journal, in reference to the Model Prison at Pentonville, but the general treatment of convicted prisoners under the associated silent system too, it must be once more distinctly set before the reader, that we have come to this absurd, this dangerous, this monstrous pass, that the dishonest felon is, in respect of cleanliness, order, diet, and accommodation, better provided for, and taken care of, than the honest pauper.

And this conveys no special imputation on the workhouse of the parish of St So-and-So, where, on the contrary, I saw many things to commend. It was very agreeable, recollecting that most infamous and atrocious enormity committed at Tooting – an enormity which, a hundred years hence, will still be vividly remembered in the bye-ways of English life, and which has done more to engender a gloomy discontent and suspicion among many thousands of the people than all the Chartist leaders could have done in all their lives – to find the pauper children in this workhouse looking robust and well, and apparently the objects of very great care. In the Infant School – a large, light, airy room at the top of the building – the little creatures, being at dinner, and eating their potatoes heartily, were not cowed by the presence of strange visitors, but stretched out their small hands to be shaken, with a very pleasant confidence. And it was comfortable to see two mangey pauper rocking-horses rampant in a corner. In the girls' school, where the dinner was also in progress, everything bore a cheerful and healthy aspect. The meal was over, in the boys' school, by the time of our arrival there, and the room was not yet quite re-arranged; but the boys were roaming unrestrained about a large and airy yard, as any other schoolboys might have done. Some of them had been drawing large ships upon the schoolroom wall; and if they had a mast with shrouds and stays set up for practice (as they have in the Middlesex House of Correction), it would be so much the better. At present, if a boy should feel a strong impulse upon him to learn the art of going aloft, he could only gratify it, I presume, as the men and women paupers gratify their aspirations after better board and lodging, by smashing as many workhouse windows as possible, and being promoted to prison.

In one place, the Newgate of the Workhouse, a company of boys and youths were locked up in a yard alone; their day-room being a kind of kennel where the casual poor used formerly to be littered down at night. Divers of them had been there some long time. 'Are they never going away?' was the natural enquiry. 'Most of them are crippled, in some form or other,' said the Wardsman, 'and not fit for anything.' They slunk about, like dispirited wolves or hyænas; and made a pounce at their food when it was served out, much as those animals do. The big-headed idiot shuffling his feet along the pavement, in the sunlight outside, was a more agreeable object everyway.

Groves of babies in arms; groves of mothers and other sick women in bed; groves of lunatics; jungles of men in stone-paved downstairs day-rooms, waiting for their dinners; longer and longer groves of old people, in upstairs Infirmary wards, wearing out life, God knows how – this was the scenery through which the walk lay, for two hours. In some of these latter chambers, there were pictures stuck against the wall, and a neat display of crockery and pewter on a kind of sideboard; now and then it was a treat to see a plant or two; in almost every ward, there was a cat.

In all of these Long Walks of aged and infirm, some old people were bed-ridden, and had been for a long time; some were sitting on their beds half-naked; some dying in their beds; some out of bed, and sitting at a table near the fire. A sullen or lethargic indifference to what was asked, a blunted sensibility to everything but warmth, and food, a moody absence of complaint as being of no use, a dogged silence and resentful desire to be left alone again, I thought were generally apparent. On our walking into the midst of one of these dreary perspectives of old men, nearly the following little dialogue took place, the nurse not being immediately at hand:

'All well here?'

No answer. An old man in a Scotch cap sitting among others on a form at the table, eating out of a tin porringer, pushes back his cap a little to look at us, claps it down on his forehead again with the palm of his hand, and goes on eating.

'All well here?' (repeated.)

No answer. Another old man sitting on his bed, paralytically peeling a boiled potato, lifts his head, and stares.

'Enough to eat?'

No answer. Another old man, in bed, turns himself and coughs.

'How are *you* today?' To the last old man.

That old man says nothing; but another old man, a tall old man of very good address, speaking with perfect correctness, comes forward from somewhere, and volunteers an answer. The reply almost always proceeds from a volunteer, and not from the person looked at or spoken to.

'We are very old, Sir,' in a mild, distinct voice. 'We can't expect to be well, most of us.'

'Are you comfortable?'

'I have no complaint to make, Sir.' With a half shake of his head, a half shrug of his shoulders, and a kind of apologetic smile.

'Enough to eat?'

'Why, Sir, I have but a poor appetite,' with the same air as before; 'and yet I get through my allowance very easily.'

'But,' showing a porringer with a Sunday dinner in it; 'here is a portion of mutton, and three potatoes. You can't starve on that?'

'Oh dear no, Sir,' with the same apologetic air. 'Not starve.'

'What do you want?'

'We have very little bread, Sir. It's an exceedingly small quantity of bread.'

The nurse, who is now rubbing her hands at the questioner's elbow, interferes with, 'It ain't much raly, Sir. You see they've only six ounces a day, and when they've took their breakfast, there *can* only be a little left for night, Sir.'

Another old man, hitherto invisible, rises out of his bedclothes, as out of a grave, and looks on.

'You have tea at night?' The questioner is still addressing the well-spoken old man.

'Yes, Sir, we have tea at night.'

'And you save what bread you can from the morning, to eat with it?'

'Yes, Sir – if we can save any.'

'And you want more to eat with it?'

'Yes, Sir.' With a very anxious face.

The questioner, in the kindness of his heart, appears a little discomposed, and changes the subject.

'What has become of the old man who used to lie in that bed in the corner?'

The nurse don't remember what old man is referred to. There has been such a many old men. The well-spoken old man is doubtful. The spectral old man who has come to life in bed, says, 'Billy Stevens.' Another old man who has previously had his head in the fireplace, pipes out,

'Charley Walters.'

Something like a feeble interest is awakened. I suppose Charley Walters had conversation in him.

'He's dead!' says the piping old man.

Another old man, the one eye screwed up, hastily displaces the piping old man, and says:

'Yes! Charley Walters died in that bed, and – and—'

'Billy Stevens,' persists the spectral old man.

'No, no! and Johnny Rogers died in that bed, and – and – they're both on 'em dead – and Sam'l Bowyer;' this seems very extraordinary to him; 'he went out!'

With this he subsides, and all the old men (having had quite enough of it) subside, and the spectral old man goes into his grave again, and takes the shade of Billy Stevens with him.

As we turn to go out at the door, another previously invisible old man, a hoarse old man in a flannel gown, is standing there, as if he had just come up through the floor.

'I beg your pardon, Sir, could I take the liberty of saying a word?'

'Yes; what is it?'

'I am greatly better in my health, Sir; but what I want, to get me quite round,' with his hand on his throat, 'is a little fresh air, Sir. It has always done my complaint so much good, Sir. The regular leave for going out, comes round so seldom, that if the gentlemen, next Friday, would give me leave to go out walking, now and then – for only an hour or so, Sir! –'

Who could wonder, looking through those weary vistas of bed and infirmity, that it should do him good to meet with some other scenes, and assure himself that there was something else on earth? Who could help wondering why the old men lived on as they did; what grasp they had on life; what crumbs of interest or occupation they could pick up from its bare board; whether Charley Walters had ever described to them the days when he kept company with some old pauper woman in the bud, or Billy Stevens ever told them of the time when he was a dweller in the far-off foreign land called Home!

The morsel of burnt child, lying in another room, so patiently, in bed, wrapped in lint, and looking stedfastly at us with his bright quiet eyes when we spoke to him kindly, looked as if the knowledge of these things, and of all the tender things there are to think about, might have been in his mind – as if he thought, with us, that there was a fellow-feeling in the pauper nurses which appeared to make them more kind to their charges than the race of common nurses in the hospitals – as if he mused upon the Future of some older children lying around him in the same place, and thought it best, perhaps, all things considered, that he should die – as if he knew, without fear, of those many coffins, made and unmade, piled up in the store below – and of his unknown friend, 'the dropped child,' calm upon the box-lid covered with a cloth. But there was something wistful and appealing, too, in his tiny face, as if, in the midst of all the hard necessities and incongruities he pondered on, he pleaded, in behalf of the helpless and the aged poor, for a little more liberty – and a little more bread.

47

Old Lamps for New Ones

Household Words, 15 June 1850 (leading article)

John Everett Millais was one of the founder-members of the Pre-Raphaelite Brotherhood with Holman Hunt and D.G. Rossetti. His first major religious painting, titled only by a Biblical text but known as 'Christ in the House of His Parents' (see *The Pre-Raphaelites*, exhibition catalogue, Tate Gallery/Penguin Books [1984], no. 26), caused immense controversy because of its determined realism when it was shown in the Royal Academy exhibition ('In all the papers ... the attack on Millais has been most virulent and audacious,' wrote W.M. Rossetti, quoted by Leonee Ormond in 'Dickens and Painting: Contemporary Art', *The Dickensian*, Vol. 80 [1984], p. 21; this article contains an excellent analysis of Dickens's reaction to Millais's painting). Dickens was a fervent admirer of Raphael and, as Ormond observes, felt that the Brotherhood's name 'implied a deliberate attack' on the great Renaissance artist. His strong hostility towards the Oxford Movement (see p. 59f.) would also have influenced his attitude towards Pre-Raphaelitism, which had clear links with it (see Tate Gallery catalogue entry; also *Pilgrim*, Vol. VI, p. 107, n. 2). This is clear from his letter to Maclise of 30 May sending him a proof of the article and saying: 'I feel perfectly sure that you will see nothing in it but what is fair public satire on a point that opens very serious social considerations. If such things were allowed to sweep on, without some vigorous protest, three fourths of this Nation would be under the feet of Priests, in ten years' (*Pilgrim*, Vol. VI, p. 106f.).

Dickens later met Millais socially and liked him, but did not change his mind about this picture. Sending the artist a copy of the first volume of *HW* five years later (it contained an article about fire-fighting which Dickens had mentioned to Millais, who was working on his picture on this subject, 'The Rescue'), Dickens wrote:

> If you have in your mind any previous association with the pages in which it appears ... it may be a rather disagreeable one. In that case I hope a word frankly said may make it pleasanter. Objecting very strongly to what I believe to be an unworthy use of your great powers, I once expressed the objection in this same journal. My opinion on that point is not in the least changed, but it has never dashed my admiration of your progress in what I suppose are higher and better things.... [*Pilgrim*, Vol. VII, p. 517]

Writing in 1903, however, Dickens's artist-daughter Kate Perugini said that it was simply the shock of seeing a sacred subject so misrepresented, as it seemed to him, that led him in his 'surprise and pain', to write 'a very harsh and hasty criticism upon it, a criticism that I have reason to believe he regretted having published in later years' (quoted by Ormond, *op. cit.*, p. 23).

The phrase about 'the Young England Hallucination' refers to a tiny and short-lived splinter-group of aristocratic young Tories who rallied round Disraeli in opposition to Peel in the early 1840s, advocating a return to feudalism as a remedy for the distress of the working classes (or 'Order of the Peasantry', as they preferred to call them). The phrase 'to "put it down"' (p. 245) echoes Sir Peter Laurie's notorious campaign against suicide (see p. 189). For the reference to 'desecration' in connection with the Post Office, see next article.

Literary and pictorial allusions (p. 243) the story of Aladdin in *The Arabian Nights*; (p. 246) 'lay that flattering unction ...': Shakespeare, *Hamlet*, Act 3, Sc. 4; (p. 247) 'Hogarth's idea of a man on a mountain ...': the reference here is to a print called 'Satire on False Perspective' published by Hogarth in 1754.

MS. Corrected proof, Forster Collection, Victoria and Albert Museum. There are, as the Pilgrim editors note, 'many small alterations ... a few making the satire less coarse', but these are unlikely to have been the result of 'tinkering' by Maclise, who would have disagreed altogether with the article. The substitution of 'some bold aspirants' (end of para. 3) for 'a mere bucket-full of young blood' is an example of the toning-down found in the proof-corrections; on the other hand, the clause in paragraph 6 'who appears ... the contemplation' is elaborated from 'who appears to have lost a game at cards and to be holding up the ace of diamonds for the contemplation'.

The Magician in 'Aladdin' may possibly have neglected the study of men, for the study of alchemical books; but it is certain that in spite of his profession he was no conjuror. He knew nothing of human nature, or the everlasting set of the current of human affairs. If, when he fraudulently sought to obtain possession of the wonderful Lamp, and went up and down, disguised, before the flying-palace, crying New Lamps for Old ones, he had reversed his cry, and made it Old Lamps for New ones, he would have been so far before his time as to have projected himself into the nineteenth century of our Christian Era.

This age is so perverse, and is so very short of faith – in consequence, as some suppose, of there having been a run on that bank for a few generations – that a parallel and beautiful idea, generally known among the ignorant as the Young England hallucination, unhappily expired before it could run alone, to the great grief of a small but a very select circle of mourners. There is something so fascinating, to a mind capable of any serious reflection, in the notion of ignoring all that has been done for the happiness and elevation of mankind during three or four centuries of slow and dearly-bought amelioration, that we have always thought it would tend soundly to the improvement of the general public, if any tangible symbol, any outward and visible sign, expressive of that admirable conception, could be held up before them. We are happy to have found such a sign at last; and although it would make a very indifferent sign, indeed, in the Licensed Victualling sense of the word, and would probably be rejected with contempt and horror by any Christian publican, it has our warmest philosophical appreciation.

In the fifteenth century, a certain feeble lamp of art arose in the Italian town of Urbino. This poor light, Raphael Sanzio by name, better known to a few miserably mistaken wretches in these later days, as Raphael (another burned at the same time called Titian), was fed with a preposterous idea of Beauty – with a ridiculous power of etherealising, and exalting to the very Heaven of Heavens, what was most sublime and lovely in the expression of the human face divine on Earth – with the truly contemptible conceit of finding in poor humanity the fallen likeness of the angels of GOD, and raising it up again to their pure spiritual condition. This very fantastic whim effected a low revolution in Art, in this wise, that Beauty came to be regarded as one of its indispensable elements. In this very poor delusion, Artists have continued until this present nineteenth century, when it was reserved for some bold aspirants to 'put it down.'

The Pre-Raphael Brotherhood, Ladies and Gentlemen, is the dread Tribunal which is to set this matter right. Walk up, walk up; and here, conspicuous on the wall of the Royal Academy of Art in England, in the eighty-second year of their annual exhibition, you shall see what this new Holy Brotherhood, this terrible Police that is to disperse all Post-Raphael offenders, has 'been and done!'

You come – in this Royal Academy Exhibition, which is familiar with the works of WILKIE, COLLINS, ETTY, EASTLAKE, MULREADY, LESLIE, MACLISE, TURNER, STANFIELD, LANDSEER, ROBERTS, DANBY, CRESWICK, LEE, WEBSTER, HERBERT, DYCE, COPE, and others who would have been renowned as great masters in any age or country – you come, in this place, to the contemplation of a Holy Family. You will have the goodness to discharge from your minds all Post-Raphael ideas, all religious aspirations, all elevating thoughts; all tender, awful, sorrowful, ennobling, sacred, graceful, or beautiful associations; and to prepare yourselves as befits such a subject – Pre-Raphaelly considered – for the

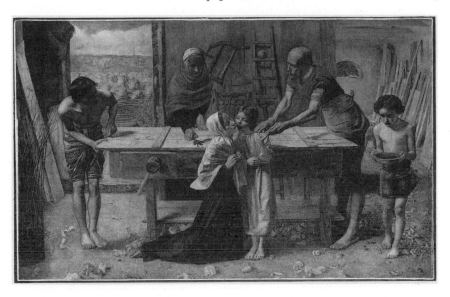

Christ in the House of His Parents by Sir John Millais.

lowest depths of what is mean, odious, repulsive, and revolting.

You behold the interior of a carpenter's shop. In the foreground of that carpenter's shop is a hideous, wry-necked, blubbering, red-headed boy, in a bed-gown; who appears to have received a poke in the hand from the stick of another boy with whom he has been playing in an adjacent gutter, and to be holding it up for the contemplation of a kneeling woman, so horrible in her ugliness, that (supposing it were possible for any human creature to exist for a moment with that dislocated throat) she would stand out from the rest of the company as a Monster, in the vilest cabaret in France, or the lowest gin-shop in England. Two almost naked carpenters, master and journeyman, worthy companions of this agreeable female, are working at their trade; a boy, with some small flavour of humanity in him, is entering with a vessel of water; and nobody is paying any attention to a snuffy old woman who seems to have mistaken that shop for the tobacconist's next door, and to be hopelessly waiting at the counter to be served with half an ounce of her favourite mixture. Wherever it is possible to express ugliness of feature, limb, or attitude, you have it expressed. Such men as the carpenters might be undressed in any hospital where dirty drunkards, in a high state of varicose veins, are received. Their very toes have walked out of Saint Giles's.

This, in the nineteenth century, and in the eighty-second year of the annual exhibition of the National Academy of Art, is the Pre-Raphael representation to us, Ladies and Gentlemen, of the most solemn passage which our minds can ever approach. This, in the nineteenth century, and in the eighty-second year of the annual exhibition of the National Academy of Art, is what Pre-Raphael Art can do to render reverence and homage to the faith in which we live and die! Consider this picture well. Consider the pleasure we should have in a similar Pre-Raphael rendering of a favourite horse, or dog, or cat; and, coming fresh from a pretty considerable turmoil about 'desecration' in connection with the National Post Office, let us extol this great achievement, and commend the National Academy!

In further considering this symbol of the great retrogressive principle, it is particularly gratifying to observe that such objects as the shavings which are strewn on the carpenter's floor are admirably painted; and that the Pre-Raphael Brother is indisputably accomplished in the manipulation of his art. It is gratifying to observe this, because the fact involves no low effort at notoriety; everybody knowing that it is by no means easier to call attention to a very indifferent pig with five legs than to a symmetrical pig with four. Also, because it is good to know that the National Academy thoroughly feels and comprehends the high range and exalted purposes of art; distinctly perceives that art includes something more than the faithful portraiture of shavings, or the skilful colouring of drapery – imperatively requires, in short, that it shall be informed with mind and sentiment; will on no account reduce it to a narrow question of trade-juggling with a palette, palette-knife, and paint box. It is likewise pleasing to reflect that the great educational establishment foresees the difficulty into which it would be led, by attaching greater weight to mere handicraft, than to any other consideration – even to considerations of common reverence or decency; which absurd principle in the event of a skilful painter of the figure becoming a very little more perverted in his taste, than certain skilful painters are just now, might place Her Gracious Majesty in a very painful position, one of these fine Private View Days.

Would it were in our power to congratulate our readers on the hopeful prospects of the great retrogressive principle, of which this thoughtful picture is the sign and emblem! Would that we could give our readers encouraging assurance of a healthy demand for Old Lamps in exchange for New ones, and a steady improvement in the Old Lamp Market! The perversity of mankind is such, and the untoward arrangements of Providence are such, that we cannot lay that flattering unction to their souls. We can only report what Brotherhoods, stimulated by this sign, are forming; and what opportunities will be presented to the people, if the people will but accept them.

In the first place, the Pre-Perspective Brotherhood will be presently incorporated, for the subversion of all known rules and principles of perspective. It is intended to swear every P.P.B. to a solemn renunciation of the art of perspective on a soup-plate of the willow pattern; and we may expect, on the occasion of the eighty-third Annual Exhibition of the Royal Academy of Art in England, to see some pictures by this pious Brotherhood, realising Hogarth's idea of a man on a mountain several miles off, lighting his pipe at the upper window of a house in the foreground. But we are informed that every brick in the house will be a portrait; that the man's boots will be copied with the utmost fidelity from a pair of Bluchers sent up out of Northamptonshire for the purpose; and that the texture of his hands (including four chilblains, a whitlow, and ten dirty nails) will be a triumph of the Painter's art.

A Society, to be called the Pre-Newtonian Brotherhood, was lately projected by a young gentleman, under articles to a Civil Engineer, who objected to being considered bound to conduct himself according to the laws of gravitation. But this young gentleman, being reproached by some aspiring companions with the timidity of his conception, has abrogated that idea in favour of a Pre Galileo Brotherhood now flourishing, who distinctly refuse to perform any annual revolution round the sun, and have arranged that the world shall not do so any more. The course to be taken by the Royal Academy of Art in reference to this Brotherhood is not yet decided upon; but it is whispered that some other large educational Institutions in the neighbourhood of Oxford are nearly ready to pronounce in favour of it.

Several promising Students connected with the Royal College of Surgeons have held a meeting, to protest against the circulation of the blood, and to pledge themselves to treat all the patients they can get, on principles condemnatory of that innovation. A Pre-Harvey Brotherhood is the result, from which a great deal may be expected – by the undertakers.

In literature, a very spirited effort has been made, which is no less than the formation of a P.G.A.P.C.B., or Pre-Gower and Pre-Chaucer-Brotherhood for the restoration of the ancient English style of spelling, and the weeding out from all libraries, public and private, of those and all later pretenders, particularly a person of loose character named SHAKESPEARE. It having been suggested, however, that this happy idea could scarcely be considered complete while the art of printing was permitted to remain unmolested, another society, under the name of the Pre-Laurentius Brotherhood, has been established in connection with it, for the abolition of all but manuscript books. These Mr PUGIN has engaged to supply, in characters that nobody on earth shall be able to read. And it is confidently expected by those who have seen the House of Lords, that he will faithfully redeem his pledge.

In Music, a retrogressive step, in which there is much hope, has been taken. The P.A.B., or Pre-Agincourt Brotherhood has arisen, nobly devoted to consign to oblivion Mozart, Beethoven, Handel, and every other such ridiculous reputation, and to fix its Millennium (as its name implies) before the date of the first regular musical composition known to have been achieved in England. As this Institution has not yet commenced active operations, it remains to be seen whether the Royal Academy of Music will be a worthy sister of the Royal Academy of Art, and admit this enterprising body to its orchestra. We have it on the best authority, that its compositions will be quite as rough and discordant as the real old original – that it will be, in a word, exactly suited to the pictorial Art we have endeavoured to describe. We have strong hopes, therefore, that the Royal Academy of Music, not wanting an example, may not want courage.

The regulation of social matters, as separated from the Fine Arts, has been undertaken by the Pre-Henry-the-Seventh Brotherhood, who date from the same period as the Pre-Raphael Brotherhood. This Society, as cancelling all the advances of nearly four hundred years, and reverting to one of the most disagreeable periods of English History, when the nation was yet very slowly emerging from barbarism, and when gentle female foreigners, come over to be the wives of Scottish Kings, wept bitterly (as well they might) at being left alone among the savage Court, must be regarded with peculiar favour. As the time of ugly religious caricatures (called mysteries), it is thoroughly Pre-Raphael in its spirit; and may be deemed the twin brother to that great society. We should be certain of the Plague among many other advantages, if this Brotherhood were properly encouraged.

All these Brotherhoods, and any other society of the like kind, now in being or yet to be, have at once a guiding star, and a reduction of their great ideas to something palpable and obvious to the senses, in the sign to which we take the liberty of directing their attention. We understand that it is in the contemplation of each Society to become possessed, with all convenient speed, of a collection of such pictures; and that once, every year, to wit, upon the first of April, the whole intend to amalgamate in a high festival, to be called the Convocation of Eternal Boobies.

48

The Sunday Screw

Household Words, 22 June 1850 (leading article)

From the time of his 1836 *Sunday Under Three Heads* (Vol. 1 of this edition, pp. 475–99), Dickens took a strongly anti-Sabbatarian stance. (For an earlier comment on this Post Office controversy, see p. 161.) The following article was provoked by the success of Lord Ashley's motion in the House of Commons on 30 May (carried by a majority of ninety-three votes to sixty-eight) asking for an Address to the Crown to end all Sunday collections and deliveries of letters throughout the country; the measure was due to come into effect on 23 June. The Postmaster-General, Rowland Hill, had been trying to accommodate Sabbatarian criticisms of Sunday working, but his plans had been misunderstood and also deliberately misrepresented; this resulted in increased pressure from the powerful and energetic Sabbatarian lobby for the total abolition of all Sunday postal services and the success of Ashley's motion (for a full discussion of all this, see Norris Pope, *Dickens and Charity* [1978], p. 63f.). *The Times*, as Dickens's allusion to it makes clear, was also very anti-Sabbatarian and declared (31 May 1850) that the success of the motion showed how 'the general interests of the public are subordinated to the fanatical persuasions of a minority'.

Ashley's speech is fully reported in *The Times* (31 May 1850, p. 4, cols 1–4). He declared that 'No other object had ever excited a deeper attention, or had created a more intense sentiment in the public mind.' The detail about the committee formed by Liverpool merchants quoted by Dickens comes from Ashley's speech and the 'perilous bombast' to which Dickens refers (p. 254) is a lengthy quotation made by Ashley from a working man's prize essay entitled 'Heaven's Antidote to the Curse of Labour'. The writer asserted that to allow workers only the minimum amount of rest and recreation that was physically necessary was to 'embrute' them, 'yea, to degrade beings originally fashioned in the image of God into mere animate machines to be used in the production of wealth, luxury and patrician indulgences in which they are never suffered to participate'. After comparing the labourer to Sisyphus condemned to endless toil, the writer goes on: 'But cheer thee, child of travail! The blessed Sabbath is thine own! It is the excellent gift of thy Maker … the heirloom of thy family – see that it be not alienated from thy possession!' The 'Sage' whom Dickens mocks on p. 253 for considering Sunday police necessary but not Sunday postmen was the Conservative MP for East Kent, John Pemberton Plumptre, and the MP for Birmingham who was 'tired of reading and writing letters on

Sunday' was the Radical George Frederick Muntz, a merchant and manufacturer who argued, for social reasons, that Parliament should defend Sunday as a day of rest, otherwise 'Masters would soon force their workmen to labour on Sunday, as some masters now compelled their men to work longer than they ought to do on week days'.

For the reference to Egyptian sorcery in paragraph 3, see George Eliot's *Adam Bede* (1859), Ch. 1, and compare Wilkie Collins's *The Moonstone* (1868), Ch. 3. Dickens refers again to this practice in *The Mystery of Edwin Drood*, Ch. 3. During his early career in Parliament, before he was created the first Baron Brougham (1830), Henry Brougham was a great champion of liberal causes and a notable law reformer. By calling his generic Sabbatarian MP 'the member for Whitened Sepulchres', Dickens is attributing hypocrisy to him as Jesus did to the scribes and Pharisees when he compared them (Matthew 23:27) to 'whited sepulchres, which indeed appear beautiful outward, but are within full of dead men's bones, and of all uncleanness'. The 'notable public example' of a violent reaction resulting from 'too tight a hand' in governing a nation alludes to the execution of Charles 1 in 1649.

Dickens's most famous novelistic onslaught on Sabbatarianism appears in *Little Dorrit*, Book 1, Ch. 3 (1857).

Literary allusions (p. 251) 'and all uncharitableness …': The Litany ('… malice and all uncharitableness'), *The Book of Common Prayer*; (p. 251) 'The Sabbath was made for man …': Mark 2:27; (p. 251) 'upstairs, downstairs …': the nursery rhyme 'Goosey goosey gander'; (p. 254) 'Tom Thumb made his giants first …': from Henry Fielding's burlesque satire *The Tragedy of Tragedies, or, The Life and Death of Tom Thumb the Great* (1731), Act 1, Sc. 5, in which Tom's envious rival Grizzle says to the Queen, 'I tell you, madam, it was all a trick,/He made the giants first, and then he killed them.'

This little instrument, remarkable for its curious twist, has been at work again. A small portion of the collective wisdom of the nation has affirmed the principle that there must be no collection or delivery of posted letters on a Sunday. The principle was discussed by something less than a fourth of the House of Commons, and affirmed by something less than a seventh.

Having no doubt whatever, that this brilliant victory is, in effect, the affirmation of the principle that there ought to be No Anything but churches and chapels on a Sunday; or, that it is the beginning of a Sabbatarian Crusade, outrageous to the spirit of Christianity, irreconcilable with the health, the rational enjoyments, and the true religious feeling, of the community; and certain to result, if successful, in a violent re-action, threatening contempt and hatred of that seventh day which it is a great religious and social object to maintain in the popular affection; it would ill become us to be deterred from speaking out upon the subject, by any fear of being misunderstood, or by any certainty of being misrepresented.

Confident in the sense of the country, and not unacquainted with the habits and exigencies of the people, we approach the Sunday question, quite undiscomposed by the late storm of mad mis-statement and all uncharitableness, which cleared the way for Lord Ashley's motion. The preparation may be likened to that which is usually described in the case of the Egyptian Sorcerer and the boy who has some dark liquid poured into the palm of his hand, which is presently to become a magic mirror. 'Look for Lord Ashley. What do you see?' 'Oh, here's some one with a broom!' 'Well! what is he doing?' 'Oh, he's sweeping away Mr Rowland Hill! Now, there is a great crowd of people all sweeping Mr Rowland Hill away; and now, there is a red flag with Intolerance on it; and now, they are pitching a great many Tents called Meetings. Now, the tents are all upset, and Mr Rowland Hill has swept everybody else away. And oh! *now* here's Lord Ashley, with a Resolution in his hand!'

One Christian sentence is all-sufficient with us, on the theological part of this subject. 'The Sabbath was made for man, and not man for the Sabbath.' No amount of signatures to petitions can ever sign away the meaning of those words; no end of volumes of Hansard's Parliamentary Debates can ever affect them in the least. Move and carry resolutions, bring in bills, have committees, upstairs, downstairs, and in my lady's chamber; read a first time, read a second time, read a third time, read thirty thousand times; the declared authority of the Christian dispensation over the letter of the Jewish Law, particularly in this especial instance, cannot be petitioned, resolved, read, or committee'd away.

It is important in such a case as this affirmation of a principle, to know what amount of practical sense and logic entered into its assertion. We will inquire.

Lord Ashley (who has done much good, and whom we mention with every sentiment of sincere respect, though we believe him to be most mischievously deluded on this question,) speaks of the people employed in the Country Post-Offices on Sunday, as though they were continually at work, all the livelong day. He asks whether they are to be 'a Pariah race, excluded from the enjoyments of the rest of the community?' He presents to our mind's eye, rows of Post-Office clerks, sitting, with dishevelled hair and dirty linen, behind small shutters, all Sunday long, keeping time with their sighs to the ringing of the church bells, and watering bushels of letters, incessantly passing through their hands, with their tears. Is this exactly the reality? The Upas tree is a figure of speech almost as ancient as our lachrymose friend the Pariah, in whom most of

us recognise a respectable old acquaintance. Supposing we were to take
it into our heads to declare in these Household Words, that every Post-
Office Clerk employed on Sunday in the country, is compelled to sit
under his own particular sprig of Upas, planted in a flower-pot beside
him for the express purpose of blighting him with its baneful shade,
should we be much more beyond the mark than Lord Ashley himself?
Did any of our readers ever happen to post letters in the Country on a
Sunday? Did they ever see a notice outside a provincial Post-Office, to
the effect that the presiding Pariah would be in attendance at such an
hour on Sunday, and not before? Did they ever wait for the Pariah, at
some inconvenience, until the hour arrived, and observe him come to
the office in an extremely spruce condition as to his shirt collar, and do
a little sprinkling of business in a very easy off-hand manner? We have
such recollections ourselves. We have posted and received letters in most
parts of this kingdom on a Sunday, and we never yet observed the Pariah
to be quite crushed. On the contrary, we have seen him at church,
apparently in the best health and spirits (notwithstanding an hour or so
of sorting, earlier in the morning), and we have met him out a-walking
with the young lady to whom he is engaged, and we have known him
meet her again with her cousin, after the dispatch of the Mails, and
really conduct himself as if he were not particularly exhausted or afflicted.
Indeed, how *could* he be so, on Lord Ashley's own showing? There
is a Saturday before the Sunday. We are a people indisposed, he
says, to business on a Sunday. More than a million of people are
known, from their petitions, to be too scrupulous to hear of such a
thing. Few counting-houses or offices are ever opened on a Sunday.
The Merchants and Bankers write by Saturday night's post. The
Sunday night's post may be presumed to be chiefly limited to letters
of necessity and emergency. Lord Ashley's whole case would break
down, if it were probable that the Post-Office Pariah had half as
much confinement on Sunday, as the He-Pariah who opens my Lord's
street door when anybody knocks, or the She-Pariah who nurses my
Lady's baby.

If the London Post-Office be not opened on a Sunday, says Lord
Ashley, why should the Post-Offices of provincial towns be opened on a
Sunday? Precisely because the provincial towns are NOT London, we
apprehend. Because London is the great capital, mart, and business-
centre of the world; because in London there are hundreds of thousands
of people, young and old, away from their families and friends; because
the stoppage of the Monday's Post Delivery in London would stop, for
many precious hours, the natural flow of the blood from every vein and
artery in the world to the heart of the world, and its return from the
heart through all those tributary channels. Because the broad difference

between London and every other place in England, necessitated this distinction, and has perpetuated it.

But, to say nothing of petitioners elsewhere, it seems that two hundred merchants and bankers in Liverpool 'formed themselves into a committee, to forward the object of this motion.' In the name of all the Pharisees of Jerusalem, could not the two hundred merchants and bankers form themselves into a committee to write or read no business-letters themselves on a Sunday – and let the Post-Office alone? The Government establishes a monopoly in the Post-Office, and makes it not only difficult and expensive for me to send a letter by any other means, but illegal. What right has any merchant or banker to stop the course of any letter that I may have sore necessity to post, or may choose to post? If any one of the two hundred merchants and bankers lay at the point of death, on Sunday, would he desire his absent child to be written to – the Sunday Post being yet in existence? And how do they take upon themselves to tell us that the Sunday Post is not a 'necessity,' when they know, every man of them, every Sunday morning, that before the clock strikes next, they and theirs may be visited by any one of incalculable millions of accidents, to make it a dire need? Not a necessity? Is it possible that these merchants and bankers suppose there is any Sunday Post, from any large town, which is not a very agony of necessity to some one? I might as well say, in my pride of strength, that a knowledge of bone-setting in surgeons is not a necessity, because I have not broken my leg.

There is a Sage of this sort in the House of Commons. He is of opinion that the Sunday Police is a necessity, but the Sunday Post is not. That is to say, in a certain house in London or Westminster, there are certain silver spoons, engraved with the family crest – a Bigot rampant – which would be pretty sure to disappear, on an early Sunday, if there were no Policemen on duty; whereas the Sage sees no present probability of his requiring to write a letter into the country on a Saturday night – and, if it should arise, he can use the Electric Telegraph. Such is the sordid balance some professing Heathens hold of their own pounds against other men's pennies, and their own selfish wants against those of the community at large! Even the Member for Birmingham, of all the towns in England, is afflicted by this selfish blindness, and, because *he* is 'tired of reading and answering letters on a Sunday,' cannot conceive the possibility of there being other people not so situated, to whom the Sunday Post may, under many circumstances, be an unspeakable blessing.

The inconsequential nature of Lord Ashley's positions, cannot be better shown, than by one brief passage from his speech. 'When he said the transmission of the Mail, he meant the Mailbags; he did not propose to interfere with the passengers.' No? Think again, Lord Ashley.

When the Honorable Member for Whitened Sepulchres moves his

resolution for the stoppage of Mail Trains – in a word, of all Railway travelling – on Sunday; and when that Honorable Gentleman talks about the Pariah clerks who take the money and give the tickets, the Pariah engine-drivers, the Pariah stokers, the Pariah porters, the Pariah police along the line, and the Pariah flys waiting at the Pariah stations to take the Pariah passengers, to be attended by Pariah servants at the Pariah Arms and other Pariah Hotels; what will Lord Ashley do then? Envy insinuated that Tom Thumb made his giants first, and then killed them, but you cannot do the like by your Pariahs. You cannot get an exclusive patent for the manufacture and destruction of Pariah dolls. Other Honorable Gentlemen are certain to engage in the trade; and when the Honorable Member for Whitened Sepulchres makes *his* Pariahs of all these people, you cannot refuse to recognise them as being of the genuine sort, Lord Ashley. Railway and all other Sunday Travelling, suppressed, by the Honorable Member for Whitened Sepulchres, the same honorable gentleman, who will not have been particularly complimented in the course of that achievement by the Times Newspaper, will discover that a good deal is done towards the Times of Monday, on a Sunday night, and will Pariah the whole of that immense establishment. For, this is the great inconvenience of Pariah-making, that when you begin, they spring up like mushrooms: insomuch, that it is very doubtful whether we shall have a house in all this land, from the Queen's Palace downward, which will not be found, on inspection, to be swarming with Pariahs. Not touch the Mails, and yet abolish the Mail-bags? Stop all those silent messengers of affection and anxiety, yet let the talking traveller, who is the cause of infinitely more employment, go? Why, this were to suppose all men Fools, and the Honorable Member for Whitened Sepulchres even a greater Noodle than he is!

Lord Ashley supports his motion by reading some perilous bombast, said to be written by a working man – of whom the intelligent body of working men have no great reason, to our thinking, to be proud – in which there is much about not being robbed of the boon of the day of rest; but, with all Lord Ashley's indisputably humane and benevolent impulses, we grieve to say we know no robber whom the working man, really desirous to preserve his Sunday, has so much to dread, as Lord Ashley himself. He is weakly lending the influence of his good intentions to a movement which would make that day no day of rest – rest to those who are overwrought, includes recreation, fresh air, change – but a day of mortification and gloom. And this not to one class only, be it understood. This is not a class question. If there be no gentleman of spirit in the House of Commons to remind Lord Ashley that the high-flown nonsense he quoted, concerning labour, is but another form of the stupidest socialist dogma, which seeks to represent that there is only one class of labourers on earth, it is well that the truth should be stated somewhere. And it is, indisputably, that three-fourths of us are laborers who work hard for our living; and that the condition of what we call the working man, has its parallel, at a remove of certain degrees, in almost all professions and pursuits. Running through the middle classes, is a broad deep vein of constant, compulsory, indispensable work. There are innumerable gentlemen, and sons and daughters of gentlemen, constantly at work, who have no more hope of making fortunes in their vocation, than the working man has in his. There are innumerable families in which the day of rest, is the only day out of the seven, where innocent domestic recreations and enjoyments are very feasible. In our mean gentility, which is the cause of so much social mischief, we may try to separate ourselves, as to this question, from the working man; and may very complacently resolve that there is no occasion for his excursion trains and tea-gardens, because we don't use them; but we had better not deceive ourselves. It is impossible that we can cramp his means of needful recreation and refreshment, without cramping our own, or basely cheating him. We cannot leave him to the Christian patronage of the Honorable Member for Whitened Sepulchres, and take ourselves off. We cannot restrain him and leave ourselves free. Our Sunday wants are pretty much the same as his, though his are far more easily satisfied; our inclinations and our feelings are pretty much the same; and it will be no less wise than honest in us, the middle classes, not to be Janus-faced about the matter.

What is it that the Honorable Member for Whitened Sepulchres, for whom Lord Ashley clears the way, wants to do? He sees on a Sunday morning, in the large towns of England, when the bells are ringing for church and chapel, certain unwashed, dim-eyed, dissipated loungers, hanging about the doors of public houses, and loitering at the street corners, to whom the day of rest appeals in much the same degree as a sunny summer day does to so many pigs. Does he believe that any weight of handcuffs on the Post-Office, or any amount of restriction imposed on decent people, will bring Sunday home to these? Let him go, any Sunday morning, from the new Town of Edinburgh where the sound of a piano would be profanation, to the old Town, and see what Sunday is in the Canongate. Or let him get up some statistics of the drunken people in Glasgow, while the churches are full – and work out the amount of Sabbath observance which is carried downward, by rigid shows and sad-colored forms.

But, there is another class of people, those who take little jaunts, and mingle in social little assemblages, on a Sunday, concerning whom the whole constituency of Whitened Sepulchres, with their Honorable Member in the chair, find their lank hair standing on end with horror, and pointing, as if they were all electrified, straight up to the skylights of Exeter Hall. In reference to this class, we would whisper in the ears of the disturbed assemblage, three short words, 'Let well alone!'

The English people have long been remarkable for their domestic habits, and their household virtues and affections. They are, now, beginning to be universally respected by intelligent foreigners who visit this country, for their unobtrusive politeness, their good-humour, and their cheerful recognition of all restraints that really originate in consideration for the general good. They deserve this testimony (which we have often heard, of late, with pride) most honorably. Long maligned and mistrusted, they proved their case from the very first moment of having it in their power to do so; and have never, on any single occasion within our knowledge, abused any public confidence that has been reposed in them. It is an extraordinary thing to know of a people, systematically excluded from galleries and museums for years, that their respect for such places, and for themselves as visitors to them, dates, without any period of transition, from the very day when their doors were freely opened. The national vices are surprisingly few. The people in general are not gluttons, nor drunkards, nor gamblers, nor addicted to cruel sports, nor to the pushing of any amusement to furious and wild extremes. They are moderate, and easily pleased, and very sensible to all affectionate influences. Any knot of holiday-makers, without a large proportion of women and children among them, would be a perfect phenomenon. Let us go into any place of Sunday enjoyment where any fair representation of the people resort, and we shall find them decent, orderly, quiet, sociable among their families and neighbours. There is a general feeling of respect for religion, and for religious observances. The churches and chapels are well filled. Very few people who keep servants or apprentices leave out of consideration their opportunities of attending church or chapel; the general demeanour within those edifices, is particularly grave and decorous; and the general recreations without, are of a harmless and simple kind. Lord Brougham never did Henry Brougham more justice, than in declaring to the House of Lords, after the success of this motion in the House of Commons, that there is no Country where the Sabbath is, on the whole, better observed than in England. Let the constituency of Whitened Sepulchres ponder, in a Christian spirit, on these things; take care of their own consciences; leave their Honorable Member to take care of his; and let well alone.

For, it is in nations as in families. Too tight a hand in these respects, is certain to engender a disposition to break loose, and to run riot. If the private experience of any reader, pausing on this sentence, cannot furnish many unhappy illustrations of its truth, it is a very fortunate experience indeed. Our most notable public example of it, in England, is just two hundred years old.

Lord Ashley had better merge his Pariahs into the body politic; and the Honorable Member for Whitened Sepulchres had better accustom his jaundiced eyes to the Sunday sight of dwellers in towns, roaming in green fields, and gazing upon country prospects. If he will look a little beyond them, and lift up the eyes of his mind, perhaps he may observe a mild, majestic figure in the distance, going through a field of corn, attended by some common men who pluck the grain as they pass along, and whom their Divine Master teaches that he is the Lord, even of the Sabbath-Day.

A brief follow-up piece to 'The Sunday Screw', by W.H. Wills, appeared in *HW* on 13 July 1850 (Vol. 1, p. 378f.) in the 'Chips' sections. Entitled 'Sunday Pariahs', it quoted a disgruntled Post Office clerk obliged to work much harder on Saturdays as a result of the new law and noted, 'Vexation has, we fear, taken the place of that religious, calm and beneficent state of mind in which the Sabbath ought to be passed.' By this time, however, the Commons had set up a committee of enquiry on the matter, as a result of which it was eventually decided that Sunday working should be left to local initiative (see Pope, *op. cit.*, p. 69).

49

The Ghost of Art

Household Words, 20 July 1850 (leading article) *(RP)*

For a discussion of Dickens's objection to conventionality in art and to the use of stereotyped models by contemporary painters, an objection frequently expressed in his novels, see L. Ormond, 'Dickens and Painting: Contemporary Art', *The Dickensian*, Vol. 80 (1984), pp. 12–16. He had already mocked this practice in *Pictures from Italy* (1846), when describing models waiting to be hired on the Spanish Steps in Rome:

I could not conceive why the faces seemed familiar to me; why they appeared to have beset me, for years, in every possible variety of action and costume; and how it came to pass that they start up before me, in

Rome, in the broad day, like so many saddled and bridled nightmares. I soon found that we had made acquaintance, and improved it, for several years, on the walls of various Exhibition Galleries. There is one old gentleman, with long white hair and an immense beard, who, to my knowledge, has gone through half the catalogue of the Royal Academy. This is the venerable, or patriarchal model. He carries a long staff; and every knot and twist in that staff I have seen, faithfully delineated, innumerable times. . . .

Ormond comments that Dickens's objection was 'more moral than aesthetic' and quotes his letter to Angela Burdett-Coutts (18 March 1845; *Pilgrim*, Vol. IV, p. 281) in which, having described the models as 'one and all the falsest Rascals in Rome or out of it', he says, 'It is a good illustration of the Student life as it is, that young men should go on copying these people elaborately time after time out of mind, and find nothing fresh or suggestive in the actual world about them.'

Dickens mocks hackneyed subjects as well as hackneyed models in his list on p. 260. This begins with Goldsmith's *The Vicar of Wakefield*, a novel always close to his heart, which perhaps accounts for the more elaborate return to it at the end of the list. Its immense popularity at this time as a source for Academy paintings is attested by R.D. Altick (*Paintings from Books* [1985], p. 405f.): during the 1840s 'almost as many pictures from [the novel] were exhibited (some thirty) as had been seen in the entire preceding sixty years'; Altick also quotes *Punch*'s humorous suggestion in 1845 that in future exhibitions a large room should be set aside solely for *Vicar* paintings.

In connection with Dickens's reference to 'the German taste' becoming popular in British art, we might note Will Vaughan's comment on p. 54 of *The Romantic Spirit in German Art 1790–1990* (ed. Vaughan [1994]): 'The 1840s was probably the only time in the history of British art when contemporary German art was imitated in a wholesale manner. . . . The "German man-ner", as it came to be known. . . .' This manner was particularly associated with the so-called 'Nazarene' painters established in Rome since 1810. They wore long hair, beards and loose-flowing, quasi-medieval costume.

Dickens seems always to have associated chambers (bachelor apartments inhabited by lawyers and others in the Inns of Court) with gloom, loneliness and startling visitations, and this essay is a comic, mock-gothic variation on the theme. In *Great Expectations* Pip and Herbert have a 'top set' in the Temple and it is there that Magwitch suddenly appears from the past one stormy night (Ch. 39). See also the *Uncommercial Traveller* essay 'Chambers' (1860). The 'tempestuous sea of chaff' image for the law in paragraph 3 looks forward to *Bleak House*.

Literary allusions (p. 259) 'the little man in the nursery story': allusion to a nursery rhyme first found in *Tommy Thumb's Pretty Song Book* (*c.*1744), the first verse of which runs: 'When I was a little boy I lived by myself,/And all the bread and cheese I got I laid upon the shelf;/The rats and the mice they made such a strife,/I had to go to London town and buy me a wife.'; (p. 260) 'the Spectator ... Coverley': Addison and Steele's periodical (1711–12, 1714) supposedly written by a 'Mr Spectator' and conducted by a small club including Sir Roger de Coverley.

I am a bachelor, residing in rather a dreary set of chambers in the Temple. They are situated in a square court of high houses, which would be a complete well, but for the want of water and the absence of a bucket. I live at the top of the house, among the tiles and sparrows. Like the little man in the nursery-story, I live by myself, and all the bread and cheese I get – which is not much – I put upon a shelf. I need scarcely add, perhaps, that I am in love, and that the father of my charming Julia objects to our union.

I mention these little particulars as I might deliver a letter of introduction. The reader is now acquainted with me, and perhaps will condescend to listen to my narrative.

I am naturally of a dreamy turn of mind; and my abundant leisure – for I am called to the bar – coupled with much lonely listening to the twittering of sparrows, and the pattering of rain, has encouraged that disposition. In my 'top set,' I hear the wind howl, on a winter night, when the man on the ground floor believes it is perfectly still weather. The dim lamps with which our Honourable Society (supposed to be as yet unconscious of the new discovery called Gas) make the horrors of the staircase visible, deepen the gloom which generally settles on my soul when I go home at night.

I am in the Law, but not of it. I can't exactly make out what it means. I sit in Westminster Hall sometimes (in character) from ten to four; and when I go out of Court, I don't know whether I am standing on my wig or my boots.

It appears to me (I mention this in confidence) as if there were too much talk and too much law – as if some grains of truth were started overboard into a tempestuous sea of chaff.

All this may make me mystical. Still, I am confident that what I am going to describe myself as having seen and heard, I actually did see and hear.

It is necessary that I should observe that I have a great delight in pictures. I am no painter myself, but I have studied pictures and written about them. I have seen all the most famous pictures in the world; my education and reading have been sufficiently general to possess me beforehand with a knowledge of most of the subjects to which a Painter is likely to have recourse; and, although I might be in some doubt as to the rightful fashion of the scabbard of King Lear's sword, for instance, I think I should know King Lear tolerably well, if I happened to meet with him.

I go to all the Modern Exhibitions every season, and of course I revere the Royal Academy. I stand by its forty Academical articles almost as firmly as I stand by the thirty-nine Articles of the Church of England. I am convinced that in neither case could there be, by any rightful possibility, one article more or less.

It is now exactly three years – three years ago, this very month – since I went from Westminster to the Temple, one Thursday afternoon, in a cheap steam-boat. The sky was black, when I imprudently walked on board. It began to thunder and lighten immediately afterwards, and the rain poured down in torrents. The deck seeming to smoke with the wet, I went below; but so many passengers were there, smoking too, that I came up again, and buttoning my pea-coat, and standing in the shadow of the paddle-box, stood as upright as I could, and made the best of it.

It was at this moment that I first beheld the terrible Being, who is the subject of my present recollections.

Standing against the funnel, apparently with the intention of drying himself by the heat as fast as he got wet, was a shabby man in threadbare black, and with his hands in his pockets, who fascinated me from the memorable instant when I caught his eye.

Where had I caught that eye before? Who was he? Why did I connect him, all at once, with the Vicar of Wakefield, Alfred the Great, Gil Blas, Charles the Second, Joseph and his Brethren, the Fairy Queen, Tom Jones, the Decameron of Boccaccio, Tam O'Shanter, the Marriage of the Doge of Venice with the Adriatic, and the Great Plague of London? Why, when he bent one leg, and placed one hand upon the back of the seat near him, did my mind associate him wildly with the words, 'Number one hundred and forty-two, Portrait of a gentleman?' Could it be that I was going mad?

I looked at him again, and now I could have taken my affidavit that he belonged to the Vicar of Wakefield's family. Whether he was the Vicar, or Moses, or Mr Burchill, or the Squire, or a conglomeration of all four, I knew not; but I was impelled to seize him by the throat, and charge him with being, in some fell way, connected with the Primrose blood. He looked up at the rain, and then – oh Heaven! – he became Saint John. He folded his arms, resigning himself to the weather, and I was frantically inclined to address him as the Spectator, and firmly demand to know what he had done with Sir Roger de Coverley.

The frightful suspicion that I was becoming deranged, returned upon me with redoubled force. Meantime, this awful stranger, inexplicably linked to my distress, stood drying himself at the funnel; and ever, as the steam rose from his clothes, diffusing a mist around him, I saw through the ghostly medium all the people I have mentioned, and a score more, sacred and profane.

I am conscious of a dreadful inclination that stole upon me, as it thundered and lightened, to grapple with this man, or demon, and plunge him over the side. But, I constrained myself – I know not how – to speak to him, and in a pause of the storm, I crossed the deck, and said:

'What are you?'

He replied, hoarsely, 'A Model.'

'A what?' said I.

'A Model,' he replied. 'I sets to the profession for a bob a-hour.' (All through this narrative I give his own words, which are indelibly imprinted on my memory.)

The relief which this disclosure gave me, the exquisite delight of the restoration of my confidence in my own sanity, I cannot describe. I should have fallen on his neck, but for the consciousness of being observed by the man at the wheel.

'You then,' said I, shaking him so warmly by the hand, that I wrung the rain out of his coat-cuff, 'are the gentleman whom I have so frequently contemplated, in connection with a high-backed chair with a red cushion, and a table with twisted legs.'

'I am that Model,' he rejoined moodily, 'and I wish I was anything else.'

'Say not so,' I returned. 'I have seen you in the society of many beautiful young women;' as in truth I had, and always (I now remembered) in the act of making the most of his legs.

'No doubt,' said he. 'And you've seen me along with warses of flowers, and any number of table-kivers, and antique cabinets, and warious gammon.'

'Sir?' said I.

'And warious gammon,' he repeated, in a louder voice. 'You might have seen me in armour, too, if you had looked sharp. Blessed if I ha'n't stood in half the suits of armour as ever came out of Pratts's shop: and sat, for weeks together, a eating nothing, out of half the gold and silver dishes as has ever been lent for the purpose out of Storrses, and Mortimerses, or Garrardses, and Davenportseseses.'

Excited, as it appeared, by a sense of injury, I thought he never would have found an end for the last word. But, at length it rolled sullenly away with the thunder.

'Pardon me,' said I, 'you are a well-favoured, well-made man, and yet – forgive me – I find, on examining my mind, that I associate you with – that my recollection indistinctly makes you, in short – excuse me – a kind of powerful monster.'

'It would be a wonder if it didn't,' he said. 'Do you know what my points are?'

'No,' said I.

'My throat and my legs,' said he. 'When I don't set for a head, I mostly sets for a throat and a pair of legs. Now, granted you was a painter, and was to work at my throat for a week together, I suppose you'd see a lot of lumps and bumps there, that would never be there at all, if you looked at me, complete, instead of only my throat. Wouldn't you?'

'Probably,' said I, surveying him.

'Why, it stands to reason,' said the Model. 'Work another week at my legs, and it'll be the same thing. You'll make 'em out as knotty and as knobbly, at last, as if they was the trunks of two old trees. Then, take and stick my legs and throat on to another man's body, and you'll make a reg'lar monster. And that's the way the public gets their reg'lar monsters, every first Monday in May, when the Royal Academy Exhibition opens.'

'You are a critic,' said I, with an air of deference.

'I'm in an uncommon ill humour, if that's it,' rejoined the Model, with great indignation. 'As if it warn't bad enough for a bob a-hour, for a man to be mixing himself up with that there jolly old furniter that one 'ud think the public know'd the wery nails in by this time – or to be putting on greasy old ats and cloaks, and playing tambourines in the Bay o' Naples, with Wesuvius a smokin' according to pattern in the background, and the wines a bearing wonderful in the middle distance – or to be unpolitely kicking up his legs among a lot o' gals, with no reason whatever in his mind, but to show 'em – as if this warn't bad enough, I'm to go and be thrown out of employment too!'

'Surely no!' said I.

'Surely yes,' said the indignant Model. 'BUT I'LL GROW ONE.'

The gloomy and threatening manner in which he muttered the last words, can never be effaced from my remembrance. My blood ran cold.

I asked of myself, what was it that this desperate Being was resolved to grow? My breast made no response.

I ventured to implore him to explain his meaning. With a scornful laugh, he uttered this dark prophecy:

'I'LL GROW ONE. AND, MARK MY WORDS, IT SHALL HAUNT YOU!'

We parted in the storm, after I had forced half-a-crown on his acceptance, with a trembling hand. I conclude that something supernatural happened to the steam-boat, as it bore his reeking figure down the river; but it never got into the papers.

Two years elapsed, during which I followed my profession without any vicissitudes; never holding so much as a motion, of course. At the expiration of that period, I found myself making my way home to the

Temple, one night, in precisely such another storm of thunder and lightning as that by which I had been overtaken on board the steam-boat – except that this storm, bursting over the town at midnight, was rendered much more awful by the darkness and the hour.

As I turned into my court, I really thought a thunderbolt would fall, and plough the pavement up. Every brick and stone in the place seemed to have an echo of its own for the thunder. The water-spouts were overcharged, and the rain came tearing down from the house-tops as if they had been mountain-tops.

Mrs Parkins, my laundress – wife of Parkins the porter, then newly dead of a dropsy – had particular instructions to place a bedroom candle and a match under the staircase lamp on my landing, in order that I might light my candle there, whenever I came home. Mrs Parkins invariably disregarding all instructions, they were never there. Thus it happened that on this occasion I groped my way into my sitting-room to find the candle, and came out to light it.

What were my emotions when, underneath the staircase lamp, shining with wet as if he had never been dry since our last meeting, stood the mysterious Being whom I had encountered on the steam-boat in a thunderstorm, two years before! His prediction rushed upon my mind, and I turned faint.

'I said I'd do it,' he observed, in a hollow voice, 'and I have done it. May I come in?'

'Misguided creature, what have you done?' I returned.

'I'll let you know,' was his reply, 'if you'll let me in.'

Could it be murder that he had done? And had he been so successful that he wanted to do it again, at my expense?

I hesitated.

'May I come in?' said he.

I inclined my head, with as much presence of mind as I could command, and he followed me into my chambers. There, I saw that the lower part of his face was tied up, in what is commonly called a Belcher handkerchief. He slowly removed this bandage, and exposed to view a long dark beard, curling over his upper lip, twisting about the corners of his mouth, and hanging down upon his breast.

'What is this?' I exclaimed involuntarily, 'and what have you become?'

'I am the Ghost of Art!' said he.

The effect of these words, slowly uttered in the thunderstorm at midnight, was appalling in the last degree. More dead than alive, I surveyed him in silence.

'The German taste came up,' said he, 'and threw me out of bread. I am ready for the taste now.'

He made his beard a little jagged with his hands, folded his arms, and said,

'Severity!'

I shuddered. It was so severe.

He made his beard flowing on his breast, and, leaning both hands on the staff of a carpet-broom which Mrs Parkins had left among my books, said:

'Benevolence.'

I stood transfixed. The change of sentiment was entirely in the beard. The man might have left his face alone, or had no face. The beard did everything.

He laid down on his back, on my table, and with that action of his head threw up his beard at the chin.

'That's death!' said he.

He got off my table and, looking up at the ceiling, cocked his beard a little awry; at the same time making it stick out before him.

'Adoration, or a vow of vengeance,' he observed.

He turned his profile to me, making his upper lip very bulgy with the upper part of his beard.

'Romantic character,' said he.

He looked sideways out of his beard, as if it were an ivy-bush. 'Jealousy,' said he. He gave it an ingenious twist in the air, and informed me that he was carousing. He made it shaggy with his fingers – and it was Despair; lank – and it was avarice; tossed it all kinds of ways – and it was rage. The beard did everything.

'I am the Ghost of Art,' said he. 'Two bob a-day now, and more when it's longer! Hair's the true expression. There is no other. I SAID I'D GROW IT, AND I'VE GROWN IT, AND IT SHALL HAUNT YOU!'

He may have tumbled downstairs in the dark, but he never walked down or ran down. I looked over the bannisters, and I was alone with the thunder.

Need I add more of my terrific fate? It HAS haunted me ever since. It glares upon me from the walls of the Royal Academy, (except when MACLISE subdues it to his genius,) it fills my soul with terror at the British Institution, it lures young artists on to their destruction. Go where I will, the Ghost of Art, eternally working the passions in hair, and expressing everything by beard, pursues me. The prediction is accomplished, and the Victim has no rest.

50

A Detective Police Party (1)

Household Words, 27 July 1850 (leading article) (*RP* as 'The Detective Police')

The Detective Branch of the Police was established in 1842 with two detectives attached to each division of the force and two inspectors and six sergeants at headquarters in Scotland Yard. Their role was primarily to prevent crime happening rather than to detect criminals after the event, and their necessary contacts with the criminal world made them initially the object of much public suspicion. A series of successful cases of tracking down perpetrators of crime, culminating in the celebrated Manning murder case referred to here by Dickens (a case in which nearly all the officers he is entertaining were directly involved), led to a change in the public's attitude and this is reflected in the intensely admiring series of articles Dickens published in *HW*. The first of these, by Wills, entitled 'The Modern Science of Thief-taking', appeared on 13 July and compared the detective to a connoisseur of paintings – he 'at once pounces upon the authors of the work of art under consideration, by the style of performance'. Wills also asserts that detectives are 'so thoroughly well acquainted' with the kind of criminals known as 'swell mobsmen' (clever confidence tricksters, superior pickpockets, etc.) that 'they frequently tell what they have been about by the expression of their eyes and their general manner' (*HW*, Vol. 1 pp. 369, 371).

In this follow-up article Dickens describes his entertainment at the journal's office opposite the Lyceum Theatre of a group of detectives from the Yard, giving them transparently fictitious names. Joan Lock points out in her *Dreadful Deeds and Awful Murders: Scotland Yard's First Detectives 1829–1878* (1990, p. 121) that Robert Walker (Dickens's 'Stalker') was not, in fact, a detective inspector but a member of Scotland Yard's Executive Branch. Three of the sergeants, 'Dornton' (Thornton), 'Witchem' (Whicher) and 'Straw' (Shaw), had been at the Yard since 1842, the two others, 'Mith' (Smith) and 'Fendall' (Kendall), were later recruits. 'Inspector Wield' was Charles Frederick Field, whom Dickens greatly admired and on whom he famously modelled Inspector Bucket in *Bleak House* (1852–4), 'corpulent forefinger' and all. For more on Field, see p. 356f., and for an excellent general discussion of Dickens and his hero-worship of the detective police, see Philip Collins, *Dickens and Crime* (1962), Ch. 9. Dickens's admiration was apparently reciprocated: he wrote to Bulwer Lytton on 9 May 1851 that Field was 'quite devoted' to him and that 'Any of the Detective men will do anything for me' (*Pilgrim*, Vol. VI, p. 380).

Field's story about 'Fikey, the man accused of forging the Sou'Western Railway debentures,' refers to a case that was *sub judice* when the article was published (William Eicke was eventually found guilty and transported for seven years) and Wills had to make some alterations to Dickens's manuscript because of this – see *Pilgrim*, Vol. VI, p. 130, n. 1. For more on this case and on Field's further dealings with the Eicke family, see W. Long, 'The "Singler Stories" of Inspector Field', *The Dickensian*, Vol. 83 (1987), pp. 141–3.

With regard to Dickens's contemptuous remarks about the old Bow Street Runners, we should note Collins's comment (*op. cit.*, p. 202) that in portraying Blathers and Duff in *Oliver Twist* (1837) Dickens showed himself 'impressed by their professional pride, expertise and patter' and that 'the tones and the relish' of the detective anecdote they relate closely anticipate his presentation of the detectives' tales in this piece.

Literary allusions (p. 268) 'Our hearts leaping up when we beheld this rainbow ...': Wordsworth, 'My heart leaps up when I behold....'

Textual note In the *RP* text the first paragraph is omitted; also the phrase 'to which our readers have already been introduced; (p. 275), and the last sentence, 'But we must reserve ... paper.'

In pursuance of the intention mentioned at the close of a former paper on 'The Modern Science of Thief-taking' we now proceed to endeavour to convey to our readers some faint idea of the extraordinary dexterity, patience, and ingenuity, exercised by the Detective Police. That our description may be as graphic as we can render it, and may be perfectly reliable, we will make it, so far as in us lies, a piece of plain truth. And first, we have to inform the reader how the anecdotes we are about to communicate, came to our knowledge.

We are not by any means devout believers in the Old Bow-Street Police. To say the truth, we think there was a vast amount of humbug about those worthies. Apart from many of them being men of very indifferent character, and far too much in the habit of consorting with thieves and the like, they never lost a public occasion of jobbing and trading in mystery and making the most of themselves. Continually puffed besides by incompetent magistrates anxious to conceal their own deficiencies, and hand-in-glove with the penny-a-liners of that time, they became a sort of superstition. Although as a Preventive Police they were utterly ineffective, and as a Detective Police were very loose and uncertain in their operations, they remain with some people, a superstition to the present day.

On the other hand, the Detective Force organised since the establishment of the existing Police, is so well chosen and trained, proceeds so systematically and quietly, does its business in such a workman-like manner, and is always so calmly and steadily engaged in the service of the public, that the public really do not know enough of it, to know a tithe of its usefulness. Impressed with this conviction, and interested in the men themselves, we represented to the authorities at Scotland Yard, that we should be glad, if there were no official objection, to have some talk with the Detectives. A most obliging and ready permission being given, a certain evening was appointed with a certain Inspector for a social conference between ourselves and the Detectives, at our Office in Wellington Street, Strand, London. In consequence of which appointment the party 'came off,' which we are about to describe. And we beg to repeat that, avoiding such topics as it might for obvious reasons be injurious to the public, or disagreeable to respectable individuals, to touch upon in print, our description is as exact as we can make it.

The reader will have the goodness to imagine the Sanctum Sanctorum of Household Words. Anything that best suits the reader's fancy, will best represent that magnificent chamber We merely stipulate for a round table in the middle, with some glasses and cigars arranged upon it; and the editorial sofa elegantly hemmed in between that stately piece of furniture and the wall.

It is a sultry evening at dusk. The stones of Wellington Street are hot and gritty, and the watermen and hackney-coachmen at the Theatre opposite, are much flushed and aggravated. Carriages are constantly setting down the people who have come to Fairy-Land; and there is a mighty shouting and bellowing every now and then, deafening us for the moment, through the open windows.

Just at dusk, Inspectors Wield and Stalker are announced; but we do not undertake to warrant the orthography of any of the names here mentioned. Inspector Wield presents Inspector Stalker. Inspector Wield is a middle-aged man of a portly presence, with a large, moist, knowing eye, a husky voice, and a habit of emphasising his conversation by the aid of a corpulent fore-finger, which is constantly in juxtaposition with his eyes or nose. Inspector Stalker is a shrewd, hard-headed Scotchman – in appearance not at all unlike a very acute, thoroughly-trained school-master, from the Normal Establishment at Glasgow. Inspector Wield one might have known, perhaps, for what he is – Inspector Stalker, never.

The ceremonies of reception over, Inspectors Wield and Stalker observe that they have brought some sergeants with them. The sergeants are presented – five in number, Sergeant Dornton, Sergeant Witchem, Sergeant Mith, Sergeant Fendall, and Sergeant Straw. We have the whole Detective Force from Scotland Yard with one exception. They sit down in a semi-circle (the two Inspectors at the two ends) at a little distance from the round table, facing the editorial sofa. Every man of them, in a glance, immediately takes an inventory of the furniture and an accurate sketch of the editorial presence. The Editor feels that any gentleman in company could take him up, if need should be, without the smallest hesitation, twenty years hence.

The whole party are in plain clothes. Sergeant Dornton, about fifty years of age, with a ruddy face and a high sun-burnt forehead, has the air of one who has been a Sergeant in the army – he might have sat to Wilkie for the Soldier in the Reading of the Will. He is famous for steadily pursuing the inductive process, and, from small beginnings, working on from clue to clue until he bags his man. Sergeant Witchem, shorter and thicker-set, and marked with the small pox, has something of a reserved and thoughtful air, as if he were engaged in deep arithmetical calculations. He is renowned for his acquaintance with the swell mob. Sergeant Mith, a smooth-faced man with a fresh bright complexion, and a strange air of simplicity, is a dab at housebreakers. Sergeant Fendall, a light-haired, well-spoken, polite person, is a prodigious hand at pursuing private inquiries of a delicate nature. Straw, a little wiry Sergeant of meek demeanour and strong sense, would knock at a door and ask a series of questions in any mild character you chose to prescribe to him, from a charity-boy upwards, and seem as innocent as an infant. They are, one and all, respectable-looking men; of perfectly good deportment and unusual intelligence; with nothing lounging or slinking in their manners; with an air of keen observation, and quick perception when addressed; and generally presenting in their faces, traces more or less marked of habitually leading lives of strong mental excitement. They have all good eyes; and they all can, and they all do, look full at whomsoever they speak to.

We light the cigars, and hand round the glasses (which are very temperately used indeed), and the conversation begins by a modest amateur reference on the Editorial part to the swell mob. Inspector Wield immediately removes his cigar from his lips, waves his right hand, and says, 'Regarding the Swell Mob, Sir, I can't do better than call upon Sergeant Witchem. Because the reason why? I'll tell you. Sergeant Witchem is better acquainted with the Swell Mob than any officer in London.'

Our heart leaping up when we beheld this rainbow in the sky, we turn to Sergeant Witchem, who very concisely, and in well-chosen language, goes into the subject forthwith. Meantime, the whole of his brother officers are closely interested in attending to what he says, and observing its effect. Presently they begin to strike in, one or two together, when an opportunity offers, and the conversation becomes general. But these brother officers only come in to the assistance of each other – not to the contradiction – and a more amicable brotherhood there could not be. From the swell mob, we diverge to the kindred topics of cracksmen, fences, public-house dancers, area-sneaks, designing young people who go out 'gonophing,' and other 'schools,' to which our readers have already been introduced. It is observable throughout these revelations, that Inspector Stalker, the Scotchman, is always exact and statistical, and that when any question of figures arises, everybody as by one consent pauses, and looks to him.

When we have exhausted the various schools of Art – during which discussion the whole body have remained profoundly attentive, except when some unusual noise at the Theatre over the way, has induced some gentleman to glance inquiringly towards the window in that direction, behind his next neighbour's back – we burrow for information on such points as the following. Whether there really are any highway robberies in London, or whether some circumstances not convenient to be mentioned by the aggrieved party, usually precede the robberies complained of, under that head, which quite change their character? Certainly the latter, almost always. Whether in the case of robberies in houses, where servants are necessarily exposed to doubt, innocence under suspicion ever becomes so like guilt in appearance, that a good officer need be cautious how he judges it? Undoubtedly. Nothing is so common or deceptive as such appearances at first. Whether in a place of public amusement, a thief knows an officer, and an officer knows a thief, – supposing them, beforehand, strangers to each other – because each recognises in the other, under all disguise, an inattention to what is going on, and a purpose that is not the purpose of being entertained? Yes. That's the way exactly. Whether it is reasonable or ridiculous to trust to the alleged experiences of thieves as narrated by themselves, in prisons, or penitentiaries, or anywhere? In general, nothing more absurd. Lying is their habit and their trade; and they would rather lie – even if they hadn't an interest in it, and didn't want to make themselves agreeable – than tell the truth.

From these topics, we glide into a review of the most celebrated and horrible of the great crimes that have been committed within the last fifteen or twenty years. The men engaged in the discovery of almost all of them, and in the pursuit or apprehension of the murderers, are here, down to the very last instance. One of our guests gave chase to and boarded the Emigrant Ship, in which the murderess last hanged in London was supposed to have embarked. We learn from him that his errand was not announced to the passengers, who may have no idea of it to this hour. That he went below, with the captain, lamp in hand – it being dark, and the whole steerage abed and seasick – and engaged the

Mrs Manning who *was* on board, in a conversation about her luggage, until she was, with no small pains, induced to raise her head, and turn her face towards the light. Satisfied that she was not the object of his search, he quietly re-embarked in the Government steamer alongside, and steamed home again with the intelligence.

When we have exhausted these subjects, too, which occupy a considerable time in the discussion, two or three leave their chairs, whisper Sergeant Witchem, and resume their seats. Sergeant Witchem, leaning forward a little, and placing a hand on each of his legs, then modestly speaks as follows:

'My brother-officers wish me to relate a little account of my taking Tally-ho Thompson. A man oughtn't to tell what he has done himself; but still, as nobody was with me, and, consequently, as nobody but myself can tell it, I'll do it in the best way I can, if it should meet your approval.'

We assure Sergeant Witchem that he will oblige us very much, and we all compose ourselves to listen with interest and attention.

'Tally-ho Thompson,' says Sergeant Witchem, after merely wetting his lips with his brandy-and-water, 'Tally-ho Thompson was a famous horse-stealer, couper, and magsman. Thompson in conjunction with a pal that occasionally worked with him, gammoned a countryman out of a good round sum of money, under pretence of getting him a situation – the regular old dodge – and was afterwards in the "Hue and Cry" for a horse – a horse that he stole, down in Hertfordshire. I had to look after Thompson, and I applied myself, of course, in the first instance, to discovering where he was. Now, Thompson's wife lived, along with a little daughter, at Chelsea. Knowing that Thompson was somewhere in the country, I watched the house – especially at post-time in the morning – thinking Thompson was pretty likely to write to her. Sure enough, one morning the postman comes up, and delivers a letter at Mrs Thompson's door. Little girl opens the door, and takes it in. We're not always sure of postmen, though the people at the post-offices are always very obliging. A postman may help us, or he may not, – just as it happens. However, I go across the road, and I say to the postman, after he has left the letter, "Good morning! how are you?" "How are *you?*" says he. "You've just delivered a letter for Mrs Thompson." "Yes, I have." "You didn't happen to remark what the post-mark was, perhaps?" "No," says he, "I didn't." "Come," says I, "I'll be plain with you. I'm in a small way of business, and I have given Thompson credit, and I can't afford to lose what he owes me. I know he's got money, and I know he's in the country, and if you could tell me what the post-mark was, I should be very much obliged to you, and you'd do a service to a tradesman in a small way of business that can't afford a loss." "Well," he said, "I do assure you that I did not observe what the post-mark was; all I know is, that there was money in the letter – I should say a sovereign." This was enough for me, because of course I knew that Thompson having sent his wife money, it was probable she'd write to Thompson, by return of post, to acknowledge the receipt. So I said "Thankee" to the postman, and I kept on the watch. In the afternoon I saw the little girl come out. Of course I followed her. She went into a stationer's shop, and I needn't say to you that I looked in at the window. She bought some writing-paper and envelopes, and a pen. I think to myself, "That'll do!" – watch her home again – and don't go away, you may be sure, knowing that Mrs Thompson was writing her letter to Tally-ho, and that the letter would be posted presently. In about an hour or so, out came the little girl again, with the letter in her hand. I went up, and said something to the child, whatever it might have been; but I couldn't see the direction of the letter, because she held it with the seal upwards. However, I observed that on the back of the letter there was what we call a kiss – a drop of wax by the side of the seal – and again, you understand, that was enough for me. I saw her post the letter, waited till she was gone, then went into the shop, and asked to see the Master. When he came out, I told him, "Now, I'm an Officer in the Detective Force; there's a letter with a kiss been posted here just now, for a man that I'm in search of; and what I have to ask of you, is, that you will let me look at the direction of that letter." He was very civil – took a lot of letters from the box in the window – shook 'em out on the counter with the faces downwards – and there among 'em was the identical letter with the kiss. It was directed, Mr Thomas Pigeon, Post-Office, B—, to be left 'till called for. Down I went to B— (a hundred and twenty miles or so) that night. Early next morning I went to the Post-Office; saw the gentleman in charge of that department; told him who I was; and that my object was to see, and track, the party that should come for the letter for Mr Thomas Pigeon. He was very polite, and said, "You shall have every assistance we can give you; you can wait inside the office; and we'll take care to let you know when anybody comes for the letter." Well, I waited there, three days, and began to think that nobody ever *would* come. At last the clerk whispered to me, "Here! Detective! Somebody's come for the letter!" "Keep him a minute," said I, and I ran round to the outside of the office. There I saw a young chap with the appearance of an Ostler, holding a horse by the bridle – stretching the bridle across the pavement, while he waited at the Post-Office Window for the letter. I began to pat the horse, and that; and I said to the boy, "Why, this is Mr Jones's Mare!" "No. It an't." "No?" said I. "She's very like Mr Jones's Mare!" "She an't Mr Jones's Mare, anyhow," says he. "It's Mr So-and-So's, of the Warwick Arms." And up he jumped, and off he went – letter and all. I got a cab, followed on the box, and was so quick after him that I came into the stable-yard of the Warwick Arms, by one gate, just as he came in by another. I went into the bar, where there was a young woman serving, and called for a glass of brandy-and-water. He came in directly, and handed her the letter. She casually looked at it, without saying anything, and stuck it up behind the glass over the chimney-piece. What was to be done next?

'I turned it over in my mind while I drank my brandy-and-water (looking pretty sharp at the letter the while), but I couldn't see my way out of it at all. I tried to get lodgings in the house, but there had been a horse-fair, or something of that sort, and it was full. I was obliged to put up somewhere else, but I came backwards and forwards to the bar for a couple of days, and there was the letter always behind the glass. At last I thought I'd write a letter to Mr Pigeon myself, and see what that would do. So I wrote one, and posted it, but I purposely addressed it, Mr John Pigeon, instead of Mr Thomas Pigeon, to see what *that* would do. In the morning (a very wet morning it was) I watched the postman down the street, and cut into the bar, just before he reached the Warwick Arms. In he came presently with my letter. "Is there a Mr John Pigeon staying here?" "No! – stop a bit though," says the barmaid; and she took down the letter behind the glass. "No," says she, "it's Thomas, and *he* is not staying here. Would you do me a favor, and post this for me, as it is so wet?" The postman said Yes; she folded it in another envelope, directed it, and gave it him. He put it in his hat, and away he went.

'I had no difficulty in finding out the direction of that letter. It was addressed, Mr Thomas Pigeon, Post-Office, R—, Northamptonshire, to be left till called for. Off I started directly for R—; I said the same at the Post-Office there, as I had said at B—; and again I waited three days before anybody came. At last another chap on horseback came. "Any letters for Mr Thomas Pigeon?" "Where do you come from?" "New Inn, near R—." He got the letter, and away *he* went – at a canter.

'I made my enquiries about the New Inn, near R—, and hearing it was a solitary sort of house, a little in the horse line, about a couple of miles from the station, I thought I'd go and have a look at it. I found it what it had been described, and sauntered in, to look about me. The landlady was in the bar, and I was trying to get into conversation with her; asked her how business was, and spoke about the wet weather, and so on; when I saw, through an open door, three men sitting by the fire in a sort of parlor, or kitchen; and one of those men, according to the description I had of him, was Tally-ho Thompson!

'I went and sat down among 'em, and tried to make things agreeable; but they were very shy – wouldn't talk at all – looked at me, and at one another, in a way quite the reverse of sociable. I reckoned 'em up, and finding that they were all three bigger men than me, and considering that their looks were ugly – that it was a lonely place – railroad station two miles off – and night coming on – thought I couldn't do better than have a drop of brandy-and-water to keep my courage up. So I called for my brandy-and-water; and as I was sitting drinking it by the fire, Thompson got up and went out.

'Now the difficulty of it was, that I wasn't sure it *was* Thompson, because I had never set eyes on him before; and what I had wanted was to be quite certain of him. However, there was nothing for it now, but to follow, and put a bold face upon it. I found him talking, outside in the yard, with the landlady. It turned out afterwards, that he was wanted by a Northampton officer for something else, and that, knowing that officer to be pock-marked (as I am myself), he mistook me for him. As I have observed, I found him talking to the landlady, outside. I put my hand upon his shoulder – this way – and said, "Tally-ho Thompson, it's no use. I know you. I'm an officer from London, and I take you into custody for felony!" "That be d——d!" says Tally-ho Thompson.

'We went back into the house, and the two friends began to cut up rough, and their looks didn't please me at all, I assure you. "Let the man go. What are you going to do with him?" "I'll tell you what I'm going to do with him. I'm going to take him to London tonight, as sure as I'm alive. I'm not alone here, whatever you may think. You mind your own business, and keep yourselves to yourselves. It'll be better for you, for I know you both very well." I'd never seen or heard of 'em in all my life, but my bouncing cowed 'em a bit, and they kept off, while Thompson was making ready to go. I thought to myself, however, that they might be coming after me on the dark road, to rescue Thompson; so I said to the landlady, "What men have you got in the house, Missis?" "We haven't got no men here," she says, sulkily. "You have got an ostler, I suppose?" "Yes, we've got an ostler." "Let me see him." Presently he came, and a shaggy-headed young fellow he was. "Now attend to me, young man," says I; "I'm a Detective Officer from London. This man's name is Thompson. I have taken him into custody for felony. I'm going to take him to the railroad station. I call upon you in the Queen's name to assist me; and mind you, my friend, you'll get yourself into more trouble than you know of, if you don't!" You never saw a person open his eyes so wide. "Now, Thompson, come along!" says I. But when I took out the handcuffs, Thompson cries, "No! None of that! I won't stand *them*! I'll go along with you quiet, but I won't bear none of that!" "Tally-ho Thompson," I said, "I'm willing to behave as a man to you, if you are willing to behave as a man to me. Give me your word that you'll come peaceably along, and I don't want to handcuff you." "I will," says Thompson, "but I'll have a glass of brandy first." "I don't care if I've another," said I. "We'll have two more, Missis," said the friends, "and con-found you, Constable, you'll give your man a drop, won't you?" I was agreeable to that, so we had it all round, and then my man and I took Tally-ho Thompson safe to the railroad, and I carried him to London that night. He was afterwards acquitted, on account of a defect in the evidence; and I understand he always praises me up to the skies, and says I'm one of the best of men.'

This story coming to a termination amidst general applause, Inspector Wield, after a little grave smoking, fixes his eye on his host, and thus delivers himself:

'It wasn't a bad plant that of mine, on Fikey, the man accused of forging the Sou' Western Railway debentures – it was only t'other day – because the reason why? I'll tell you.

'I had information that Fikey and his brother kept a factory over yonder there,' indicating any region on the Surrey side of the river, 'where he bought second-hand carriages; so after I'd tried in vain to get hold of him by other means, I wrote him a letter in an assumed name, saying that I'd got a horse and shay to dispose of, and would drive down next day, that he might view the lot, and make an offer – very reasonable it was, I said – a reg'lar bargain. Straw and me then went off to a friend of mine that's in the livery and job business, and hired a turn-out for the day, a precious smart turn-out, it was – quite a slap-up thing! Down we drove, accordingly with a friend (who's not in the Force himself); and leaving my friend in the shay near a public-house, to take care of the horse, we went to the factory, which was some little way off. In the factory, there was a number of strong fellows at work, and after reckoning 'em up, it was clear to me that it wouldn't do to try it on there. They were too many for us. We must get our man out of doors. "Mr Fikey at home?" "No, he ain't." "Expected home soon?" "Why, no, not soon." "Ah! is his brother here?" "*I'm* his brother." "Oh! well, this is an ill-conwenience, this is. I wrote him a letter yesterday, saying I'd got a little turn-out to dispose of, and I've took the trouble to bring the turn-out down, a' purpose, and now he ain't in the way." "No, he an't in the way. You couldn't make it convenient to call again, could you?" "Why, no, I couldn't. I want to sell; that's the fact; and I can't put it off. Could you find him anywheres?" At first he said No, he couldn't, and then he wasn't sure about it, and then he'd go and try. So, at last he went upstairs, where there was a sort of loft, and presently down comes my man himself, in his shirt sleeves.

' "Well," he says, "this seems to be rayther a pressing matter of yours." "Yes," I says, "it *is* rayther a pressing matter, and you'll find it a bargain – dirt cheap." "I ain't in partickler want of a bargain just now," he says, "but where is it?" "Why," I says, "the turn-out's just outside. Come and look at it." He hasn't any suspicions, and away we go. And the first thing that happens is, that the horse runs away with my friend (who knows no more of driving than a child) when he takes a little trot along the road to show his paces. You never saw such a game in your life!

'When the bolt is over, and the turn-out has come to a stand-still again, Fikey walks round and round it, as grave as a judge — me too. "There, Sir!" I says. "There's a neat thing!" "It an't a bad style of thing," he says. "I believe you," says I. "And there's a horse!" — for I saw him looking at it. "Rising eight!" I says, rubbing his fore-legs. (Bless you, there an't a man in the world knows less of horses than I do, but I'd heard my friend at the Livery Stables say he was eight year old, so I says, as knowing as possible, "Rising Eight.") "Rising eight, is he?" says he. "Rising eight," says I. "Well," he says, "what do you want for it?" "Why, the first and last figure for the whole concern is five-and-twenty pound!" "That's very cheap!" he says, looking at me. "An't it?" I says. "I told you it was a bargain! Now, without any higgling and haggling about it, what I want is to sell, and that's my price. Further, I'll make it easy to you, and take half the money down and you can do a bit of stiff* for the balance." "Well," he says again, "that's very cheap." "I believe you," says I; "get in and try it, and you'll buy it. Come! take a trial!"

'Ecod, he gets in, and we get in, and we drive along the road, to show him to one of the railway clerks that was hid in the public-house window to identify him. But the clerk was bothered, and didn't know whether it was him, or wasn't — because the reason why? I'll tell you, on account of his having shaved his whiskers. "It's a clever little horse," he says, "and trots well; and the shay runs light." "Not a doubt about it," I says. "And now, Mr Fikey, I may as well make it all right, without wasting any more of your time. The fact is, I'm Inspector Wield, and you're my prisoner." "You don't mean that?" he says. "I do, indeed." "Then burn my body," says Fikey, "if this ain't *too* bad!"

'Perhaps you never saw a man so knocked over with surprise. "I hope you'll let me have my coat?" he says. "By all means." "Well, then, let's drive to the factory." "Why, not exactly that, I think," said I; "I've been there, once before, today. Suppose we send for it." He saw it was no go so he sent for it, and put it on, and we drove him up to London, comfortable.'

This reminiscence is in the height of its success, when a general proposal is made to the fresh-complexioned, smooth-faced officer, with the strange air of simplicity, to tell the 'Butcher's story.' But we must reserve the Butcher's story, together with another not less curious in its way, for a concluding paper.

* Give a bill.

51

A Detective Police Party (II)

Household Words, 10 August 1850 (leading article) (*RP* as 'The Detective Police')

This is a straight continuation of article 50. Dickens visited the Tombs Prison in New York in 1842 and described it, very unfavourably, in *American Notes* ('a dismal-fronted pile of bastard Egyptian, like an enchanter's palace in a melodrama'), hence the allusion on p. 281.

The fresh-complexioned, smooth-faced officer, with the strange air of simplicity, began, with a rustic smile, and in a soft, wheedling tone of voice, to relate the Butcher's Story, thus:

'It's just about six years ago, now, since information was given at Scotland Yard of there being extensive robberies of lawns and silks going on, at some wholesale houses in the City. Directions were given for the business being looked into; and Straw, and Fendall, and me, we were all in it.'

'When you received your instructions,' said we, 'you went away, and held a sort of Cabinet Council together?'

The smooth-faced officer coaxingly replied, 'Ye-es. Just so. We turned it over among ourselves a good deal. It appeared, when we went into it, that the goods were sold by the receivers extraordinarily cheap – much cheaper than they could have been if they had been honestly come by. The receivers were in the trade, and kept capital shops – establishments of the first respectability – one of 'em at the West End, one down in Westminster. After a lot of watching and inquiry, and this and that among ourselves, we found that the job was managed, and the purchases of the stolen goods made, at a little public-house near Smithfield, down by Saint Bartholomew's; where the Warehouse Porters, who were the thieves, took 'em for that purpose, don't you see? and made appointments to meet the people that went between themselves and the receivers. This public-house was principally used by journeymen butchers from the country, out of place, and in want of situations; so, what did we do, but – ha, ha, ha! – we agreed that I should be dressed up like a butcher myself, and go and live there!'

Never, surely, was a faculty of observation better brought to bear upon a purpose, than that which picked out this officer for the part. Nothing in all creation, could have suited him better. Even while he spoke, he became a greasy, sleepy, shy, good-natured, chuckle-headed, unsuspicious, and confiding young butcher. His very hair seemed to have suet in it, as he made it smooth upon his head, and his fresh complexion to be lubricated by large quantities of animal food.

—'So I – ha, ha, ha!' (always with the confiding snigger of the foolish young butcher) 'so I dressed myself in the regular way, made up a little bundle of clothes, and went to the public-house, and asked if I could have a lodging there? They says, "yes, you can have a lodging here," and I got a bedroom, and settled myself down in the tap. There was a number of people about the place, and coming backwards and forwards to the house; and first one says, and then another says, "Are you from the country, young man?" "Yes," I says, "I am. I'm come out of Northamptonshire, and I'm quite lonely here, for I don't know London at all, and it's such a mighty big town?" "It *is* a big town," they says. "Oh, it's a *very* big town!" I says. "Really and truly I never was in such a town. It quite confuses of me!" – and all that, you know.

'When some of the Journeymen Butchers that used the house found that I wanted a place, they says, "Oh, we'll get you a place!" And they actually took me to a sight of places, in Newgate market, Newport Market, Clare, Carnaby – I don't know where all. But the wages was – ha, ha, ha! – was not sufficient, and I never could suit myself, don't you see? Some of the queer frequenters of the house, were a little suspicious of me at first, and I was obliged to be very cautious indeed, how I communicated with Straw or Fendall. Sometimes, when I went out, pretending to stop and look into the shop-windows, and just casting my eye round, I used to see some of 'em following me; but, being perhaps better accustomed than they thought for, to that sort of thing, I used to lead 'em on as far as I thought necessary or convenient – sometimes a long way – and then turn sharp round, and meet 'em, and say, "Oh, dear, how glad I am to come upon you so fortunate! This London's such a place, I'm blowed if I an't lost again!" And then we'd go back all together, to the public-house, and – ha, ha, ha! and smoke our pipes, don't you see?

'They were very attentive to me, I am sure. It was a common thing, while I was living there, for some of 'em to take me out, and show me London. They showed me the Prisons – showed me Newgate – and when they showed me Newgate, I stops at the place where the Porters pitch their loads, and says, "Oh dear," "is this where they hang the men! Oh Lor!" "That!" they says, "what a simple cove he is! *That* ain't it!" And then, they pointed out which *was* it, and I says "Lor!" and they says, "Now you'll know it agen, won't you?" And I said I thought I should if I tried hard – and I assure you I kept a sharp look out for the

City Police when we were out in this way, for if any of 'em had happened to know me, and had spoke to me, it would have been all up in a minute. However, by good luck such a thing never happened, and all went on quiet: though the difficulties I had in communicating with my brother officers were quite extraordinary.

'The stolen goods that were brought to the public-house, by the Warehouse Porters, were always disposed of in a back parlor. For a long time, I never could get into this parlor, or see what was done there. As I sat smoking my pipe, like an innocent young chap, by the tap-room fire, I'd hear some of the parties to the robbery, as they came in and out, say softly to the landlord, "Who's that? What does *he* do here?" "Bless your soul," says the landlord, "He's only a' – ha, ha, ha! – "he's only a green young fellow from the country, as is looking for a butcher's sitiwation. Don't mind *him!*" So, in course of time, they were so convinced of my being green, and got to be so accustomed to me, that I was as free of the parlor as any of 'em, and I have seen as much as Seventy Pounds worth of fine lawn sold there, in one night, that was stolen from a warehouse in Friday Street. After the sale, the buyers always stood treat – hot supper, or dinner, or what not – and they'd say on those occasions, "Come on, Butcher! Put your best leg foremost, young'un, and walk into it!" Which I used to do – and hear, at table, all manner of particulars that it was very important for us Detectives to know.

'This went on for ten weeks. I lived in the public-house all the time, and never was out of the Butcher's dress – except in bed. At last, when I had followed seven of the thieves, and set 'em to rights – that's an expression of ours, don't you see, by which I mean to say that I traced 'em, and found out where the robberies were done, and all about 'em – Straw, and Fendall, and I, gave one another the office, and at a time agreed upon, a descent was made upon the public-house, and the apprehensions effected. One of the first things the officers did, was to collar me – for the parties to the robbery wasn't to suppose yet, that I was anything but a Butcher – on which the landlord cries out, "Don't take *him*," he says, "whatever you do! He's only a poor young chap from the country and butter wouldn't melt in his mouth!" However, they – ha, ha, ha! – they took me, and pretended to search my bedroom, where nothing was found but an old fiddle belonging to the landlord, that had got there somehow or another. But, it entirely changed the landlord's opinion, for when it was produced, he says "My fiddle! The Butcher's a purloiner! I give him into custody for the robbery of a musical instrument!"

'The man that had stolen the goods in Friday Street was not taken yet. He had told me, in confidence, that he had his suspicions there was something wrong (on account of the City Police having captured one of the party), and that he was going to make himself scarce. I asked him, "Where do you mean to go, Mr Shepherdson?" "Why, Butcher," says he, "the Setting Moon, in the Commercial Road, is a snug house and I shall hang out there for a time. I shall call myself Simpson, which appears to me to be a modest sort of a name. Perhaps you'll give us a look in, Butcher?" "Well," says I, "I think I *will* give you a call" – which I fully intended, don't you see, because, of course, he was to be taken! I went over to the Setting Moon next day, with a brother officer, and asked at the bar for Simpson. They pointed out his room, upstairs. As we were going up, he looks down over the bannisters, and calls out, "Halloa, Butcher! is that you?" "Yes, it's me. How do you find yourself?" "Bobbish," he says; "but who's that with you?" "It's only a young man, that's a friend of mine," I says. "Come along, then," says he; "any friend of the Butcher's is as welcome as the Butcher!" So, I made my friend acquainted with him, and we took him into custody.

'You have no idea, Sir, what a sight it was, in Court, when they first knew that I wasn't a Butcher, after all! I wasn't produced at the first examination, when there was a remand; but I was, at the second. And when I stepped into the box, in full police uniform, and the whole party saw how they had been done, actually a groan of horror and dismay proceeded from 'em in the dock!

'At the Old Bailey, when their trials came on, Mr Clarkson was engaged for the defence, and he *couldn't* make out how it was, about the Butcher. He thought, all along, it was a real Butcher. When the counsel for the prosecution said, "I will now call before you, gentlemen, the Police-officer," meaning myself, Mr Clarkson says, "Why Police-officer? Why more Police-officers? I don't want Police. We have had a great deal too much of the Police. I want the Butcher!" However, Sir, he had the Butcher and the Police-officer, both in one. Out of seven prisoners committed for trial, five were found guilty, and some of 'em were transported. The respectable firm at the West End got a term of imprisonment; and that's the Butcher's Story!'

The story done, the chuckle-headed Butcher again resolved himself into the smooth-faced Detective. But, he was so extremely tickled by their having taken him about, when he was that Dragon in disguise, to show him London, that he could not help reverting to that point in his narrative; and gently repeating, with the Butcher snigger, ' "Oh, dear!" I says, "is that where they hang the men? Oh, Lor!" "*That!*" says they. "What a simple cove he is!" '

It being now late, and the party very modest in their fear of being too diffuse, there were some tokens of separation; when Serjeant Dornton, the soldierly-looking man, said, looking round him with a smile:

'Before we break up, Sir, perhaps you might have some amusement in hearing of the Adventures of a Carpet Bag. They are very short; and, I think, curious.'

We welcomed the Carpet Bag, as cordially as Mr Shepherdson welcomed the false Butcher at the Setting Moon. Serjeant Dornton proceeded:

'In 1847, I was dispatched to Chatham, in search of one Mesheck, a Jew. He had been carrying on, pretty heavily, in the bill-stealing way, getting acceptances from young men of good connexions (in the army chiefly), on pretence of discount, and bolting with the same.

'Mesheck was off, before I got to Chatham. All I could learn about him was, that he had gone, probably to London, and had with him – a Carpet Bag.

'I came back to town, by the last train from Blackwall, and made inquiries concerning a Jew passenger with – a Carpet Bag.

'The office was shut up, it being the last train. There were only two or three porters left. Looking after a Jew with a Carpet Bag, on the Blackwall Railway, which was then the high road to a great Military Depôt, was worse than looking after a needle in a hayrick. But it happened that one of these porters had carried, for a certain Jew, to a certain public-house, a certain – Carpet Bag.

'I went to the public-house, but the Jew had only left his luggage there for a few hours, and had called for it in a cab, and taken it away. I put such questions there, and to the porter, as I thought prudent, and got at this description of – the Carpet Bag.

'It was a bag which had, on one side of it, worked in worsted, a green parrot on a stand. A green parrot on a stand was the means by which to identify that – Carpet Bag.

'I traced Mesheck, by means of this green parrot on a stand, to Cheltenham, to Birmingham, to Liverpool, to the Atlantic Ocean. At Liverpool he was too many for me. He had gone to the United States, and I gave up all thoughts of Mesheck, and likewise of his – Carpet Bag.

'Many months afterwards – near a year afterwards – there was a Bank in Ireland robbed of seven thousand pounds, by a person of the name of Doctor Dundey, who escaped to America; from which country some of the stolen notes came home. He was supposed to have bought a farm in New Jersey. Under proper management, that estate could be seized and sold, for the benefit of the parties he had defrauded. I was sent off to America for this purpose.

'I landed at Boston. I went on to New York. I found that he had lately changed New York paper-money for New Jersey paper-money, and had banked cash in New Brunswick. To take this Doctor Dundey, it was necessary to entrap him into the State of New York, which required a deal of artifice and trouble. At one time, he couldn't be drawn into an appointment. At another time, he appointed to come to meet me, and a New York officer, on a pretext I made; and then his children had the measles. At last, he came, per steamboat, and I took him, and lodged him in a New York Prison called the Tombs; which I dare say you know, Sir?'

Editorial acknowledgment to that effect.

'I went to the Tombs, on the morning after his capture, to attend the examination before the magistrate. I was passing through the magistrate's private room, when, happening to look round me to take notice of the place, as we generally have a habit of doing, I clapped my eyes, in one corner, on a – Carpet Bag.

'What did I see upon that Carpet Bag, if you'll believe me, but a green parrot on a stand, as large as life!

' "That Carpet Bag, with the representation of a green parrot on a stand," said I, "belongs to an English Jew, named Aaron Mesheck, and to no other man, alive or dead!"

'I give you my word the New York Police officers were doubled up with surprise.

' "How do you ever come to know that?" said they.

' "I think I ought to know that green parrot by this time," said I; "for I have had as pretty a dance after that bird, at home, as ever I had, in all my life!" '

'And *was* it Mesheck's?' we submissively inquired.

'Was it, Sir? Of course it was! He was in custody for another offence, in that very identical Tombs, at that very identical time. And, more than that! Some memoranda, relating to the fraud for which I had vainly endeavoured to take him, were found to be, at that moment, lying in that very same individual – Carpet Bag!'

Such are the curious coincidences and such is the peculiar ability, always sharpening and being improved by practice, and always adapting itself to every variety of circumstances, and opposing itself to every new device that perverted ingenuity can invent, for which this important social branch of the public service is remarkable! For ever on the watch, with their wits stretched to the utmost, these officers have, from day to day and year to year, to set themselves against every novelty of trickery and dexterity that the combined imaginations of all the lawless rascals in England can devise, and to keep pace with every such invention that comes out. In the Courts of Justice, the materials of thousands of such stories as we have narrated – often elevated into the marvellous and romantic, by the circumstances of the case – are dryly compressed into the set phrase, 'in consequence of information I received, I did so and so,' Suspicion was to be directed, by careful inference and deduction, upon the right person; the right person was to be taken, wherever he had gone, or whatever he was doing to avoid detection: he is taken; there he is at the bar; that is enough. From information I, the officer, received, I did it; and, according to the custom in these cases, I say no more.

These games of chess, played with live pieces, are played before small audiences, and are chronicled nowhere. The interest of the game supports the player. Its results are enough for Justice. To compare great things with small, suppose LEVERRIER or ADAMS informing the public that from information he had received he had discovered a new planet; or COLUMBUS informing the public of his day that from information he had received, he had discovered a new continent; so the Detectives inform it that they have discovered a new fraud or an old offender, and the process is unknown.

Thus, at midnight, closed the proceedings of our curious and interesting party. But one other circumstance finally wound up the evening, after our Detective guests had left us. One of the sharpest among them, and the officer best acquainted with the Swell Mob, had his pocket picked, going home!

Dickens wrote up yet another sequence of detective reminiscences which was published as the lead article under the title 'Three "Detective" Anecdotes' in *HW*, 14 September 1850, and later collected in *RP*. Two are told by 'Inspector Wield', one of them relating to the famous Waterloo Road murder (May 1838) of a prostitute called Eliza Grimwood, and the third is told by 'Sergeant Dornton'. For detailed discussion of Field's two anecdotes, see W. Long, 'The "Singler Stories" of Inspector Field', *The Dickensian*, Vol. 83 (1987), pp. 153–62.

52

Chips: The Individuality of Locomotives

Household Words, 21 September 1850

In the fifteenth number of *HW* (6 July 1850) Dickens introduced a new feature called 'Chips' ('There is a saying that a good workman is known by his chips. Such a prodigious accumulation of chips takes place in our Manufactory, that we infer we must have some first-rate workmen about us ...'). 'Chips' was to consist of short pieces (they would vary from a quarter of a column to four columns in length) on all sorts of topics, contributed by Wills and other staff writers as well as by others, and – very occasionally – by Dickens himself. The total number of Dickens 'Chips' in *MP* is six and the one reprinted below is the only imaginative one. This feature appeared irregularly (less frequently in later volumes) and could be used to add a footnote or a correction to an article in an earlier issue (for an example, see p. 257). Mainly, however, it was devoted to the presentation of curious facts and anecdotes about the natural world, scientific or historical titbits, notes on aspects of contemporary life at home and overseas, and so on. Matters in which *HW* took a keen interest, such as emigration to Australia and cruelty to livestock, naturally tended to crop up fairly often.

It is a remarkable truth, and, well applied, it might be profitable to us, in helping us to make fair allowance for the differences between the temperaments of different men – that every Locomotive Engine running on a Railway, has a distinct individuality and character of its own.

It is perfectly well known to experienced practical engineers, that if a dozen different Locomotive Engines were made, at the same time, of the same power, for the same purpose, of like materials, in the same factory – each of those Locomotive Engines would come out with its own peculiar whims and ways, only ascertainable by experience. One engine will take a great meal of coke and water at once; another will not hear of such a thing, but will insist on being coaxed by spades-full and buckets-full. One is disposed to start off, when required, at the top of his speed; another must have a little time to warm at his work, and to get well into it. These peculiarities are so accurately mastered by skilful drivers, that only particular men can persuade particular engines to do their best. It would seem as if some of these 'excellent monsters' declared, on being brought out of the stable, 'If it's Smith who is to drive me, I won't go. If it's my friend Stokes, I am agreeable to anything!'

All Locomotive Engines are low-spirited in damp and foggy weather. They have a great satisfaction in their work when the air is crisp and frosty. At such a time they are very cheerful and brisk; but they strongly object to haze and Scotch mists. These are points of character on which they are all united. It is in their peculiarities and varieties of character that they are most remarkable.

The Railway Company who should consign all their Locomotives to one uniform standard of treatment, without any allowance for varying shades of character and opinion, would soon fall as much behind-hand in the world as those greater Governments are, and ever will be, who pursue the same course with the finer piece of work called Man.

53

A Poor Man's Tale of a Patent

Household Words, 19 October 1850 (leading article) *(RP)*

For the detailed background to this anticipation of the great Circumlocution Office satire in *Little Dorrit*, see N. Davenport, *The United Kingdom Patent System: A Brief History with Bibliography* (1979). On pp. 15–17 Davenport, who quotes Dickens, sets out the stages of obtaining a patent in 1850, together with the fees payable at each stage, and notes that 'it normally took six to eight weeks to obtain an English patent by this procedure' at a total cost of £94 17s 0d (= £94.85). This gave protection in England and Wales only; full UK patenting cost £310 and 'If, as likely, the inventor employed an agent to help him through the maze of procedures, the cost was considerably more.' The Patent Law Amendment Act of 1852 ameliorated the situation by establishing the Patent Office as a single office where all the procedures could be carried out under the control of the Commissioners of Patents. It also considerably reduced the costs (one patent now gave protection for the whole of the UK), though this was offset by the introduction of new fees payable to keep the patent in force. An article by the miscellaneous writer and regular *HW* contributor George Dodd, entitled 'A Room Near Chancery Lane' and published in *HW* on 21 February 1857 (Vol. XV, pp. 190–2), welcomed the reforms brought about by the 1852 Act, noting, however, that 'it does not sever us from contact with routine and red tape, but it renders [them] less obstructive and annoying than before'.

The conception of the inventor Daniel Doyce in *Little Dorrit* (1855–7) and his ordeal by bureaucracy is clearly related to the following narrative. Humphry House notes (*The Dickens World* [1960 edn], p. 175) that Doyce's troubles 'were rather out of date when they were published', but of course Dickens sets the action of the novel thirty years before the time of writing.

The reference to 'Physical force' Chartists in paragraph 5 is to that branch of the Chartist movement associated with Feargus O'Connor, a branch that believed in what we should now call 'direct action' and was one of the greatest bogeys of the early Victorian middle classes. By 1850, however, Chartism was generally on the decline following the fiasco of 1848.

I am not used to writing for print. What working-man that never labours less (some Mondays, and Christmas Time and Easter Time, excepted) than twelve or fourteen hour a day, is? But I have been asked to put down, plain, what I have got to say; and so I take pen-and-ink, and do it to the best of my power, hoping defects will find excuse.

I was born, nigh London, but have worked in a shop at Birmingham (what you would call Manufactories, we call Shops), almost ever since I was out of my time. I served my apprenticeship at Deptford, nigh where I was born, and I am a smith by trade. My name is John. I have been called 'Old John' ever since I was nineteen year of age, on account of not having much hair. I am fifty-six year of age at the present time, and I don't find myself with more hair, nor yet with less, to signify, than at nineteen year of age aforesaid.

I have been married five and thirty years, come next April. I was married on All Fools' Day. Let them laugh that win. I won a good wife that day, and it was as sensible a day to me, as ever I had.

We have had a matter of ten children, six whereof are living. My eldest son is engineer in the Italian steam-packet, 'Mezzo Giorno, plying between Marseilles and Naples, and calling at Genoa, Leghorn, and Civita Vecchia.' He was a good workman. He invented a many useful little things that brought him in – nothing. I have two sons doing well at Sydney, New South Wales – single, when last heard from. One of my sons (James) went wild and for a soldier, where he was shot in India, living six weeks in hospital with a musket ball lodged in his shoulder-blade, which he wrote with his own hand. He was the best looking. One of my two daughters (Mary) is comfortable in her circumstances, but water on the chest. The other (Charlotte), her husband run away from her in the basest manner, and she and her three children live with us. The youngest, six year old, has a turn for mechanics.

I am not a Chartist, and I never was. I don't mean to say but what I see a good many public points to complain of, still I don't think that's the way to set them right. If I did think so, I should be a Chartist. But I don't think so, and I am not a Chartist. I read the paper, and hear discussion, at what we call 'a parlor' in Birmingham, and I know many good men and workmen who are Chartists. Note. Not Physical force.

It won't be took as boastful in me, if I make the remark (for I can't put down what I have got to say, without putting that down before going any further), that I have always been of an ingenious turn. I once got

'A Poor Man's Tale of a Patent' by Fred Walker.

twenty pound by a screw, and it's in use now. I have been twenty year, off and on, completing an Invention and perfecting it. I perfected of it, last Christmas Eve at ten o'clock at night. Me and my wife stood and let some tears fall over the Model, when it was done and I brought her in to take a look at it.

A friend of mine, by the name of William Butcher, is a Chartist. Moderate. He is a good speaker. He is very animated. I have often heard him deliver that what is, at every turn, in the way of us working-men, is, that too many places have been made, in the course of time, to provide for people that never ought to have been provided for; and that we have to obey forms and to pay fees to support those places when we shouldn't ought. 'True,' (delivers William Butcher), 'all the public has to do this, but it falls heaviest on the working man, because he has least to spare; and likewise because impediments shouldn't be put in his way, when he wants redress of wrong, or furtherance of right.' Note. I have wrote down those words from William Butcher's own mouth. W. B. delivering them fresh for the aforesaid purpose.

Now, to my Model again. There it was, perfected of, on Christmas Eve, gone nigh a year, at ten o'clock at night. All the money I could spare I had laid out upon the Model; and when times was bad, or my daughter Charlotte's children sickly, or both, it had stood still, months at a spell. I had pulled it to pieces, and made it over again with improvements, I don't know how often. There it stood, at last, a perfected Model as aforesaid.

William Butcher and me had a long talk, Christmas Day, respecting of the Model. William is very sensible. But sometimes cranky. William said, 'What will you do with it, John?' I said, 'Patent it.' William said, 'How Patent it, John?' I said, 'By taking out a Patent.' William then delivered that the law of Patent was a cruel wrong. William said, 'John, if you make your invention public, before you get a Patent, anyone may rob you of the fruits of your hard work. You are put in a cleft stick, John. Either you must drive a bargain very much against yourself, by getting a party to come forward beforehand with the great expenses of the Patent; or, you must be put about, from post to pillar, among so many parties, trying to make a better bargain for yourself, and showing your invention, that your invention will be took from you over your head.' I said, 'William Butcher, are you cranky? You are sometimes cranky.' William said, 'No John, I tell you the truth;' which he then delivered more at length. I said to W. B. I would Patent the invention myself.

My wife's brother, George Bury of West Bromwich (his wife unfortunately took to drinking, made away with everything, and seventeen times committed to Birmingham Jail before happy release in every point of view), left my wife, his sister, when he died, a legacy of one hundred and twenty-eight pound ten, Bank of England Stocks. Me and my wife had never broke into that money yet. Note. We might come to be old, and past our work. We now agreed to Patent the invention. We said we would make a hole in it – I mean in the aforesaid money – and Patent the invention. William Butcher wrote me a letter to Thomas Joy, in London. T. J. is a carpenter; six foot four in height, and plays quoits well. He lives in Chelsea, London, by the church. I got leave from the shop, to be took on again when I come back. I am a good workman. Not a Teetotaller; but never drunk. When the Christmas holidays were over, I went up to London by the Parliamentary Train, and hired a lodging for a week with Thomas Joy. He is married. He has one son gone to sea.

Thomas Joy delivered (from a book he had) that the first step to be took, in Patenting the invention, was to prepare a petition unto Queen Victoria. William Butcher had delivered similar, and drawn it up. Note, William is a ready writer. A declaration before a Master in Chancery was to be added to it. That, we likewise drew up. After a deal of trouble I found out a Master, in Southampton Buildings, Chancery Lane, nigh Temple Bar, where I made the declaration, and paid eighteenpence. I was told to take the declaration and petition to the Home Office, in Whitehall, where I left it to be signed by the Home Secretary (after I had found the office out) and where I paid two pound, two, and sixpence. In six days he signed it, and I was told to take it to the Attorney-general's chambers, and leave it there for a report. I did so, and paid four pound, four. Note. Nobody, all through, ever thankful for their money, but all uncivil.

My lodging at Thomas Joy's was now hired for another week, whereof five days were gone. The Attorney-General made what they called a Report-of-course (my invention being, as William Butcher had delivered before starting, unopposed), and I was sent back with it to the Home Office. They made a Copy of it, which was called a Warrant. For this warrant, I paid seven pound, thirteen, and six. It was sent to the Queen, to sign. The Queen sent it back, signed. The Home Secretary signed it again. The gentleman throwed it at me when I called, and said, 'Now take it to the Patent Office in Lincoln's Inn.' I was then in my third week at Thomas Joy's, living very sparing, on account of fees. I found myself losing heart.

At the Patent Office in Lincoln's Inn, they made 'a draft of the Queen's bill,' of my invention and a 'docket of the bill.' I paid five pound, ten, and six, for this. They 'engrossed two copies of the bill; one for the Signet Office, and one for the Privy-Seal Office.' I paid one pound, seven, and six, for this. Stamp duty over and above, three pound.

The Engrossing Clerk of the same office engrossed the Queen's bill for signature. I paid him one pound, one. Stamp-duty, again, one pound, ten. I was next to take the Queen's bill to the Attorney-General again, and get it signed again. I took it, and paid five pound more. I fetched it away, and took it to the Home Secretary again. He sent it to the Queen again. She signed it again. I paid seven pound, thirteen, and six, more, for this. I had been over a month at Thomas Joy's. I was quite wore out, patience and pocket.

Thomas Joy delivered all this, as it went on, to William Butcher. William Butcher delivered it again to three Birmingham Parlors, from which it got to all the other Parlors, and was took, as I have been told since, right through all the shops in the North of England. Note. William Butcher delivered, at his Parlor, in a speech, that it was a Patent way of making Chartists.

But I hadn't nigh done yet. The Queen's bill was to be took to the Signet Office in Somerset House, Strand – where the stamp shop is. The Clerk of the Signet made 'a Signet bill for the Lord Keeper of the Privy Seal.' I paid him four pound, seven. The Clerk of the Lord Keeper of the Privy Seal made, 'a Privy-Seal bill for the Lord Chancellor.' I paid him, four pound, two. The Privy-Seal bill was handed over to the Clerk of the Patents, who engrossed the aforesaid. I paid him five pound, seventeen, and eight; at the same time, I paid Stamp-duty for the Patent, in one lump, thirty pound. I next paid for 'boxes for the Patent,' nine and sixpence. Note. Thomas Joy would have made the same at a profit for eighteen-pence. I next paid 'fees to the Deputy, the Lord Chancellor's Purse-bearer,' two pound, two. I next paid 'fees to the Clerk of the Hanaper,' seven pound, thirteen. I next paid 'fees to the Deputy Clerk of the Hanaper,' ten shillings. I next paid to the Lord Chancellor again, one pound, eleven, and six. Last of all, I paid 'fees to the Deputy Sealer, and Deputy Chaff-Wax,' ten shillings and sixpence. I had lodged at Thomas Joy's over six weeks, and the unopposed Patent for my invention, for England only, had cost me ninety-six pound, seven, and eightpence. If I had taken it out for the United Kingdom, it would have cost me more than three hundred pound.

Now, teaching had not come up but very limited when I was young. So much the worse for me you'll say. I say the same. William Butcher is twenty year younger than me. He knows a hundred year more. If William Butcher had wanted to Patent an invention, he might have been sharper than myself when hustled backwards and forwards among all those offices, though I doubt if so patient. Note. William being sometimes cranky, and consider Porters, Messengers, and Clerks.

Thereby I say nothing of my being tired of my life, while I was Patenting my invention. But I put this: Is it reasonable to make a man feel as if, in inventing an ingenious improvement meant to do good, he had done something wrong? How else can a man feel, when he is met by such difficulties at every turn? All inventors taking out a Patent MUST feel so. And look at the expense. How hard on me, and how hard on the country if there's any merit in me (and my invention is took up now, I am thankful to say, and doing well), to put me to all that expense before I can move a finger! Make the addition yourself, and it'll come to ninety-six pound, seven, and eightpence. No more, and no less.

What can I say against William Butcher, about places? Look at the Home Secretary, the Attorney-General, the Patent Office, the Engrossing Clerk, the Lord Chancellor, the Privy Seal, the Clerk of the Patents, the Lord Chancellor's Purse-bearer, the Clerk of the Hanaper, the Deputy Clerk of the Hanaper, the Deputy Sealer, and the Deputy Chaff-wax. No man in England could get a Patent for an India-rubber band, or an iron hoop, without feeing all of them. Some of them, over and over again. I went through thirty-five stages. I began with the Queen upon the Throne. I ended with the Deputy Chaff-wax. Note. I should like to see the Deputy Chaff-wax. Is it a man, or what is it?

What I had to tell, I have told. I have wrote it down. I hope it's plain. Not so much in the handwriting (though nothing to boast of there), as in the sense of it. I will now conclude with Thomas Joy. Thomas said to me, when we parted, 'John, if the laws of this country were as honest as they ought to be, you would have come to London – registered an exact description and drawing of your invention – paid half-a-crown or so for doing of it – and therein and thereby have got your Patent.'

My opinion is the same as Thomas Joy. Further. In William Butcher's delivering 'that the whole gang of Hanapers and Chaff-waxes must be done away with, and that England has been chaffed and waxed sufficient,' I agree.

54

Lively Turtle

Household Words, 26 October 1850 (leading article)

The Aldermen of the Court of Common Council, the governing body of the City of London, had long been the butt of jokes in *Punch* and other satirical papers for their reactionary stupidity and complacency and their gormandising feasts (always involving turtle soup). Their strenuous opposition to the application to the City of the Public Health Act of 1848, and to the removal of Smithfield Meat market from the city centre, particularly angered Dickens. On 12 July he noticed a report in *The Times* (which was also campaigning for the removal of Smithfield) of 'a most intolerably asinine Speech about Smithfield, made in the Common Council by one Taylor' and asked Wills to get him further material about 'absurdities enunciated by this wiseacre' so that he could write up something about him for *HW* (*Pilgrim*, Vol. VI, p. 129). Snoady's wonderful vision of Alderman Groggles as a 'lively turtle' is the result.

How closely Dickens catches the very accent of the sort of Common Councilman's speech he is here mocking can be seen by a comparison of Snoady's rhetoric with the *Times* report (12 July 1850, p. 8, col. 3) of Taylor's speech. Taylor, a wholesale ironmonger and Chairman of the Markets Improvement Committee, said in the course of his speech against the proposal to move Smithfield:

> It was sought to make the city adopt the continental system, and have abattoirs. Now, he would prefer to remain English. (Cheers.) He did not want to go to France to learn how to live. (Continued cheering.) The citizens of London did not want to have any trees of liberty planted in Cheapside. (Loud cheers.) They would rather remain as they are. ... It was notorious that the people in France lived on soup made of very poor beef (Mr G. Taylor – 'Frogs, too'). ...

Concerning the Smithfield debate, see further headnote to article 60.

Literary allusions (p. 292) 'The Negro is a man and a brother': in propaganda pamphlets of the Anti-Slavery Society a picture of a slave being whipped was captioned, 'Am I not a man and a brother?'; (p. 293) 'whatever is, is right': Pope, *An Essay on Man*, Ep. i, 1. 294; (p. 293) 'the whole duty of man': title of a famous devotional work by Richard Allestree (1680); (p. 294) 'Rule Britannia ...': James Thomson, *Alfred*, Act 2, scene the last (1740).

I have a comfortable property. What I spend, I spend upon myself; and what I don't spend I save. Those are my principles. I am warmly attached to my principles, and stick to them on all occasions.

I am not, as some people have represented, a mean man. I never denied myself anything that I thought I should like to have. I may have said to myself 'Snoady' – that is my name – 'you will get those peaches cheaper if you wait till next week'; or, I may have said to myself, 'Snoady, you will get that wine for nothing, if you wait till you are asked out to dine;' but I never deny myself anything. If I can't get what I want without buying it, and paying its price for it, I *do* buy it and pay its price for it. I have an appetite bestowed upon me; and, if I baulked it, I should consider that I was flying in the face of Providence.

I have no near relation but a brother. If he wants anything of me, he don't get it. All men are my brothers; and I see no reason why I should make his, an exceptional case.

I live at a cathedral town where there is an old corporation. I am not in the Church, but it may be that I hold a little place of some sort. Never mind. It may be profitable. Perhaps yes, perhaps no. It may, or it may not, be a sinecure. I don't choose to say. I never enlightened my brother on these subjects, and I consider all men my brothers. The Negro is a man and a brother – should I hold myself accountable for my position in life, *to him?* Certainly not.

I often run up to London. I like London. The way I look at it, is this. London is not a cheap place, but, on the whole, you can get more of the real thing for your money there – I mean the best thing, whatever it is – than you can get in most places. Therefore, I say to the man who has got the money, and wants the thing, 'Go to London for it, and treat yourself.'

When *I* go, I do it in this manner. I go to Mrs Skim's Private Hotel and Commercial Lodging House, near Aldersgate Street, City (it is advertised in 'Bradshaw's Railway Guide,' where I first found it), and there I pay, 'for bed and breakfast, with meat, two and ninepence per day, including servants.' Now, I have made a calculation, and I am satisfied that Mrs Skim cannot possibly make much profit out of *me.* In fact, if all her patrons were like me, my opinion is, the woman would be in the Gazette next month.

Why do I go to Mrs Skim's when I could go to the Clarendon, you may ask? Let us argue that point. If I went to the Clarendon I could get nothing in bed but sleep; could I? No. Now, sleep at the Clarendon is an expensive article; whereas sleep, at Mrs Skim's, is decidedly cheap. I have made a calculation, and I don't hesitate to say, all things considered, that it's cheap. Is it an inferior article, as compared with the Clarendon sleep, or is it of the same quality? I am a heavy sleeper, and it is of the same quality. Then why should I go to the Clarendon?

But as to breakfast? you may say. – Very well. As to breakfast. I could get a variety of delicacies for breakfast at the Clarendon, that are out of the question at Mrs Skim's. Granted. But I don't want to have them! My opinion is, that we are not entirely animal and sensual. Man has an intellect bestowed upon him. If he clogs that intellect by too good a breakfast, how can he properly exert that intellect in meditation, during the day, upon his dinner? That's the point. We are not to enchain the soul. We are to let it soar. It is expected of us.

At Mrs Skim's, I get enough for breakfast (there is no limitation to the bread and butter, though there is to the meat) and not too much. I have all my faculties about me, to concentrate upon the object I have mentioned, and I can say to myself besides, 'Snoady, you have saved six, eight, ten, fifteen, shillings, already today. If there is anything you fancy for your dinner, have it. Snoady, you have earned your reward.'

My objection to London, is, that it is the headquarters of the worst radical sentiments that are broached in England. I consider that it has a great many dangerous people in it. I consider the present publication (if it's 'Household Words') very dangerous, and I write this with the view of neutralising some of its bad effects. My political creed is, let us be comfortable. We are all very comfortable as we are – *I* am very comfortable as I am – leave us alone!

All mankind are my brothers, and I don't think it Christian – if you come to that – to tell my brother that he is ignorant, or degraded, or dirty, or anything of the kind. I think it's abusive, and low. You meet me with the observation that I am required to love my brother. I reply, 'I do.' I am sure I am always willing to say to my brother, 'My good fellow, I love you very much; go along with you; keep to your own road; leave me to mine; whatever is, is right; whatever isn't, is wrong; don't make a disturbance!' It seems to me, that this is at once the whole duty of man, and the only temper to go to dinner in.

Going to dinner in this temper in the City of London, one day not long ago, after a bed at Mrs Skim's, with meat-breakfast and servants included, I was reminded of the observation which, if my memory does not deceive me, was formerly made by somebody on some occasion, that man may learn wisdom from the lower animals. It is a beautiful fact, in my opinion, that great wisdom is to be learnt from that noble animal the Turtle.

I had made up my mind, in the course of the day I speak of, to have a Turtle dinner. I mean a dinner mainly composed of Turtle. Just a comfortable tureen of soup, with a pint of punch; and nothing solid to follow, but a tender juicy steak. I like a tender juicy steak. I generally say to myself when I order one, 'Snoady, you have done right.'

When I make up my mind to have a delicacy, expense is no consideration. The question resolves itself, then, into a question of the very best. I went to a friend of mine who is a Member of the Common Council, and with that friend I held the following conversation.

Said I to him, 'Mr Groggles, the best Turtle is where?'

Says he, 'If you want a basin for lunch, my opinion is, you can't do better than drop into Birch's.'

Said I, 'Mr Groggles, I thought you had known me better, than to suppose me capable of a basin. My intention is to dine. A tureen.'

Says Mr Groggles, without a moment's consideration, and in a determined voice, 'Right opposite the India House, Leadenhall Street.'

We parted. My mind was not inactive during the day, and at six in the afternoon I repaired to the house of Mr Groggles's recommendation. At the end of the passage, leading from the street into the coffee-room, I observed a vast and solid chest, in which I then supposed that a Turtle of unusual size might be deposited. But, the correspondence between its bulk and that of the charge made for my dinner, afterwards satisfied me that it must be the till of the establishment.

I stated to the waiter what had brought me there, and I mentioned Mr Groggles's name. He feelingly repeated after me, 'A tureen of Turtle, and a tender juicy steak.' His manner, added to the manner of Mr Groggles in the morning, satisfied me that all was well. The atmosphere of the coffee-room was odoriferous with Turtle, and the steams of thousands of gallons, consumed within its walls, hung, in savoury grease, upon their surface. I could have inscribed my name with a penknife, if I had been so disposed, in the essence of innumerable Turtles. I preferred to fall into a hungry reverie, brought on by the warm breath of the place, and to think of the West Indies and the Island of Ascension.

My dinner came – and went. I will draw a veil over the meal, I will put the cover on the empty tureen, and merely say that it was wonderful – and that I paid for it.

I sat meditating, when all was over, on the imperfect nature of our present existence, in which we can eat only for a limited time, when the waiter roused me with these words.

Said he to me, as he brushed the crumbs off the table, 'Would you like to see the Turtle, Sir?'

'To see what Turtle, waiter?' said I (calmly) to him.

'The tanks of Turtle below, Sir,' said he to me.

Tanks of Turtle! Good Gracious! 'Yes!'

The waiter lighted a candle, and conducted me downstairs to a range of vaulted apartments, cleanly whitewashed and illuminated with gas, where I saw a sight of the most astonishing and gratifying description, illustrative of the greatness of my native country. 'Snoady,' was my first observation to myself, 'Rule Britannia, Britannia rules the waves!'

There were two or three hundred Turtle in the vaulted apartments – all alive. Some in tanks, and some taking the air in long dry walks littered down with straw. They were of all sizes; many of them enormous. Some of the enormous ones had entangled themselves with the smaller ones, and pushed and squeezed themselves into corners, with their fins over water-pipes, and their heads downwards, where they were apoplectically struggling and splashing, apparently in the last extremity. Others were calm at the bottom of the tanks; others languidly rising to the surface. The Turtle in the walks littered down with straw, were calm and motionless. It was a thrilling sight. I admire such a sight. It rouses my imagination. If you wish to try its effect on yours, make a call right opposite the India House any day you please – dine – pay – and ask to be taken below.

Two athletic young men, without coats, and with the sleeves of their shirts tucked up to the shoulders, were in attendance on these noble animals. One of them, wrestling with the most enormous Turtle in company, and dragging him up to the edge of the tank, for me to look at, presented an idea to me which I never had before. I ought to observe that I like an idea. I say, when I get a new one, 'Snoady, book that!'

My idea, on the present occasion, was, – Mr Groggles! It was not a Turtle that I saw, but Mr Groggles. It was the dead image of Mr Groggles. He was dragged up to confront me, with his waistcoat – if I may be allowed the expression – towards me; and it was identically the waistcoat of Mr Groggles. It was the same shape, very nearly the same colour, only wanted a gold watch-chain and a bunch of seals, to BE the waistcoat of Mr Groggles. There was what I should call a bursting expression about him in general, which was accurately the expression of Mr Groggles. I had never closely observed a Turtle's throat before. The folds of his loose cravat, I found to be precisely those of Mr Groggles's cravat. Even the intelligent eye – I mean to say, intelligent enough for a person of correct principles, and not dangerously so – was the eye of Mr Groggles. When the athletic young man let him go, and, with a roll of his head, he flopped heavily down into the tank, it was exactly the manner of Mr Groggles as I have seen him ooze away into his seat, after opposing a sanitary motion in the Court of Common Council!

'Snoady,' I couldn't help saying to myself, 'you have done it. You have got an idea, Snoady, in which a great principle is involved. I congratulate you!' I followed the young man, who dragged up several Turtle to the brinks of the various tanks. I found them all the same – all varieties of Mr Groggles – all extraordinarily like the gentlemen who usually eat them. 'Now, Snoady,' was my next remark, 'what do you deduce from this?'

'Sir,' said I, 'what I deduce from this, is, confusion to those Radicals and other Revolutionists who talk about improvement. Sir,' said I, 'what I deduce from this, is, that there isn't this resemblance between the Turtles and the Groggleses for nothing. It's meant to show mankind that the proper model for a Groggles, is a Turtle; and that the liveliness we want in a Groggles, is the liveliness of a Turtle, and no more.' 'Snoady,' was my reply to this, 'You have hit it. You are right!'

I admired the idea very much, because, if I hate anything in the world, it's change. Change has evidently no business in the world, has nothing to do with it, and isn't intended. What we want is (as I think I have mentioned) to be comfortable. I look at it that way. Let us be comfortable, and leave us alone. Now, when the young man dragged a Groggles – I mean a Turtle – out of his tank, this was exactly what the noble animal expressed as he floundered back again.

I have several friends besides Mr Groggles in the Common Council, and it might be a week after this, when I said, 'Snoady, if I was you, I would go to that court, and hear the debate today.' I went. A good deal of it was what I call a sound, old English discussion. One eloquent speaker objected to the French as wearing wooden shoes; and a friend of his reminded him of another objection to that foreign people, namely, that they eat frogs. I had feared, for many years, I am sorry to say, that these wholesale principles were gone out. How delightful to find them still remaining among the great men of the City of London, in the year one thousand eight hundred and fifty! It made me think of the Lively Turtle.

But, I soon thought more of the Lively Turtle. Some Radicals and Revolutionists have penetrated even to the Common Council – which otherwise I regard as one of the last strongholds of our afflicted constitution; and speeches were made, about removing Smithfield Market – which I consider to be a part of that Constitution – and about appointing a Medical officer for the City, and about preserving the public health; and other treasonable practices, opposed to Church and State. These proposals Mr Groggles, as might have been expected of such a man, resisted; so warmly, that, as I afterwards understood from Mrs Groggles, he had rather a sharp attack of blood to the head that night. All the Groggles party resisted them too, and it was a fine constitutional sight to see waistcoat after waistcoat rise up in resistance of them and subside. But what struck me in the sight was this. 'Snoady,' said I, 'here is your idea carried out, Sir! These Radicals and Revolutionists are the athletic young men in shirt sleeves, dragging the Lively Turtle to the edges of the tank. The Groggleses are the Turtle, looking out for a moment, and flopping down again. Honour to the Groggleses! Honour to the Court of Lively Turtle! The wisdom of the Turtle is the hope of England!'

There are three heads in the moral of what I had to say. First, Turtle and Groggles are identical; wonderfully alike externally, wonderfully alike mentally. Secondly, Turtle is a good thing every way, and the liveliness of the Turtle is intended as an example for the liveliness of man; you are not to go beyond that. Thirdly, we are all quite comfortable. Leave us alone!

55

A Crisis in the Affairs of Mr John Bull,
As Related by Mrs Bull to the Children

Household Words, 23 November 1850 (leading article)

On 29 September 1850 the Pope issued a formal declaration, commonly called a 'bull', restoring the Roman Catholic hierarchy in England, creating Nicholas Wiseman Archbishop of Westminster (Wiseman was also made a cardinal the following day) and establishing twelve bishoprics. On 7 October Wiseman issued his first pastoral letter, 'from out of the Flaminian Gate', to the Catholic clergy of England, the triumphalist tone of which further inflamed Protestant antagonism to what became known as the 'Papal Aggression'. The result was a wave of anti-Catholic hysteria as 'the latent and historic prejudices of the English people rose to the surface' (Owen Chadwick, *The Victorian Church*, Part 1 [1966], p. 294). The Ritualist or Tractarian Movement in the Anglican Church, associated with Dr Pusey (see p. 59), was also fiercely assailed as having been a sort of fifth column within the Church of England consisting of clergymen who had, according to the Bishop of London, brought 'their flocks, step by step, to the very verge of the precipice' of Romanism.

In the following ferociously partisan piece, Dickens's contribution to the anti-Papal outcry, 'Master C.J. London' is Charles James Blomfield, Bishop of London, who had seemed, in his 1842 charge to his diocesan clergy, to be supporting the Tractarians (who were closely associated with the 'Young England' movement in politics). In his insistence that priests should scrupulously obey all rubrics in the Prayer book, in permitting candles to be placed on the altar, in requiring the wearing of surplices at morning service, and so on, Blomfield 'precipitated the first of the ritual controversies' (Chadwick, *op. cit.*, p. 215). In 1849 he had officiated at the consecration of St Barnabas, Pimlico, the first full-blown Tractarian church, having 'previously approved its Popish foppery of decoration' (*Household Narrative* for November 1850, p. 244; the *Narrative* also notes the anti-Papal so-called 'surplice riots' that took place during divine service at St Barnabas in November).

The Prime Minister, Lord John Russell, raised the temperature by writing, and allowing the publication of, a strongly anti-Catholic and anti-Tractarian letter to the Bishop of Durham in which he referred to 'unworthy sons of the Church of England' and 'the mummeries of superstition' (see Spencer Walpole, *The Life of Lord John Russell*, Vol. II [1889], pp. 120–1). Chadwick calls this 'the most foolish act of Russell's political career' (p. 296), but it won him immense popularity in a country now thoroughly

'The Pope "Trying it on" Mr Bull', Punch, *2 November 1850.*

alarmed by a fear that Rome was about to take over the national church, and Dickens here adds his voice to the chorus of praise for Russell with whom he was friendly and generally in agreement.

The reference to the Bulls of Rome 'getting into difficulties' (p. 303) concerns the flight of Pius IX from Rome to Gaeta in November 1848, after the Roman uprising against Papal rule. The Roman republic was proclaimed by Mazzini and others in February 1849, but was suppressed four months later by French troops sent by Louis Napoleon, President of the Second Republic, and the Pope was restored to his temporal power.

'Miss Eringobragh' represents Catholic Ireland, of course, and Dickens's comments here both about Ireland and the juxtaposition of Catholic squalor and Protestant order in Switzerland (p. 303) recall his 1846 letter to Forster in which he describes a valley in the Simplon, where, at the border of two cantons,

> you might separate two perfectly distinct and different conditions of humanity by drawing a line with your stick in the dust on the ground. On the Protestant side, neatness; cheerfulness; industry; education; continual aspiration, at least after better things. On the Catholic side, dirt, disease, ignorance, squalor, and misery. I have so constantly observed the like of this ... that I have a sad misgiving that the religion of Ireland lies as deep at the root of all its sorrows, even as English misgovernment and Tory villainy. [Pilgrim, Vol. iv, p. 611]

The reference to John Bull dancing about 'on the Platform in the Hall' (p. 305) is an allusion to Evangelical rallies at Exeter Hall, a frequent target of Dickens's satire.

The 'new plaything' about which the Americans ('Young Jonathan') are making such an uproar refers to the Swedish soprano Jenny Lind, who was touring the States under the management of P.T. Barnum and creating a huge sensation wherever she went. Dickens's comment that 'Jonathan' will soon quarrel with his 'new toy' would have reminded his readers of his own embittering experience in this respect.

Literary allusions (p. 304) 'a great gulf fixed': Luke 16:26.

Mrs Bull and her rising family were seated round the fire, one November evening at dusk, when all was mud, mist, and darkness, out of doors, and a good deal of fog had even got into the family parlour. To say the truth, the parlour was on no occasion fog-proof, and had, at divers notable times, been so misty as to cause the whole Bull family to grope about, in a most confused manner, and make the strangest mistakes. But, there was an excellent ventilator over the family fire-place (not one of Dr Arnott's, though it was of the same class, being an excellent invention, called Common Sense), and hence, though the fog was apt to get into the parlour through a variety of chinks, it soon got out again, and left the Bulls at liberty to see what o'clock it was, by the solid, steady-going, family time-piece: which went remarkably well in the long run, though it was apt, at times, to be a trifle too slow.

Mr Bull was dozing in his easy-chair, with his pocket-handkerchief drawn over his head. Mrs Bull, always industrious, was hard at work, knitting. The children were grouped in various attitudes around the blazing fire. Master C.J. London (called after his Godfather), who had been rather late at his exercise, sat with his chin resting, in something of a thoughtful and penitential manner, on his slate, and his slate resting on his knees. Young Jonathan – a cousin of the little Bulls, and a noisy, overgrown lad – was making a tremendous uproar across the yard, with a new plaything. Occasionally, when his noise reached the ears of Mr Bull, the good gentleman moved impatiently in his chair, and muttered 'Con—found that boy in the stripes, I wish he wouldn't make such a fool of himself!'

'He'll quarrel with his new toy soon, I know,' observed the discreet Mrs Bull, 'and then he'll begin to knock it about. But we mustn't expect to find old heads on young shoulders.'

'That can't be, Ma,' said Master C.J. London, who was a sleek, shining-faced boy.

'And why, then, did you expect to find an old head on Young England's shoulders?' retorted Mrs Bull, turning quickly on him.

'I didn't expect to find an old head on Young England's shoulders!' cried Master C.J. London, putting his left-hand knuckles to his right eye.

'You didn't expect it, you naughty boy?' said Mrs Bull.

'No!' whimpered Master C.J. London. 'I am sure I never did. Oh, oh, oh!'

'Don't go on in that way, don't!' said Mrs Bull, 'but behave better in future. What did you mean by playing with Young England at all?'

'I didn't mean any harm!' cried Master C.J. London, applying, in his increased distress, the knuckles of his right hand to his right eye, and the knuckles of his left hand to his left eye.

'I dare say you didn't!' returned Mrs Bull. 'Hadn't you had warning enough about playing with candles and candlesticks? How often had you been told that your poor father's house, long before you were born, was in danger of being reduced to ashes by candles and candlesticks? And when Young England and his companions began to put their shirts on, over their clothes, and to play all sorts of fantastic tricks in them, why didn't you come and tell your poor father and me, like a dutiful C.J. London?'

'Because the rubric—' Master C.J. London was beginning, when Mrs Bull took him up short.

'Don't talk to me about the Rubric, or you'll make it worse!' said Mrs Bull, shaking her head at him. 'Just exactly what the Rubric meant then, it means now; and just exactly what it didn't mean then, it don't mean now. You are taught to act, according to the spirit, not the letter; and you know what its spirit must be, or *you* wouldn't be. No, C.J. London!' said Mrs Bull, emphatically. 'If there were any candles or candlesticks in the spirit of your lesson-book, Master Wiseman would have been my boy, and not you!'

Here, Master C.J. London fell a-crying more grievously than before, sobbing, 'Oh, Ma! Master Wiseman with his red legs, your boy! Oh, oh, oh!'

'Will you be quiet,' returned Mrs Bull, 'and let your poor father rest? I am ashamed of you. *You* to go and play with a parcel of sentimental girls, and dandy boys! Is *that* your bringing up?'

'I didn't know they were fond of Master Wiseman,' protested Master C.J. London, still crying.

'You didn't know, Sir!' retorted Mrs Bull. 'Don't tell me! Then you ought to have known. Other people knew. You were told often enough, at the time, what it would come to. You didn't want a ghost, I suppose, to warn you that when they got to candlesticks, they'd get to candles; and that when they got to candles, they'd get to lighting 'em; and that when they began to put their shirts on outside, and to play at monks and friars, it was as natural that Master Wiseman should be encouraged to put on a pair of red-stockings, and a red hat, and to commit I don't know what other Tom-fooleries and make a perfect Guy Fawkes of himself in more ways than one. Is it because you are a Bull, that you are not to be roused till they shake scarlet close to your very eyes?' said Mrs Bull indignantly.

Master C.J. London still repeating 'Oh, oh, oh!' in a very plaintive manner, screwed his knuckles into his eyes until there appeared considerable danger of his screwing his eyes out of his head. But, little John (who though of a spare figure was a very spirited boy), started up from the little bench on which he sat; gave Master C.J. London a hearty pat on the back (accompanied, however, with a slight poke in the ribs); and told him that if Master Wiseman, or Young England, or any of those fellows, wanted anything for himself, he (little John) was the boy to give it him. Hereupon, Mrs Bull, who was always proud of the child, and always had been, since his measure was first taken for an entirely new suit of clothes, to wear in Common, could not refrain from catching him up on her knee and kissing him with great affection, while the whole family expressed their delight in various significant ways.

'You are a noble boy, little John,' said Mrs Bull, with a mother's pride, 'and that's the fact, after everything is said and done!'

'I don't know about that, Ma,' quoth little John, whose blood was evidently up; 'but if these chaps and their backers, the Bulls of Rome'—

Here Mr Bull, who was only half asleep, kicked out in such an alarming manner, that for some seconds, his boots gyrated fitfully all over the family hearth, filling the whole circle with consternation. For, when Mr Bull *did* kick, his kick was tremendous. And he always kicked, when the Bulls of Rome were mentioned.

Mrs Bull holding up her finger as an injunction to the children to keep quiet, sagely observed Mr Bull from the opposite side of the fireplace, until he calmly dozed again, when she recalled the scattered family to their former positions, and spoke in a low tone.

'You must be very careful,' said the worthy lady, 'how you mention that name; for, your poor father has so many unpleasant experiences of those Bulls of Rome – Bless the man! he'll do somebody a mischief.'

Mr Bull, lashing out again more violently than before, upset the fender, knocked down the fire-irons, kicked over the brass footman, and, whisking his silk handkerchief off his head, chased the Pussy on the rug clean out of the room into the passage, and so out of the street-door into the night; the Pussy having, (as was well known to the children in general,) originally strayed from the Bulls of Rome into Mr Bull's assembled family. After the achievement of this crowning feat, Mr Bull came back, and in a highly excited state performed a sort of war-dance in his top-boots, all over the parlour. Finally, he sank into his arm-chair, and covered himself up again.

Master C.J. London, who was by no means sure that Mr Bull in his heat would not come down upon him for the lateness of his exercise, took refuge behind his slate and behind little John, who was a perfect gamecock. But, Mr Bull having concluded his war-dance without injury to any one, the boy crept out, with the rest of the family, to the knees of Mrs Bull, who thus addressed them, taking little John into her lap before she began:

'The B.'s of R.,' said Mrs Bull, getting, by this prudent device, over the obnoxious words, 'caused your poor father a world of trouble, before any one of you were born. They pretended to be related to us, and to have some influence in our family; but it can't be allowed for a single moment – nothing will ever induce your poor father to hear of it; let them disguise or constrain themselves now and then, as they will, they are, by nature, an insolent, audacious, oppressive, intolerable race.'

Here little John doubled his fists, and began squaring at the Bulls of Rome, as he saw those pretenders with his mind's eye. Master C.J. London, after some considerable reflection, made a show of squaring, likewise.

'In the days of your great, great, great, great grandfather,' said Mrs Bull, dropping her voice still lower, as she glanced at Mr Bull in his repose, 'the Bulls of Rome were not so utterly hateful to our family as they are at present. We didn't know them so well, and our family were very ignorant and low in the world. But, we have gone on advancing in every generation since then; and now we are taught, by all our family history and experience, and by the most limited exercise of our national faculties, that our knowledge, liberty, progress, social welfare and happiness, are wholly irreconcileable and inconsistent with them. That the Bulls of Rome are not only the enemies of our family, but of the whole human race. That wherever they go, they perpetuate misery, oppression, darkness, and ignorance. That they are easily made the tools of the worst of men for the worst of purposes; and that they *cannot* be endured by your poor father, or by any man, woman, or child, of common sense, who has the least connexion with us.'

Little John, who had gradually left off squaring, looked hard at his aunt, Miss Eringobragh, Mr Bull's sister, who was grovelling on the ground, with her head in the ashes. This unfortunate lady had been, for a length of time, in a horrible condition of mind and body, and presented a most lamentable spectacle of disease, dirt, rags, superstition and degradation.

Mrs Bull, observing the direction of the child's glance, smoothed little John's hair, and directed her next observation to him.

'Ah! You may well look at the poor thing, John!' said Mrs Bull; 'for the Bulls of Rome have had far too much to do with her present state. There have been many other causes at work to destroy the strength of her constitution, but the Bulls of Rome have been at the bottom of it; and, depend upon it, wherever you see a condition at all resembling hers, you will find, on inquiry, that the sufferer has allowed herself to be dealt with by the Bulls of Rome. The cases of squalor and ignorance, in all the world most like your aunt's, are to be found in their own household; on the steps of their doors; in the heart of their homes. In Switzerland, you may cross a line, no broader than a bridge or a hedge, and know, in an instant, where the Bulls of Rome have been received, by the condition of the family. Wherever the Bulls of Rome have the most influence, the family is sure to be the most abject. Put your trust in those Bulls, John, and it's in the inevitable order and sequence of things, that you must come to be something like your Aunt, sooner or later.'

'I thought the Bulls of Rome had got into difficulties, and run away, Ma?' said little John, looking up into his mother's face inquiringly.

'Why, so they did get into difficulties, to be sure, John,' returned Mrs Bull, 'and so they did run away; but, even the Italians, who had got thoroughly used to them, found them out, and they were obliged to go and hide in a cupboard, where they still talked big through the key-hole, and presented one of the most contemptible and ridiculous exhibitions that ever were seen on earth. However, they were taken out of the cupboard by some friends of theirs – friends, indeed! who care as much about them as I do for the sea-serpent; but who happened, at the moment, to find it necessary to play at soldiers, to amuse their fretful children, who didn't know what they wanted, and, what was worse, would have it – and so the Bulls got back to Rome. And at Rome they are anything but safe to stay, as you'll find, my dear, one of these odd mornings.'

'Then, if they are so unsafe, and so found out, Ma,' said Master C.J. London, 'how come they to interfere with us, now?'

'Oh, C.J. London!' returned Mrs Bull, 'what a sleepy child you must be, to put such a question! Don't you know that the more they are found out, and the weaker they are, the more important it must be to them to impose upon the ignorant people near them, by pretending to be closely connected with a person so much looked up to as your poor father?'

'Why, of course!' cried little John to his brother. 'Oh, you stupid!'

'And I am ashamed to have to repeat, C.J. London,' said Mrs Bull, 'that, but for your friend, Young England, and the encouragement you gave to that mewling little Pussy, when it strayed here – don't say you didn't, you naughty boy, for you did!' –

'You know you did!' said little John.

Master C.J. London began to cry again.

'Don't do that,' said Mrs Bull, sharply, 'but be a better boy in future! I say, I am ashamed to have to repeat, that, but for that, the Bulls of Rome would never have had the audacity to call their connexion, Master Wiseman, your poor father's child, and to appoint him, with his red hat and stockings, and his mummery and flummery, to a portion of your father's estates – though, for the matter of that, there is nothing to prevent their appointing him to the Moon, except the difficulty of getting him there! And so, your poor father's affairs have been brought to this crisis: that he has to deal with an insult which is perfectly absurd, and yet which he must, for the sake of his family, in all time to come, decisively and seriously deal with, in order to detach himself, once and for ever, from these Bulls of Rome; and show how impotent they are. There's difficulty and vexation, you have helped to bring upon your father, you bad child!'

'Oh, oh, oh!' cried Master C.J. London. 'Oh, I never went to do it. Oh, oh, oh!'

'Hold your tongue!' said Mrs Bull, 'and do a good exercise! Now that your father has turned that Pussy out of doors, go on with your exercise, like a man; and let us have no more playing with any one connected with those Bulls of Rome; between whom and you there is a great gulf fixed, as you ought to have known in the beginning. Take your fingers out of your eyes, Sir, and do your exercise!'

'—Or I'll come and pinch you!' said little John.

'John,' said Mrs Bull, 'you leave him alone. Keep your eye upon him, and, if you find him relapsing, tell your father.'

'Oh, won't I neither!' cried little John.

'Don't be vulgar,' said Mrs Bull. 'Now, John, I can trust *you*. Whatever you do, I know you won't wake your father unnecessarily. You are a bold, brave child, and I highly approve of your erecting yourself against Master Wiseman and all that bad set. But, be wary John; and, as you have, and deserve to have, great influence with your father, I am sure you will be careful how you wake him. If he was to make a wild rush, and begin to dance about, on the Platform in the Hall, I don't know where he'd stop.'

Little John, getting on his legs, began buttoning his jacket with great firmness and vigor, preparatory to action. Master C.J. London, with a dejected aspect and an occasional sob, went on with his exercise.

56

A December Vision

Household Words, 14 December 1850 (leading article)

This powerful and menacing denunciation of the failure of the great institutions of Victorian society to address the terrible problems of mass poverty and deprivation can be seen as a continuation of a recurrent theme in Dickens's Christmas Books (1843–9). 'A December Vision' reiterates, in sombre vein, the message of the first of these, *A Christmas Carol*, in which Scrooge is warned to beware of the two 'yellow, meagre, scowling, wolfish' children, Ignorance and Want; and it naturally follows on from *The Haunted Man*, the last of the series. In this book a 'baby savage' appears, the hunted, desperate child of the London streets, 'a creature ... who ... would live and perish a mere beast'. This child is the subject of a fearful warning: 'Woe ... to the nation that shall count its monsters such as this, lying here, by hundreds and by thousands! ... From every seed of evil in this boy, a field of ruin is grown that shall be gathered in....'

'A December Vision' can also be read as an overture to *Bleak House*, which Dickens was to begin writing a year later. Reprinting the piece as the title item in their anthology *Charles Dickens: A December Vision. His Social Journalism* (1986), Neil Philip and Victor Neuburg compare it with the description (*Bleak House*, Ch. 46) of the fetid squalor of Tom-all-Alone's infecting more prosperous areas of London, and many other links can be

made. Poor Jo the crossing-sweeper, constantly harried and 'moved on' by
the police and preached at by Mr Chadband, but taught and helped by
no authority figure, is the fictional representative of the 'Thirty Thousand
children, hunted, flogged, imprisoned, but not taught' of this essay; and
the squabbling teachers and preachers condemned here reappear in his
deathbed words (Ch. 47):

> ... genlemen came down Tom-all-Alone's a-prayin, but they all mostly
> sed as the to'other wuns prayed wrong, and all mostly sounded to be ...
> a-passin blame on the t'others, and not a-talkin to us.

The master-motif of the whole novel, the ruinous delays and labyrinthine
complexity of the law, especially the Court of Chancery, is also first sounded
here, and we even find an anticipation of Sir Leicester Dedlock's 'family
gout' (*Bleak House*, Ch. 16).

Literary allusions (p. 307) 'BUT IT WILL LAST MY TIME': possibly echoes
Carlyle's 'The foul sluggard's comfort: "It will last my time"' (*Critical and
Miscellaneous Essays*, Literary Edition (1869), Vol. 4, p. 338, 'Count Cagliostro.
Flight last'); (p. 309) 'Rule Britannia', James Thomson, *Alfred*, Act 2, scene
the last (1740).

I saw a mighty Spirit, traversing the world without any rest or pause. It
was omnipresent, it was all-powerful, it had no compunction, no pity, no
relenting sense that any appeal from any of the race of men could reach.
It was invisible to every creature born upon the earth, save once to each.
It turned its shaded face on whatsoever living thing, one time; and
straight the end of that thing was come. It passed through the forest,
and the vigorous tree it looked on shrunk away; through the garden, and
the leaves perished and the flowers withered; through the air, and the
eagles flagged upon the wing and dropped; through the sea, and the
monsters of the deep floated, great wrecks, upon the waters. It met the
eyes of lions in their lairs, and they were dust; its shadow darkened the
faces of young children lying asleep, and they awoke no more.

It had its work appointed; it inexorably did what was appointed to it
to do; and neither sped nor slackened. Called to, it went on unmoved,
and did not come. Besought, by some who felt that it was drawing near,
to change its course, it turned its shaded face upon them, even while
they cried, and they were dumb. It passed into the midst of palace
chambers, where there were lights and music, pictures, diamonds, gold
and silver; crossed the wrinkled and the grey, regardless of them; looked
into the eyes of a bright bride; and vanished. It revealed itself to the
baby on the old crone's knee, and left the old crone wailing by the fire.

But, whether the beholder of its face were, now a King, or now a labourer, now a Queen, or now a seamstress; let the hand it palsied be on the sceptre, or the plough, or yet too small and nerveless to grasp anything: the Spirit never paused in its appointed work, and, sooner or later, turned its impartial face on all.

I saw a Minister of State, sitting in his Closet; and round about him, rising from the country which he governed, up to the Eternal Heavens, was a low dull howl of Ignorance. It was a wild, inexplicable mutter, confused, but full of threatening, and it made all hearers' hearts to quake within them. But, few heard. In the single city where this Minister of State was seated, I saw Thirty Thousand children, hunted, flogged, imprisoned, but not taught – who might have been nurtured by the wolf or bear, so little of humanity had they, within them or without – all joining in this doleful cry. And, ever among them, as among all ranks and grades of mortals, in all parts of the globe, the Spirit went; and ever by thousands, in their brutish state, with all the gifts of God perverted in their breasts or trampled out, they died.

The Minister of State, whose heart was pierced by even the little he could hear of these terrible voices, day and night rising to Heaven, went among the Priests and Teachers of all denominations, and faintly said:

'Hearken to this dreadful cry! What shall we do to stay it?'

One body of respondents answered, 'Teach this!'

Another said, 'Teach that!'

Another said, 'Teach neither this nor that, but t'other!'

Another quarrelled with all the three; twenty others quarrelled with all the four, and quarrelled no less bitterly among themselves. The voices, not stayed by this, cried out day and night; and still, among those many thousands, as among all mankind, went the Spirit, who never rested from its labour; and still, in brutish sort, they died.

Then, a whisper murmured to the Minister of State:

'Correct this for thyself. Be bold! Silence these voices, or virtuously lose thy power in the attempt to do it. Thou can'st not sow a grain of good seed in vain. Thou knowest it well. Be bold, and do thy duty!'

The Minister shrugged his shoulders, and replied 'It is a great wrong – BUT IT WILL LAST MY TIME.' And so he put it from him.

Then, the whisper went among the Priests and Teachers, saying to each, 'In thy soul thou knowest it is a truth, O man, that there are good things to be taught, on which all men may agree. Teach those, and stay this cry.'

To which, each answered in like manner, 'It is a great wrong – BUT IT WILL LAST MY TIME.' And so *he* put it from him.

I saw a poisoned air, in which Life drooped. I saw Disease, arrayed in all its store of hideous aspects and appalling shapes, triumphant in every alley, bye-way, court, back-street, and poor abode, in every place where human beings congregated – in the proudest and most boastful places, most of all. I saw innumerable hosts fore-doomed to darkness, dirt, pestilence, obscenity, misery, and early death. I saw, wheresoever I looked, cunning preparations made for defacing the Creator's Image, from the moment of its appearance here on earth, and stamping over it the image of the Devil. I saw, from those reeking and pernicious stews, the avenging consequences of such Sin issuing forth, and penetrating to the highest places. I saw the rich struck down in their strength, their darling children weakened and withered, their marriageable sons and daughters perish in their prime. I saw that not one miserable wretch breathed out his poisoned life in the deepest cellar of the most neglected town, but, from the surrounding atmosphere, some particles of his infection were borne away, charged with heavy retribution on the general guilt.

There were many attentive and alarmed persons looking on, who saw these things too. They were well clothed, and had purses in their pockets; they were educated, full of kindness, and loved mercy. They said to one another, 'This is horrible, and shall not be!' and there was a stir among them to set it right. But, opposed to these, came a small multitude of noisy fools and greedy knaves, whose harvest was in such horrors; and they, with impudence and turmoil, and with scurrilous jests at misery and death, repelled the better lookers-on, who soon fell back, and stood aloof.

Then, the whisper went among those better lookers-on, saying, 'Over the bodies of those fellows, to the remedy!'

But, each of them moodily shrugged his shoulders, and replied, 'It is a great wrong – BUT IT WILL LAST MY TIME!' And so they put it from them.

I saw a great library of laws and law-proceedings, so complicated, costly, and unintelligible, that, although numbers of lawyers united in a public fiction that these were wonderfully just and equal, there was scarcely an honest man among them, but who said to his friend, privately consulting him, 'Better put up with a fraud or other injury than grope for redress through the manifold blind turnings and strange chances of this system.'

I saw a portion of the system, called (of all things) EQUITY, which was ruin to suitors, ruin to property, a shield for wrong-doers having money, a rack for right-doers having none: a byword for delay, slow agony of mind, despair, impoverishment, trickery, confusion, insupportable injustice. A main part of it, I saw prisoners wasting in jail; mad people babbling in hospitals; suicides chronicled in the yearly records; orphans robbed of their inheritance; infants righted (perhaps) when they were grey.

Certain lawyers and laymen came together, and said to one another, 'In only one of these our Courts of Equity, there are years of this dark perspective before us at the present moment. We must change this.'

Uprose, immediately, a throng of others, Secretaries, Petty Bags, Hanapers, Chaff-waxes, and what not, singing (in answer) 'Rule Britannia,' and 'God save the Queen;' making flourishing speeches, pronouncing hard names, demanding committees, commissions, commissioners, and other scarecrows, and terrifying the little band of innovators out of their five wits.

Then, the whisper went among the latter, as they shrunk back, saying, 'If there is any wrong within the universal knowledge, this wrong is. Go on! Set it right!'

Whereon, each of them sorrowfully thrust his hands in his pockets, and replied, 'It is indeed a great wrong – BUT IT WILL LAST MY TIME!' – and so *they* put it from them.

The Spirit, with its face concealed, summoned all the people who had used this phrase about their Time, into its presence. Then, it said, beginning with the Minister of State:

'Of what duration is *your* Time?'

The Minister of State replied, 'My ancient family has always been long-lived. My father died at eighty-four; my grandfather, at ninety-two. We have the gout, but bear it (like our honours) many years.'

'And you,' said the Spirit to the Priests and Teachers, 'what may *your* time be?'

Some, believed they were so strong, as that they should number many more years than threescore and ten; others, were the sons of old incumbents who had long outlived youthful expectants. Others, for any means they had of calculating, might be long-lived or short-lived – generally (they had a strong persuasion) long. So, among the well-clothed lookers on. So among the lawyers and laymen.

'But, every man, as I understand you, one and all,' said the Spirit, 'has his time?'

'Yes!' they exclaimed together.

'Yes,' said the Spirit: 'and it is – ETERNITY! Whosoever is a consenting party to a wrong, comforting himself with the base reflection that it will last his time, shall bear his portion of that wrong throughout ALL TIME. And, in the hour when he and I stand face to face, he shall surely know it, as my name is Death!'

It departed, turning its shaded face hither and thither as it passed along upon its ceaseless work, and blighting all on whom it looked.

Then went among many trembling hearers the whisper, saying, 'See, each of you, before you take your ease, O wicked, selfish, men, that what will "last your time," be Just enough to last for ever!'

57

The Last Words of the Old Year

Household Words, 4 January 1851 (leading article)

In this piece Dickens seizes the opportunity both to mock political slo-
ganeering in general and to remind his readers of particular scandals of
the previous year. The Old Year's words, 'I have been a Year of Ruin ...
I have been a Year of Commercial Prosperity' look forward to the famous
opening of *A Tale of Two Cities* (1859): 'It was the best of times, it was the worst
of times. . . .' Turning to particularities, Dickens mocks the Metropolitan
Commission of Sewers (est. 1847), which had decreed the abolition of all
cesspits with the catastrophic result that London's sewage was now discharged direct into the Thames. The Commissioners were able to resist
the General Board of Health's plans (drawn up by Edwin Chadwick) for a
total reorganisation of London's water-supply and drainage system because
the metropolis was specifically excluded from the Board's remit. Dickens
also reverts to the scandal of London's neglected children so powerfully
raised in 'A December Vision' (article 56). He refers back to literacy
statistics given in the preceding number of *HW*, in the lead article for 28
December, 'Mr Bendigo Buster on Our National Defences against Education', written jointly by himself and Henry Morley (reprinted in Stone,
Vol. I, pp. 191–203); also to the *Household Narrative* for May and its mention
of the case of the two starving children whipped for stealing a loaf.

Dickens refers to a number of individuals singled out for praise or blame:
Robert Stephenson, the builder of the Britannia Bridge; Joseph Paxton,
creator of the Crystal Palace ('a great natural genius, self-improved');
Charles Blomfield, Bishop of London ('My Right Reverend Brother'), who
first made a name for himself as an editor of Euripides and other Greek
dramatists (see p. 313); Sir Robert Peel ('a great Statesman'), who died in
a riding accident on 29 June; King Louis-Philippe, who arrived an exile in
England in 1848 and died (aged seventy-seven) on 26 August 1850; Cardinal
Wiseman (see p. 297); and Dr Gilbert Elliot, Dean of Bristol and a personal
friend of Dickens's, whose vigorously anti-Tractarian speech at a meeting
of Bristol clergy on 6 November had been extensively quoted and commended in the *Household Narrative* for November (p. 246; the author of the
article was presumably Forster). The wish that the Dean might be translated
to the see of Exeter is a hit at the High Church Bishop Philpotts (see p. 191).

Literary allusions (p. 312) 'sound and fury': Shakespeare, *Macbeth*, Act

5, Sc. 3; (p. 313) 'the night cometh when no man can work': John, 9:4; (p. 315) 'With twelve great shocks of sound ...': Tennyson, 'Godiva' (1842), 11.73–6, omitting the words 'the shameless noon' after 'sound'.

This venerable gentleman, christened (in the Church of England) by the names One Thousand Eight Hundred and Fifty, who had attained the great age of three hundred and sixty-five (days), breathed his last, at midnight, on the thirty-first of December, in the presence of his confidential business-agents, the Chief of the Grave Diggers, and the Head Registrar of Births. The melancholy event took place at the residence of the deceased, on the confines of Time; and it is understood that his ashes will rest in the family vault, situated within the quiet precincts of Chronology.

For some weeks, it had been manifest that the venerable gentleman was rapidly sinking. He was well aware of his approaching end, and often predicted that he would expire at twelve at night, as the whole of his ancestors had done. The result proved him to be correct, for he kept his time to the moment.

He had always evinced a talkative disposition, and latterly became extremely garrulous. Occasionally, in the months of November and December, he exclaimed, 'No Popery!' with some symptoms of a disordered mind; but, generally speaking, was in the full possession of his faculties, and very sensible.

On the night of his death, being then perfectly collected, he delivered himself in the following terms, to his friends already mentioned, the Chief of the Grave Diggers and the Head Registrar of Births:

'We have done, my friends, a good deal of business together, and you are now about to enter into the service of my successor. May you give every satisfaction to him and his!

'I have been,' said the good old gentleman, penitently, 'a Year of Ruin. I have blighted all the farmers, destroyed the land, given the final blow to the Agricultural Interest, and smashed the Country. It is true, I have been a Year of Commercial Prosperity, and remarkable for the steadiness of my English Funds, which have never been lower than ninety-four, or higher than ninety-seven and three-quarters. But you will pardon the inconsistencies of a weak old man.

'I had fondly hoped,' he pursued, with much feeling, addressing the Chief of the Grave Diggers, 'that, before my decease, you would have finally adjusted the turf over the ashes of the Honourable Board of Commissioners of Sewers; the most feeble and incompetent Body that ever did outrage to the common sense of any community, or was ever beheld by any member of my family. But, as this was not to be, I charge you, do your duty by them in the days of my successor!'

The Chief of the Grave Diggers solemnly pledged himself to observe this request. The Abortion of Incapables referred to, had (he said) done much for him, in the way of preserving his business, endangered by the recommendations of the Board of Health; but, regardless of all personal obligations, he thereby undertook to lay them low. Deeper than they were already buried in the contempt of the public, (this he swore upon his spade) he would shovel the earth over their preposterous heads!

The venerable gentleman, whose mind appeared to be relieved of an enormous load by this promise, stretched out his hand, and tranquilly returned, 'Thank you! Bless you!'

'I have been,' he said, resuming his last discourse, after a short interval of silent satisfaction, 'doomed to witness the sacrifice of many valuable and dear lives, in steamboats, because of the want of commonest and easiest precautions for the prevention of those legal murders. In the days of my great-grandfather, there yet existed an invention called Paddle-box Boats. Can either of you gild the few remaining sands fast running through my glass, with the hope that my great-grandson may see its adoption made compulsory on the owners of passenger steam-ships?'

After a despondent pause, the Head Registrar of Births gently observed that, in England, the recognition of any such invention by the legislature – particularly if simple, and of proved necessity – could scarcely be expected under a hundred years. In China, such a result might follow in fifty, but in England (he considered) in not less than a hundred. The venerable invalid replied, 'True, true!' and for some minutes appeared faint, but afterwards rallied.

'A stupendous material work;' these were his next words; 'has been accomplished in my time. Do I, who have witnessed the opening of the Britannia Bridge across the Menai Straits, and who claim the man who made that bridge for one of my distinguished children, see through the Tube, as through a mighty telescope, the Education of the people coming nearer?'

He sat up in his bed, as he spoke, and a great light seemed to shine from his eyes.

'Do I,' he said, 'who have been deafened by a whirlwind of sound and fury, consequent on a demand for Secular Education, see *any* Education through the opening years, for those who need it most?'

A film gradually came over his eyes, and he sunk back on his pillow. Presently, directing his weakened glance towards the Head Registrar of Births, he asked that personage:

'How many of those whom Nature brings within your province, in the spot of earth called England, can neither read nor write in after years?'

The Registrar answered (referring to the last number of the present publication), 'about forty-five in every hundred.'

'And in my History for the month of May,' said the old year with a heavy groan, 'I find it written: "Two little children whose heads scarcely reached the top of the dock, were charged at Bow Street on the seventh, with stealing a loaf out of a baker's shop. They said, in defence, that they were starving, and their appearance showed that they spoke the truth. They were sentenced to be whipped in the House of Correction." To be whipped! Woe, woe! can the State devise no better sentence for its little children! Will it never sentence them to be taught!'

The venerable gentleman became extremely discomposed in his mind, and would have torn his white hair from his head, but for the soothing attentions of his friends.

'In the same month,' he observed, when he became more calm, 'and within a week, an English Prince was born. Suppose him taken from his Princely home, (Heaven's blessing on it!), cast like these wretched babies on the streets, and sentenced to be left in ignorance, what difference, soon, between him, and the little children sentenced to be whipped? Think of it, Great Queen, and become the Royal Mother of them all!'

The Head Registrar of Births and the Chief of the Grave Diggers, both of whom have great experience of infancy, predestined, (they do not blasphemously suppose, by God, but know, by man) to vice and shame, were greatly overcome by the earnestness of their departing friend.

'I have seen,' he presently said, 'a project carried into execution for a great assemblage of the peaceful glories of the world. I have seen a wonderful structure, reared in glass, by the energy and skill of a great natural genius, self-improved: worthy descendant of my Saxon ancestors: worthy type of industry and ingenuity triumphant! Which of my children shall behold the Princes, Prelates, Nobles, Merchants, of England, equally united, for another Exhibition — for a great display of England's sins and negligences, to be, by steady contemplation of all eyes, and steady union of all hearts and hands, set right? Come hither my Right Reverend Brother, to whom an English tragedy presented in the theatre is contamination, but who art a Bishop, none the less, in right of the translation of Greek Plays; come hither, from a life of Latin Verses and Quantities, and study the Humanities through *these* transparent windows! Wake, Colleges of Oxford, from day-dreams of ecclesiastical melo-drama, and look in on these realities in the daylight, for the night cometh when no man can work! Listen, my Lords and Gentlemen, to the roar within, so deep, so real, so low down, so incessant and accumulative! Not all the reedy pipes of all the shepherds that eternally play one little tune — not twice as many feet of Latin verses as would reach from this globe to the

Moon and back – not all the Quantities that are, or ever were, or will be, in the world – Quantities of Prosody, or Law, or State, or Church, or Quantities of anything but work in the right spirit, will quiet it for a second, or clear an inch of space in this dark Exhibition of the bad results of our doings! Where shall we hold it? When shall we open it? What courtier speaks?'

After the foregoing rhapsody, the venerable gentleman became, for a time, much enfeebled; and the Chief of the Grave Diggers took a few minutes' repose.

As the hands of the clock were now rapidly advancing towards the hour which the invalid had predicted would be his last, his attendants considered it expedient to sound him as to his arrangements in connection with his worldly affairs; both, being in doubt whether these were completed, or, indeed, whether he had anything to leave. The Chief of the Grave Diggers, as the fittest person for such an office, undertook it. He delicately enquired, whether his friend and master had any testamentary wishes to express? If so, they should be faithfully observed.

'Thank you,' returned the old gentleman, with a smile, for he was once more composed; 'I have Something to bequeath to my successor; but not so much (I am happy to say) as I might have had. The Sunday Postage question, thank God, I have got rid of; and the Nepaulese Ambassadors are gone home. May they stay there!'

This pious aspiration was responded to, with great fervour, by both the attendants.

'I have seen you,' said the venerable Testator, addressing the Chief of the Grave Diggers, 'lay beneath the ground, a great Statesman and a fallen King of France.'

The Chief of the Grave Diggers replied, 'It is true.'

'I desire,' said the Testator, in a distinct voice, 'to entail the remembrance of them on my successors for ever. Of the Statesman, as an Englishman who rejected an adventitious nobility, and composedly knew his own. Of the King, as a great example that the monarch who addresses himself to the meaner passions of humanity, and governs by cunning and corruption, makes his bed of thorns, and sets his throne on shifting sand.'

The Head Registrar of Births took a note of the bequest.

'Is there any other wish?' enquired the Chief of the Grave Diggers, observing that his patron closed his eyes.

'I bequeath to my successor,' said the aged gentleman, opening them again, 'a vast inheritance of degradation and neglect in England; and I charge him, if he be wise, to get speedily through it. I do hereby give and bequeath to him, also, Ireland. And I admonish him to leave it to his successor in a better condition than he will find it. He can hardly leave it in a worse.'

The scratching of the pen used by the Head Registrar of Births, was the only sound that broke the ensuing silence.

'I do give and bequeath to him, likewise,' said the Testator, rousing himself by a vigorous effort, 'the Court of Chancery. The less he leaves of it to his successor, the better for mankind.'

The Head Registrar of Births wrote as expeditiously as possible, for the clock showed that it was within five minutes of midnight.

'Also, I do give and bequeath to him,' said the Testator, 'the costly complications of the English law in general. With which I do hereby couple the same advice.'

The Registrar, coming to the end of his note, repeated, 'The same advice.'

'Also, I do give and bequeath to him,' said the Testator, 'the Window Tax. Also, a general mismanagement of all public expenditure, revenues, and property, in Great Britain and its possessions.'

The anxious Registrar, with a glance at the clock, repeated, 'And its possessions.'

'Also, I do give and bequeath to him,' said the Testator, collecting his strength once more, by a surprising effort, 'Nicholas Wiseman and the Pope of Rome.'

The two attendants breathlessly inquired together, 'With what injunctions?'

'To study well,' said the Testator, 'the speech of the Dean of Bristol, made at Bristol aforesaid; and to deal with them and the whole vexed question, according to that speech. And I do hereby give and bequeath to my successor the said speech and the said faithful Dean, as great possessions and good guides. And I wish with all my heart, the said faithful Dean were removed a little farther to the West of England and made Bishop of Exeter!'

With this, the Old Year turned serenely on his side, and breathed his last in peace. Whereon,

> – With twelve great shocks of sound,
> Was clash'd and hammer'd from a hundred towers,
> One after one,

the coming of the New Year. He came on, joyfully. The Head Registrar, making, from mere force of habit, an entry of his birth, while the Chief of the Grave Diggers took charge of his predecessor; added these words in Letters of Gold. MAY IT BE A WISE AND HAPPY YEAR, FOR ALL OF US!

58

Railway Strikes

Household Words, 11 January 1851 (leading article)

Dickens is here responding, as he makes clear, to a report in *The Times* of 27 December (p. 5, cols 5–6) of a meeting of the engine-drivers and firemen of the southern division of the London and North Western Railway, held at the Railway Tavern, Hampstead Road, on 26 December. The meeting was to hear delegates from the northern division and to decide whether to support them in threatening to strike. Delegates from the Great Western and other lines also attended. The northern men's grievances seem to have centred around the Company's decision to require three months' notice from employees wishing to leave its service. Simpson, a GWR driver, counselled caution and compromise: 'The more strikes there are the worse for ourselves, for we always find a certain set of men who have no character while things are straight, but who are taken on to supply the places of honest men if a strike occurs.' Alluding to a recent strike on the London and Eastern Counties line, he said that good men had been 'dictated to and led away by bad counsel and by the advice of men who ought not to be relied upon'. The letter from the Bedford men cited by Dickens similarly argued for compromise and the avoidance of a strike: 'Look at the consequences of losing and the ruinous result of defeat to so many families. ... Mr Carr Glyn [presumably the locomotive superintendent of the LNW] has always been favourably disposed towards us....'

Railway strikes were, in fact, very rare during the first forty years of the industry's history (see P.W. Kingford, 'Labour Relations on the Railways 1835–75', *Journal of Transport History*, Vol. 1 [1953], pp. 65–81) and this particular conflict was settled without one. Given the intensity of public concern about railway safety (accidents were quite frequent and widely reported – four are described in *The Household Narrative* for January 1850, for example), Dickens's characterisation of a railway strike as 'rather a murdering mode of action' would have struck a chord with his readers.

Dickens's contention, expressed here, that industrial workers were often misled by 'designing persons', who sought to involve them in 'a system of tyranny and oppression', looks forward to his presentation of Slackbridge, the manipulative trades union official, in *Hard Times* just over three years later.

Everything that has a direct bearing on the prosperity, happiness, and reputation of the working-men of England should be a Household Word.

We offer a few remarks on a subject which has recently attracted their attention, and on which one particular and important branch of industry has made a demonstration, affecting, more or less, every other branch of industry, and the whole community; in the hope that there are few among the intelligent body of skilled mechanics who will suspect us of entertaining any other than friendly feelings towards them, or of regarding them with any sentiment but one of esteem and confidence.

The Engine Drivers and Firemen on the North Western line of Railway – the great iron high-road of the Kingdom, by which communication is maintained with Ireland, Scotland, Wales, the chief manufacturing towns of Great Britain, and the port which is the main artery of her commerce with the world – have threatened, for the second time, a simultaneous abandonment of their work, and relinquishment of their engagements with the Company they have contracted to serve.

We dismiss from consideration, the merits of the case. It would be easy, we conceive, to show, that the complaints of the men, even assuming them to be beyond dispute, were not, from the beginning of the manifestation, of a grave character, or by any means hopeless of fair adjustment. But, we purposely dismiss that question. We purposely dismiss, also, the character of the Company, for careful, business-like, generous, and honourable management. We are content to assume that it stands no higher than the level of the very worst public servant bearing the name of railway, that the public possesses. We will suppose MR GLYN's communications with the men, to have been characterised by overbearing evasion, and not (as they undoubtedly have been) by courtesy, good temper, self-command, and the perfect spirit of a gentleman. We will suppose the case of the Company to be the worst that such a case could be, in this country, and in these times. Even with such a reduction of it to its lowest possible point, and a corresponding elevation of the case of the skilled Railway servants to its highest, we must deny the moral right or justification of the latter to exert the immense power they accidentally possess, to the public detriment and danger.

We say, accidentally possess, because this power has not been raised up by themselves. If there be ill-conditioned spirits among them who represent that it has been, they represent what is not true, and what a minute's rational consideration will show to be false. It is the result of a vast system of skilful combination, and a vast expenditure of wealth. The construction of the line, alone, against all the engineering difficulties it presented, involved an amount of outlay that was wonderful, even in England. To bring it to its present state of working efficiency, a thousand ingenious problems have been studied and solved, stupendous machines have been constructed, a variety of plans and schemes have been matured with incredible labour: a great whole has been pieced together by numerous capacities and appliances, and kept incessantly in motion. Even the character of the men, which stands deservedly high, has not been set up by themselves alone, but has been assisted by large contributions from these various sources. Without a good permanent way, and good engine power, they could not have established themselves in the public confidence as good drivers. Without good business-management in the complicated arrangements of trains for goods and passengers, they could not possibly have avoided accidents. They have done their part manfully; but they could not have done it, without efficient aid in like manful sort, from every department of the great executive staff. And because it happens that the whole machine is dependent upon them in one important stage, and is delivered necessarily into their control – and because it happens that Railway accidents, when they do occur, are of a frightful nature, attended with horrible mutilation and loss of life – and because such accidents, with the best precautions, probably *must* occur, in the event of their resignation in a body – is it, therefore, defensible to strike?

To that, the question comes. It is just so narrow, and no broader. We all know, perfectly well, that there would be no strike, but for the extent of the power possessed. Can such an exercise of it be defended, after due consideration, by any honest man?

We firmly believe that these are honest men – as honest men as the world can produce. But, we believe, also, that they have not well considered what it is that they do. They are laboriously and constantly employed; and it is the habit of many men, so engaged, to allow other men to think for them. These deputy-thinkers are not always the most judicious order of intellects. They are something quick at grievances. They drive Express Trains to that point, and Parliamentary to all other points. They are not always, perhaps, the best workmen, and are not so satisfied as the best workmen. They are, sometimes, not workmen at all, but designing persons, who have, for their own base purposes, immeshed the workmen in a system of tyranny and oppression. Through these, on the one hand, and through an imperfect or misguided view of the details of a case on the other, a strike (always supposing this great power in the strikers) may be easily set a going. Once begun, there is aroused a chivalrous spirit – much to be respected, however mistaken its manifestation – which forbids all reasoning. 'I will stand by my order, and do as the rest do. I never flinch from my fellow-workmen. I should not have thought of this myself; but I wish to be true to the backbone, and here I put my name among the others.' Perhaps in no class of society, in any country, is this principle of honour so strong, as among most great bodies of English artisans.

But there is a higher principle of honour yet; and it is that, we suggest to our friends the Engine Drivers and Firemen on the North Western Railway, which would lead to these greater considerations. First, what is my duty to the public, who are, after all, my chief employers? Secondly, what is my duty to my fellow-workmen of all denominations: not only here, upon this Railway, but all over England?

We will suppose Engine Driver, John Safe, entering upon these considerations with his Fireman, Thomas Sparks. Sparks is one of the best of men, but he has a great belief in Caleb Coke, of Wolverhampton, and Coke says (because somebody else has said so, to him) 'Strike!'

'But, Sparks,' argues John Safe, sitting on the side of the tender, waiting for the Down Express, 'to look at it in these two ways, before we take any measures – Here we are, a body of men with a great public charge; hundreds and thousands of lives every day. Individuals among us may, of course, and of course do, every now and again give up their part of that charge, for one reason or another – and right too! But I'm not so sure that we can all turn our backs upon it at once, and do right.'

Thomas Sparks inquires 'Why not?'

'Why, it seems to me, Sparks,' says John Safe, 'rather a murdering mode of action.'

Sparks, to whom the question has never presented itself in this light, turns pale.

'You see,' John Safe pursues, 'when I first came upon this line, I didn't know – how could I? – where there was a bridge and where a tunnel – where we took the turnpike road – where there was a cutting – where there was an embankment – where there was an incline – when full speed, when half, when slacken, when shut off, when your whistle going, when not. I got to know all such, by degrees; first, from them that was used to it; then, from my own use, Sparks.'

'So you did, John,' said Sparks.

'Well, Sparks! When we and all the rest that are used to it, Engine Drivers and Firemen, all down the line and up again, lay our heads together, and say to the public, "if you don't back us up in what we want, we'll all go to the right-about, such a-day, so that Nobody shall know all such" – that's rather a murdering mode of action, it appears to me.'

Thomas Sparks, still uncomfortably pale, wishes Coke of Wolverhampton were present to reply.

'Because, it's saying to the public, "If you *don't* back us up, we'll do our united best towards your being run away with, and run into, and smashed, and jammed, and dislocated, and having your heads took off, and your bodies gleaned for, in small pieces – and we hope you may!" Now, you know, that has a murdering appearance, Sparks, upon the whole!' says John Safe.

Sparks, much shocked, suggests that 'it mightn't happen.'

'True. But it might,' returns John Safe, 'and we know it might – no men better. We threaten that it might. Now, when we entered into this employment, Sparks, I doubt if it was any part of our fair bargain, that we should have a monopoly of this line, and a manslaughtering sort of a power over the public. What do *you* think?'

Thomas Sparks thinks certainly not. But, Coke of Wolverhampton said, last Wednesday (as somebody else had said to him), that every man worthy of the name of Briton must stick up for his rights.

'There again!' says John Safe. 'To my mind, Sparks, it's not at all clear that any person's rights *can be* another person's wrongs. And, that our strike must be a wrong to the persons we strike against, call 'em Company or Public, seems pretty plain.'

'What do they go and unite against us for, then?' demands Thomas Sparks.

'I don't know that they do,' replies John Safe. 'We took service with this company, as Individuals, ourselves, and not as a body; and you know very well we no more ever thought, then, of turning them off, as one man, than they ever thought of turning us off as one man. If the Company is a body, now, it was a body all the same when we came into its employment with our eyes wide open, Sparks.'

'Why do they make aggravating rules then, respecting the Loco-motives?' demands Mr Sparks, 'which, Coke of Wolverhampton says, is Despotism!'

'Well, anyways they're made for the public safety, Sparks,' returns John Safe; 'and what's for the public safety, is for yours and mine. The first thing to go, in a smash, is, generally, the Engine and Tender.'

'*I* don't want to be made more safe,' growls Thomas Sparks. '*I* am safe enough, *I* am.'

'But, it don't signify a cinder whether you want it or don't want it,' returns his companion. 'You must be made safe, Sparks, whether you like or not, – if not on your own account, on other people's.'

'Coke of Wolverhampton says, Justice! That's what Coke says!' observes Mr Sparks, after a little deliberation.

'And a very good thing it is to say,' returns John Safe. 'A better thing to do. But, let's be sure we do it. I can't see that we good workmen do it to ourselves and families, by letting in bad un's that are out of employment. That's as to ourselves. I am sure we don't do it to the Company or Public, by conspiring together, to turn an accidental advantage against 'em. Look at other people! Gentlemen don't strike.

Union doctors are bad enough paid (which we are not), but *they* don't strike. Many dispensary and hospital-doctors are not over well treated, but *they* don't strike, and leave the sick a groaning in their beds. So much for the use of power. Then for taste. The respectable young men and women that serve in the shops, *they* didn't strike, when they wanted early closing.'

'All the world wasn't against *them*,' Thomas Sparks puts in.

'No; if it had been, a man might have begun to doubt their being in the right,' returns John Safe.

'Why, you don't doubt *our* being in the right, I hope?' says Sparks.

'If I do, I an't alone in it. You know there are scores and scores of us that, of their own accord, don't want no striking, nor anything of the kind.'

'Suppose we all agreed that we was a prey to despotism, what then?' asks Sparks.

'Why, even then, I should recommend our doing our work, true to the public, and appealing to the public feeling against the same,' replies John Safe. 'It would very soon act on the Company. As to the Company and the Public siding together against us, I don't find the Public too apt to go along with the Company when it can help it.'

'Don't we owe nothing to our order?' inquires Thomas Sparks.

'A good deal. And when we enter on a strike like this, we don't appear to me to pay it. We are rather of the upper sort of our order; and what we owe to our workmen, is, to set 'em a good example, and to represent them well. Now, there is, at present, a deal of general talk (here and there, with a great deal of truth in it) of combinations of capital, and one power and another, against workmen. I leave you to judge how it serves the workman's case, at such a time, to show a small body of his order, combined, in a misuse of power, against the whole community!'

It appears to us, not only that John Safe might reasonably urge these arguments and facts; but, that John Safe did actually present many of them, and not remotely suggest the rest, to the consideration of an aggregate meeting of the Engine Drivers and Firemen engaged on the Southern Division of the line, which was held at Camden Town on the day after Christmas Day. The sensible, moderate, and upright tone of some men who spoke at that meeting, as we find them reported in The Times, commands our admiration and respect, though it by no means surprises us. We would especially commend to the attention of our readers, the speech of an Engine Driver on the Great Western Railway, and the letter of the Enginemen and Firemen at the Bedford Station. Writing, in submission to the necessities of this publication, immediately after that meeting was held, we are, of course, in ignorance of the issue of the question, though it will probably have transpired before the present number appears. It can, however, in no wise affect the observations we have made, or those with which we will conclude.

To the men, we would submit, that if they fail in adjusting the difference to their complete satisfaction, the failure will be principally their own fault, as inseparable, in a great measure, from the injudicious and unjustifiable threat into which the more sensible portion of them have allowed themselves to be betrayed. What the Directors might have conceded to temperate remonstrance, it is easy to understand they may deem it culpable weakness to yield to so alarming a combination against the public service and safety.

To the Public, we would submit, that the steadiness and patriotism of English workmen may, in the long run, be safely trusted; and that this mistake, once remedied, may be calmly dismissed. It is natural, in the first hot reception of such a menace, to write letters to newspapers, urging strong-handed legislation, or the enforcement of pains and penalties, past, present, or to come, on such deserters from their posts. But, it is not agreeable, on calmer reflection, to contemplate the English artisan as working under a curb or yoke, or even as being supposed to require one. His spirit is of the highest; his nature is of the best. He comes of a great race, and his character is famous in the world. If a false step on the part of any man should be generously forgotten, it should be forgotten in him.

59

'Births. Mrs Meek, of a Son'

Household Words, 22 February 1851 (leading article) *(RP)*

In the midwife or monthly nurse sketched here Dickens presents, as T.W. Hill observes (unpub. notes to *RP*, Dickens House), 'a more respectable Mrs Gamp'. Alone among European countries, England had no regulations regarding the practice of midwifery (this remained the case until 1902): 'Any person, however ignorant and untrained, could describe herself as a midwife and practise for gain' (*Encyclopedia Britannica*, 11th edn, s.v. 'midwife'). The custom of 'swaddling' new-born infants, wrapping them up in narrow lengths of bandage to prevent free movement of the limbs, had been condemned as far back as 1826 (see W.P. Dewees's *Physical Treatment of Children*, cited in *OED*, s.v. 'swaddling'), but persisted far into Victorian times. The phrase 'the brushes of All Nations' is a playful allusion to the coming Great Exhibition of the Works of All Nations (opened 1 May 1851).

My name is Meek. I am, in fact, Mr Meek. That son is mine and Mrs Meek's. When I saw the announcement in the Times, I dropped the paper. I had put it in, myself, and paid for it, but it looked so noble that it overpowered me. As soon as I could compose my feelings, I took the paper up to Mrs Meek's bedside. 'Maria Jane,' said I (I allude to Mrs Meek), 'you are now a public character.' We read the review of our child, several times, with feelings of the strongest emotion; and I sent the boy who cleans the boots and shoes, to the office, for fifteen copies. No reduction was made on taking that quantity.

It is scarcely necessary for me to say, that our child had been expected. In fact, it had been expected, with comparative confidence, for some months. Mrs Meek's mother, who resides with us – of the name of Bigby – had made every preparation for its admission to our circle.

I hope and believe I am a quiet man. I will go farther. I *know* I am a quiet man. My constitution is tremulous, my voice was never loud, and, in point of stature, I have been from infancy, small. I have the greatest respect for Maria Jane's Mama. She is a most remarkable woman. I honour Maria Jane's Mama. In my opinion she would storm a town, single-handed, with a hearth-broom, and carry it. I have never known her to yield any point whatever, to mortal man. She is calculated to terrify the stoutest heart.

Still – but I will not anticipate.

The first intimation I had, of any preparations being in progress, on the part of Maria Jane's Mama, was one afternoon, several months ago. I came home earlier than usual from the office, and, proceeding into the dining-room, found an obstruction behind the door, which prevented it from opening freely. It was an obstruction of a soft nature. On looking in, I found it to be a female.

The female in question stood in the corner behind the door, consuming Sherry Wine. From the nutty smell of that beverage pervading the apartment, I have no doubt she was consuming a second glassful. She wore a black bonnet of large dimensions, and was copious in figure. The expression of her countenance was severe and discontented. The words to which she gave utterance on seeing me, were these, 'Oh git along with you, Sir, if *you* please; me and Mrs Bigby don't want no male parties here!'

That female was Mrs Prodgit.

I immediately withdrew, of course. I was rather hurt, but I made no remark. Whether it was that I showed a lowness of spirits after dinner, in consequence of feeling that I seemed to intrude, I cannot say. But, Maria Jane's Mama said to me on her retiring for the night: in a low distinct voice, and with a look of reproach that completely subdued me: 'George Meek, Mrs Prodgit is your wife's nurse!'

I bear no ill-will towards Mrs Prodgit. Is it likely that I, writing this with tears in my eyes, should be capable of deliberate animosity towards a female, so essential to the welfare of Maria Jane? I am willing to admit that Fate may have been to blame, and not Mrs Prodgit; but, it is undeniably true, that the latter female brought desolation and devastation into my lowly dwelling.

We were happy after her first appearance; we were sometimes exceedingly so. But, whenever the parlor door was opened, and 'Mrs Prodgit!' announced (and she was very often announced), misery ensued. I could not bear Mrs Prodgit's look. I felt that I was far from wanted, and had no business to exist in Mrs Prodgit's presence. Between Maria Jane's Mama, and Mrs Prodgit, there was a dreadful, secret, understanding – a dark mystery and conspiracy, pointing me out as a being to be shunned. I appeared to have done something that was evil. Whenever Mrs Prodgit called, after dinner, I retired to my dressing-room – where the temperature is very low, indeed, in the wintry time of the year – and sat looking at my frosty breath as it rose before me, and at my rack of boots: a serviceable article of furniture, but never, in my opinion, an exhilarating object. The length of the councils that were held with Mrs Prodgit, under these circumstances, I will not attempt to describe. I will merely remark, that Mrs Prodgit always consumed Sherry Wine while the deliberations were in progress; that they always ended in Maria Jane's being in wretched spirits on the sofa; and that Maria Jane's Mama always received me, when I was recalled, with a look of desolate triumph that too plainly said, '*Now*, George Meek! You see my child, Maria Jane, a ruin, and I hope you are satisfied!'

I pass, generally, over the period that intervened between the day when Mrs Prodgit entered her protest against male parties, and the ever-memorable midnight when I brought her to my unobtrusive home in a cab, with an extremely large box on the roof, and a bundle, a bandbox, and a basket, between the driver's legs. I have no objection to Mrs Prodgit, (aided and abetted by Mrs Bigby, who I never can forget is the parent of Maria Jane), taking entire possession of my unassuming establishment. In the recesses of my own breast, the thought may linger that a man in possession cannot be so dreadful as a woman, and that woman Mrs Prodgit; but, I ought to bear a good deal, and I hope I can, and do. Huffing and snubbing, prey upon my feelings; but, I can bear them without complaint. They may tell in the long run; I may be hustled about, from post to pillar, beyond my strength; nevertheless, I wish to avoid giving rise to words in the family.

The voice of Nature, however, cries aloud in behalf of Augustus George, my infant son. It is for him that I wish to utter a few plaintive household words. I am not at all angry; I am mild – but miserable.

I wish to know why, when my child, Augustus George, was expected in our circle, a provision of pins was made, as if the little stranger were a criminal who was to be put to the torture immediately on his arrival, instead of a holy babe? I wish to know why haste was made to stick those pins all over his innocent form, in every direction? I wish to be informed why light and air are excluded from Augustus George, like poisons? Why, I ask, is my unoffending infant so hedged into a basket-bedstead, with dimity and calico, with miniature sheets and blankets, that I can only hear him snuffle (and no wonder!) deep down under the pink hood of a little bathing-machine, and can never peruse even so much of his lineaments as his nose.

Was I expected to be the father of a French Roll, that the brushes of All Nations were laid in, to rasp Augustus George? Am I to be told that his sensitive skin was ever intended by Nature to have rashes brought out upon it, by the premature and incessant use of those formidable little instruments?

Is my son a Nutmeg, that he is to be grated on the stiff edges of sharp frills? Am I the parent of a Muslin boy, that his yielding surface is to be crimped and small-plaited? Or is my child composed of Paper or of Linen, that impressions of the finer getting-up art, practised by the laundress, are to be printed off, all over his soft arms and legs, as I constantly observe them? The starch enters his soul; who can wonder that he cries?

Was Augustus George intended to have limbs, or to be born a Torso? I presume that limbs were the intention, as they are the usual practice. Then, why are my poor child's limbs fettered and tied up? Am I to be told that there is any analogy between Augustus George Meek, and Jack Sheppard?

Analyse Castor Oil at any Institution of Chemistry that may be agreed upon, and inform me what resemblance, in taste, it bears to that natural provision which it is at once the pride and duty of Maria Jane, to administer to Augustus George! Yet, I charge Mrs Prodgit (aided and abetted by Mrs Bigby) with systematically forcing Castor Oil on my innocent son, from the first hour of his birth. When that medicine, in its efficient action, causes internal disturbance to Augustus George, I charge Mrs Prodgit (aided and abetted by Mrs Bigby) with insanely and inconsistently administering opium to allay the storm she has raised! What is the meaning of this?

If the days of Egyptian Mummies are past, how dare Mrs Prodgit require, for the use of my son, an amount of flannel and linen that would carpet my humble roof? Do I wonder that she requires it? No! This morning, within an hour, I beheld this agonising sight. I beheld my son – Augustus George – in Mrs Prodgit's hands, and on Mrs Prodgit's knee being dressed. He was at the moment, comparatively speaking, in a state of nature; having nothing on, but an extremely short shirt, remarkably disproportionate to the length of his usual outer garments. Trailing from Mrs Prodgit's lap, on the floor, was a long narrow roller or bandage – I should say, of several yards in extent. In this, I saw Mrs Prodgit tightly roll the body of my unoffending infant, turning him over and over, now presenting his unconscious face upwards, now the back of his bald head, until the unnatural feat was accomplished, and the bandage secured by a pin, which I have every reason to believe entered the body of my only child. In this tourniquet, he passes the present phase of his existence. Can I know it, and smile!

I fear I have been betrayed into expressing myself warmly, but I feel deeply. Not for myself; for Augustus George. I dare not interfere. Will any one? Will any publication? Any doctor? Any parent? Any body? I do not complain that Mrs Prodgit (aided and abetted by Mrs Bigby) entirely alienates Maria Jane's affections from me, and interposes an impassable barrier between us. I do not complain of being made of no account. I do not want to be of any account. But, Augustus George is a production of Nature (I cannot think otherwise), and I claim that he should be treated with some remote reference to Nature. In my opinion, Mrs Prodgit is, from first to last, a convention and a superstition. Are all the faculty afraid of Mrs Prodgit? If not, why don't they take her in hand and improve her?

P.S. Maria Jane's Mama boasts of her own knowledge of the subject, and says she brought up seven children besides Maria Jane. But, how do *I* know that she might not have brought them up, much better? Maria Jane herself, is far from strong, and is subject to headaches, and nervous indigestion. Besides which, I learn from the statistical tables that one child in five, dies within the first year of its life; and one child in three, within the fifth. That don't look as if we could never improve in these particulars, I think!

P.P.S. Augustus George is in convulsions.

'Punch and the Smithfield Savages', Punch, *24 April 1847.*

60

A Monument of French Folly

Household Words, 8 March 1851 (leading article) *(RP)*

Dickens here continues his vigorous support of the public pressure on the City of London's governing body, the Court of Common Council, to accept the 1849 Royal Commission on Smithfield's recommendation that the market be relocated in a less central and densely populated part of London. The Council's extreme reluctance to adopt this course was hardly surprising given that the City was, according to A. Forshaw and T. Bergström (*Smithfield Past and Present*, 2nd edn [1990], p. 57) raking in a net profit of almost £10,000 a year from tolls imposed on Smithfield traders (one old penny per head per beast and one shilling per score of sheep – W. Thornbury, *Old and New London* [n.d.], Vol. 2, p. 350).

This 'reeking central abomination', as a correspondent of *The Times* called it (31 January 1851, p. 6, col. 4), had been the subject of attack for many years, one of the most memorable depictions of its horrors being Dickens's own in *Oliver Twist* (Ch. 21). Dickens had also collaborated with Wills on an early *HW* article, 'The Heart of Mid-London' (4 May 1850), containing harrowing descriptions of the suffering inflicted on the animals at Smithfield (see Stone, Vol. I, pp. 101–11); and published (29 June 1850) an even more horrifying account, 'The Cattle-road to Ruin' by R.H. Horne, describing how livestock was got to Smithfield and the appalling conditions obtaining in London slaughterhouses. Horne also contributed some verses on the subject, 'The Smithfield Bull to his Cousin of Nineveh', to the 15 March issue of *HW*. In 'Lively Turtle' (article 54) Dickens had mocked a fatuous pro-Smithfield speech by Councilman Henry Taylor and he recalls it in the first paragraph of this piece.

The distinguished scientist Sir Richard Owen was a member of the Royal Commission (in his speech Taylor had raised a laugh by objecting to this on the grounds that Owen 'had some crotchets in his head about sanitary reform') and a vigorous proponent of the idea of moving the livestock market to a healthier site. Parliament eventually passed the Smithfield Market Removal Bill in 1852 and the last market was held on the old site in 1855, the new one being located in Copenhagen Fields, north of Islington.

For this article Dickens made a special trip (10–15 February) to Paris to inspect the Poissy market and the city abattoirs ('they will make a decent description, I think,' he wrote to Wills [*Pilgrim*, Vol. VI, p. 290]). Napoleon had issued regulations concerning the long-established livestock market at Poissy and ordered the construction of five clean new slaughterhouses in Paris 'outside the populated areas to replace the old abattoirs in the heart of the city which were real hives of infection' (M. Guerrini, *Napoleon and Paris* [1970], p. 177). These slaughterhouses, one of which was at Montmartre, were all put into use in 1818.

The reference to James Bruce concerns his *Travels to Discover the Source of the Nile in the Years 1768, 1769 [etc]* (5 vols, Edinburgh, 1790). In Abyssinia Bruce found that the corpses of criminals 'slain for treason, murder, and violence, on the high-way at certain times' were seldom buried: 'the streets of Gondar are strewed with pieces of their carcases, which bring the wild beasts in multitudes into the city as soon as it becomes dark.... The dogs used to bring pieces of human bodies into the house and court-yard, to eat them in greater security' (Vol. III, p. 288).

The Times, which campaigned relentlessly against the continuance of Smithfield Market, reprinted Dickens's description of Poissy under the heading of 'The Smithfield of Paris' (6 March 1851, p. 4, col. 5).

There are two characteristically Dickensian language-games in this piece: the rendering of idiomatic French into the literal rather than the idiomatic

English equivalent ('brave infants' instead of 'lads', etc.); and the periphrastic avoidance of swear words (p. 335: 'Damn your eyes!' was a common nineteenth-century oath).

Literary allusions (p. 330) 'all who run . . . may read': John Keble's *Christian Year*, 'There is a book, who runs may read'; (p. 331) 'the roast beef of England': Fielding's *Grub Street Opera*, Act 3, Sc. 3; (p. 331) 'prunes are ill for a green wound': Shakespeare, *Henry IV Part Two*, Act 2, Sc. 1 (the correct reading is 'prawns'); (p. 331) 'Britons never, never': James Thomson's 'Rule, Britannia', *Alfred*, Act 2, scene the last (1740); (p. 338) 'potent, grave and common counselling Signors': adapted from Shakespeare, *Othello*, Act 1, Sc. 3.

It was profoundly observed by a witty member of the Court of Common Council, in Council assembled in the City of London, in the year of our Lord one thousand eight hundred and fifty, that the French are a frog-eating people, who wear wooden shoes.

We are credibly informed, in reference to the nation whom this choice spirit so happily disposed of, that the caricatures and stage representations which were current in England some half a century ago, exactly depict their present condition. For example, we understand that every French-man, without exception, wears a pigtail and curl-papers. That he is extremely sallow, thin, long-faced, and lantern-jawed. That the calves of his legs are invariably undeveloped; that his legs fail at the knees, and that his shoulders are always higher than his ears. We are likewise assured that he rarely tastes any food but soup maigre, and an onion; that he always says, 'By Gar! Aha! Vat you tell me, Sare?' at the end of every sentence he utters; and that the true generic name of his race is the Mounseers, or the Parly-voos. If he be not a dancing-master, or a barber, he must be a cook; since no other trades but those three are congenial to the tastes of the people, or permitted by the Institutions of the country. He is a slave, of course. The ladies of France (who are also slaves) invariably have their heads tied up in Belcher handkerchiefs, wear long ear-rings, carry tambourines, and beguile the weariness of their yoke by singing in head voices through their noses – principally to barrel-organs.

It may be generally summed up, of this inferior people, that they have no idea of anything.

Of a great Institution like Smithfield, they are unable to form the least conception. A Beast Market in the heart of Paris would be regarded as an impossible nuisance. Nor have they any notion of slaughter-houses in the midst of a city. One of these benighted frog-eaters would scarcely understand your meaning, if you told him of the existence of such a British bulwark.

It is agreeable, and perhaps pardonable, to indulge in a little self-complacency when our right to it is thoroughly established. At the present time, to be rendered memorable by a final attack on that good old market which is the (rotten) apple of the Corporation's eye, let us compare ourselves, to our national delight and pride, as to these two subjects of slaughter-house and beast-market, with the outlandish foreigner.

The blessings of Smithfield are too well understood to need recapitulation; all who run (away from mad bulls and pursuing oxen) may read. Any market-day, they may be beheld in glorious action. Possibly, the merits of our slaughter-houses are not yet quite so generally appreciated.

Slaughter-houses, in the large towns of England, are always (with the exception of one or two enterprising towns) most numerous in the most densely crowded places, where there is the least circulation of air. They are often underground, in cellars; they are sometimes in close back yards; sometimes (as in Spitalfields) in the very shops where the meat is sold. Occasionally, under good private management, they are ventilated and clean. For the most part, they are unventilated and dirty; and, to the reeking walls, putrid fat and other offensive animal matter clings with a tenacious hold. The busiest slaughter-houses in London are in the neighbourhood of Smithfield, in Newgate Market, in Whitechapel, in Newport market, in Leadenhall Market, in Clare Market. All these places are surrounded by houses of a poor description, swarming with inhabitants. Some of them are close to the worst burial-grounds in London. When the slaughter-house is below the ground, it is a common practice to throw the sheep down areas, neck and crop – which is exciting, but not at all cruel. When it is on the level surface, it is often extremely difficult to approach. Then, the beasts have to be worried, and goaded, and pronged, and tail-twisted for a long time before they can be got in – which is entirely owing to their natural obstinacy. When it is not difficult of approach, but is in a foul condition, what they see and scent makes them still more reluctant to enter – which is their natural obstinacy again. When they do get in at last, after no trouble and suffering to speak of (for, there is nothing in the previous journey into the heart of London, the night's endurance in Smithfield, the struggle out again, among the crowded multitude, the coaches, carts, waggons, omnibuses, gigs, chaises, phaetons, cabs, trucks, dogs, boys, whoopings, roarings, and ten thousand other distractions), they are represented to be in a most unfit state to be killed, according to microscopic examinations made of their fevered blood by one of the most distinguished physiologists in the world, PROFESSOR OWEN – but that's humbug. When they *are* killed, at last, their reeking carcases are hung in impure air, to become, as the same Professor will explain to you, less nutritious and more unwholesome – but he is only an *un*common counsellor, so don't mind *him*. In half a quarter of a mile's length of Whitechapel, at one time, there shall be six hundred newly slaughtered oxen hanging up, and seven hundred sheep – but, the more the merrier – proof of prosperity. Hard by Snow Hill and Warwick Lane, you shall see the little children, inured to sights of brutality from their birth, trotting along the alleys, mingled with troops of horribly busy pigs, up to their ankles in blood – but it makes the young rascals hardy. Into the imperfect sewers of this overgrown city, you shall have the immense mass of corruption, engendered by these practices, lazily thrown out of sight, to rise in poisonous gases, into your house at night, when your sleeping children will most readily absorb them, and to find its languid way, at last, into the river that you drink – but, the French are a frog-eating people who wear wooden shoes, and it's O the roast beef of England, my boy, the jolly old English roast beef!

It is quite a mistake – a new-fangled notion altogether – to suppose that there is any natural antagonism between putrefaction and health. They know better than that, in the Common Council. You may talk about Nature, in her wisdom, always warning man through his sense of smell, when he draws near to something dangerous; but, that won't go down in the city. Nature very often don't mean anything. Mrs Quickly says that prunes are ill for a green wound; but, whosoever says that putrid animal substances are ill for a green wound, or for robust vigor, or for any thing or for any body, is a humanity-monger and a humbug. Britons never, never, never, &c., therefore. And prosperity to cattle-driving, cattle-slaughtering, bone-crushing, blood-boiling, trotter-scraping, tripe-dressing, paunch-cleaning, gut-spinning, hide-preparing, tallow-melting, and other salubrious proceedings, in the midst of hospitals, church-yards, workhouses, schools, infirmaries, refuges, dwellings, provision-shops, nurseries, sick-beds, every stage and baiting-place in the journey from birth to death!

These *un*common counsellors, your Professor Owens and fellows, will contend that to tolerate these things in a civilised city, is to reduce it to a worse condition than Bruce found to prevail in Abyssinnia. For, there (say they) the jackals and wild dogs came at night to devour the offal; whereas here there are no such natural scavengers, and quite as savage customs. Further, they will demonstrate that nothing in Nature is intended to be wasted, and that besides the waste which such abuses occasion in the articles of health and life – main sources of the riches of any community – they lead to a prodigious waste of changing matters, which might, with proper preparation, and under scientific direction, be safely applied to the increase of the fertility of the land. Thus (they argue) does Nature ever avenge infractions of her beneficent laws, and so surely as Man is determined to warp any of her blessings into curses, shall they become curses, and shall he suffer heavily. But, this is cant. Just as it is cant of the worst description to say to the London Corporation, 'How can you exhibit to the people so plain a spectacle of dishonest equivocation, as to claim the right of holding a market in the midst of the great city, for one of your vested privileges, when you know that when your last market-holding charter was granted to you by King Charles the First, Smithfield stood IN THE SUBURBS OF LONDON, and is in that very charter so described in those five words?' – which is certainly true, but has nothing to do with the question.

Now to the comparison, in these particulars of civilisation, between the capital of England, and the capital of that frog-eating and wooden-shoe wearing country, which the illustrious Common Councilman so sarcastically settled.

In Paris, there is no Cattle Market. Cows and calves are sold within the city, but the Cattle Markets are at Poissy, about thirteen miles off, on a line of Railway; and at Sceaux, about five miles off. The Poissy market is held every Thursday; the Sceaux market, every Monday. In Paris, there are no slaughter-houses, in our acceptation of the term. There are five public Abattoirs – within the walls, though in the suburbs – and in these all the slaughtering for the city must be performed. They are managed by a Syndicat or Guild of Butchers, who confer with the Minister of the Interior on all matters affecting the trade, and who are consulted when any new regulations are contemplated for its government. They are, likewise, under the vigilant superintendance of the Police. Every butcher must be licensed: which proves him at once to be a slave, for we don't license butchers in England – we only license apothecaries, attorneys, postmasters, publicans, hawkers, retailers of tobacco, snuff, pepper, and vinegar – and one or two other little trades not worth mentioning. Every arrangement in connexion with the slaughtering and sale of meat, is matter of strict police regulation. (Slavery again, though we certainly have a general sort of a Police Act here.)

But, in order that the reader may understand what a monument of folly these frog-eaters have raised in their abattoirs and cattle markets, and may compare it with what common counselling has done for us all these years, and would still do but for the innovating spirit of the times, here follows a short account of a recent visit to these places: –

It was as sharp a February morning as you would desire to feel at your fingers' ends when I turned out – tumbling over a chiffonier with his little basket and rake, who was picking up the bits of colored paper that had been swept out, overnight, from a Bon-Bon shop – to take the Butchers' Train to Poissy. A cold dim light just touched the high roofs of the Tuileries which have seen such changes, such distracted crowds, such riot and bloodshed; and they looked as calm, and as old, all covered with white frost, as the very Pyramids. There was not light enough, yet, to strike upon the towers of Notre Dame across the water; but I thought of the dark pavement of the old Cathedral as just beginning to be streaked with grey; and of the lamps in the 'House of God,' the Hospital close to it, burning low and being quenched; and of the keeper of the Morgue going about with a fading lantern, busy in the arrangement of his terrible waxwork for another sunny day.

The sun was up, and shining merrily when the butchers and I, announcing our departure with an engine-shriek to sleepy Paris, rattled away for the Cattle Market. Across the country, over the Seine, among a forest of scrubby trees – the hoar frost lying cold in shady places, and glittering in the light – and here we are at Poissy! Out leap the butchers who have been chattering all the way like madmen, and off they straggle for the Cattle Market (still chattering, of course, incessantly), in hats and caps of all shapes, in coats and blouses, in calf-skins, cow-skins, horse-skins, furs, shaggy mantles, hairy coats, sacking, baize, oil-skin, anything you please that will keep a man and a butcher warm, upon a frosty morning.

Many a French town have I seen, between this spot of ground and Strasburgh or Marseilles, that might sit for your picture, little Poissy! Barring the details of your old church, I know you well, albeit we make acquaintance, now, for the first time. I know your narrow, straggling, winding streets, with a kennel in the midst, and lamps slung across. I know your picturesque street-corners, winding up-hill Heaven knows why or where! I know your tradesmen's inscriptions, in letters not quite fat enough; your barbers' brazen basins dangling over little shops; your Cafés and Estaminets, with cloudy bottles of stale syrup in the windows, and pictures of crossed billiard-cues outside. I know this very grey horse with his tail rolled up in a knot like the 'back-hair' of an untidy woman, who won't be shod, and who makes himself heraldic by clattering across the street on his hind legs, while twenty voices shriek and growl at him as a Brigand, an accursed Robber, and an everlastingly-doomed Pig. I know your sparkling town-fountain too, my Poissy, and am glad to see it near a cattle market, gushing so freshly, under the auspices of a gallant little sublimated Frenchman wrought in metal, perched upon the top. Through all the land of France I know this unswept room at The Glory, with its peculiar smell of beans and coffee, where the butchers crowd about the stove, drinking the thinnest of wine from the smallest of tumblers; where the thickest of coffee-cups mingle with the longest of loaves, and the weakest of lump sugar; where Madame at the counter easily acknowledges the homage of all entering and departing butchers;

where the billiard-table is covered up in the midst like a great bird-cage – but the bird may sing by-and-bye!

A bell! The Calf Market! Polite departure of butchers. Hasty payment and departure on the part of amateur Visitor. Madame reproaches Ma'amselle for too fine a susceptibility in reference to the devotion of a Butcher in a bear-skin. Monsieur, the landlord of The Glory, counts a double handful of sous, without an unobliterated inscription, or an undamaged crowned head, among them.

There is little noise without, abundant space, and no confusion. The open area devoted to the market, is divided into three portions: the Calf Market, the Cattle Market, the Sheep Market. Calves at eight, cattle at ten, sheep at mid-day. All is very clean.

The Calf Market is a raised platform of stone, some three or four feet high, open on all sides, with a lofty over-spreading roof, supported on stone columns, which give it the appearance of a sort of vineyard from Northern Italy. Here, on the raised pavement, lie innumerable calves, all bound hind-legs and fore-legs together, and all trembling violently – perhaps with cold, perhaps with fear, perhaps with pain; for, this mode of tying, which seems to be an absolute superstition with the peasantry, can hardly fail to cause great suffering. Here, they lie, patiently in rows, among the straw, with their stolid faces and inexpressive eyes: superintended by men and women, boys and girls; here, they are inspected by our friends, the butchers, bargained for, and bought. Plenty of time; plenty of room; plenty of good humour. 'Monsieur François in the bear-skin, how do you do, my friend? You come from Paris by the train? The fresh air does you good. If you are in want of three or four fine calves this market-morning, my angel, I, Madame Doche, shall be happy to deal with you. Behold these calves, Monsieur François! Great Heaven, you are doubtful! Well, sir, walk round and look about you. If you find better for the money, buy them. If not, come to me!' Monsieur François goes his way leisurely, and keeps a wary eye upon the stock. No other butcher jostles Monsieur François; Monsieur François jostles no other butcher. Nobody is flustered and aggravated. Nobody is savage. In the midst of the country blue frocks and red handkerchiefs, and the butchers' coats, shaggy, furry, and hairy: of calf-skin, cow-skin, horse-skin, and bear-skin: towers a cocked hat and a blue cloak. Slavery! For *our* Police wear great coats and glazed hats.

But now the bartering is over, and the calves are sold. 'Ho! Gregorie, Antoine, Jean, Louis! Bring up the carts, my children! Quick, brave infants! Hola! Hi!'

The carts, well littered with straw, are backed up to the edge of the raised pavement, and various hot infants carry calves upon their heads, and dexterously pitch them in, while other hot infants, standing in the carts, arrange the calves, and pack them carefully in straw. Here is a promising young calf, not sold, whom Madame Doche unbinds. Pardon me, Madame Doche, but I fear this mode of tying the four legs of a quadruped together, though strictly à la mode, is not quite right. You observe, Madame Doche, that the cord leaves deep indentations in the skin, and that the animal is so cramped at first as not to know, or even remotely suspect, that he *is* unbound, until you are so obliging as to kick him, in your delicate little way, and pull his tail like a bell-rope. Then, he staggers to his knees, not being able to stand, and stumbles about like a drunken calf, or the horse at Franconi's, whom you may have seen, Madame Doche, who is supposed to have been mortally wounded in battle. But, what is this rubbing against me, as I apostrophise Madame Doche? It is another heated infant, with a calf upon his head. 'Pardon, Monsieur, but will you have the politeness to allow me to pass?' 'Ah, Sir, willingly. I am vexed to obstruct the way.' On he staggers, calf and all, and makes no allusion whatever either to my eyes or limbs.

Now, the carts are all full. More straw, my Antoine, to shake over these top rows; then, off we will clatter, rumble, jolt, and rattle, a long row of us, out of the first town-gate, and out at the second town-gate, and past the empty sentry-box, and the little thin square bandbox of a guardhouse, where nobody seems to live; and away for Paris, by the paved road, lying, a straight straight line, in the long long avenue of trees. We can neither choose our road, nor our pace, for that is all prescribed to us. The public convenience demands that our carts should get to Paris by such a route, and no other (Napoleon had leisure to find that out, while he had a little war with the world upon his hands), and woe betide us if we infringe orders.

Droves of oxen stand in the Cattle Market, tied to iron bars fixed into posts of granite. Other droves advance slowly down the long avenue, past the second town-gate, and the first town-gate, and the sentry-box, and the bandbox, thawing the morning with their smoky breath as they come along. Plenty of room; plenty of time. Neither man nor beast is driven out of his wits by coaches, carts, waggons, omnibuses, gigs, chaises, phaetons, cabs, trucks, boys, whoopings, roarings, and multitudes. No tail-twisting is necessary – no iron pronging is necessary. There are no iron prongs here. The market for cattle is held as quietly as the market for calves. In due time, off the cattle go to Paris; the drovers can no more choose their road, nor their time, nor the numbers they shall drive, than they can choose their hour for dying in the course of nature.

Sheep next. The Sheep-pens are up here, past the Branch Bank of Paris established for the convenience of the butchers, and behind the two pretty fountains they are making in the Market. My name is Bull: yet I think I should like to see as good twin fountains – not to say in

Smithfield, but in England anywhere. Plenty of room; plenty of time. And here are sheep-dogs, sensible as ever, but with a certain French air about them – not without a suspicion of dominoes – with a kind of flavor of moustache and beard – demonstrative dogs, shaggy and loose where an English dog would be tight and close – not so troubled with business calculations as our English drovers' dogs, who have always got their sheep upon their minds, and think about their work, even resting, as you may see by their faces; but, dashing, showy, rather unreliable dogs: who might worry me instead of their legitimate charges if they saw occasion – and might see it somewhat suddenly. The market for sheep passes off like the other two; and away they go, by *their* allotted road to Paris. My way being the Railway, I make the best of it at twenty miles an hour; whirling through the now high-lighted landscape; thinking that the inexperienced green buds will be wishing before long, they had not been tempted to come out so soon; and wondering who lives in this or that château, all window and lattice, and what the family may have for breakfast this sharp morning.

After the market comes the Abattoir. What abattoir shall I visit first? Montmartre is the largest. So, I will go there.

The abattoirs are all within the walls of Paris, with an eye to the receipt of the octroi duty; but, they stand in open places in the suburbs, removed from the press and bustle of the city. They are managed by the Syndicat or Guild of Butchers under the inspection of the Police. Certain smaller items of the revenue derived from them are in part retained by the Guild for the payment of their expenses, and in part devoted by it to charitable purposes in connexion with the trade. They cost six hundred and eighty thousand pounds; and they return to the City of Paris an interest on that outlay, amounting to nearly six and a half per cent.

Here, in a sufficiently dismantled space is the Abattoir of Montmartre, covering nearly nine acres of ground, surrounded by a high wall, and looking from the outside like a cavalry barrack. At the iron gates is a small functionary in a large cocked hat. 'Monsieur desires to see the abattoir? Most certainly.' State being inconvenient in private transactions, and Monsieur being already aware of the cocked hat, the functionary puts it into a little official bureau which it almost fills, and accompanies me in the modest attire – as to his head – of ordinary life.

Many of the animals from Poissy have come here. On the arrival of each drove, it was turned into yonder ample space, where each butcher who had bought, selected his own purchases. Some, we see now, in these long perspectives of stalls with a high overhanging roof of wood and open tiles rising above the walls. While they rest here, before being slaughtered, they are required to be fed and watered, and the stalls must be kept clean. A stated amount of fodder must always be ready in the loft above; and the supervision is of the strictest kind. The same regulations apply to sheep and calves; for which, portions of these perspectives are strongly railed off. All the buildings are of the strongest and most solid description.

After traversing these lairs, through which, besides the upper provision for ventilation just mentioned, there may be a thorough current of air from opposite windows in the side walls, and from doors at either end, we traverse the broad, paved, court-yard until we come to the slaughter-houses. They are all exactly alike, and adjoin each other, to the number of eight or nine together, in blocks of solid building. Let us walk into the first.

It is firmly built and paved with stone. It is well lighted, thoroughly aired, and lavishly provided with fresh water. It has two doors opposite each other; the first, the door by which I entered from the main yard; the second, which is opposite, opening on another smaller yard, where the sheep and calves are killed on benches. The pavement of that yard, I see, slopes downward to a gutter, for its being more easily cleansed. The slaughter-house is fifteen feet high, sixteen feet and a half wide, and thirty-three feet long. It is fitted with a powerful windlass, by which one man at the handle can bring the head of an ox down to the ground to receive the blow from the pole-axe that is to fell him – with the means of raising the carcase and keeping it suspended during the after-operation of dressing – and with hooks on which carcases can hang, when completely prepared, without touching the walls. Upon the pavement of this first stone chamber, lies an ox scarcely dead. If I except the blood draining from him, into a little stone well in a corner of the pavement, the place is as free from offence as the Place de la Concorde. It is infinitely purer and cleaner, I know, my friend the functionary, than the Cathedral of Notre Dame. Ha, ha! Monsieur is pleasant, but, truly, there is reason, too, in what he says.

I look into another of these slaughter-houses. 'Pray enter,' says a gentleman in bloody boots. 'This is a calf I have killed this morning. Having a little time upon my hands, I have cut and punctured this lace pattern in the coats of his stomach. It is pretty enough. I did it to divert myself.' – 'It is beautiful, Monsieur, the slaughterer!' He tells me I have the gentility to say so.

I look into rows of slaughter-houses. In many, retail dealers, who have come here for the purpose, are making bargains for meat. There is killing enough, certainly, to satiate an unused eye; and there are steaming carcases enough, to suggest the expediency of a fowl and salad for dinner; but, everywhere, there is an orderly, clean, well-systematised routine of work in progress – horrible work at the best, if you please; but, so much the greater reason why it should be made the best of. I don't know (I think I have observed, my name is Bull) that a Parisian of the lowest order is particularly delicate, or that his nature is remarkable for an infinitesimal infusion of ferocity; but, I do know, my potent, grave, and common counselling Signors, that he is forced, when at this work, to submit himself to a thoroughly good system, and to make an Englishman very heartily ashamed of you.

Here, within the walls of the same abattoir, in other roomy and commodious buildings, are a place for converting the fat into tallow and packing it for market – a place for cleansing and scalding calves' heads and sheeps' feet – a place for preparing tripe – stables and coach-houses for the butchers – innumerable conveniences, aiding in the diminution of offensiveness to its lowest possible point, and the raising of cleanliness and supervision to their highest. Hence, all the meat that goes out of the gate is sent away in clean covered carts. And if every trade connected with the slaughtering of animals were obliged by law to be carried on in the same place, I doubt, my friend, now reinstated in the cocked hat (whose civility these two francs imperfectly acknowledge, but appear munificently to repay) whether there could be better regulations than those which are carried out at the Abattoir of Montmartre. Adieu, my friend, for I am away to the other side of Paris, to the Abattoir of Grenelle! And there, I find exactly the same thing on a smaller scale, with the addition of a magnificent Artesian well, and a different sort of conductor, in the person of a neat little woman, with neat little eyes, and a neat little voice, who picks her neat little way among the bullocks in a very neat little pair of shoes and stockings.

Such is the Monument of French Folly which a foreigneering people have erected, in a national hatred and antipathy for common counselling wisdom. That wisdom, assembled in the City of London, having distinctly refused, after a debate three days long, and by a majority of nearly seven to one, to associate itself with any Metropolitan Cattle Market unless it be held in the midst of the City, it follows that we shall lose the inestimable advantages of common counselling protection, and be thrown, for a market, on our own wretched resources. In all human probability we shall thus come, at last, to erect a monument of folly very like this French monument. If that be done, the consequences are obvious. The leather trade will be ruined, by the introduction of American timber, to be manufactured into shoes for the fallen English; the Lord Mayor will be required, by the popular voice, to live entirely on frogs; and both these changes will (how, is not at present quite clear, but certainly somehow or other) fall on that unhappy landed interest which is always being killed, yet is always found to be alive – and kicking.

61

Bill-Sticking

Household Words, 22 March 1851 (leading article); *(RP)*

'External paper-hanging', or the pasting up of advertising posters on every available square foot of space on walls, fences, hoardings, etc., reached epidemic proportions during the 1830s and 1840s, one of the things that encouraged the practice being the exemption of such posters from the tax levied on newspaper advertisements. Advertising vans, parading the streets at a walking pace, constituted a major nuisance to other traffic. W. Weir, writing a chapter on 'Advertisements' in Vol. 5 (1843) of Charles Knight's *London* (1841–4), comments:

> The rude structure of boards stuck round with placards has of late given way to natty vans, varnished like coaches, and decorated with emblematic paintings. The first of these that met our eye had emblazoned on its stern an orange sky bedropped with Cupids or cherubs, and ... an energetic Fame puffing lustily at a trumpet. Below this allegorical device was ... a placard displaying in large letters the name of 'the monster murderer, Daniel Good'. There was an apotheosis!

For an illustration of a van advertising the last State Lottery (1826), see H. Sampson's *History of Advertising* (1874), opposite p. 464. Sampson notes (p. 31) that 'the huge vans, plastered all over with bills which used to traverse London, to the terror of the horses and wonder of the yokels, were improved off the face of the earth a quarter of a century ago'.

Hill points out (unpub. notes to *RP*, Dickens House) that most of the advertisers Dickens refers to in paragraph 3 regularly advertised in the monthly numbers of his novels. Moses and Son, Mechi, Nicoll, Du Barry & Co. (manufacturers of 'Revalenta Arabica') all advertised in the monthly parts of *David Copperfield* (1849–50), for example – see entries in Index and Glossary. The 'head eternally being measured for a wig' appears in an advertisement for F. Browne's 'Gentlemen's Real Head of Hair, or Invisible Peruke', which was one of the most regular of all items in the advertising supplements to Dickens's novels (see Bernard Darwin, *The Dickens Advertiser* [1930], p. 130); there were also any number of 'balsam' hair-restorers advertised (Darwin, p. 135).

The 'bill-sticking clause' in the 1839 (Metropolitan) Police Act referred to (p. 347) was one that penalised 'every person who, without the consent of the owner or occupier, shall affix any posting bill or other paper against or upon any building, wall, fence or pale'.

Literary allusions (para. 1) 'Belshazzar's Palace': Daniel 5: 5–6; (p. 341) 'Sleeping Beauty': allusion to the fairy-tale 'La Belle au bois dormant' by Charles Perrault (1697); (p. 344) 'taking tea ... according to the song': allusions to the contemporary popular song, 'Come and take Tea in the Arbour'; (p. 345) Hood's 'surprising fancy': untraced.

If I had an enemy whom I hated – which Heaven forbid! – and if I knew of something that sat heavy on his conscience, I think I would introduce that something into a Posting-Bill, and place a large impression in the hands of an active sticker. I can scarcely imagine a more terrible revenge. I should haunt him, by this means, night and day. I do not mean to say that I would publish his secret, in red letters two feet high, for all the town to read: I would darkly refer to it. It should be between him, and me, and the Posting-Bill. Say, for example, that, at a certain period of his life, my enemy had surreptitiously possessed himself of a key. I would then embark my capital in the lock business, and conduct that business on the advertising principle. In all my placards and advertisements, I would throw up the line SECRET KEYS. Thus, if my enemy passed an uninhabited house, he would see his conscience glaring down on him from the parapets, and peeping up at him from the cellars. If he took a dead wall in his walk, it would be alive with reproaches. If he sought refuge in an omnibus, the panels thereof would become Belshazzar's palace to him. If he took boat, in a wild endeavour to escape, he would see the fatal words lurking under the arches of the bridges over the Thames. If he walked the streets with downcast eyes, he would recoil from the very stones of the pavement, made eloquent by lamp-black lithograph. If he drove or rode, his way would be blocked up, by enormous vans, each proclaiming the same words over and over again from its whole extent of surface. Until, having gradually grown thinner and paler, and having at last totally rejected food, he would miserably perish, and I should be revenged. This conclusion I should, no doubt, celebrate by laughing a hoarse laugh in three syllables, and folding my arms tight upon my chest agreeably to most of the examples of glutted animosity that I have had an opportunity of observing in connexion with the Drama – which, by the bye, as involving a good deal of noise, appears to me to be occasionally confounded with the Drummer.

The foregoing reflections presented themselves to my mind, the other day, as I contemplated (being newly come to London from the East Riding of Yorkshire, on a house-hunting expedition for next May), an old warehouse which rotting paste and rotting paper had brought down to the condition of an old cheese. It would have been impossible to say, on the most conscientious survey, how much of its front was brick and mortar, and how much decaying and decayed plaster. It was so thickly encrusted with fragments of bills, that no ship's keel after a long voyage could be half so foul. All traces of the broken windows were billed out, the doors were billed across, the water-spout was billed over. The building was shored up to prevent its tumbling into the street; and the very beams erected against it, were less wood than paste and paper, they had been so continually posted and reposted. The forlorn dregs of old posters so encumbered this wreck, that there was no hold for new posters, and the stickers had abandoned the place in despair, except one enterprising man who had hoisted the last masquerade to a clear spot near the level of the stack of chimnies where it waved and drooped like a shattered flag. Below the rusty cellar-grating, crumpled remnants of old bills torn down; rotted away in wasting heaps of fallen leaves. Here and there, some of the thick rind of the house had peeled off in strips, and fluttered heavily down, littering the street; but, still, below these rents and gashes, layers of decomposing posters showed themselves, as if they were interminable. I thought the building could never even be pulled down, but in one adhesive heap of rottenness and poster. As to getting in – I don't believe that if the Sleeping Beauty and her Court had been so billed up, the young Prince could have done it.

Knowing all the posters that were yet legible, intimately, and pondering on their ubiquitous nature, I was led into the reflections with which I began this paper, by considering what an awful thing it would be, ever to have wronged – say M. JULLIEN for example – and to have his avenging name in characters of fire incessantly before my eyes. Or to have injured MADAME TUSSAUD, and undergo a similar retribution. Has any man a self-reproachful thought associated with pills, or ointment? What an avenging spirit to that man is PROFESSOR HOLLOWAY! Have I sinned in oil? CABBURN pursues me. Have I a dark remembrance associated with any gentlemanly garments, bespoke or ready made? MOSES and SON are on my track. Did I ever aim a blow at a defenceless fellow-creature's head? That head eternally being measured for a wig, or that worse head which was bald before it used the balsam, and hirsute afterwards – enforcing the benevolent moral, 'Better to be bald as a Dutch-cheese than come to this,' – undoes me. Have I no sore places in my mind which MECHI touches – which NICOLL probes – which no registered article whatever lacerates? Does no discordant note within me thrill responsive to mysterious watchwords, as 'Revalenta Arabica,' or 'Number One St Paul's Church-yard'? Then may I enjoy life, and be happy.

Lifting up my eyes, as I was musing to this effect, I beheld advancing towards me (I was then on Cornhill near to the Royal Exchange), a solemn procession of three advertising vans, of first-class dimensions, each drawn by a very little horse. As the cavalcade approached, I was at a loss to reconcile the careless deportment of the drivers of these vehicles, with the terrific announcements they conducted through the city, which, being a summary of the contents of a Sunday newspaper, were of the most thrilling kind. Robbery, fire, murder, and the ruin of the united kingdom – each discharged in a line by itself, like a separate broadside of red-hot shot – were among the least of the warnings addressed to an unthinking people. Yet, the Ministers of Fate who drove the awful cars, leaned forward with their arms upon their knees in a state of extreme lassitude, for want of any subject of interest. The first man, whose hair I might naturally have expected to see standing on end, scratched his head – one of the smoothest I ever beheld – with profound indifference. The second whistled. The third yawned.

Pausing to dwell upon this apathy, it appeared to me, as the fatal cars came by me, that I descried in the second car, through the portal in which the charioteer was seated, a figure stretched upon the floor. At the same time, I thought I smelt tobacco. The latter impression passed quickly from me; the former remained. Curious to know whether this prostrate figure was the one impressible man of the whole capital who had been stricken insensible by the terrors revealed to him, and whose form had been placed in the car by the charioteer, from motives of humanity, I followed the procession. It turned into Leadenhall-market, and halted at a public-house. Each driver dismounted. I then distinctly heard, proceeding from the second car, where I had dimly seen the prostrate form, the words:

'And a pipe!'

The driver entering the public-house with his fellows, apparently for purposes of refreshment, I could not refrain from mounting on the shaft of the second vehicle, and looking in at the portal. I then beheld, reclining on his back upon the floor, on a kind of mattress or divan, a little man in a shooting-coat. The exclamation 'Dear me!' which irresistibly escaped my lips, caused him to sit upright, and survey me. I found him to be a good-looking little man of about fifty, with a shining face, a tight head, a bright eye, a moist wink, a quick speech, and a ready air. He had something of a sporting way with him.

He looked at me, and I looked at him, until the driver displaced me by handing in a pint of beer, a pipe, and what I understand is called 'a screw' of tobacco – an object which has the appearance of a curl-paper taken off the barmaid's head, with the curl in it.

'I beg your pardon,' said I, when the removed person of the driver again admitted of my presenting my face at the portal. 'But – excuse my curiosity, which I inherit from my mother – do you live here?'

'That's good, too!' returned the little man, composedly laying aside a pipe he had smoked out, and filling the pipe just brought to him.

'Oh, you *don't* live here then?' said I.

He shook his head, as he calmly lighted his pipe by means of a German tinder-box, and replied, 'This is my carriage. When things are flat, I take a ride sometimes, and enjoy myself. I am the inventor of these wans.'

His pipe was now alight. He drank his beer all at once, and he smoked and he smiled at me.

'It was a great idea!' said I.

'Not so bad,' returned the little man, with the modesty of merit.

'Might I be permitted to inscribe your name upon the tablets of my memory?' I asked.

'There's not much odds in the name,' returned the little man, ' – no name particular – I am the King of the Bill-Stickers.'

'Good gracious!' said I.

The monarch informed me, with a smile, that he had never been crowned or installed with any public ceremonies, but, that he was peaceably acknowledged as King of the Bill-Stickers in right of being the oldest and most respected member of 'the old school of bill-sticking.' He likewise gave me to understand that there was a Lord Mayor of the Bill-Stickers, whose genius was chiefly exercised within the limits of the city. He made some allusion, also, to an inferior potentate, called 'Turkey-legs;' but, I did not understand that this gentleman was invested with much power. I rather inferred that he derived his title from some peculiarity of gait, and that it was of an honorary character.

'My father,' pursued the King of the Bill-Stickers, 'was Engineer, Beadle, and Bill-Sticker to the parish of St Andrew's, Holborn, in the year one thousand seven hundred and eighty. My father stuck bills at the time of the riots of London.'

'You must be acquainted with the whole subject of bill-sticking, from that time to the present!' said I.

'Pretty well so,' was the answer.

'Excuse me,' said I; 'but I am a sort of collector —'

'Not Income-tax?' cried His Majesty, hastily removing his pipe from his lips.

'No, no,' said I.

'Water-rate?' said His Majesty.

'No, no,' I returned.

'Gas? Assessed? Sewers?' said His Majesty.

'You misunderstand me,' I replied soothingly. 'Not that sort of collector at all: a collector of facts.'

'Oh! if it's only facts,' cried the King of the Bill-Stickers, recovering his good-humour, and banishing the great mistrust that had suddenly fallen upon him, 'come in and welcome! If it had been income, or winders, I think I should have pitched you out of the wan, upon my soul!'

Readily complying with the invitation, I squeezed myself in at the small aperture. His Majesty, graciously handing me a little three-legged stool on which I took my seat in a corner, inquired if I smoked?

'I do; – that is, I can,' I answered.

'Pipe and a screw!' said His Majesty to the attendant charioteer. 'Do you prefer a dry smoke, or do you moisten it?'

As unmitigated tobacco produces most disturbing effects upon my system (indeed, if I had perfect moral courage, I doubt if I should smoke at all, under any circumstances), I advocated moisture, and begged the Sovereign of the Bill-Stickers to name his usual liquor, and to concede to me the privilege of paying for it. After some delicate reluctance on his part, we were provided, through the instrumentality of the attendant charioteer, with a can of cold rum-and-water, flavoured with sugar and lemon. We were also furnished with a tumbler, and I was provided with a pipe. His Majesty, then, observing that we might combine business with conversation, gave the word for the car to proceed; and, to my great delight, we jogged away at a foot pace.

I say to my great delight, because I am very fond of novelty, and it was a new sensation to be jolting through the tumult of the city in that secluded Temple, partly open to the sky, surrounded by the roar without, and seeing nothing but the clouds. Occasionally, blows from whips fell heavily on the Temple's walls, when by stopping up the road longer than usual, we irritated carters and coachmen to madness; but, they fell harmless upon us within and disturbed not the serenity of our peaceful retreat. As I looked upward, I felt, I should imagine, like the Astronomer Royal. I was enchanted by the contrast between the freezing nature of our external mission on the blood of the populace, and the perfect composure reigning within those sacred precincts: where His Majesty, reclining easily on his left arm, smoked his pipe and drank his rum-and-water from his own side of the tumbler, which stood impartially between us. As I looked down from the clouds and caught his royal eye, he understood my reflections. 'I have an idea,' he observed, with an up-ward glance, 'of training scarlet runners across in the season, – making a arbor of it, – and sometimes taking tea in the same, according to the song.'

I nodded approval.

'And here you repose and think?' said I.

'And think,' said he; 'of posters – walls – and hoardings.'

We were both silent, contemplating the vastness of the subject. I remembered a surprising fancy of dear THOMAS HOOD's, and wondered whether this monarch ever sighed to repair to the great wall of China, and stick bills all over it.

'And so,' said he, rousing himself, 'it's facts as you collect?'

'Facts,' said I.

'The facts of bill-sticking,' pursued His Majesty, in a benignant manner, 'as known to myself, air as following. When my father was Engineer, Beadle, and Bill-Sticker to the parish of St Andrew's, Holborn, he employed women to post bills for him. He employed women to post bills at the time of the riots of London. He died at the age of seventy-five year, and was buried by the murdered Eliza Grimwood, over in the Waterloo-road.'

As this was somewhat in the nature of a royal speech, I listened with deference and silently. His Majesty, taking a scroll from his pocket, proceeded, with great distinctness, to pour out the following flood of information: –

' "The bills being at that period mostly proclamations and declarations, and which were only a demy size, the manner of posting the bills (as they did not use brushes) was by means of a piece of wood which they called a "dabber." Thus things continued till such time as the State Lottery was passed, and then the printers began to print larger bills, and men were employed instead of women, as the State Lottery Commissioners then began to send men all over England to post bills, and would keep them out for six or eight months at a time, and they were called by the London bill-stickers "*trampers*," their wages at the time being ten shillings per day, besides expenses. They used sometimes to be stationed in large towns for five or six months together, distributing the schemes to all the houses in the town. And then there were more caricature wood-block engravings for posting-bills than there are at the present time, the principal printers, at that time, of posting-bills being Messrs Evans and Ruffy, of Budge-row; Thoroughgood and Whiting, of the present day; and Messrs Gye and Balne, Gracechurch Street, City. The largest bills printed at that period were a two-sheet double crown; and when they commenced printing four-sheet bills, two bill-stickers would work together. They had no settled wages per week, but had a fixed price for their work, and the London bill-stickers, during a lottery week, have been known to earn, each eight or nine pounds per week, till the day of drawing; likewise the men who carried boards in the street used to have one pound per week, and the bill-stickers at that time would not allow any one to wilfully cover or destroy their bills, as they had a society amongst themselves, and very frequently dined together at some public-house where they used to go of an evening to have their work delivered out untoe 'em." '

All this His Majesty delivered in a gallant manner; posting it, as it were, before me, in a great proclamation. I took advantage of the pause he now made, to inquire what a 'two-sheet double crown' might express?

'A two-sheet double crown,' replied the King, 'is a bill thirty-nine inches wide by thirty inches high.'

'Is it possible,' said I, my mind reverting to the gigantic admonitions we were then displaying to the multitude – which were as infants to some of the posting-bills on the rotten old warehouse – 'that some few years ago the largest bill was no larger than that?'

'The fact,' returned the King, 'is undoubtedly so.' Here he instantly rushed again into the scroll.

' "Since the abolishing of the State Lottery all that good feeling has gone, and nothing but jealousy exists, through the rivalry of each other. Several bill-sticking companies have started, but have failed. The first party that started a company was twelve year ago; but what was left of the old school and their dependents joined together and opposed them. And for some time we were quiet again, till a printer of Hatton Garden formed a company by hiring the sides of houses; but he was not supported by the public, and he left his wooden frames fixed up for rent. The last company that started, took advantage of the New Police Act, and hired of Messrs Grisell and Peto the hoarding of Trafalgar Square, and established a bill-sticking office in Cursitor-street, Chancery-lane, and engaged some of the new bill-stickers to do their work, and for a time got the half of all our work, and with such spirit did they carry on their opposition towards us, that they used to give us in charge before the magistrate, and get us fined; but they found it so expensive, that they could not keep it up, for they were always employing a lot of ruffians from the Seven Dials to come and fight us; and on one occasion the old bill-stickers went to Trafalgar Square to attempt to post bills, when they were given in custody by the watchman in their employ, and fined at Queen Square five pounds, as they would not allow any of us to speak in the office; but when they were gone, we had an interview with the magistrate, who mitigated the fine to fifteen shillings. During the time the men were waiting for the fine, this company started off to a public-house that we were in the habit of using, and waited for us coming back, where a fighting scene took place that beggars description. Shortly after this, the principal one day came and shook hands with us, and acknowledged that he had broken up the company, and that he himself had lost five hundred pound in trying to overthrow us. We then took possession of the hoarding in Trafalgar Square; but Messrs Grisell and Peto would not allow us to post our bills on the said hoarding without paying them – and from first to last we paid upwards of two hundred pounds for that hoarding, and likewise the hoarding of the Reform Club-house, Pall Mall." '

His Majesty, being now completely out of breath, laid down his scroll (which he appeared to have finished), puffed at his pipe, and took some rum-and-water. I embraced the opportunity of asking how many divisions the art and mystery of bill-sticking comprised? He replied, three – auctioneers' bill-sticking, theatrical bill-sticking, general bill-sticking.

'The auctioneers' porters,' said the King, 'who do their bill-sticking, are mostly respectable and intelligent, and generally well paid for their work, whether in town or country. The price paid by the principal auctioneers for country work, is nine shillings per day; that is, seven shillings for day's work, one shilling for lodging, and one for paste. Town work is five shillings a day, including paste.'

'Town work must be rather hot-work,' said I, 'if there be many of those fighting scenes that beggar description, among the bill-stickers?'

'Well,' replied the King, 'I an't a stranger, I assure you, to black eyes; a bill-sticker ought to know how to handle his fists a bit. As to that row I have mentioned, that grew out of competition, conducted in an uncompromising spirit. Besides a man in a horse-and-shay continually following us about, the company had a watchman on duty, night and day, to prevent us sticking bills upon the hoarding in Trafalgar Square. We went there, early one morning, to stick bills and to black-wash their bills if we were interfered with. We *were* interfered with, and I gave the word for laying on the wash. It *was* laid on – pretty brisk – and we were all taken to Queen Square: but they couldn't fine *me*. *I* knew that,' – with a bright smile – 'I'd only given directions – I was only the General.'

Charmed with this monarch's affability, I inquired if he had ever hired a hoarding himself.

'Hired a large one,' he replied, 'opposite the Lyceum Theatre, when the buildings was there. Paid thirty pound for it; let out places on it, and called it "The External Paper-Hanging Station." But it didn't answer. Ah!' said His Majesty thoughtfully, as he filled the glass, 'Bill-stickers have a deal to contend with. The bill-sticking clause was got into the Police Act by a member of parliament that employed me at his election. The clause is pretty stiff respecting where bills go; but *he* didn't mind where *his* bills went. It was all right enough, so long as they was *his* bills!'

Fearful that I observed a shadow of misanthropy on the King's cheerful face, I asked whose ingenious invention that was, which I greatly admired, of sticking bills under the arches of the bridges.

'Mine!' said His Majesty, 'I was the first that ever stuck a bill under a bridge! Imitators soon rose up, of course. – When don't they? But they stuck 'em at low-water, and the tide came and swept the bills clean away. *I* knew that!' The King laughed.

'What may be the name of that instrument, like an immense fishing-rod,' I inquired, 'with which bills are posted on high places?'

'The joints,' returned His Majesty. 'Now, we use the joints where formerly we used ladders – as they do still in country places. Once, when Madame' (Vestris, understood) 'was playing in Liverpool, another bill-sticker and me were at it together on the wall outside the Clarence Dock – me with the joints – him on a ladder. Lord! I had my bill up, right over his head, yards above him, ladder and all, while he was crawling to his work. The people going in and out of the docks, stood and laughed! – It's about thirty years since the joints come in.'

'Are there any bill-stickers who can't read?' I took the liberty of inquiring.

'Some,' said the King. 'But they know which is the right side up'ards of their work. They keep it as it's given out to 'em. I have seen a bill or so stuck wrong side up'ards. But it's very rare.'

Our discourse sustained some interruption at this point, by the procession of cars occasioning a stoppage of about three quarters of a mile in length, as nearly as I could judge. His Majesty, however, entreating me not to be discomposed by the contingent uproar, smoked with great placidity, and surveyed the firmament.

When we were again in motion, I begged to be informed what was the largest poster His Majesty had ever seen. The King replied, 'A thirty-six sheet poster.' I gathered, also, that there were about a hundred and fifty bill-stickers in London, and that His Majesty considered an average hand equal to the posting of one hundred bills (single sheets) in a day. The King was of opinion, that, although posters had much increased in size, they had not increased in number; as the abolition of the State Lotteries had occasioned a great falling off, especially in the country. Over and above which change, I bethought myself that the custom of advertising in newspapers had greatly increased. The completion of many London improvements, as Trafalgar-square (I particularly observed the singularity of His Majesty's calling *that* an improvement), the Royal Exchange, &c., had of late years reduced the number of advantageous posting-places. Bill-stickers at present rather confined themselves to districts, than to particular descriptions of work. One man would strike over Whitechapel; another would take round Houndsditch, Shoreditch, and the City Road; one (the King said) would stick to the Surrey side; another would make a beat of the West-end.

His Majesty remarked, with some approach to severity, on the neglect of delicacy and taste, gradually introduced into the trade by the new school: a profligate and inferior race of impostors who took jobs at almost any price, to the detriment of the old school, and the confusion of their own misguided employers. He considered that the trade was overdone with competition, and observed, speaking of his subjects, 'There are too many of 'em.' He believed, still, that things were a little better than they had been; adducing, as a proof, the fact that particular posting-places were now reserved, by common consent, for particular posters; those places, however, must be regularly occupied by those posters, or, they lapsed and fell into other hands. It was of no use giving a man a Drury Lane bill this week and not next. Where was it to go? He was of opinion that going to the expense of putting up your own board on which your sticker could display your own bills, was the only complete way of posting yourself at the present time; but, even to effect this, on payment of a shilling a week to the keepers of steamboat piers and other such places, you must be able, besides, to give orders for theatres and public exhibitions, or you would be sure to be cut out by somebody. His Majesty regarded the passion for orders, as one of the most inappeasable appetites of human nature. If there were a building, or if there were repairs, going on, anywhere, you could generally stand something and make it right with the foreman of the works; but, orders would be expected from you, and the man who could give the most orders was the man who would come off best. There was this other objectionable point, in orders, that workmen sold them for drink, and often sold them to persons who were likewise troubled with the weakness of thirst: which led (His Majesty said) to the presentation of your orders at Theatre doors, by individuals who were 'too shakery' to derive intellectual profit from the entertainments, and who brought a scandal on you. Finally, His Majesty said that you could hardly put too little in a poster; what you wanted, was, two or three good catch-lines for the eye to rest on – then, leave it alone – and there you were!

These are the minutes of my conversation with His Majesty, as I noted them down shortly afterwards. I am not aware that I have been betrayed into any alteration or suppression. The manner of the King was frank in the extreme; and he seemed to me to avoid, at once that slight tendency to repetition which may have been observed in the conversation of His Majesty King George the Third, and that slight under-current of egotism which the curious observer may perhaps detect in the conversation of Napoleon Buonaparte.

I must do the King the justice to say that it was I, and not he, who closed the dialogue. At this juncture, I became the subject of a remarkable optical delusion; the legs of my stool appeared to me to double up; the car to spin round and round with great violence; and a mist to arise between myself and His Majesty. In addition to these sensations, I felt extremely unwell. I refer these unpleasant effects, either to the paste with which the posters were affixed to the van: which may have contained some small portion of arsenic; or, to the printer's ink, which may have contained some equally deleterious ingredient. Of this, I cannot be sure. I am only sure that I was not affected, either by the smoke, or the rum-and-water. I was assisted out of the vehicle, in a state of mind which I have only experienced in two other places – I allude to the Pier at Dover, and to the corresponding portion of the town of Calais – and sat upon a door-step until I recovered. The procession had then disappeared. I have since looked anxiously for the King in several other cars, but I have not yet had the happiness of seeing His Majesty.

62

The Finishing Schoolmaster

Household Words, 17 May 1850 (leading article)

This article relates closely to Dickens's long-standing concern with the issue of capital punishment. He had contributed a powerful series of letters advocating total abolition of the death penalty to the *Daily News* (23 February – 16 March 1846). The previous year he had offered to write an article on capital punishment for the *Edinburgh Review*, but never did so (see *Pilgrim*, Vol. IV, pp. 340–1). By the time of his two 1849 letters to *The Times* deploring the disgusting scenes at the Mannings' execution (*Pilgrim*, Vol. V, pp. 644–5 and 651), he had come to believe that total abolition was not a practical possibility and concentrated on arguing for the abolition of *public* executions. For the texts of the five *Daily News* letters, see D. Paroissien (ed.), *Selected Letters of Charles Dickens* (1985), pp. 213–55; for an excellent detailed discussion of them, and Dickens's attitude to capital punishment generally, see Philip Collins, *Dickens and Crime* (1962), Ch. 10.

In this piece (described as a 'striking article' by Collins, *op. cit.*, p. 245) Dickens links one of the main themes of his opposition to capital punishment – the degrading effect it has on the public and the morbid fascination it engenders – with his angry concern about successive British governments' neglect of education for the poor (cf. articles 23, 24 and 56). The grim pun of his title (a 'finishing school' draws its pupils from privileged backgrounds and trains them in the social graces) welds the two things together.

Maria Clarke was a twenty-two-year-old woman tried at Bury St Edmunds on 18 March for the murder of her illegitimate infant son by burying him alive. The defence plea of insanity was not admitted by the judge and she was found guilty and sentenced to death (*The Times*, 7 April 1851, p. 8, col. 1). On 19 April *The Times* reprinted (p. 7, col. 6) a report from the *Standard* describing the Sheriff of Suffolk's dilemma resulting from the non-availability of William Calcraft, the public hangman, to carry out the execution of Clarke on the appointed day. If no substitute could be found and the date could not be altered, the Sheriff would have 'to perform a duty repugnant to the feelings of thousands of Her Majesty's subjects'. In the event, however, 'a statement of circumstances indicating the woman's insanity was forwarded to the Home Secretary, and her execution, consequently respited' (*Household Narrative* for April 1851, p. 87).

It was recently supposed and feared that a vacancy had occurred in this great national office. One of the very few public Instructors – we had almost written the only one – as to whose moral lessons all sorts of Administrations and Cabinets are united in having no kind of doubt, was so much engaged in enlightening the people of England, that an occasion for his services arose, when it was dreaded they could not be rendered. It is scarcely necessary to say who this special public instructor is. Our administrative legislators cannot agree on the teaching of The Lord's Prayer, the Sermon on the Mount, the Christian History; but they are all quite clear as to the public teaching of the Hangman. The scaffold is the blessed neutral ground on which conflicting Governments may all accord, and Mr John Ketch is the great state Schoolmaster.

Maria Clarke was left for execution at Ipswich, Suffolk, on Tuesday the 22nd of April. It was Easter Tuesday; and besides the decent compliment to the Festival of Easter that may be supposed to be involved in a Public Execution at that time, it was important that the woman should be hanged upon a holiday, as so many country people were then at leisure to profit by the improving spectacle. It happened, however, that the great finishing Schoolmaster was pre-engaged to lecture, that morning, to other pupils in another part of the country, and thus a paragraph found its way into the newspapers announcing that his humanising office might, perhaps, be open for the nonce to competition.

A gentleman of the county, distinguished for his truth and goodness, has placed in our hands copies of the letters addressed to the Sheriff by the various candidates for this post of instruction. We proceed to lay them before our readers, as we have received them, without names or addresses. In all other respects they are exact copies from the originals. This is no jest, we beg it to be understood. The letters we present, are literal transcripts of the letters written to the High Sheriff of Suffolk, on the occasion in question.

The first, is in the form of a polite note, and has an air of genteel common-place – like an invitation, or an answer to one.

Mr   residing at   Southwark will accept the office unavoidably declined by Calcraft on Wednesday next viz to execute Maria Clarke a speedy answer will oblige stating terms say not less than £20.

To the High Sheriff of Suffolk.

The second, has a Pecksniffian morality in it, which is very edifying.

Sir   20 *April*
This day i Was Reading the newspaper When i saw the advertise for A hangman for that unfortunate Woman if there is not A person come fored and and that you cannot Get no one by the time i Will come as A suBstitute to finish that wich the law require

> Yours respect
> fully

for the Govener of the
prepaid   *ips Wich Goal*
Suffolk

The third, is respectful towards the great finishing Schoolmaster, though – such is fame! – it mis-spells a name, with which (as we have elsewhere observed) the public has become familiarised.

Sir   *Saturday April* 19/51
Seeing a statement in the Times of this day that you wanted a person to execute Maria Clarke & you could not get a substitute as Mr Calcroft was engagd on Wednesday next if well Paid I am Redey to do it myself an early communication will oblige yours   &c
    P.S. You must pay all expences Down as I am in Desperate Cir-
    cumstances hoping this is in secreecy I am

In the fourth, the writer modestly recommends himself as a self-reliant trustworthy person.

Sir   *April th*21/51
    having understood you Want a Man on Wednesday Morning to Perform the Office Of hangman i beg most respectfully To Offer Myself to your Notice feeling Confident i Am Abel to undertake it.

From your obedient
Servant   No
    Street   Square
White Chappel

The fifth, appears to know his value as Public Instructor, and Head of the National System of Education, if elected.

Southwark London
April 20*th* 1851

Mr Sherriff
Sir I will perform the duties of Hangman for the execution of Maria Clarke on Wednesday in consideration of sixty pounds for my services

Yours respectfully

to the High Sheriff of
   Suffolk
      on haste
        to the
          High Sheriff for the
            County of Suffolk
p. paid   *Ipswhich*

The sixth, is workmanlike.

Honoured Sir   *Deal. April* 21/51
    Understanding that you cannot get a man to take the job of hanging the Woman on Wednesday next I will volunteer to do the business if the terms are liberal and suit me

I remain your respected
Servant

The seventh, is also business-like, and is more particular. The writer's mention of himself as a married man shows considerable delicacy.

Sir   *Manchester April* 19/51
    Seeing the enclosed printed paper in the Newspaper if it is a facte I am your man if your trums will suit me that is what am I to have for the work and how am I to get there

I am yours &c

P S. my height is 5 feet 5 and my age is 32 years – and I am a married man

The writer of the eighth, is, we may infer from his tone respecting the eminent 'Calcraft,' a Constant Reader.

To the Sheriff of Ipswitch

Sir   *April* 20

Hearing that Calcraft is unable to attend on Wednesday next to execute Maria Clarke I offer myself as a substitute being able and competent to fullfill his place on this occasion upon the same terms as Calcraft if you think proper to engage me a note addressed to me will meet with immediate attention

Your humble Servant

The ninth, is cautious and decisive, though it evidently proceeds from a Saxon, and is characteristically unjust toward the only part of the earth which is in no way responsible for its own doings.

Honor'd Sir   *April* 20*th*/51.

Seeing that you ware at present in some difficulty to find an Executioner to perform your Duties on the person of Maria Clarke whose execution is fixed for Wednesday next I beg to offer to perform the office of hangsman on that occasion for the sum of £50 to be paid on the completion of the same In order to prevent the public from Knowing my real name and address I shall request you to address to M. B. care of

should you accede to my proposal an answer per return of Post will reach me on Tuesday morning which will afford me time to make the Journey per Rail

I of course shall expect my expences paid in addition to the sum named

This is no idle offer as I shall most Certainly attend to perform the duties imposed on you, at the time required Should you accept this offer

I have the Honor to be

Honord Sir

Your Obdt Servt

To the High Sheriff
of the County of Suffolk
P.S I of course expect the name to be kept a secret should you not accept the offer And if the offer be accepted I shall assume the name of Patrick Keley of Kildare Ireland

The tenth, as proceeding from an individual who is honored with the acquaintance of the real finishing Schoolmaster, and who even aspires to succeed him, claims great respect. If we selected any particular beauty from the rest, it would be his mention of the post as a 'birth.'

Gentlemen   *April* 19*th* 1851
    Seeing a paragraph in the paper of this day that you are in want of an executioner in the place of Calcraft I have taken the liberty to inform you that you can have me the writer of this note. I have been for some time after the birth and am well acquainted with calcraft and I wonder he did not mention my name when you dispatched a messenger to him. I made application at horsemonger lane for the last job there but Calcraft attended himself Gentlemen if you should think fit to nominate me for the job, you will find me a fitt and proper person to fulfill it
                An Answer to this application
          will oblidge
              Your Most Humble Servant

And will meet with immediate attention

Gent^en
    Should this meet your approbation you will oblidge by sending me instructions when and how to come down
    You will be Kind enough to communicate this to the High Sheriff as soon as Convenient
To the Governer
    of Ipswich Gaol

The connexion of 'the sad office,' in the eleventh, with 'the amount,' unites a heart of sentiment with an eye to business.

                    Cockermouth Apl 21 1851
    Sir having seen in the paper that Calcraft cannot come up. I will undertake the sad Office if well remunerated and as time is short please to say the amount and I will come by return of Post you may depend on me
                      Yours.

This is the twelfth and last − from a plain man accustomed to job-work.

Sir   *Wigan April* 20 1851
Having seen in the Newspaper that you was in want of a Man to oficiate in the place of Calcraft at the execution of Maria Clarke if you will pay my expences from Wigan & Back & 5 pounds for the Job Please to send my expences from Wigan to Ipswich & direct to the
                                & he will let me Know
                                Your obedient Servant

These letters, we repeat, are genuine. They may set our readers thinking. It may be well to think a little now and then, however distasteful it be to do so, of this public teaching by the finishing Schoolmaster, and to consider how often he has at once begun and ended − and how long he should continue to begin and end − the only State Education the State can adjust to the perfect satisfaction of its conscience.

63

On Duty with Inspector Field

Household Words, 14 June 1851 (leading article) *(RP)*

Charles Frederick Field, an amateur actor in his youth, joined the New Police in 1829 and worked first in Holborn Division, which included the notorious slum area of St Giles. He was made an inspector in 1833 and may well have been Dickens's guide on the occasion in 1839 when, together with Maclise, Forster and the actor James R. Anderson, Dickens made a nocturnal tour to the St Giles 'Rookery', which ended up in a brawl from which the gentlemen visitors had to be hastily extricated (J.R. Anderson,

Inspector Charles Frederick Field.

An Actor's Life [1902], pp. 87–8). In 1846 Field became Chief of the Detective Department at Scotland Yard. He retired in 1852 (Dickens subscribed £300 to a testimonial for him) and opened a private detective agency. In 1867, talking to an American visitor about his past visits to 'the dens of thieves and other haunts of infamy', Dickens mentioned that he was always accompanied by 'a brace of policemen who are well versed in the ways of the localities ... and who introduced me as an old friend ...'. He went on to make a pun that was lost on his visitor: 'These were what I called my field-days' (see *The Dickensian*, Vol. 63 [1967], p. 116). In this piece Field appears under his own name instead of the transparent 'Wield' alias of articles 50 and 51. For more on Field, his character and prowess, and his modelling for Bucket in *Bleak House*, see Philip Collins, *Dickens and Crime* [1962], pp. 206–11; also Collins's article, 'Inspector Bucket visits the Princess Puffer', *The Dickensian*, Vol. 60 (1964), pp. 88–90, and W. Long, 'The "Singler Stories" of Inspector Field', *The Dickensian*, Vol. (1987), pp. 149–62.

Forster records (Book 3, Ch. 8) that Dickens took Henry Wadsworth Longfellow on a tour of 'the worst haunts of the most dangerous classes' in 1842 and adds that when he toured them again for this *HW* essay, he 'found important changes effected whereby these human dens, if not less dangerous, were becoming certainly more decent' (on the 1842 expedition Maclise was so nauseated by the atmosphere of the first Old Mint lodging-house that he had to wait outside). Dickens makes the point himself in this piece (p. 364).

Dickens and Field cover a great deal of ground in the course of their night's tour. Beginning in St Giles, recently cut through by the building of New Oxford Street (1847), they visit Rats' Castle, a notorious pub in Dyot Street (not the modern street of that name). Then they proceed east and south by cab, probably crossing the Thames by Waterloo Bridge, to the Old Mint just off the Borough High Street, Southwark. They then cross back to the north bank of the river, probably by London Bridge, to visit the Ratcliffe Highway (now called The Highway) skirting the northern boundary of the London Docks. 'It was', writes Millicent Rose (*The East End of London* [1951], p. 58), 'one function of the Ratcliffe Highway, and more especially of its tributary courts and alleys, to provide sailors with the means of losing a voyage's earnings in three days' dissipation, and then of pawning the shirts off their backs'. (Rose also mentions the German sugar-bakers Dickens encountered: the refining of the raw sugar imported from the West Indies 'was carried out ... under conditions so dreadful that even the ... Irish would not tolerate them, and the industry had to be manned by German labour, the cheapest in the whole East End' [p. 139]). From the Ratcliffe Highway Dickens and Field strike north to Whitechapel and finally west to Holborn Hill, a steep decline to the Fleet Ditch with the equally steep ascent of Snow Hill the other side (bridged over by Holborn Viaduct 1863–9).

The allusions to 'Red Tape' (pp. 360 and 363) look back to an earlier *HW* article of that title (15 February 1851; see *MP*) in which Dickens inveighs against the addiction of civil servants and politicians to bureaucratic practices which 'tidy away' social problems:

Your public functionary who delights in Red Tape – the purpose of whose existence is to tie up public questions, great and small, in an abundance of this official article – to make the neatest possible parcels of them, ticket them, and carefully put them away on a top shelf out of human reach – is the peculiar curse and nuisance of England.

Literary allusions (p. 363) 'the plagues of Egypt': refers to Exodus 8–12; (p. 367) 'the best of friends must part': from the old song 'There is a Tavern in the Town'; (p. 367) 'marshal us the way that we are going': Shakespeare, *Macbeth*, Act 2, Sc. 1; (p. 369) 'almost at odds with morning ...': *Ibid.*, Act 3, Sc. 4; (p. 369) 'the wicked cease from troubling ...': Job 3:17.

How goes the night? Saint Giles's clock is striking nine. The weather is dull and wet, and the long lines of street-lamps are blurred, as if we saw them through tears. A damp wind blows, and rakes the pieman's fire out, when he opens the door of his little furnace, carrying away an eddy of sparks.

Saint Giles's clock strikes nine. We are punctual. Where is Inspector Field? Assistant Commissioner of Police is already here, enwrapped in oil-skin cloak, and standing in the shadow of Saint Giles's steeple. Detective Serjeant, weary of speaking French all day to foreigners unpacking at the Great Exhibition, is already here. Where is Inspector Field?

Inspector Field is, tonight, the guardian genius of the British Museum. He is bringing his shrewd eye to bear on every corner of its solitary galleries, before he reports 'all right.' Suspicious of the Elgin marbles, and not to be done by cat-faced Egyptian giants, with their hands upon their knees, Inspector Field, sagacious, vigilant, lamp in hand, throwing monstrous shadows on the walls and ceilings, passes through the spacious rooms. If a mummy trembled in an atom of its dusty covering, Inspector Field would say, 'Come out of that, Tom Green. I know you!' If the smallest 'Gonoph' about town were crouching at the bottom of a classic bath, Inspector Field would nose him with a finer scent than the ogre's, when adventurous Jack lay trembling in his kitchen copper. But all is quiet, and Inspector Field goes warily on, making little outward show of attending to anything in particular, just recognising the Ichthyosaurus as a familiar acquaintance, and wondering, perhaps, how the detectives did it in the days before the Flood.

Will Inspector Field be long about this work? He may be half-an-hour longer. He sends his compliments by Police Constable, and proposes that we meet at Saint Giles's Station House, across the road. Good. It were as well to stand by the fire, there, as in the shadow of Saint Giles's steeple.

Anything doing here tonight? Not much. We are very quiet. A lost boy, extremely calm and small, sitting by the fire, whom we now confide to a constable to take home, for the child says that if you show him Newgate Street, he can show you where he lives – a raving drunken woman in the cells, who has screeched her voice away, and has hardly power enough left to declare, even with the passionate help of her feet and arms, that she is the daughter of a British officer, and, strike her blind and dead, but she'll write a letter to the Queen! but who is soothed with a drink of water – in another cell, a quiet woman with a child at her breast, for begging – in another, her husband in a smock-frock, with a basket of watercresses – in another, a pick-pocket – in another, a meek tremulous old pauper man who has been out for a holiday 'and has took but a little drop, but it has overcome him arter so many months in the house' – and that's all, as yet. Presently, a sensation at the Station House door. Mr Field, gentlemen!

Inspector Field comes in, wiping his forehead, for he is of a burly figure, and has come fast from the ores and metals of the deep mines of the earth, and from the Parrot Gods of the South Sea Islands, and from the birds and beetles of the tropics, and from the Arts of Greece and Rome, and from the Sculptures of Nineveh, and from the traces of an elder world, when these were not. Is Rogers ready? Rogers is ready, strapped and great-coated, with a flaming eye in the middle of his waist, like a deformed Cyclops. Lead on, Rogers, to Rats' Castle!

How many people may there be in London, who, if we had brought them deviously and blindfold, to this street, fifty paces from the Station House, and within call of Saint Giles's church, would know it for a not remote part of the city in which their lives are passed? How many, who amidst this compound of sickening smells, these heaps of filth, these tumbling houses, with all their vile contents, animate and inanimate, slimily overflowing into the black road, would believe that they breathe *this* air? How much Red Tape may there be, that could look round on the faces which now hem us in – for our appearance here has caused a rush from all points to a common centre – the lowering foreheads, the sallow cheeks, the brutal eyes, the matted hair, the infected, vermin-haunted heaps of rags – and say 'I have thought of this. I have not dismissed the thing. I have neither blustered it away, nor frozen it away, nor tied it up and put it away, nor smoothly said pooh, pooh! to it, when it has been shown to me'?

This is not what Rogers wants to know, however. What Rogers wants to know, is, whether you *will* clear the way here, some of you, or whether you won't; because if you don't do it right on end, he'll lock you up! What! *You* are there, are you, Bob Miles? You haven't had enough of it yet, haven't you? You want three months more, do you? Come away from that gentleman! What are you creeping round there for?

'What am I a doing, thinn, Mr Rogers?' says Bob Miles, appearing, villanous, at the end of a lane of light, made by the lantern.

'I'll let you know pretty quick, if you don't hook it. WILL you hook it?'

A sycophantic murmur rises from the crowd. 'Hook it, Bob, when Mr Rogers and Mr Field tells you! Why don't you hook it, when you are told to?'

The most importunate of the voices strikes familiarly on Mr Rogers's ear. He suddenly turns his lantern on the owner.

'What! *You* are there, are you, Mister Click? You hook it too – come!'

'What for?' says Mr Click, discomfited.

'You hook it, will you!' says Mr Rogers with stern emphasis.

Both Click and Miles *do* 'hook it,' without another word, or, in plainer English, sneak away.

'Close up there, my men!' says Inspector Field to two constables on duty who have followed. 'Keep together gentlemen; we are going down here. Heads!'

Saint Giles's church strikes half-past ten. We stoop low, and creep down a precipitous flight of steps into a dark close cellar. There is a fire. There is a long deal table. There are benches. The cellar is full of company, chiefly very young men in various conditions of dirt and raggedness. Some are eating supper. There are no girls or women present. Welcome to Rats' Castle, gentlemen, and to this company of noted thieves!

'Well, my lads! How are you, my lads! What have you been doing today? Here's some company come to see you, my lads! *There's* a plate of beefsteak, Sir, for the supper of a fine young man! And there's a mouth for a steak, Sir! Why, I should be too proud of such a mouth as that, if I had it myself! Stand up and show it, Sir! Take off your cap. There's a fine young man for a nice little party, Sir! An't he?'

Inspector Field is the bustling speaker. Inspector Field's eye is the roving eye that searches every corner of the cellar as he talks. Inspector Field's hand is the well-known hand that has collared half the people here, and motioned their brothers, sisters, fathers, mothers, male and female friends, inexorably, to New South Wales. Yet Inspector Field stands in this den, the Sultan of the place. Every thief here, cowers before him, like a schoolboy before his schoolmaster. All watch him, all answer when addressed, all laugh at his jokes, all seek to propitiate him. This cellar-company alone – to say nothing of the crowd surrounding the entrance from the street above, and making the steps shine with eyes – is strong enough to murder us all, and willing enough to do it; but, let Inspector Field have a mind to pick out one thief here, and take him; let him produce that ghostly truncheon from his pocket, and say, with his business-air, 'My lad, I want you!' and all Rats' Castle shall be stricken with paralysis, and not a finger move against him, as he fits the handcuffs on!

Where's the Earl of Warwick? – Here he is, Mr Field! Here's the Earl of Warwick, Mr Field! – O there you are, my Lord. Come for'ard. There's a chest, Sir, not to have a clean shirt on. An't it? Take your hat off, my Lord. Why, I should be ashamed if I was you – and an Earl, too – to show myself to a gentleman with my hat on! – The Earl of Warwick laughs, and uncovers. All the company laugh. One pickpocket, especially, laughs with great enthusiasm. O what a jolly game it is, when Mr Field comes down – and don't want nobody!

So, *you* are here, too, are you, you tall, grey, soldierly-looking, grave man, standing by the fire? – Yes, Sir. Good evening, Mr Field! – Let us see. You lived servant to a nobleman once? – Yes, Mr Field. – And what is it you do now; I forget? – Well, Mr Field, I job about as well as I can. I left my employment on account of delicate health. The family is still kind to me. Mr Wix of Piccadilly is also very kind to me when I am hard up. Likewise Mr Nix of Oxford Street. I get a trifle from them occasionally, and rub on as well as I can, Mr Field. Mr Field's eye rolls enjoyingly, for this man is a notorious begging-letter writer. – Good night, my lads! – Good night, Mr Field, and thank'ee, Sir!

Clear the street here, half a thousand of you! Cut it, Mrs Stalker – none of that – we don't want you! Rogers of the flaming eye, lead on to the tramps' lodging-house!

A dream of baleful faces attends to the door. Now, stand back all of you! In the rear, Detective Serjeant plants himself, composedly whistling, with his strong right arm across the narrow passage. Mrs Stalker, I am something'd that need not be written here, if you won't get yourself into trouble, in about half a minute, if I see that face of yours again!

Saint Giles's church clock, striking eleven, hums through our hand from the dilapidated door of a dark outhouse as we open it, and are stricken back by the pestilent breath that issues from within. Rogers, to the front with the light, and let us look!

Ten, twenty, thirty – who can count them! Men, women, children, for the most part naked, heaped upon the floor like maggots in a cheese! Ho! In that dark corner yonder! Does anybody lie there? Me Sir, Irish me, a widder, with six children. And yonder? Me Sir, Irish me, with me wife and eight poor babes. And to the left there? Me Sir, Irish me, along with two more Irish boys as is me friends. And to the right there? Me Sir and the Murphy fam'ly, numbering five blessed souls. And what's this, coiling, now, about my foot? Another Irish me, pitifully in want of shaving, whom I have awakened from sleep – and across my other foot lies his wife – and by the shoes of Inspector Field lie their three eldest – and their three youngest are at present squeezed between the open door and the wall. And why is there no one on that little mat before the sullen fire? Because O'Donovan, with wife and daughter, is not come in yet from selling Lucifers! Nor on the bit of sacking in the nearest corner? Bad luck! Because that Irish family is late tonight, a-cadging in the streets!

They are all awake now, the children excepted, and most of them sit up, to stare. Wheresoever Mr Rogers turns the flaming eye, there is a spectral figure rising, unshrouded, from a grave of rags. Who is the landlord here? – I am, Mr Field! says a bundle of ribs and parchment against the wall, scratching itself. – Will you spend this money fairly, in the morning, to buy coffee for 'em all? – Yes Sir, I will! – O he'll do it Sir, he'll do it fair. He's honest! cry the spectres. And with thanks and Good Night sink into their graves again.

Thus, we make our New Oxford Streets, and our other new streets, never heeding, never asking, where the wretches whom we clear out, crowd. With such scenes at our doors, with all the plagues of Egypt tied up with bits of cobweb in kennels so near our homes, we timorously make our Nuisance Bills and Boards of Health, nonentities, and think to keep away the Wolves of Crime and Filth, by our electioneering ducking to little vestry-men, and our gentlemanly handling of Red Tape!

Intelligence of the coffee money has got abroad. The yard is full, and Rogers of the flaming eye is beleaguered with entreaties to show other Lodging Houses. Mine next! Mine! Mine! Rogers, military, obdurate, stiff-necked, immovable, replies not, but leads away; all falling back before him. Inspector Field follows. Detective Serjeant, with his barrier of arm across the little passage, deliberately waits to close the procession. He sees behind him, without any effort, and exceedingly disturbs one individual far in the rear by coolly calling out, 'It won't do Mr Michael! Don't try it!'

After council holden in the street, we enter other lodging houses, public-houses, many lairs and holes; all noisome and offensive; none so filthy and so crowded as where Irish are. In one, the Ethiopian party are expected home presently – were in Oxford Street when last heard of – shall be fetched, for our delight, within ten minutes. In another, one of the two or three Professors who draw Napoleon Buonaparte and a couple of mackarel, on the pavement, and then let the work of art out to a speculator, is refreshing after his labors. In another, the vested interest of the profitable nuisance has been in one family for a hundred years, and the landlord drives in comfortably from the country to his snug little stew in town. In all, Inspector Field is received with warmth. Coiners and smashers droop before him; pickpockets defer to him; the gentle sex

(not very gentle here) smile upon him. Half-drunken hags check themselves in the midst of pots of beer, or pints of gin, to drink to Mr Field,
and pressingly to ask the honor of his finishing the draught. One beldame
in rusty black has such admiration for him, that she runs a whole street's
length to shake him by the hand; tumbling into a heap of mud by the
way, and still pressing her attentions when her very form has ceased to
be distinguishable through it. Before the power of the law, the power of
superior sense − for common thieves are fools beside these men − and
the power of a perfect mastery of their character, the garrison of Rats'
Castle and the adjacent Fortresses make but a skulking show indeed
when reviewed by Inspector Field.

Saint Giles's clock says it will be midnight in half-an-hour, and
Inspector Field says we must hurry to the Old Mint in the Borough. The
cab-driver is low-spirited, and has a solemn sense of his responsibility.
Now, what's your fare, my lad? − O *you* know, Inspector Field, what's
the good of asking *me*!

Say, Parker, strapped and great-coated, and waiting in dim Borough
doorway by appointment, to replace the trusty Rogers whom we left
deep in Saint Giles's, are you ready? Ready, Inspector Field, and at a
motion of my wrist behold my flaming eye.

This narrow street, sir, is the chief part of the Old Mint, full of low
lodging-houses, as you see by the transparent canvas-lamps and blinds,
announcing beds for travellers! But it is greatly changed, friend Field,
from my former knowledge of it; it is infinitely quieter and more subdued
than when I was here last, some seven years ago? O yes! Inspector
Haynes, a first-rate man, is on this station now and plays the Devil with
them!

Well, my lads! How are you tonight, my lads! Playing cards here, eh?
Who wins? − Why, Mr Field, I, the sulky gentleman with the damp flat
side-curls, rubbing my bleared eye with the end of my neck-kerchief
which is like a dirty eel-skin, am losing just at present, but I suppose I
must take my pipe out of my mouth, and be submissive to *you* − I hope
I see you well, Mr Field? − Aye, all right, my lad. Deputy, who have you
got upstairs? Be pleased to show the rooms!

Why Deputy, Inspector Field can't say. He only knows that the man
who takes care of the beds and lodgers is always called so. Steady, O
Deputy, with the flaring candle in the blacking bottle, for this is a slushy
back-yard, and the wooden staircase outside the house creaks and has
holes in it.

Again, in these confined intolerable rooms, burrowed out like the holes
of rats or the nests of insect vermin, but fuller of intolerable smells, are
crowds of sleepers, each on his foul truckle-bed coiled up beneath a rug.
Halloa here! Come! Let us see you! Shew your face! Pilot Parker goes

from bed to bed and turns their slumbering heads towards us, as a salesman might turn sheep. Some wake up with an execration and a threat. – What! who spoke? O! If it's the accursed glaring eye that fixes me, go where I will, I am helpless. Here! I sit up to be looked at. Is it me you want? – Not you, lie down again! – and I lie down, with a woeful growl.

Wherever the turning lane of light becomes stationary for a moment, some sleeper appears at the end of it, submits himself to be scrutinised, and fades away into the darkness.

There should be strange dreams here, Deputy. They sleep sound enough, says Deputy, taking the candle out of the blacking bottle, snuffing it with his fingers, throwing the snuff into the bottle, and corking it up with the candle; that's all *I* know. What is the inscription, Deputy, on all the discolored sheets? A precaution against loss of linen. Deputy turns down the rug of an unoccupied bed and discloses it. STOP THIEF!

To lie at night, wrapped in the legend of my slinking life; to take the cry that pursues me, waking, to my breast in sleep; to have it staring at me, and clamouring for me, as soon as consciousness returns; to have it for my first-foot on New-Year's day, my Valentine, my Birthday salute, my Christmas greeting, my parting with the old year. STOP THIEF!

And to know that I *must* be stopped, come what will. To know that I am no match for this individual energy and keenness, or this organised and steady system! Come across the street, here, and, entering by a little shop, and yard, examine these intricate passages and doors contrived for escape, flapping and counter-flapping, like the lids of the conjuror's boxes. But what avail they? Who gets in by a nod, and shews their secret working to us? Inspector Field.

Don't forget the old Farm House, Parker! Parker is not the man to forget it. We are going there, now. It is the old Manor-House of these parts, and stood in the country once. Then, perhaps, there was something, which was not the beastly street, to see from the shattered low fronts of the overhanging wooden houses we are passing under – shut up now, pasted over with bills about the literature and drama of the Mint, and mouldering away. This long paved yard was a paddock or a garden once, or a court in front of the Farm House. Perchance, with a dovecot in the centre, and fowls pecking about – with fair elm trees, then, where discolored chimney-stacks and gables are now – noisy, then, with rooks which have yielded to a different sort of rookery. It's likelier than not, Inspector Field thinks, as we turn into the common kitchen, which is in the yard, and many paces from the house.

Well my lads and lasses, how are you all! Where's Blackey, who has stood near London Bridge these five-and-twenty years, with a painted skin to represent disease? – Here he is, Mr Field! – How are you,

Blackey? – Jolly, sa! – Not playing the fiddle tonight, Blackey? – Not a night, sa! – A sharp, smiling youth, the wit of the kitchen, interposes. He an't musical tonight, sir. I've been giving him a moral lecture; I've been a talking to him about his latter end, you see. A good many of these are my pupils, sir. This here young man (smoothing down the hair of one near him, reading a Sunday paper) is a pupil of mine. I'm a teaching of him to read, sir. He's a promising cove, sir. He's a smith, he is, and gets his living by the sweat of the brow, sir. So do I myself, sir. This young woman is my sister, Mr Field. *She's* a getting on very well too. I've a deal of trouble with 'em, sir, but I'm richly rewarded, now I see 'em all a doing so well, and growing up so creditable. That's a great comfort, that is, an't it, sir? – In the midst of the kitchen (the whole kitchen is in ecstacies with this impromptu 'chaff') sits a young, modest, gentle-looking creature, with a beautiful child in her lap. She seems to belong to the company, but is so strangely unlike it. She has such a pretty, quiet face and voice, and is so proud to hear the child admired – thinks you would hardly believe that he is only nine months old! Is she as bad as the rest, I wonder? Inspectorial experience does not engender a belief contrariwise, but prompts the answer, Not a ha'porth of difference!

There is a piano going in the old Farm House as we approach. It stops. Landlady appears. Has no objections, Mr Field, to gentlemen being brought, but wishes it were at earlier hours, the lodgers complaining of ill-conwenience. Inspector Field is polite and soothing – knows his woman and the sex. Deputy (a girl in this case) shows the way up a heavy broad old staircase, kept very clean, into clean rooms where many sleepers are, and where painted panels of an older time look strangely on the truckle beds. The sight of white-wash and the smell of soap – two things we seem by this time to have parted from in infancy – make the old Farm House a phenomenon, and connect themselves with the so curiously misplaced picture of the pretty mother and child long after we have left it, – long after we have left, besides, the neighbouring nook with something of a rustic flavor in it yet, where once, beneath a low wooden colonnade still standing as of yore, the eminent Jack Sheppard condescended to regale himself, and where, now, two old bachelor brothers in broad hats (who are whispered in the Mint to have made a compact long ago that if either should ever marry, he must forfeit his share of the joint property) still keep a sequestered tavern, and sit o' nights smoking pipes in the bar, among ancient bottles and glasses, as our eyes behold them.

How goes the night now? Saint George of Southwark answers with twelve blows upon his bell. Parker, good night, for Williams is already waiting over in the region of Ratcliffe Highway, to show the houses where the sailors dance.

I should like to know where Inspector Field was born. In Ratcliffe Highway, I would have answered with confidence, but for his being equally at home wherever we go. *He* does not trouble his head as I do, about the river at night. *He* does not care for its creeping, black and silent, on our right there, rushing through sluice gates, lapping at piles and posts and iron rings, hiding strange things in its mud, running away with suicides and accidentally drowned bodies faster than a midnight funeral should, and acquiring such various experience between its cradle and its grave. It has no mystery for *him*. Is there not the Thames Police!

Accordingly, Williams lead the way. We are a little late, for some of the houses are already closing. No matter. You show us plenty. All the landlords know Inspector Field. All pass him, freely and good-humouredly, wheresoever he wants to go. So thoroughly are all these houses open to him and our local guide, that, granting that sailors must be entertained in their own way – as I suppose they must, and have a right to be – I hardly know how such places could be better regulated. Not that I call the company very select, or the dancing very graceful – even so graceful as that of the German Sugar Bakers, whose assembly, by the Minories, we stopped to visit – but there is watchful maintenance of order in every house, and swift expulsion where need is. Even in the midst of drunkenness, both of the lethargic kind and the lively, there is sharp landlord supervision, and pockets are in less peril than out of doors. These houses show, singularly, how much of the picturesque and romantic there truly is in the sailor, requiring to be especially addressed. All the songs (sung in a hailstorm of halfpence, which are pitched at the singer without the least tenderness for the time or tune – mostly from great rolls of copper carried for the purpose – and which he occasionally dodges like shot as they fly near his head) are of the sentimental sea sort. All the rooms are decorated with nautical subjects. Wrecks, engagements, ships on fire, ships passing lighthouses on iron-bound coasts, ships blowing up, ships going down, ships running ashore, men lying out upon the main yard in a gale of wind, sailors and ships in every variety of peril, constitute the illustrations of fact. Nothing can be done in the fanciful way, without a thumping boy upon a scaly dolphin.

How goes the night now? Past one. Black and Green are waiting in Whitechapel to unveil the mysteries of Wentworth Street. Williams, the best of friends must part. Adieu!

Are not Black and Green ready at the appointed place? O yes! They glide out of shadow as we stop. Imperturbable Black opens the cab-door; Imperturbable Green takes a mental note of the driver. Both Green and Black then open, each his flaming eye, and marshal us the way that we are going.

The lodging-house we want, is hidden in a maze of streets and courts.

It is fast shut. We knock at the door, and stand hushed looking up for a light at one or other of the begrimed old lattice windows in its ugly front when another constable comes up – supposes that we want 'to see the school.' Detective Serjeant meanwhile has got over a rail, opened a gate, dropped down an area, overcome some other little obstacles, and tapped at a window. Now returns. The landlord will send a deputy immediately.

Deputy is heard to stumble out of bed. Deputy lights a candle, draws back a bolt or two, and appears at the door. Deputy is a shivering shirt and trousers by no means clean, a yawning face, a shock head much confused externally and internally. We want to look for some one. You may go up with the light, and take 'em all, if you like, says Deputy, resigning it, and sitting down upon a bench in the kitchen with his ten fingers sleepily twisting in his hair.

Halloa here! Now then! Show yourselves. That'll do. It's not you. Don't disturb yourself any more! So on, through a labyrinth of airless rooms, each man responding, like a wild beast, to the keeper who has tamed him, and who goes into his cage. What, you haven't found him, then? says Deputy, when we came down. A woman mysteriously sitting up all night in the dark by the smouldering ashes of the kitchen fire, says it's only tramps and cadgers here; it's gonophs over the way. A man, mysteriously walking about the kitchen all night in the dark, bids her hold her tongue. We come out. Deputy fastens the door and goes to bed again.

Black and Green, you know Bark, lodging-house keeper and receiver of stolen goods! – O yes, Inspector Field. – Go to Bark's next.

Bark sleeps in an inner wooden hutch, near his street-door. As we parley on the step with Bark's Deputy, Bark growls in his bed. We enter, and Bark flies out of bed. Bark is a red villain and a wrathful, with a sanguine throat that looks very much as if it were expressly made for hanging, as he stretches it out, in pale defiance, over the half-door of his hutch. Bark's parts of speech are of an awful sort – principally adjectives. I won't, says Bark, have no adjective police and adjective strangers in my adjective premises! I won't, by adjective and substantive! Give me my trousers, and I'll send the whole adjective police to adjective and substantive! Give me, says Bark, my adjective trousers! I'll put an adjective knife in the whole bileing of 'em. I'll punch their adjective heads. I'll rip up their adjective substantives. Give me my adjective trousers! says Bark, and I'll spile the bileing of em!

Now, Bark, what's the use of this? Here's Black and Green, Detective Serjeant, and Inspector Field. You know we will come in. – I know you won't! says Bark. Somebody give me my adjective trousers! Bark's trousers seem difficult to find. He calls for them, as Hercules might for his club.

Give me my adjective trousers! says Bark, and I'll spile the bileing of 'em!

Inspector Field holds that it's all one whether Bark likes the visit or don't like it. He, Inspector Field, is an Inspector of the Detective Police, Detective Serjeant *is* Detective Serjeant, Black and Green are constables in uniform. Don't you be a fool, Bark, or you know it will be the worse for you. – I don't care, says Bark. Give me my adjective trousers!

At two o'clock in the morning, we descend into Bark's low kitchen, leaving Bark to foam at the mouth above, and Imperturbable Black and Green to look at him. Bark's kitchen is crammed full of thieves, holding a *conversazione* there by lamp-light. It is by far the most dangerous assembly we have seen yet. Stimulated by the ravings of Bark, above, their looks are sullen, but not a man speaks. We ascend again. Bark has got his trousers, and is in a state of madness in the passage with his back against a door that shuts off the upper staircase. We observe, in other respects, a ferocious individuality in Bark. Instead of 'STOP THIEF!' on his linen, he prints 'STOLEN FROM Bark's!'

Now, Bark, we are going up stairs! – No, you an't! – You refuse admission to the Police, do you, Bark? – Yes, I do! I refuse it to all the adjective police, and to all the adjective substantives. If the adjective coves in the kitchen was men they'd come up now, and do for you! Shut me that there door! says Bark, and suddenly we are enclosed in the passage. They'd come up and do for you! cries Bark, and waits. Not a sound in the kitchen! They'd come up and do for you! cries Bark again, and waits. Not a sound in the kitchen! We are shut up, half-a-dozen of us, in Bark's house, in the innermost recesses of the worst part of London, in the dead of the night – the house is crammed with notorious robbers and ruffians – and not a man stirs. No, Bark. They know the weight of the law, and they know Inspector Field and Co. too well.

We leave Bully Bark to subside at leisure out of his passion and his trousers, and, I dare say, to be inconveniently reminded of this little brush before long. Black and Green do ordinary duty here, and look serious.

As to White, who waits on Holborn Hill to show the courts that are eaten out of Rotten Gray's Inn Lane, where other lodging-houses are, and where (in one blind alley) the Thieves' Kitchen and Seminary for the teaching of the art to children, is, the night has so worn away, being now

almost at odds with morning, which is which,

that they are quiet, and no light shines through the chinks in the shutters. As undistinctive Death will come here, one day, sleep comes now. The wicked cease from troubling sometimes, even in this life.

APPENDIX A

Descriptive headlines added by Dickens to articles in this volume from *HW* which were included in *RP*.

In the Charles Dickens Edition of Dickens's works, the last one to be published during his lifetime, *RP* was included in the same volume as *American Notes*. For all volumes in this edition Dickens added descriptive headlines or running titles at the top of each right-hand page. These are listed below, keyed to the appropriate pages of the present volume.

'A Child's Dream of a Star'
Accomplished (p. 188)

'The Begging-Letter Writer'
He is Seven-and-Sixpence Short of Independence (p. 228)
He enchants a Magistrate (p. 231)
He is a mere Robber (p. 234)

'A Walk in a Workhouse'
Inmates (p. 237)
Among the Old Men (p. 239)

'The Ghost of Art'
A Model (p. 261)
The German Taste (p. 264)

'A Detective Police Party (1)' (renamed 'The Detective Police')
Little Party in Wellington Street (p. 267)
Sergeant Witchem and Tally-ho Thompson (p. 270)
Sticking to the Letter (p. 271)
Mr Fikey disconcerted (p. 275)
The Young Man from the Country (p. 277)

'A Poor Man's Tale of a Patent'
Autobiographical (p. 286)
A Costly Pilgrimage (p. 289)

'*Births: Mrs Meek, of a Son*'
Mrs Prodgit and Maria Jane's Mama (p. 324)

'*A Monument of French Folly*'
The jolly old English Roast Beef (p. 331)
Poissy and its Calf Market (p. 334)
The Abattoir of Montmartre (p. 336)

'*Bill-Sticking*'
Moral Philosophy of Bill-sticking (p. 341)
The King of the Bill-stickers (p. 343)
His Majesty's Scroll (p. 345)
Speech from the Throne (p. 346)

'*On Duty with Inspector Field*'
Rats' Castle (p. 361)
The Old Mint (p. 364)
Ratcliffe Highway (p. 367)
At Bully Bark's (p. 368)

APPENDIX B

Complete listing of Dickens's known
journalism, December 1833–June 1851

NOTE: Letters to the Editor and editorial addresses to Dickens's readers have
not been included in this listing, with the exception of his 'Preliminary Word'
in the first number of *HW* and his 1846 letters on Ragged Schools and on
Capital Punishment to the *Daily News* (see n. 25 to Introduction, p. xxii). A
parenthetical question-mark following an item means that it cannot be established
as Dickens's by external evidence, but that there is circumstantial evidence for
the ascription (for such evidence as regards the *Morning Chronicle* theatre reviews,
see W.J. Carlton's 'Charles Dickens, Dramatic Critic', *The Dickensian*, Vol. 56
[1960], pp. 11–27).

The stories and sketches collected in *Sketches by Boz* are indicated by SB; they,
together with Dickens's contributions to *Bentley's Miscellany*, appear in Vol. 1 of
the present edition.

An asterisk indicates that the article was a collaboration. In the case of
collaborative *HW* essays these are indicated by 'Stone', which refers to Harry
Stone's edition of *Uncollected Writings*, where these items may be found. Essays
included by Dickens in *RP* (1858) are indicated by RP.

Bold type indicates that an item is reprinted in the present volume.

Key to Titles of Periodicals:

BLL	*Bell's Life in London*
BM	*Bentley's Miscellany*
BWM	*Bell's Weekly Magazine*
CC	*Carlton Chronicle*
DJSM	*Douglas Jerrold's Shilling Magazine*
DN	*Daily News*
EC	*Evening Chronicle*
Ex	*The Examiner*
HM	*Hood's Magazine*
HW	*Household Words*
LF	*Library of Fiction*
MM	*Monthly Magazine*

MC   *Morning Chronicle*

Date	Title	Periodical
12/33	A Dinner at Poplar Walk (SB)	MM
1/34	Mrs Joseph Porter 'Over the Way' (SB)	MM
2/34	Horatio Sparkins (SB)	MM
4/34	The Bloomsbury Christening (SB)	MM
5/34	The Boarding House (SB)	MM
7/6/34	Sentiment(!) (SB)	BWM
8/34	The Boarding House – No. 2 (SB)	MM
17/9/34	**Report from Edinburgh on Preparations for the Grey Festival**	MC
18/9/34	**Report of the Edinburgh Dinner to Lord Grey**	MC
26/9/34	Omnibuses (SB)	MC
10/34	The Steam Excursion (SB)	MM
10/10/34	Shops and their Tenants (SB)	MC
14/10/34	**Theatre Review: *The Christening***	MC
23/10/34	The Old Bailey (SB)	MC
5/11/34	Shabby-genteel People (SB)	MC
1/12/34	Report on meeting of Birmingham Liberals	MC
5/12/34	Report of Southwark parish meeting (?)	MC
15/12/34	Brokers' and Marine Store Shops (SB)	MC
18/12/34	**'The Story Without a Beginning'**	MC
1/35	A Passage in the Life of Mr Watkins Tottle, Chapter the First (SB)	MM
10/1/35	**Election Report from Colchester**	MC
12/1/35	Election Report from Braintree	MC
13/1/35	Election Report from Chelmsford	MC
14/1/35	Election Report from Sudbury	MC
17/1/35	Election Report from Bury St Edmunds	MC
22/1/35	Theatre Review: *The Maid of Castile*, etc. (?)	MC
31/1/35	Hackney Coach Stands (SB)	EC
2/35	A Passage in the Life of Mr Watkins Tottle, Chapter the Second (SB)	MM
7/2/35	Gin Shops (SB)	EC
19/2/35	Early Coaches (SB)	EC
28/2/35	The Parish (The Beadle – The Parish Engine – The Schoolmaster) (SB)	EC
7/3/35	The 'House' (SB)	EC
17/3/35	London Recreations (SB)	EC
7/4/35	Public Dinners (SB)	EC
11/4/35	Bellamy's (SB)	EC

16/4/35	Greenwich Fair (SB)	EC
23/4/35	Thoughts about People (SB)	EC
2/5/35	Election Report from Exeter	MC
9/5/35	Astley's (SB)	EC
19/5/35	Our Parish (The Curate – The Old Lady – The Half Pay Captain) (SB)	EC
6/6/35	The River (SB)	EC
18/6/35	Our Parish (The Four Sisters) (SB)	EC
30/6/35	The Pawnbroker's Shop (SB)	EC
8/7/35	The Colosseum	MC
10/7/35	**Grand Colosseum Fête**	MC
14/7/35	Our Parish (The Election for Beadle) (SB)	EC
21/7/35	The Streets – Morning (SB)	EC
28/7/35	Our Parish (The Broker's Man) (SB)	EC
11/8/35	Private Theatres (SB)	EC
20/8/35	Our Parish (The Ladies' Societies) (SB)	EC
8/9/35	Theatre Review: *Zarah*, etc. (?)	MC
27/9/35	Seven Dials (SB)	BLL
29/9/35	Theatre Review: *Christening*, etc.	MC
4/10/35	Miss Evans and 'The Eagle' (SB)	BLL
9/10/35	Theatre Review: *Rival Pages*, etc.	MC
11/10/35	The Dancing Academy (SB)	BLL
13/10/35	**The Reopening of the Colosseum**	MC
18/10/35	Making a Night of It (SB)	BLL
20/10/35	Theatre Review: *Truth, or a Glass Too Much*, etc. (?)	MC
25/10/35	Love and Oysters (SB)	BLL
27/10/35	Theatre Review: *The King's Command* (?)	MC
1/11/35	Some Account of an Omnibus Cad (SB)	BLL
4/11/35	Theatre Review: *The Castilian Noble and the Contra-bandista*	MC
11/11/35	Report of Speech by Lord John Russell in Bristol (also 12/11)	MC
13/11/35	Report of Political Dinner at Bath	MC
17/11/35	Reopening of the Adelphi under Mrs Nisbett's management	MC
22/11/35	The Vocal Dressmaker (SB)	BLL
24/11/35	**Theatre Review: *The Dream at Sea***	MC
29/11/35	The Prisoners' Van (SB)	BLL
2/12/35	**Report on the Fire at Hatfield House** (also 3 and 4/12)	MC
13/12/35	The Parlour (SB)	BLL
16/12/35	**Report on the Northamptonshire Election** (also 19/12)	MC

27/12/35	Christmas Festivities (SB)	BLL
3/1/36	The New Year (SB)	BLL
12/1/36	Theatre Review: *One Hour, or a Carnival Ball*	MC
15/1/36	Theatre Review: *The Waterman*, etc.	MC
17/1/36	The Streets at Night (SB)	BLL
19/1/36	Theatre Review: *Brown's Horse*	MC
22/1/36	Report of Foundation Stone Laying by Lord Melbourne	MC
4/2/36	Theatre Review: *Rienzi*	MC
18/3/36	Our Next-door Neighbours (SB)	MC
4/36	The Tuggs's at Ramsgate (SB)	LF
28/5/36	Report of Reform Dinner at Ipswich	MC
6/36	A Little Talk about Spring and the Sweeps (SB)	LF
23/6/36	Report of Norton/Melbourne Trial	MC
6/8/36	The Hospital Patient (SB)	CC
17/9/36	Hackney Cabs, and Their Drivers (SB)	CC
24/9/36	Meditations in Monmouth Street (SB)	MC
4/10/36	Scotland Yard (SB)	MC
11/10/36	Doctors' Commons (SB)	MC
26/10/36	Vauxhall – Gardens by Day (SB)	MC
3/37	The Pantomime of Life	BM
5/37	Some Particulars concerning a Lion	BM
10/37	Full Report of the First Meeting of the Mudfog Association for the Advancement of Everything	BM
3/12/37	Theatre Review: *Joan of Arc*, etc.	Ex
17/12/37	**Theatre Review: *Pierre Bertrand***	Ex
28/1/38	Book Review: *The Ages of Female Beauty*	Ex
28/1/38	Book Review: *Sporting. Edited by Nimrod*	Ex
1/7/38	Report of Coronation Fair in Hyde Park*	Ex
9/38	Full Report of the Second Meeting of the Mudfog Association for the Advancement of Everything	BM
2/9/38	**Book Review: Refutations of the Misstatements ... in Mr Lockhart's Life of Sir Walter Scott (I)**	Ex
2/39	Familiar Epistle from a Parent to a Child Aged Two Years and Two Months	BM
3/2/39	**Book Review: *Hood's Comic Annual* for 1839**	Ex
31/3/39	Scott and His Publishers II	Ex
7/4/39	Book Review: *The Boy's Country Book* (?)	Ex
29/9/39	Scott and His Publishers III	Ex
26/7/40	Theatre Review: *Lady of Lyons*, etc.	Ex
20/10/42	**Book Review: *A Letter to Lord Ashley* ...**	MC

27/10/49	**Demoralisation and Total Abstinence**	Ex
27/10/49	**Theatre Review: Macready as King Lear**	Ex
8/12/49	Central Criminal Court (?)	Ex
15/12/49	**Court Ceremonies**	Ex
30/3/50	**A Preliminary Word**	HW
30/3/50	**The Amusements of the People (I)**	HW
30/3/50	Valentine's Day at the Post Office (Stone)	HW
30/3/50	A Bundle of Emigrants' Letters (Stone)	HW
6/4/50	**A Child's Dream of a Star (*RP*)**	HW
6/4/50	**Perfect Felicity in a Bird's-Eye View**	HW
13/4/50	**The Amusements of the People (II)**	HW
20/4/50	**Some Account of an Extraordinary Traveller**	HW
20/4/50	Supposing!	HW
27/4/50	**Pet Prisoners**	HW
4/5/50	The Heart of Mid-London (Stone)	HW
11/5/50	From the Raven in the Happy Family	HW
18/5/50	**The Begging-Letter Writer (*RP*)**	HW
18/5/50	A Card from Mr Booley	HW
27/5/50	**A Walk in the Workhouse (*RP*)**	HW
1/6/50	A Popular Delusion (Stone)	HW
8/6/50	From the Raven in the Happy Family (II)	HW
15/6/50	**Old Lamps for New Ones**	HW
22/6/50	**The Sunday Screw**	HW
6/7/50	The Old Lady in Threadneedle Street (Stone)	HW
20/7/50	**The Ghost of Art (*RP*)**	HW
27/7/50	**A Detective Police Party (I) (*RP*)**	HW
10/8/50	**A Detective Police Party (II) (*RP*)**	HW
10/8/50	Supposing (II)	HW
24/8/50	From the Raven in the Happy Family (III)	HW
31/8/50	A Paper-Mill (Stone)	HW
14/9/50	Three 'Detective' Anecdotes (*RP*)	HW
21/9/50	Foreigners' Portraits of Englishmen (Stone)	HW
21/9/50	**Chips: The Individuality of Locomotives**	HW
21/9/50	Two Chapters on Bank Note Forgeries: Chapter II (Stone)	HW
28/9/50	The Doom of English Wills (Stone)	HW
5/10/50	The Doom of English Wills: Cathedral Number Two (Stone)	HW
12/10/50	The 'Good' Hippopotamus	HW
19/10/50	**A Poor Man's Tale of a Patent (*RP*)**	HW
26/10/50	**Lively Turtle**	HW
23/11/50	**A Crisis in the Affairs of Mr John Bull...**	HW

INDEX AND GLOSSARY

NOTE: This Index and Glossary covers both Dickens's texts and all editorial material. It includes modern scholars and critics referred to in the editorial material but, with the exception of certain earlier Dickens scholars, does not supply dates for them. Persons and places are indexed only when there is substantial reference to them; passing mentions, facetious allusions and the like are not indexed, nor are individuals about whom no information was found.

Dickens's writings, whether separately published works or not, are indexed under their titles. His many literary quotations and allusions are identified in the Headnotes and are here indexed only as page-references to the Headnotes under the relevant authors' names and under ARABIAN NIGHTS, BIBLE, FAIRY TALES AND FOLKLORE, and NURSERY RHYMES.

The following abbreviations are used: *b.* = born; *c.* = *circa*; CD = Charles Dickens; *coll.* = colloquial; *d.* = died; *Fr.* = French; *HW* = *Household Words*; *Lat.* = Latin; *sl.* = slang.

COLOSSUS OF RHODES gigantic statue straddling the harbour of Rhodes, one of the Seven Wonders of the ancient world 15

COLUMBUS, CHRISTOPHER (1451–1506) discoverer of America 282

COMMERCIAL ROAD built (1804) as a direct route for commercial traffic between the City of London and the new East and West India Docks 279

COMMON COUNCIL, COURT OF court which manages the affairs of the City of London 191, 290–6, 327, 329, 331; *see also* TAYLOR, HENRY

COMMONS, HOUSE OF xi, xiii, xiv, 11, 14, 44, 45, 46, 49, 60, 70, 72, 79, 249, 250, 253, 254, 256, 257

COMPANY, THE *see* EAST INDIA COMPANY

COMPTON, HENRY (1805–77) actor 58

COMUS masque by Milton (performed 1634, published 1637) 56, 59

CONSERVATISM the Tory Party was renamed the Conservative Party by Peel (1841) 55, 65; *see also* TORIES AND TORYISM

CONSTITUTION, THE BRITISH 68, 69, 70, 72, 296

CONVICTS in Australia 207, 219

COOK, CAPTAIN JAMES (1728–79) circumnavigator, killed by native Hawaiians 206

COOKE, T. P. (1786–1864) actor celebrated for his sailor roles 157

COPE, CHARLES WEST (1811–90) historical painter 244

COPENHAGEN FIELDS north London pleasure-gardens and large open space often used for mass meetings; became the site of the new Metropolitan Cattle Market (1852) 328

COPTS Egyptian Christians 209

COPYRIGHT, LAW OF 69–70

CORAL REEFS 132

CORK Ireland 202

CORN LAWS laws (introduced 1804) to protect British farmers from foreign competition by placing a heavy duty on foreign corn (repealed 1846) xvii, xxii, 64, 65

CORNHILL principal east-west thoroughfare in the City of London 341

CORONERS 148, 149, 151; *see also* WAKLEY, THOMAS

CORPORATION, THE *see* CITY OF LONDON

COUPER (*sl.*) sometimes called a chaunter, a dealer in worthless horses 270

COURT CIRCULAR report of royal engagements and activities published in the daily press 70, 191

COURT GUIDE 232

COURT JOURNAL 17

COURT OF ARCHES diocesan court of the Archbishop of Canterbury 19

COUTTS AND CO. bankers to the aristocracy and others including CD 48

COUTTS, ANGELA BURDETT *see* BURDETT-COUTTS, ANGELA

COVENT GARDEN THEATRE one of the two Patent Theatres (rebuilt 1809, 1858), managed by Macready (1837–9) 29, 59, 65, 68, 157, 170, 171; *see also* PATENT THEATRES

COX, J. E. 52

CRACKSMEN (*sl.*) housebreakers 269

CRANKY (*sl.*) eccentric, having a bee in one's bonnet, inclined to object to things 287

CRESWICK, THOMAS (1811–69) landscape painter 244

CRIME 91–5, 219, 265–82; AND ILLITERACY 93–4; AND OCCUPATION 93; AND UNEMPLOYMENT 93; CAUSES OF 163–4; *see also* AREA-SNEAKS; CRACKSMEN; DRUNKENNESS; FENCES; GONOPH; HORSE-STEALING; INFANTICIDE; MAGSMAN; MURDER AND MURDERERS; PICKPOCKETS; POLICE; PRISONS; PROSTITUTION; PUBLIC-HOUSE DANCERS; SMASHERS; SUICIDE; SWELL MOB, THE; THEFT

CRIMEAN WAR (1853–6) xxi, 10

CROMWELL, OLIVER (1599–1658) Lord Protector (1653–8); supposed to have said, 'Take away that bauble!', referring to the Mace, when he dissolved the so-called 'Long Parliament' (1652) 72

CROUPIER vice-chairman at a public banquet 6, 7

CROWDER, MICHAEL 108, 109

CROWE, CATHERINE (1800?–76) novelist and writer on the supernatural 80–9

CRUIKSHANK, GEORGE (1792–1878) artist and caricaturist, illustrator of *Sketches by Boz* and *Oliver Twist* 102–7, 143, 147

CRYSTAL PALACE, THE built of glass and iron, designed by Joseph Paxton to house the Great Exhibition (1851) xvii, 310

CUT IT FAT, TO (*sl.*) to swagger, show off 16

CYCLOPS in Homer's *Odyssey* a giant with one eye in the middle of his forehead 360

DAILY NEWS xvii, xviii, xxii, 350

DALKEITH Scotland 5